Brief Contents

Contents

KV 07.24.2019 0810

IDEAS
& Aims

for College Writing

Tim Taylor

Eastern Illinois University

Linda Copeland

St. Louis Community College

New!
2016
MLA
Updates

PEARSON

Boston   Columbus   Hoboken   Indianapolis   New York   San Francisco
Amsterdam   Cape Town   Dubai   London   Madrid   Milan   Munich   Paris   Montréal   Toronto
Delhi   Mexico City   São Paulo   Sydney   Hong Kong   Seoul   Singapore   Taipei   Tokyo

Executive Acquisition Editor: Matthew Wright
Product Marketing Manager: Jennifer Edwards
Senior Development Editor: Gillian Cook
Executive Digital Producer: Stefanie Snajder
Content Specialist: Erin E. Reilly
Program Manager: Anne Shure
Project Manager: Denise Phillip Grant
Project Coordination, Text Design, and
    Electronic Page Makeup: Cenveo®
    Publisher Services

Design Lead/Cover Designer: Beth Paquin
Cover Photo: Chones/Shutterstock
Senior Manufacturing Buyer:
    Roy L. Pickering, Jr.
Printer/Binder: LSC Communications/Harrisonburg
Cover Printer: Phoenix Color/Hagerstown

Acknowledgments of third-party content appear on page[s] 513–514, which constitute an extension of
this copyright page.

PEARSON, ALWAYS LEARNING, and MYWRITINGLAB are exclusive trademarks owned by Pearson
Education, Inc. or its affiliates in the United States and/or other countries.

Unless otherwise indicated herein, any third-party trademarks that may appear in this work are the
property of their respective owners and any references to third-party trademarks, logos, or other trade
dress are for demonstrative or descriptive purposes only. Such references are not intended to imply
any sponsorship, endorsement, authorization, or promotion of Pearson's products by the owners of
such marks, or any relationship between the owner and Pearson Education, Inc., or its affiliates,
authors, licensees, or distributors.

Lexile® is a trademark of MetaMetrics Inc., and is registered in the United States and abroad. The
trademarks and names of other companies and products mentioned herein are the property of
their respective owners. Copyright © 2014 Metametrics, Inc. All rights reserved.

Library of Congress Cataloging-in-Publication Data
Taylor, Tim N., author.
    IDEAS & aims for college writing / Tim N. Taylor, Eastern Illinois University ; Linda
Copeland, St. Louis Community College.
        pages cm
    Includes index.
    ISBN 978-0-205-83060-2 (Student Edition) — ISBN 0-205-83060-9 (Student Edition) –
ISBN 978-0-321-95603-3 (A la Carte) – ISBN 0-321-95603-6 (A la Carte)
1. English language–Rhetoric. 2. Report writing. 3. College readers. I. Copeland,
Linda, author. II. Title. III. Title: IDEAS and aims for college writing.
    PE1408.T366 2015
    808'.042–dc23

                                                                                    2014041653

www.pearsonhighered.com

Student Edition ISBN 10: 0-13-459089-9
Student Edition ISBN 13: 978-0-13-459089-9
A la Carte ISBN 10: 0-13-464488-3
A la Carte ISBN 13: 978-0-13-464488-2

4 2019

3 Writing and the Process of Writing   55

5 Paragraphs Working Together: The Essay **127**

6 Descriptive Writing **153**

7 Reflective Writing   187

10 Evaluative Writing   285

Consider the Criteria for Success   286

Show How a Subject Is (or Is Not) a Success   288

Put I D E A S to Work in Evaluative Writing   289

11 Persuasive Writing   313

PART 4   RESEARCH

12 Working with Sources   350

13 Documenting Sources   377

14 Style Matters   414

Purpose

IDEAS & Aims fulfills a growing need in college writing classrooms. From our interactions with colleagues at conferences, meetings, and listservs, along with our years of teaching and administrative experience, we have found many instructors who are not satisfied with textbooks organized by the modes of discourse (also called the patterns of organization). They are looking for a new approach and a different type of textbook, one that emphasizes the following:

- Rhetorical purpose
- College-level reading skills
- Critical thinking skills
- Academic, professional, and personal writing

IDEAS & Aims emphasizes each of these areas. The book reflects the reality that most people do not sit down and think, "I need to write a division/classification paper." Instead, an overarching rhetorical purpose (the *aim* of the writing) directs what is written with a specific audience in mind. Therefore, the rhetorical aim of a piece of writing is key. Depending on the situation, a writer needs to primarily describe, reflect, inform, analyze, evaluate, or persuade an audience. This text's consistent focus on subject, purpose, audience, and genre leads students to effectively analyze writing situations they will encounter in their classes and beyond.

Audience

This textbook is targeted to students who are taking basic writing classes or college composition courses in stretch, studio, integrated reading-writing, and accelerated learning programs. We wanted to create a writing textbook that acknowledges the needs of these students yet also respects their abilities and the fact they are in a college class.

I D E A S & the Reading-Writing Connection

IDEAS & Aims is written in a common-sense, conversational style supported by diverse reading selections tied to a variety of writing assignments. The text uses an easy-to-remember analytical template called ⓘ Ⓓ Ⓔ Ⓐ Ⓢ (Ⓘnterest, Ⓓetails, Ⓔxplanation, Ⓐudience, and Ⓢtyle) for analyzing readings and generating content for paragraphs, essays, and professional documents. Overall, the text helps students see writing not only as an important academic tool but also as a career-enhancing skill in their professions.

Organization

IDEAS & Aims has five parts. Part One focuses on college expectations and codes, reading strategies and the process of reading, and writing and the process of writing. Part Two teaches students how to write cohesive, unified, and fully developed paragraphs and essays. The chapters in Part Three are organized by rhetorical purpose via six aims—writing that is descriptive, reflective, informative, analytical, evaluative, and persuasive. Each chapter showcases diverse readings that range from short selections (one to four paragraphs) to longer essays. Part Four addresses working with sources, research, and MLA and APA documentation. In Part Five, the book concludes with Chapter 14, "Style Matters," which provides important sentence-level information and exercises and Chapter 15, "Handbook for Correcting Sentence Errors," which addresses grammatical and mechanical issues.

Notable Features

The following features distinguish *IDEAS & Aims* as an innovative textbook that addresses the needs of today's writing classrooms:

- **An aims-based approach**   By using an aims-based approach, the textbook shows how rhetorical aim is key to a writer's purpose and how paragraphs work toward that overarching goal. Chapters 4 and 5 explain and illustrate the traditional methods of paragraph development—process, comparison and contrast and so on—but then place these methods within the larger aims of describing, reflecting, informing, analyzing, evaluating, and persuading. Also, *IDEAS & Aims* presents writing tasks relative to academia, the workplace, and one's personal life. The assignments within each of the aims-based chapters allow students to incorporate rhetorical strategies that best suit their purpose and audience.

- **The ⓘ Ⓓ Ⓔ Ⓐ Ⓢ template**   The text introduces students to the ⓘ Ⓓ Ⓔ Ⓐ Ⓢ template (Ⓘnterest, Ⓓetails, Ⓔxplanation, Ⓐudience, and Ⓢtyle). Students can use this easy-to-remember and useful tool to examine and critique readings and as a method to brainstorm ideas for their papers. Within every aims-based chapter (6–11), a "Put IDEAS to

Work" section provides a sample of how a student generated content for a paper, followed by the student's final paper, and an "IDEAS in Action" section features a professional essay with annotations keyed to IDEAS to model analytical reading. In addition, all of the essays in these chapters are followed by questions organized by the IDEAS template.

- **Concise instruction and accessible readings**   Each aims-based chapter offers concise instruction about writing for that purpose and an inviting mix of readings that offer fresh perspectives on important issues that clearly connect to that rhetorical purpose. Instructors can choose from these selections based on their knowledge of their students' needs. The readings are accessible yet challenging, and all are prefaced by pre-reading questions to stimulate critical thinking. After each reading, there are thought-provoking questions for discussion along with writing assignments tied to the reading material and aim of the chapter.

- **A focus on critical reading, thinking, and writing**   *IDEAS & Aims* challenges students to become critical thinkers who engage in deep analytical reading and writing. Students are guided to look at an author's assumptions, evidence, and presentation of material, and they are asked to think about their own assumptions and use of evidence.

- **Chapter One: What It Means to Be a College Student**   The opening chapter of *IDEAS & Aims* addresses the dual nature of many developing writers who are particularly proud of their accomplishment of reaching college but need extra guidance in understanding the expectations and demands of college-level courses. The chapter offers insights and suggestions about the broader experience of being a college student as it prepares these new students for the writing tasks and audiences they will encounter. This chapter's emphasis on civility and respect lays the groundwork for the text's focus on critical thinking in reading and writing.

- **Diverse writing assignments for varied audiences**   *IDEAS & Aims* provides detailed writing assignments at the end of each chapter: one is a paragraph-length assignment, one is an academic essay, and the last one is a professional writing case. In these cases, students have to take on the role of a certain individual and write in a professional writing genre in response to a rhetorical situation. In addition, after each major reading in the aims-based chapters (6–11), there are short writing assignments following every reading selection that instructors can use for journals or expand for larger writing assignments.

The writing assignments, while accessible and focused, allow students to choose and practice various rhetorical tasks as well as formats for presenting their work such as reports, advertisements, letters, paragraphs, essays, and even historical markers. Instructors using this text may choose from a variety of assignments suited to the particular strengths and needs of their students. Regardless of length or format, all of the assignments encourage students to practice strategies required for writing situations they will encounter in their academic work and in their professional and private lives.

- **Comprehensive coverage of editing, grammar, and style**   In Part Five, Chapter 14 offers coverage of typical sentence-level concerns and provides smart exercises that address important sentence-based issues. Chapter 15, "Handbook for Correcting Sentence Errors," is a resource guide for grammar, style, and usage. Sentence-level exercises are provided in this part along with connections to Pearson's MyWritingLab.

- **Lexiled Readings**   A Lexile® measure—the most widely used reading metric in U.S. schools—provides valuable information about a student's reading ability and the complexity of text. It helps match students with reading resources and activities that are targeted to their ability level. Lexile measures indicate the reading levels of content in MyWritingLab and the longer selections in the Annotated Instructor's Editions of all Pearson's developmental textbooks. See the Annotated Instructor's Edition and the Instructor's Manual of *IDEAS & Aims* for more details.

These notable features within *IDEAS & Aims* form an innovative core for teaching developing writers the reading, writing, and critical thinking skills they will need in their academic, professional, and personal lives.

Chapter-Specific Features

- **Learning objectives**   Each chapter begins by providing clear learning objectives to focus the attention of students and to lay the foundation for the principles and skills the chapter covers.

- **Visuals for critical thinking**   Each chapter uses visual aids (photographs, diagrams, and cartoons) throughout to stimulate analytical thinking related to the learning goals of each chapter. Sometimes serious or sometimes humorous, they reflect the focus of each chapter and make students look beyond the obvious as critical thinkers.

- **Examples/student models**   Most chapters demonstrate how students have gone through the process of writing a paper for a college class—their brainstorming and then the final product, the paper. These "Put IDEAS to Work" sections provide positive modeling for what students can do in their writing courses.

- **Exercises**   The textbook provides exercises that link directly to concepts presented. Instructors can use these exercises for in-class activities (individuals or small groups) or homework assignments that then can be used to foster discussion within the classroom. Most of the exercises can be completed online in MyWritingLab; look for the logo—MyWritingLab—which appears to the right of the exercise.

- **Reading and Writing: I D E A S in Action**   To reinforce the IDEAS template, many chapters offer professional essays that are annotated via IDEAS to model the type of analytical reading students are required to do.

- **Ideas for Your Own Writing**   After each reading selection in the aims-based chapters (6–11), there are typically two different assignments that instructors can use for directed journal assignments, or they could use them for larger assignments.

- **Additional Reading Assignments**   Chapters 6–11 close with a section of detailed writing assignments for writing a paragraph, an academic essay, and a professional writing case.

- **Chapter at a Glance**   At the end of each chapter, there is a visual that reinforces the learning objectives of the chapter with concise detail about each learning goal.

Writing Resources and Supplements

Annotated Instructor's Edition for *IDEAS & Aims*
(**ISBN:** 0205830625 / 9780205830626)
Instructor's Resource Manual (Download only) for *IDEAS & Aims*
(**ISBN:** 0205830633 / 9780205830633)

The Instructor's Resource Manual (IRM) for *IDEAS & Aims* provides clear guidance for instructors. The IRM offers additional assignments, ideas for activities for classrooms and out-of-class work, and points to consider when an instructor is using the chapter in the classroom. In addition, the IRM provides sample syllabi that show how instructors can organize the course, readings, and assignments into a cohesive and meaningful learning experience for students. Also, the IRM has an answer key for the exercises within the chapters.

Test Bank (Download only) for *IDEAS & Aims*
ISBN: (0133928659 / 9780133928655)
PowerPoint Presentation for *IDEAS & Aims*
(ISBN: 0321956060 / 9780321956064)

MyWritingLab

Where practice, application, and demonstration meet to improve writing.

MyWritingLab, a complete online learning program, provides additional resources and effective practice exercises for developing writers. MyWritingLab accelerates learning through layered assessment and a personalized learning path utilizing the Knewton Adaptive Learning Platform™, which customizes standardized educational content to piece together the perfect personalized bundle of content for each student. With over eight thousand exercises and immediate feedback to answers, the integrated learning aids of MyWritingLab reinforce learning throughout the semester.

What makes MyWritingLab more effective?

- **Diagnostic Testing:** MyWritingLab's diagnostic Path Builder test comprehensively assesses students' skills in grammar. Students are provided with an individualized learning path based on the diagnostic's results, identifying the areas where they most need help.

- **Progressive Learning:** The heart of MyWritingLab is the progressive learning that takes place as students complete the Overview, Animation, Recall, Apply, and Write exercises along with the Post-test within each topic. Students move from preparation (Overview, Animation) to literal comprehension (Recall) to critical understanding (Apply) to the ability to demonstrate a skill in their own writing (Write) to total mastery (Post-test). This progression of critical thinking enables students to truly master the skills and concepts they need to become successful writers.

- **Online Gradebook:** All student work in MyWritingLab is captured in the Online Gradebook. Instructors can see what and how many topics their students have mastered. They can also view students' individual scores on all assignments throughout MyWritingLab, as well as overviews by student, and class performance by module. Students can monitor their progress in new Completed Work pages, which show them their totals, scores, time on task, and the date and time of their work by module.

- **A Deeper Connection between Print and Media:** The MyWritingLab logo is used throughout the book to indicate exercises and writing activities that can be completed and submitted through MyWritingLab (appropriate results flow directly to the Instructor Gradebook). The *IDEAS & Aims* book-specific module in **MyWritingLab** also includes unique videos that provide an overview of the **I D E A S** tool and reinforce the individual aspects of the five parts (**I** nterest, **D** etails, **E** xplanation, **A** udience, and **S** tyle).

Acknowledgments

We would like to thank Pearson for its commitment to this project. We are particularly grateful for the continued support of Matthew Wright, Executive Editor, throughout this process. He shared our vision of this innovative approach to developmental writing and kept the project afloat during its years of development. And we give special thanks to Gill Cook, Senior Development Editor, who was able to navigate two new textbook authors through countless revisions. Her editorial expertise and commitment to quality work were the keys to this project's completion.

The insights and suggestions of our many reviewers helped us immensely as we developed this text. We so appreciate the time and care they took to give us the critical commentary we needed to make this text a better tool for achieving student success.

Karen L. Blount, Miami University Hamilton; Karen Brown, Wallace Community College Selma; Gloria Browning, Bluegrass Community & Technical College; Joy Clark, Yakima Valley Community College; Kennette Crockett, City Colleges of Chicago; Karen Culver, University of Miami; Patricia R. DiMond, University of South Dakota; Scott Douglass, Chattanooga State Community College; Alexandra Duckworth, Richard Bland College; Jennifer Dunn, Rio Hondo College; Carol Friend, Mercer County Community College; Tatiana Gorbunova, Owens Community College; Cynthia L Gribas, Hennepin Technical College; Beth Hammett, College of the Mainland; Sue Henderson, East Central College; Thomas Patrick Henry, Utah Valley University; Michael D. Hill, Henry Ford Community College; Megan V. Howard, Montgomery College–Rockville; T. Michelle Hudgens, Ozarks Technical Community College; Laura Jeffries, Florida State College at Jacksonville; Stanley W. Johnson, Southside Virginia Community College; Elaine N. Jolayemi, Ivy Tech Community College; Heather Jordan, Bowling Green State University; Wendy King, Arizona State University; Jill A. Kinkade, University of Southern Indiana; Aimee Krall-Lanoue, Concordia University Chicago; William B. Lalicker, West Chester University; Lori Lawson, Northern Illinois University; Gloria Lester Browning, Bluegrass Community & Technical College; Lindsay Lewan, Arapahoe Community College; Lydia Lynn Lewellen, Tacoma Community College; Beverly Lucas, Trinity Washington University; Jane Maher, Nassau Community College; Bonnie Lini Markowski, University of Scranton; Laura May, Yakima Valley Community College; Beatrice Mendez Newman, The University of Texas–Pan American; Christa Higgins Raney, University of North Alabama; Joan

Reeves, Northeast Alabama Community College; Marcea Seible, Hawkeye Community College; Erin Everett Severs, Mohawk Valley Community College; Ann Tousley, Pima Community College Christine Tutlewski, University of Wisconsin–Parkside; Karen S. Uehling, Boise State University; Jennifer K. Weaver, Wayne State University; Stephen H. Wells, Community College of Alleghany; Courtney Huse Wika, Black Hills State University; Kelly Lynn Ford Zepp, Community College of Denver.

Ralph Voss and Michael Keene offered valuable advice about creating a textbook and the publishing process. Our colleagues at Eastern Illinois University and St. Louis Community College have inspired us through the years with their commitment to helping students who might otherwise fail to achieve their dreams of a college education. We are so appreciative of the help of two special adjunct instructors—Glenna Gelfand and Tina Newberry—who have helped to test and refine many of the assignments and exercises in this text.

Special thanks go to our families: Diana, Hannah, and Quinn Taylor—"the people who keep me afloat in life"—and Jeffrey Copeland—"who keeps me motivated, encouraged, and, most importantly, laughing during our years together."

The book is dedicated to our parents, Virg and Deloras Taylor and Doug and Joyce Wiegand. Though none of them went to college, they taught us what we needed to excel at college and then become college professors. Those characteristics are grit, discipline, compassion, persistence, curiosity, open-mindedness, responsibility, and a solid work ethic. From them we also learned that having a sense of humor and not taking ourselves too seriously are necessary in life.

Tim Taylor
Linda Copeland

What It Means to Be a College Student: Following the Codes

1

Learning Objectives

In this chapter, you will learn how to . . .

1. Be an active learner.
2. Show good character.
3. Practice critical thinking.
4. Be aware of college discourse communities as different audiences.
5. Meet the expectations of college writing assignments.

In college you will write many different kinds of papers. This chapter provides guidance on how to be a successful student and a strong writer. How have you been an active learner in the past? How can you show good character in classes? How can you improve as a critical thinker?

Whether you have come to college right from high school or resumed your education after taking time to pursue other endeavors, you are likely to find the experience exciting, challenging, and possibly intimidating.

Of course, college should be exciting. Being a college student is in itself quite an accomplishment, opening up limitless opportunities for you. Also, college *should* be challenging, or the final degree would not mean very much. However, college should *not* be intimidating. Learning the codes—that is, learning what is expected of you—will reduce and may even eliminate fears you may have.

The word **code** has a couple of meanings. In one respect, a code is a way of living in the world, a way of presenting oneself and a standard for treating others. For example, during the Middle Ages, knights followed a code of chivalry that included such principles as serving their lord with courage and faith, fighting for the welfare of all, and respecting the honor of women. Even the American cowboy had a code, at least in the movies, that required he never shoot first, never go back on his word, always help those in distress, and unfailingly uphold our nation's laws.

In another respect, a code is a language or dialect used by insiders, people "in the know." Think of how people in certain workplaces use jargon. A waiter may "86" a rude customer or ask the cook for a "hockey puck" with an order of fries. A realtor may offer to do a "CMA" on a property and check the "MLS" to see what properties are available. These professionals use language specific to their workplaces.

To be a successful college student, you need to learn both **codes of college**: the code of behavior and the code of communication. Knowing these codes will show your peers and professors you are an insider.

❶ Be an active learner.

The Code of Behavior

There are three principles of the code of behavior we believe students should follow: *be an active learner*, *show good character*, and *practice critical thinking*.

Be an Active Learner

Movie director Woody Allen once said, "Eighty percent of success is showing up." He makes a good point because you cannot be a successful college student if you frequently miss class. However, simply showing up is not enough to succeed in college. The code of the successful college student requires you to be an *active* learner.

Active learners show that they want to learn and that they care about the quality of their work by following these strategies:

Strategies for Active Learning . . .

1. **Take Responsibility for Learning:** Active learners arrange their work schedules and home routines to support their learning rather than compete with it. When they must miss a class, they know they are still responsible for the material covered and any assignments due. Active learners also stay informed about how well they are doing in their courses by keeping track of their grades and consistently thinking about how to improve.

2. **Participate:** Active learners come to class prepared with completed assignments. In class they take good notes, ask questions, make comments, and engage with the material. They interact with others both in the classroom and outside the classroom if a class uses online systems like Blackboard, blogs, or wikis.

3. **Take Advantage of Resources:** Active learners use services many colleges have developed to help students such as writing centers, math centers, library services, career centers, and disability services. They also meet with their professors during office hours to go over comments on papers, to ask questions, to clarify what is needed on an assignment, or to talk about ideas relevant to the course.

One key to being an active learner is practicing self-control. Are you able to put off what you *want* to do for what you *should* and *need* to do? Do you have the discipline to turn off the TV or to say no to time with friends, so you can meet the obligations of your classes? The following article describes a study that found the ability to exercise self-control is a strong indicator of a person's potential to be successful in college and beyond.

Self-Control Is the Key to Success

by David Brooks

PRE-READING PROMPTS

1. What characteristics do you think are necessary for a person to be successful in college?
2. Do you think people have to be born with these characteristics, or can they be learned?
3. What do you think parents can and should do to help their children be successful in school and in life?

1   Around 1970, psychologist Walter Mischel launched a classic experiment. He left a succession of 4-year-olds in a room with a bell and a marshmallow. If they rang the bell, he would come back and they could eat the marshmallow. If, however, they didn't ring the bell and waited for him to come back on his own, they could then have two marshmallows.

2   In videos of the experiment, you can see the children squirming, kicking, hiding their eyes—desperately trying to exercise self-control so they can wait and get two marshmallows. Their performance varied widely. Some broke down and rang the bell within a minute. Others lasted 15 minutes.

     The children who waited longer went on to get higher SAT scores. They got into better colleges and had, on average, better adult outcomes. The children who rang the bell quickest were more likely to become bullies. They received worse teacher and parental evaluations 10 years later and were more likely to have drug problems at age 32.

3   The Mischel experiments are worth noting because people in the policy world spend a lot of time thinking about how to improve education, how to reduce poverty, how to make the most of the nation's human capital. But when policymakers address these problems, they come up with structural remedies: reduce class sizes, create more charter schools, increase teacher pay, mandate universal day care and try vouchers.

4   The results of these structural reforms are almost always disappointingly modest. Yet policymakers rarely ever probe deeper into problems and ask the core questions, such as how do we get people to master the sort of self-control that leads to success? To ask that question is to leave the policymakers' comfort zone—which is the world of inputs and outputs, appropriations and bureaucratic reform—and to enter the murky world of psychology and human nature.

5   Yet the Mischel experiments, along with everyday experience, tell us that self-control is essential. Young people who can delay gratification can sit through sometimes boring classes to get a degree. They can perform rote tasks in order to, say, master a language. They can avoid drugs and alcohol. For people without self-control skills, however, school is a series of failed ordeals. No wonder they drop out. Life is a parade of foolish decisions: teenage pregnancy, drug use, gambling, truancy and crime.

6   If you're a policymaker and you are not talking about core psychological traits such as delayed gratification skills, then you're just dancing around with proxy issues. The research we do have on delayed gratification tells us that differences in self-control skills are deeply rooted but also **malleable**. Differences in the ability to focus attention and exercise control emerge very early, perhaps as soon as nine months. But there is no consensus on how much of the ability to exercise self-control is hereditary and how much is environmental.

7   The ability to delay gratification, like most skills, **correlates** with socioeco-nomic status and parenting styles. Children from poorer homes do much worse

malleable: easily shaped

correlates: shares a relationship with, is connected to

on delayed gratification tests than children from middle-class homes. That's probably because children from poorer homes are more likely to have their lives disrupted by marital breakdown, violence, moving, etc. They think in the short term because there is no predictable long term.

8   The good news is that while differences in the ability to delay gratification emerge early and persist, that ability can be improved with conscious effort. Moral lectures don't work. Sheer willpower doesn't seem to work either. The children who resisted eating the marshmallow didn't stare directly at it and exercise iron discipline. On the contrary, they were able to resist their appetites because they were able to think about other things.

9   What works, says Jonathan Haidt, the author of *The Happiness Hypothesis*, is creating stable, predictable environments for children, in which good behavior pays off—and practice. Young people who are given a series of tests that demand self-control get better at it.

10   This pattern would be too obvious to mention if it weren't so largely ignored by educators and policymakers. Somehow we've entered a world in which we obsess over structural reforms and standardized tests, but skirt around the moral and psychological traits that are at the heart of actual success. Mischel tried to interest New York schools in programs based on his research. Needless to say, he found almost no takers.

QUESTIONS FOR DISCUSSION

1. Brooks begins with a description of an experiment conducted on four-year-olds and then jumps years ahead to the children's performance in college and beyond. What impact on his readers do you think he is trying to create? Is this approach effective in capturing your interest? Explain.
2. What is meant by "delayed gratification"? Give examples of life experiences that require the ability to delay gratification.
3. Why does Brooks think children from lower socioeconomic backgrounds are likely to perform poorly on delayed gratification tests?
4. What is the key to being able to resist eating the marshmallow?
5. What can you do as a college student to improve your self-control?

MyWritingLab Visit Ch. 2 The Reading Process in MyWritingLab to access the IDEAS videos.

I D E A S for Your Own Writing

Self-Control Self-Assessment

How well are you able to deal with delayed gratification? Write a paragraph about your self-control strengths and weaknesses by giving examples of times when you were or were not able to delay gratification.

(continued)

Resisting the Marshmallow

Brooks writes, "Sheer willpower doesn't seem to work either. The children who resisted eating the marshmallow didn't stare directly at it and exercise iron discipline. On the contrary, they were able to resist their appetites because they were able to think about other things." How can you apply what Mischel learned to your own experiences of dealing with the temptations that may keep you from succeeding in college? In other words, how can you work to improve your ability to delay gratification?

❷ Show good character.

Show Good Character

Repeatedly coming to class late, talking while others are talking, texting during class, interrupting people, not doing assigned tasks during class, and other such disrespectful behavior will not help students succeed in any course. Therefore, the second principle in the successful college student's code is to *show good character*.

Negative behavior is going to hurt your *ethos*, the term the ancient Greeks used to describe a person's credibility and character. A person who behaves in a respectful and ethical manner is generally considered by others to be a more credible person, one whose ideas are more likely to be listened to and respected.

Most professors feel their classroom communities demand good manners, careful listening, and respect for diverse backgrounds and opinions. They expect students to act in a mature and mutually respectful manner. College students should strive to be seen as professionals and should act accordingly. What follows is an exercise to raise your awareness of how to demonstrate your good character—your *ethos*—in a college classroom.

EXERCISE 1.1   Guidelines to Abide by in Any College Course

Directions: Think about ways you, your classmates, and your instructor can make the classroom a place where you can exchange ideas in a civil and comfortable atmosphere. Working with your peers, come up with additional guidelines for behavior you think is desirable in any college classroom. The following list should get you started.

1. Come to class on time and stay the entire period.

2. Bring texts, paper, and writing utensils.

3. Have opinions and ideas and support them with details and examples.

4. Respect your classmates' opinions and be open to them.

5. Do not confront your professor about a grade dispute or policy issue during class time; instead, make an appointment to discuss the matter during the professor's office hours.

❸ Practice critical thinking.

Practice Critical Thinking

Throughout your college career, you will work with many professors who will have a variety of expectations. We believe there is one expectation nearly all professors share: **Students should think critically.** But what exactly does critical thinking *mean*? Although you may associate the word *critical* with *criticize*, thinking critically does not mean simply looking for what is wrong about something.

Essentially, critical thinkers are explorers. They seek answers to questions and solutions to problems through reflection and responsible research. They gather relevant information, look for connections, analyze, and apply logical reasoning to arrive at informed opinions.

Critical thinkers avoid bias and prejudice. Just as they evaluate whether evidence is relevant and accurate, critical thinkers question their own views and recognize their own potential for errors in judgment. While they understand the cliché "everyone has a right to an opinion," critical thinkers know that all opinions are not equally valid. Some opinions are poorly formulated, weakly supported, or totally off base. **Informed opinions** *are supported by ideas, facts, details, examples, and experiences.* Thinking critically—the third principle in our college student's code of behavior—is thinking that leads to an informed opinion.

EXERCISE 1.2   Who's the Critical Thinker?

Directions: In each of the following items, we present two ways of resolving a problem or answering a question. Determine which individual demonstrates critical thinking and explain why.

_____ 1. a. Tamika writes a research paper, using peer-reviewed journals she found through the college library's databases.

b. Jenna writes a research paper using Wikipedia and the first five sources that came up when she did a Google search of her topic.

_____ 2. a. Jayden always votes a straight ticket because his family has always supported the **** party.

b. Ethan researches each candidate's position on the economy, the environment, and education before casting a vote.

_____ 3. a. Mia underwent a stomach stapling procedure because she wanted to lose weight fast.

b. After exploring a number of weight-loss programs and discussing weight loss surgery with her doctor, Sofia joined Weight Watchers.

_____ 4. a. Lejla hired Ellen to work at the hair salon because they both graduated from the same high school.

b. Lilly hired Margaret to work at the hair salon because Margaret had graduated from a top cosmetology school, had five years' experience, and provided excellent references.

_____ 5. a. Youssef bought an X-phone after reading in _Consumer Reports_ about the various cell phones' strengths and weaknesses. He also spoke with friends who had cell phones and compared several phones' features by checking company websites.

b. Eric bought a Y-phone because he enjoyed the humorous television commercials that touted the phone's features.

The Code of Communication

Now that we have explored one meaning of code—a way of living and presenting oneself—let us examine the other code: a language or a dialect used by insiders.

In everyday conversations, you adjust how you talk or write to someone. If, for example, you had to explain why you like a certain band to your six-year-old cousin, to your best friend, or to your grandfather, you would use different language tactics and levels of formality to get your message across. Similarly, you adjust your messages according to _how_ you are communicating by using different strategies to speak, send a text message, compose an email, or write a paper.

If you think about it, you already understand the basics of adapting your messages for different audiences and purposes. The writing you do in college is simply a different form of communication you have to be familiar with and use effectively. This section will focus on two key expectations of the college code:

- Being aware of the college discourse communities as different audiences.
- Meeting the expectations of college writing assignments.

Discourse Communities as Different Audiences

4 Be aware of college discourse communities as different audiences.

To put it simply, a **discourse community** is a group of people united or bonded by

- similar values and beliefs.
- similar habits of thinking, problem solving, and communicating.
- common language, jargon, or dialect.

Within college there are different discourse communities, or groups of people who use the same "codes." After you have taken a number of classes in different disciplines, you will likely notice that lab reports, papers for an American literature class, memos for a business class, and papers for history courses have significant differences in how they are organized, the vocabulary that is expected, and the overall purpose of the writing.

An academic discipline such as history, physics, or sociology can be seen as a distinctive discourse community with specific values, beliefs, ways of problem solving, habits of mind, and conventions of writing tied to that community. Whether speaking or writing, you will find your ideas are more respected when you present them with an awareness of and a respect for the discourse community that is your audience, so you need to be sure to express your ideas in a way that connects with "how the job gets done" in that community. Showing that you are reasonable and avoiding biased and discourteous language are also ways to make your readers open to your ideas and points.

EXERCISE 1.3   Describe a Workplace Code

Directions: Many students come to college with work experience of some kind. Using your own work experience, describe the ways of thinking, problem solving, and communicating in that profession. Be sure to use specific details and real examples from your experience about how this type of job has a certain mindset and particular ways of speaking and writing.

To further explain the code connected to communicating with professors via email, here is an article that provides some perspectives of college professors on student emails.

To: Professor@University.edu Subject: Why It's All About Me

by Jonathan D. Glater

PRE-READING PROMPT

1. Have you ever emailed a teacher? If so, why?
2. Should teachers respond quickly to every email they receive? Why or why not?
3. Why might a teacher choose to not respond to a student's email?
4. What do you consider inappropriate content in emails to teachers?

[1]   One student skipped class and then sent the professor an e-mail message asking for copies of her teaching notes. Another did not like her grade, and wrote a petulant message to the professor. Another explained that she was late for a Monday class because she was recovering from drinking too much at a wild weekend party.

[2]   Jennifer Schultens, an associate professor of mathematics at the University of California, Davis, received this e-mail message last September from a student in her calculus course: "Should I buy a binder or a subject notebook? Since I'm a freshman, I'm not sure how to shop for school supplies. Would you let me know your recommendations? Thank you!"

[3]   At colleges and universities nationwide, e-mail has made professors much more approachable. But many say it has made them too accessible, erasing boundaries that traditionally kept students at a healthy distance. These days, they say, students seem to view them as available around the clock, sending a steady stream of e-mail messages—from 10 a week to 10 after every class—that are too informal or downright inappropriate.

[4]   "The tone that they would take in e-mail was pretty astounding," said Michael J. Kessler, an assistant dean and a lecturer in theology at Georgetown University. "'I need to know this and you need to tell me right now,' with a familiarity that can sometimes border on imperative." He added: "It's a real fine balance to accommodate what they need and at the same time maintain a level of legitimacy as an instructor and someone who is institutionally authorized to make demands on them, and not the other way round."

[5]   While once professors may have expected deference, their expertise seems to have become just another service that students, as consumers, are buying. So

students may have no fear of giving offense, imposing on the professor's time or even of asking a question that may reflect badly on their own judgment.

6   For junior faculty members, the barrage of e-mail has brought new tension into their work lives, some say, as they struggle with how to respond. Their tenure prospects, they realize, may rest in part on student evaluations of their accessibility.

7   The stakes are different for professors today than they were even a decade ago, said Patricia Ewick, chairwoman of the sociology department at Clark University in Massachusetts, explaining that "students are constantly asked to fill out evaluations of individual faculty." Students also frequently post their own evaluations on Web sites like *ratemyprofessors.com* and describe their impressions of their professors on blogs.

8   Last fall, undergraduate students at Syracuse University set up a group in Facebook.com, an online network for students, and dedicated it to maligning one particular instructor. The students were reprimanded.

9   Professor Ewick said 10 students in one class e-mailed her drafts of their papers days before they were due, seeking comments. "It's all different levels of presumption," she said. "One is that I'll be able to drop everything and read 250 pages two days before I'm going to get 50 of these." Kathleen E. Jenkins, a sociology professor at the College of William and Mary in Virginia, said she had even received e-mail requests from students who missed class and wanted copies of her teaching notes. Alexandra Lahav, an associate professor of law at the University of Connecticut, said she felt pressured by the e-mail messages. "I feel sort of responsible, as if I ought to be on call all the time," she said.

10   Many professors said they were often uncertain how to react. Professor Schultens, who was asked about buying the notebook, said she debated whether to tell the student that this was not a query that should be directed to her, but worried that "such a message could be pretty scary." "I decided not to respond at all," she said.

11   Christopher J. Dede, a professor at the Harvard Graduate School of Education who has studied technology in education, said these e-mail messages showed how students no longer deferred to their professors, perhaps because they realized that professors' expertise could rapidly become outdated.

"The deference was probably driven more by the notion that professors were infallible sources of deep knowledge," Professor Dede said, and that notion has weakened.

12   Meanwhile, students seem unaware that what they write in e-mail could adversely affect them, Professor Lahav said. She recalled an e-mail message from a student saying that he planned to miss class so he could play with his son. Professor Lahav did not respond. "It's graduate school, he's an adult human being, he's obviously a parent, and it's not my place to tell him how to run his life," she said. But such e-mail messages can have consequences, she added.

"Students don't understand that what they say in e-mail can make them seem very unprofessional, and could result in a bad recommendation."

13   Still, every professor interviewed emphasized that instant feedback could be invaluable. A question about a lecture or discussion "is for me an indication of a blind spot, that the student didn't get it," said Austin D. Sarat, a professor of political science at Amherst College.

14   College students say that e-mail makes it easier to ask questions and helps them to learn. "If the only way I could communicate with my professors was by going to their office or calling them, there would be some sort of ranking or prioritization taking place," said Cory Merrill, 19, a sophomore at Amherst. "Is this question worth going over to the office?"

15   But student e-mail can go too far, said Robert B. Ahdieh, an associate professor at Emory Law School in Atlanta. He paraphrased some of the comments he had received: "I think you're covering the material too fast, or I don't think we're using the reading as much as we could in class, or I think it would be helpful if you would summarize what we've covered at the end of class in case we missed anything."

16   Students also use e-mail to criticize one another, Professor Ahdieh said. He paraphrased this comment: "You're spending too much time with my moron classmates and you ought to be focusing on those of us who are getting the material."

17   Michael Greenstone, an economics professor at the Massachusetts Institute of Technology, said he once received an e-mail message late one evening from a student who had recently come to the realization that he was gay and was struggling to cope. Professor Greenstone said he eventually helped the student get an appointment with a counselor. "I don't think we would have had the opportunity to discuss his realization and accompanying feelings without e-mail as an icebreaker," he said.

18   A few professors said they had rules for e-mail and told their students how quickly they would respond, how messages should be drafted and what types of messages they would answer. Meg Worley, an assistant professor of English at Pomona College in California, said she told students that they must say thank you after receiving a professor's response to an e-mail message. "One of the rules that I teach my students is, the less powerful person always has to write back," Professor Worley said.

QUESTIONS FOR DISCUSSION

1. Glater begins his article with four examples of email messages from students to teachers. What characteristics do all the messages share?
2. What can be some of the negative consequences for students if they send inappropriate emails to teachers? What are some of the negative consequences for teachers if students send them inappropriate emails?

3. How can emails be a positive and useful means to connect with teachers?
4. Glater develops this article primarily through the use of examples. How effective is this approach?
5. Does this article give you a clear sense of what is an appropriate email to send to a teacher? Why or why not?

I D E A S For Your Own Writing

Revise It

A friend of yours is getting ready to send the following email off to her professor and has asked you to look it over. Revise the email to make it more appropriate for its intended audience and purpose.

From:	marshallg@university.edu
Sent:	Friday, February 15, 2015 1:09 PM
To:	Henry.Taylor@university.edu
Subject:	todays class

Hey Dr Taylor!
Some friends r going to a U of I football game this wkend and asked me along so Ill miss class this Fri. R we doing anything important in class that day? Send me any notes and assignments 4 class that day.
If u have any questions call me at 555-1234.
Gretchen

Write a Course Policy

Glater's article mentions some professors "had rules for e-mail and told their students how quickly they would respond, how messages should be drafted and what types of messages they would answer." Write an email policy your instructor could include in a future course document. As you design the policy guidelines, keep in mind the needs and concerns of the instructor as well as the students.

❺ Meet the expectations of college writing assignments.

Meet the Expectations of College Writing Assignments

Whether you are writing for a composition course, a biology course, a business course, or any other course during your college career, there are basic expectations professors have for the way you will communicate with them in writing. In short, all professors expect you to do the following:

- Connect with an audience.
- Cover the basics of the assignment.
- Produce quality writing.

Connect with an Audience

What you have learned about discourse communities relates directly to how strong writing connects with an audience. As a writer, you must have audience awareness. Successful college students will navigate various classes and adjust how they write according to the expectations of each class and each teacher.

An old saying goes, "To catch a fish, you have to think like a fish." In order to write a successful paper in a geology, English, history, consumer science, biology, or business class, you have to think about what your audience expects and what they value. You have to think like the fish you are trying to catch.

Cover the Basics of the Assignment

One of the challenges of being a college student is being able to navigate a variety of discourse communities successfully. You have to learn what is expected for each of your writing assignments, and you have to ask the right questions, such as these:

- What makes a paper earn an A, B, C, D, or F?
- What does a successful paper have to do?
- What different features (thesis, development, organization, readability, style, grammar) of the paper will the instructor be analyzing? Which ones will the instructor weigh more heavily?
- What's most important in this paper?
- How much does grammar matter?
- Are there examples of what is an average to excellent response to the assignment?

To provide a wider perspective on college writing in general, here are some basic requirements of academic writing that seem to be valued by most professors across the disciplines:

Basic Requirements for Academic Writing

- **The paper shows you have done what is asked for**. It is important that you carefully read and follow your instructor's assignment guidelines. You must address the overall purpose of the assignment. If, for example, the assignment asks you to respond to an author's ideas by connecting them to a personal experience you had, you must do that. Also, pay close attention to particulars like number of words or pages required and due dates.

- **The paper shows you have put time into it**. Since you might be working with difficult material and complex ideas, writing a successful paper will take time and effort. College writing should not be done the night before. Following an effective and productive writing process can lead to the kind of *polished* writing professors expect. (See Chapter 3 for more details on the writing process.)

- **The paper should be free of errors**. Grammatical and proofreading errors distract readers and hurt the credibility of a paper. You should take the time to edit and proofread a paper thoroughly—*multiple* times. Do not simply rely upon grammar and spell-checker systems. Also, keep in mind you need to use language appropriate for the discourse community. (See pp. 83–84 in Chapter 3 about editing and proofreading techniques.)

Produce Quality Writing

Meeting the basic expectations is only the beginning of writing a successful college paper. The college papers that earn the best grades are those that go beyond the basics and demonstrate quality writing.

While specific majors and disciplines might have different ideas about what constitutes quality writing, there are some common features:

Common Features of Quality Writing

- **A quality paper demonstrates the writer's engagement with the subject**. Writers who take the time to connect to and understand their subjects and become excited by them often convey that engagement to their readers.

- **A quality paper shows the individuality of the writer**. A writer who does not settle for commonplace ideas or predictable examples, but instead is a risk taker, will produce a quality paper that has a freshness and inventiveness that comes from a distinctively individual take on the subject.
- **A quality paper shows awareness of style**. A writer of a quality paper goes beyond proofreading and looks for ways to improve the variety of sentences and the choice of words. At the same time, the writer follows the conventions of the discourse community.

Learning to produce quality writing is like any other activity. Becoming a stronger writer takes practice, a smart process, and a willingness to learn from mistakes. Remember to use your resources—your instructor and the writing center—and take advantage of any opportunities to revise and refine your papers.

EXERCISE 1.4   Define Quality Writing

Directions: Working individually or in small groups, list and detail the components of quality writing. As you work, consider these questions:

- What is "quality" writing?
- What in particular makes a strong piece of writing effective?
- What components, details, or values must a strong piece of writing have? Be specific and detailed.

Once you or your group has brainstormed a definition of quality writing, compare results and ideas as a class. Where is there agreement, and where is there disagreement and why?

As another perspective about "quality" work, the following article from the *New York Times* provides a glimpse of the different perceptions about expectations and grades.

Student Expectations Seen As Causing Grade Disputes
by Max Roosevelt

PRE-READING PROMPT

1. What, in your opinion, are the criteria for earning an F, D, C, B, or A in a college course?
2. Should a student who received high grades in high school expect similarly high grades in college? Why or why not?

3. When might a student be justified in complaining about a grade?
4. How important are grades in motivating you to learn? Why?

1   Prof. Marshall Grossman has come to expect complaints whenever he returns graded papers in his English classes at the University of Maryland. "Many students come in with the conviction that they've worked hard and deserve a higher mark," Professor Grossman said. "Some assert that they have never gotten a grade as low as this before." He attributes those complaints to his students' sense of entitlement. "I tell my classes that if they just do what they are supposed to do and meet the standard requirements, that they will earn a C," he said. "That is the default grade. They see the default grade as an A."

2   A recent study by researchers at the University of California, Irvine, found that a third of students surveyed said that they expected B's just for attending lectures, and 40 percent said they deserved a B for completing the required reading. "I noticed an increased sense of entitlement in my students and wanted to discover what was causing it," said Ellen Greenberger, the lead author of the study, called "Self-Entitled College Students: Contributions of Personality, Parenting, and Motivational Factors," which appeared last year in *The Journal of Youth and Adolescence*. Professor Greenberger said that the sense of entitlement could be related to increased parental pressure, competition among peers and family members and a heightened sense of achievement anxiety.

3   Aaron M. Brower, the vice provost for teaching and learning at the University of Wisconsin-Madison, offered another theory. "I think that it stems from their K–12 experiences," Professor Brower said. "They have become ultra-efficient in test preparation. And this hyper-efficiency has led them to look for a magic formula to get high scores."

4   James Hogge, associate dean of the Peabody School of Education at Vanderbilt University, said: "Students often confuse the level of effort with the quality of work. There is a mentality in students that 'if I work hard, I deserve a high grade.'" In line with Dean Hogge's observation are Professor Greenberger's test results. Nearly two-thirds of the students surveyed said that if they explained to a professor that they were trying hard, that should be taken into account in their grade.

5   Jason Greenwood, a senior kinesiology major at the University of Maryland echoed that view. "I think putting in a lot of effort should merit a high grade," Mr. Greenwood said. "What else is there really than the effort that you put in?"

6   "If you put in all the effort you have and get a C, what is the point?" he added. "If someone goes to every class and reads every chapter in the book and does everything the teacher asks of them and more, then they should be getting an A like their effort deserves. If your maximum effort can only be average in a teacher's mind, then something is wrong." Sarah Kinn, a junior English major at the University of Vermont, agreed, saying, "I feel that if I do all of the readings and attend class regularly that I should be able to achieve a grade of at least a B."

7   At Vanderbilt, there is an emphasis on what Dean Hogge calls "the locus of control." The goal is to put the academic burden on the student. "Instead of getting an A, they make an A," he said. "Similarly, if they make a lesser grade, it is not the teacher's fault. Attributing the outcome of a failure to someone else is a common problem." Additionally, Dean Hogge said, "professors often try to outline the 'rules of the game' in their syllabi," in an effort to curb haggling over grades.

8   Professor Brower said professors at Wisconsin emphasized that students must "read for knowledge and write with the goal of exploring ideas." This informal mission statement, along with special seminars for freshmen, is intended to help "re-teach students about what education is."

9   The seminars are integrated into introductory courses. Examples include the conventional, like a global-warming seminar, and the more obscure, like physics in religion. The seminars "are meant to help students think differently about their classes and connect them to real life," Professor Brower said. He said that if students developed a genuine interest in their field, grades would take a back seat, and holistic and intrinsically motivated learning could take place.

10   "College students want to be part of a different and better world, but they don't know how," he said. "Unless teachers are very intentional with our goals, we play into the system in place."

QUESTIONS FOR DISCUSSION

1. What do you think Professor Grossman means when he states that his students have a "sense of entitlement"?
2. How does "effort" differ from the actual quality of the final product?
3. "Instead of getting an A, they [students] make an A," says Dean James Hogge. What is the difference?
4. Is it realistic to expect grades "to take a back seat"? Why or why not?
5. According to this article, what can professors do to avoid conflicts over grades? What additional measures do you think both students and teachers can take?

EXERCISE 1.5   Breaking the Code of a College Writing Assignment

Directions: Imagine your English instructor gave you the following assignment. First, carefully read the assignment. Next, answer the questions that follow. Compare your answers to the analysis of the assignment that follows the exercise.

Assignment: Read Max Roosevelt's article "Student Expectations Seen as Causing Grade Disputes" and write a 500-word essay in which you respond to the reasons Roosevelt cites for why college students dispute their grades. Do you agree or disagree that these are typical reasons? Might Roosevelt have overlooked key reasons for grade disputes? Draw from your own first-hand knowledge and experiences as a college student to support your points. Imagine your readers are instructors at this institution who would like to prevent the misunderstandings that lead to grade disputes.

1. According to the assignment, what is the topic of this paper? What repeated words give you a clue?

2. Who is the audience for this paper? Could there be more than one audience?

3. What is your purpose for writing about this topic for this audience? What other purposes might you have in completing this assignment?

4. What special requirements does this assignment call for?

Now check to see if your analysis of the writing assignment has cracked the "code."

Analyzing the Breaking the Code of College Writing Assignment

First, determine the **topic**, audience, and **purpose** of the writing assignment.

Topic

The **topic** is the *causes of grade disputes*. Notice how the key words of the topic are repeated in the assignment.

Read Max Roosevelt's article "Student Expectations Seen as Causing **Grade Disputes**" and write a *500-word essay in which you respond to the reasons Roosevelt cites* for why college students dispute their grades. Do you agree or disagree that these are typical reasons? Might Roosevelt have overlooked key **reasons for grade disputes**? *Draw from your own first-hand knowledge and experiences as a college student* to support your points. Imagine your readers are instructors at this institution who would like to prevent the misunderstandings that lead to grade disputes.

Audience

This assignment has two audiences. One is *your instructor*. This assignment also asks you to "imagine" a more general audience of college instructors who want to avoid grade disputes.

Purpose

Your **purpose** in writing to the more general audience is pretty straightforward: By informing your readers of the causes of grade disputes, you can then show ways to prevent such disputes. Your **purpose** in writing for your instructor is a bit more complex. One purpose is to show that you have read and understood the article. You should also demonstrate that you can connect with a particular audience by choosing the appropriate style and level of language. Finally, a purpose common to all of your assignments is to show that you can write well.

Requirements

Your instructor wants an *essay*, so that means an introduction, a body, and a conclusion—a piece with multiple paragraphs. There is also a *specific word count*, so you will want to stay in that range. This assignment asks that you *draw your support from two sources: the assigned article and your own knowledge and experiences*. So be sure to show evidence of both in your paper.

EXERCISE 1.6   **Analyze a Student's Writing**   MyWritingLab
                    Assignment

Directions: Here is one student's response to the assignment. Read it carefully and respond to the questions that follow, giving specific reasons and examples to support your opinions.

Grades

I agree with some of the reasons in the article but not all of them. There are other reasons for grade disputes that Max does not point out that are also very important. He says students argue about grades because they feel entitled, they want a magic formula and they want credit for effort. All in all, in my opinion, grades are very important, and instructors should do all they can to make sure there students get good grades.

One reason Max Roosevelt says students argue about grades is they feel entitled to good grades. He says, "He attributes those complaints to his students' sense of entitlement." Pressure, competition, and anxiety can cause this belief. I agree that pressure can make students want good grades. I have to make good grades or lose my financial aid. Another friend of mine has a job that will pay for his courses if he makes a B or higher. I think pressure leads to anxiety about grades, but I don't think that means we expect good grades.

Another reason Max Roosevelt says students argue about grades is they are good at preparing for tests in high school, so they want a "magic formula" to pass college courses. I think the tests in college are much harder than they were in high school, and not all teachers give study guides. In high school the teacher covered in class everything that would be on the test. College teachers do not do that. Some expect you to know what's in class and what's in the textbook, too. They expect students to do what they think is important, and that's not fair. There's just too much to learn. My psychology teacher did this, and now most of the students think he's a lousy teacher and the class is stupid. I agree.

Lastly, Max Roosevelt says students argue about grades because they want credit for effort. I defiantly think teachers should give credit for effort. If I go to class and do all the work, I should get a decent grade—period! Not to mention the fact that I pay a lot of money for these courses. Grades will never take a back seat like Max says they should because they are to important when it comes time to get a job.

Besides these reasons I think some students argue about grades because they are given unfairly. The teachers don't explain why the grades are what they are or else grade hard. Some teachers make students do less work than others. Like I know one of my friends has to write only two papers this semester while I have to write six. His teacher is not so picky either. One teacher online suggests that teachers "review materials for clarity, spell out expectations and minimize miscommunication" to avoid grade disputes. Those sound like good suggestions to me. Max Roosevelt writes about a serious problem in "Student Expectations Seen as Causing Grade Disputes," and that problem is probably not going to be solved soon. (505 words)

1. Does the writer connect with the audience?
   - Does the writer generate interest in the opening paragraph?
   - Is the writing style—tone and word choice—appropriate for the audience? Why or why not?
   - Does the writer include information that supports the assignment's purposes?

2. Does the paper show the writer has done what was asked for?
   - Is the paper in a proper essay form?
   - Does it meet the minimum length requirement?
   - Do the supporting details come from the assigned article and the author's experience?
   - Are there enough supporting details to achieve the writer's purpose?

3. Does the paper show that the writer put time into it?
   - What indicates the writer's effort or lack of effort in this paper?
   - Is the paper neatly presented with clean pages and clear print?

4. Does the paper avoid distracting errors?

5. How do you think the instructor will respond to this paper?

Learning Objectives	How they connect to learning, reading, and writing at college . . .
❶ Be an active learner.	Successful college students attend class, but active learners also . . . • Take responsibility for their learning. • Participate both in and outside of class. • Engage with the material in a personal and professional way. • Respect, interact with, and listen to students and professors. • Take advantage of resources such as writing centers and other on-campus resources to help them succeed.
❷ Show good character.	Students who demonstrate respectful and ethical behavior are, in turn, respected and treated fairly.
❸ Practice critical thinking.	Critical thinkers avoid bias and prejudice. They support their opinions with careful reflection and thoughtful research.
❹ Be aware of college discourse communities as different audiences.	Different academic disciplines, majors, and professions typically have their own ways of writing, speaking, and doing research. Successful students learn and work within the expectations for writing in each discipline.
❺ Meet the expectations of college writing assignments.	Professors who assign writing have some basic expectations. Students should . . . • Connect with their audience. • Cover the basics of the assignment. • Produce quality writing.

> **MyWritingLab** Visit **Chapter 1, "What It Means to Be a College Student: Following the Codes,"** in MyWritingLab to test your understanding of the chapter objectives.

The Reading
Process

2

Learning Objectives

In this chapter, you will learn how to . . .

1. Engage in a conversation with an author through active reading.

2. Read as a believer and as a doubter.

3. Put **I D E A S** to work when reading.

4. Demonstrate your understanding of a text through summarizing, paraphrasing, and quoting.

Like these students, you are a reader, and strong readers, like strong writers, use a process. How can you become a more active and critical reader, someone who sees beyond the obvious?

The ability to read actively is vitally important in college because you will have to work with, connect with, and be tested on texts all the time. Being a good reader is also important in your workplace and personal life.

There have been many surveys about what qualities employers want most in their workers, and survey after survey indicates employers hire analytical thinkers—people who read actively and critically—and strong communicators—people who write and speak well. In your personal life, you can broaden your general knowledge, expand your vocabulary, and improve your writing ability by reading from a variety of sources such as newspapers, magazines, blogs, websites, novels, and nonfiction texts. Being an active and critical reader will benefit you in all areas of your life.

❶ Engage in a conversation with an author through active reading.

Active Reading: A Conversation with an Author

When you sit down to read something for a class or for your own enjoyment, how do you go about it?

- Do you take notes?
- If you are reading a book or a handout from class, do you write in the margins?
- Do you underline important passages in your own books and react to them in the margins?
- Do you note parts of the writing that confuse you?
- Do you look up words you do not understand?

When you read in your college courses, think of reading an essay or an article as *being in a conversation*. Respond to what is written. Connect and talk back to what is stated. Be an **active reader**.

Strategies for Active Reading

The following strategies will help you become a strong reader, whether you are reading for your classes, for your job, or for enjoyment:

- **Know the context:** When you read, think about where the writing was published and who is its intended audience. Was it published in a newspaper, on a blog, on a corporation's website, or in a textbook? Are the intended readers specialists, or are they part of a general audience? Knowing the audience a writer is trying to reach will give you insights into the writer's purpose and the strategies used to achieve that purpose.

- **Determine the author's thesis or controlling idea:** Everything you read has a subject, and each writer also has a point to make about that subject. This point, called a **thesis**, is the stand—the position on the subject—that the rest of the document details and supports. The thesis is also called a **controlling idea** because this main point *controls* the action of an essay, memo, or report.

  When you read, always try to determine the writer's thesis because the function of the entire piece of writing is to support or back up that thesis. Some writers will state their thesis clearly and explicitly, often in the beginning of their work, but more often the thesis is an underlying foundation. You will not be able to underline a single sentence and say, "That's the thesis!" But all good writing is developed and organized around a point about the subject—an opinion the writer holds and will have to support if readers are to agree with it.

- **Use a dictionary as you read:** It is easy to find inexpensive but good dictionaries and even simpler to look up words online. If there is a word that you do not understand, LOOK IT UP! Active readers look up words as they read because they know they will better understand the material, and they will build their vocabulary in their own writing and speaking.

- **Read once for enjoyment and twice for analysis:** We suggest you generally read essays and articles twice, the first time for enjoyment and the second time as an exercise in analysis. As you become more skilled at college-level reading, the two steps might combine into one. You will enjoy reading the document and breaking it down, looking at how the writer uses specific details, examples, beliefs, anecdotes, and facts to support a thesis.

- **Annotate the text as you read:** As you *converse* with a text, use a pencil or pen to highlight specific, important passages or words you need to remember. Write your own thoughts or summarize the author's ideas in the margins. If the author states something confusing, put a question mark in the margin and ask your professor about it. If the author says something you really connect to—an experience much like your own—write a short note in the margins to remind yourself of the connection. If the author makes a statement that seems inappropriate or wrong, write comments that challenge him or her. Your marginal notes can work as a guide for discussing the reading in class, or as a model for your own writing if you are assigned to write about the article.

- **Take notes:** If you cannot write in a text or you are reading something published on the Web, simply take notes, using the same strategies for marking up a printed text. Strong readers both write in their texts and take notes because in their notes they can extend their conversation with the piece of writing.

- **Make connections:** Can you talk about how a piece of writing makes you feel and why? How has the text made you think about the subject differently? More importantly, can you make connections among various readings in the same course or to something you have read elsewhere? In what way does the text reinforce, question, or go against other essays or articles you have read or ideas you have encountered from family and friends or various media?

EXERCISE 2.1   Practice Active Reading   MyWritingLab

Directions: Describe the reading process you have followed up until now. Of the active reading strategies described so far, how many have you used? Choose one of the active reading strategies that you have seldom or never used. Make practicing that strategy a priority as you go through the rest of this chapter. After you have finished reading this chapter, write a short description of how using this strategy helped you become a more active reader.

In the following excerpt from a famous essay in the journal *The American Scholar*, William Cronon, a professor of history, geography, and environmental studies, provides inside knowledge about what professors want and expect; how strong reading, writing, and critical thinking skills are crucial; and how students need to be active readers and thinkers who make connections.

As you read Cronon's article, practice the active reading strategies introduced in this chapter.

"Only Connect . . .": The Goals of a Liberal Education   MyWritingLab
by William Cronon

PRE-READING PROMPT

1. How can you tell if a person is educated? In other words, what is your definition of an educated person?
2. What do you think are the advantages of being educated?
3. What do you think are the responsibilities of being educated?

genuflect: to bend on one's knee in order to worship

mantra-like: words that are repeated in prayers

invocations: when speakers appeal to a certain idea in a speech

indoctrinates: brainwashes or creates bias toward issues

liberalism: a political stance that generally supports a strong central government through regulations and federal assistance

reviled: criticized harshly

1   What does it mean to be a liberally educated person? It seems such a simple question, especially given the frequency with which colleges and universities **genuflect** toward this well-worn phrase as the central icon of their institutional missions. **Mantra-like**, the words are endlessly repeated, starting in the glossy admissions brochures that high school students receive by the hundreds in their mailboxes and continuing right down to the last tired **invocations** they hear on commencement day . . . So what exactly do we mean by liberal education, and why do we care so much about it?

2   In speaking of "liberal" education, we certainly do *not* mean an education that **indoctrinates** students in the values of political **liberalism**, at least not in the most obvious sense of the latter phrase. Rather, we use these words to describe an educational tradition that celebrates and nurtures human freedom. These days *liberal* and *liberty* have become words so mired in controversy, embraced and **reviled** as they have been by the far ends of the political spectrum, that we scarcely know how to use them without turning them into slogans—but they can hardly be separated from this educational tradition. *Liberal* derives from the Latin *liberalis,* meaning "of or relating to the liberal arts," which in turn derives from the Latin word *liber,* meaning "free." But the word actually has much deeper roots, being akin to the Old English word *leodan,* meaning "to grow," and *leod,* meaning "people." It is also related to the Greek word *eleutheros,* meaning "free," and goes all the way back to the Sanskrit word *rodhati,* meaning "one climbs," "one grows." *Freedom* and *growth:* here, surely, are values that lie at the very core of what we mean when we speak of a liberal education.

3   Liberal education is built on these values: it aspires to nurture the growth of human talent in the service of human freedom. So one very simple answer to my question is that liberally educated people have been liberated by their education to explore and fulfill the promise of their own highest talents. But what might an education for human freedom actually look like? There's the rub. . . .

4   I would therefore like to return to my opening question and try to answer it (since I too find lists irresistible) with a list of my own. My list consists not of required courses but of personal qualities: the ten qualities I most admire in the people I know who seem to embody the values of a liberal education. How does one recognize liberally educated people?

1. They listen and they hear.

5   This is so simple that it may not seem worth saying, but in our distracted and over-busy age, I think it's worth declaring that educated people know how to pay attention—to others and to the world around them. They work hard to hear what other people say. They can follow an argument, track logical reasoning, detect illogic, hear the emotions that lie behind both the logic and the illogic, and ultimately **empathize** with the person who is feeling those emotions.

empathize: identify with another's situation

2. They read and they understand.

6   This too is ridiculously simple to say but very difficult to achieve, since there are so many ways of reading in our world. Educated people can appreciate not only the front page of the *New York Times* but also the arts section, the sports section, the business section, the science section, and the editorials. They can gain insight from not only *The American Scholar* and the *New York Review of Books* but also from *Scientific American,* the *Economist,* the *National Enquirer, Vogue,* and *Reader's Digest.* They can enjoy John Milton and John Grisham. But skilled readers know how to read far more than just words. They are moved by what they see in a great art museum and what they hear in a concert hall. They recognize extraordinary athletic achievements; they are engaged by classic and contemporary works of theater and cinema; they find in television a valuable window on popular culture. When they wander through a forest or a wetland or a desert, they can identify the wildlife and interpret the lay of the land. They can glance at a farmer's field and tell the difference between soy beans and alfalfa. They recognize fine craftsmanship, whether by a cabinetmaker or an auto mechanic. And they can surf the World Wide Web. All of these are ways in which the eyes and the ears are attuned to the wonders that make up the human and the natural worlds. None of us can possibly master all these forms of "reading," but educated people should be competent in many of them and curious about all of them.

3. They can talk with anyone.

7   Educated people know how to talk. They can give a speech, ask thoughtful questions, and make people laugh. They can hold a conversation with a high school dropout or a Nobel laureate, a child or a nursing-home resident, a factory worker or a corporate president. Moreover, they participate in such conversations not because they like to talk about themselves but because they are genuinely interested in others. A friend of mine says one of the most important things his father ever told him was that whenever he had a conversation, his job was "to figure out what's so neat about what the other person does." I cannot imagine a more **succinct** description of this critically important quality.

> **succinct:** concise and to-the-point description

4. They can write clearly and persuasively and movingly.

8   What goes for talking goes for writing as well: educated people know the craft of putting words on paper. I'm not talking about **parsing** a sentence or composing a paragraph, but about expressing what is in their minds and hearts so as to teach, persuade, and move the person who reads their words. I am talking about writing as a form of touching, akin to the touching that happens in an **exhilarating** conversation.

> **parsing:** breaking down to analyze its parts

> **exhilarating:** exciting and thought provoking

5. They can solve a wide variety of puzzles and problems.

9   The ability to solve puzzles requires many skills, including a basic comfort with numbers, a familiarity with computers, and the recognition that many problems that appear to turn on questions of quality can in fact be reinterpreted as subtle problems of quantity. These are the skills of the analyst, the manager, the engineer, the critic: the ability to look at a complicated reality, break it into pieces, and figure out how it works in order to do practical things in the real world. Part of the challenge in this, of course, is the ability to put reality back together again after having broken it into pieces—for only by so doing can we accomplish practical goals without violating the integrity of the world we are trying to change.

6. They respect rigor not so much for its own sake but as a way of seeking truth.

10   Truly educated people love learning, but they love wisdom more. They can appreciate a closely reasoned argument without being unduly impressed by mere logic. They understand that knowledge serves values, and they strive to put these two—knowledge and values—into constant dialogue with each other. The ability to recognize true rigor is one of the most important achievements in any education, but it is worthless, even dangerous, if it is not placed in the service of some larger vision that also renders it humane.

7. They practice humility, tolerance, and self-criticism.

11   This is another way of saying that they can understand the power of other people's dreams and nightmares as well as their own. They have the intellectual range and emotional generosity to step outside their own experiences and prejudices, thereby opening themselves to perspectives different from their own. From this commitment to tolerance flow all those aspects of a liberal education that oppose **parochialism** and celebrate the wider world: studying foreign languages, learning about the cultures of distant peoples, exploring the history of long ago times, discovering the many ways in which men and women have known the sacred and given names to their gods. Without such encounters, we cannot learn how much people differ—and how much they have in common.

> **parochialism:** a mindset that only cares about what's happening locally

8. They understand how to get things done in the world.

12   In describing the goal of his Rhodes Scholarships, Cecil Rhodes spoke of trying to identify young people who would spend their lives engaged in what he called "the world's fight," by which he meant the struggle to leave the world a better place than they had found it. Learning how to get things done in the world in order to leave it a better place is surely one of the most practical and important lessons we can take from our education. It is **fraught** with peril because the power to act in the world can so easily be abused—but we fool

> **fraught:** filled with

ourselves if we think we can avoid acting, avoid exercising power, avoid joining the world's fight. And so we study power and struggle to use it wisely and well.

9. They nurture and empower the people around them.

13   Nothing is more important in **tempering** the exercise of power and shaping right action than the recognition that no one ever acts alone. Liberally educated people understand that they belong to a community whose prosperity and well-being are crucial to their own, and they help that community flourish by making the success of others possible. If we speak of education for freedom, then one of the crucial insights of a liberal education must be that the freedom of the individual is possible only in a free community, and vice versa. It is the community that empowers the free individual, just as it is free individuals who lead and empower the community. The fulfillment of high talent, the just exercise of power, the celebration of human diversity: nothing so redeems these things as the recognition that what seem like personal triumphs are in fact the achievements of our common humanity.

> **tempering:** to modify or weaken

10. They follow E. M. Forster's injunction from *Howards End*: "Only connect. . . ."

14   More than anything else, being an educated person means being able to see connections that allow one to make sense of the world and act within it in creative ways. Every one of the qualities I have described here—listening, reading, talking, writing, puzzle solving, truth seeking, seeing through other people's eyes, leading, working in a community—is finally about connecting. A liberal education is about gaining the power and the wisdom, the generosity and the freedom to connect.

15   I believe we should measure our educational system—whether we speak of grade schools or universities—by how well we succeed in training children and young adults to aspire to these ten qualities. I believe we should judge ourselves and our communities by how well we succeed in fostering and celebrating these qualities in each of us.

QUESTIONS FOR DISCUSSION

1. Cronon begins his essay with a question. How does he try to make his audience interested in knowing the answer to the question?
2. In his second paragraph, Cronon distinguishes his definition of *liberal education* from the political definition of *liberal*. Why do you think he does this?
3. Cronon writes that liberal education "aspires to nurture the growth of human talent in the service of human freedom." What does he mean? Explain this point in your own words.
4. Cronon has chosen to present in a list form the qualities he believes exist in an educated person. Why do you think he chose this approach, and how effective is it?

5. Why do you think educated people must "work hard" to listen? What difficulties have you encountered in trying to listen?
6. How do you think Cronon defines "reading," since it involves so much more than the printed word?
7. How will awareness of audience help a person achieve the third and fourth traits Cronon describes?
8. Explain what you think Cronon means when he writes, "knowledge serves values."
9. As you continue your education, what practical steps can you take to learn the kind of tolerance Cronon describes?
10. When Cronon says that ultimately, a liberal education is about the "freedom to connect," what does he mean? Connect to what?

MyWritingLab Visit Ch. 2 The Reading Process in MyWritingLab to access the IDEAS videos.

I D E A S for Your Own Writing

Pick One

If you are a relatively new student with a lot of years of formal education still ahead of you, Cronon's list of ten traits may seem a bit overwhelming at this point. Make the "list" manageable by picking one trait that you think you can focus on developing this semester. Which trait have you chosen, and what are some steps you will take this semester to start developing that trait within yourself?

Connect Cronon to a Career

If you have already determined the career you hope to achieve through your education, you probably have some idea about the kinds of knowledge you will need to be successful. For example, a medical professional will need to know biology and chemistry. An aspiring accountant will need to know mathematics. Now think about the broader-reaching characteristics of an educated person that Cronon describes. How will having these traits help you in your specific career? Choose the two or three traits that you see as being most valuable, and describe how having them will help you be successful in your particular field.

---

❷ Read as a believer and as a doubter.

Read as a Believer and as a Doubter

Probably without being aware of it, you have been playing what writer and teacher Peter Elbow calls the "believing and doubting games." You respond to some readings in a positive way, connecting to and agreeing with what the author states. Then you encounter other readings that you disagree with or seriously question. For anyone who wants to become an active and successful reader in college, playing the believing and doubting games on a higher level is necessary.

Reading as a Believer

If you **read as a believer**, you read with an open mind and try to understand what a writer is saying. You think deeply about the writer's ideas, and you open yourself up to the writer's perspective—how he or she sees the world, why the information is important, and how the writer convinces you to accept his or her point. You have to think as you read and ask questions:

- Does the writer have a good point? Why?
- What examples and details reinforce what the writer wants me to think, feel, or understand?
- What does the text make me think about and why?
- How do my own experiences and ideas help me better understand what the writer says?
- How does the writer try to connect with readers?
- Where does the writer connect with me in particular?
- What particular examples or details explain, convince, or entertain me?

Reading as a Doubter

In contrast, when you **read as a doubter**, you are a hardcore skeptic who does not want to believe or who needs to question the points and supporting evidence the writer provides. When you read as a doubter, you actively question what the writer says. You listen, but you question. You inspect. You judge. You read closely in respectful disagreement and, again, ask questions:

- Are there any weak points in the writing? What are they?
- Where does the writer assume something he or she should not? How does that assumption hurt the piece of writing?

- What examples and details do not work and why?
- What examples or details could the writer have added to support the main points more effectively?
- How do my own experiences and ideas go against what the writer is saying?
- Where could the author have better connected to the reader?
- How could the writer have created more interest in the subject?
- What are particular examples or details that do not inform, persuade, or entertain me?

EXERCISE 2.2   Read as a Believer and a Doubter   MyWritingLab

Directions: Imagine a psychology teacher has asked you to do some reading about how personalities can be shaped by environment. You find the following article on birth order. First, carefully read the article as a believer and answer the questions that follow.

Adler's Theory of Birth Order

1   In the 1920s, Alfred Adler, a physician and one-time colleague of Sigmund Freud, was among the first to suggest that birth order had much to do with shaping an individual's personality. According to Adler's theory, each place in a family structure comes with a role, which then shapes the personality of the family member in that role. Later theorists have expanded upon Adler's work and propose that a child's place in the family structure not only shapes personality but has implications for the child's future in school and in the workplace.

2   The oldest child begins life with both parents' attention, and with a lot of adult interaction tends to develop strong people skills. First borns are often intelligent and assertive. And because these children lose their parents' complete attention when siblings arrive, first borns tend to be ambitious and disciplined perfectionists as they try to regain their parents' attention and to assert their superiority over the other children. Their leadership role in the family may also lead first borns to be controlling and to place great importance on being right. First borns carry their high-achieving ways into their careers. They often choose professions that require higher education such as science, law, government and engineering. In business, first borns hold most senior management positions. Interestingly, over half of U.S. presidents and Nobel Prize winners are first borns. Winston Churchill, Oprah Winfrey, and Bill and Hillary Clinton are some famous first borns.

3   The typical middle child's competitiveness may stem from trying to keep up with or surpass the older sibling. With this competitive nature comes flexibility and diplomacy since the middle child must deal with older and young siblings. At the same time, middle children may become rebellious as they try to win attention. A search for their

own identity leads many middles to move far from home once they are grown. More laid back and flexible than first borns, typical middles have good communication skills and enjoy socializing. Middles often choose careers in nursing, law enforcement, social work and support services. While middles do not typically earn as much as first borns, they report greater satisfaction with their jobs. Famous middles include such great communicators as Martin Luther King and John F. Kennedy as well as Bill Gates, Madonna, and Princess Diana.

4   The stereotype of the youngest child being pampered and spoiled often is the reality according to birth order theorists. Even though their parents are the most experienced, youngest children are frequently the least disciplined, possibly because their parents have grown more relaxed or just more tired from child-raising. Although used to being the center of attention and expecting others to provide for them, the youngest children can also be creative and delightful, winning over parents and siblings with charm and humor. Having been perceived as the smallest and weakest in their own families, last borns often swell the ranks of reform movements and champion the causes of the underdog, the downtrodden. Their creativity and love of attention draw last borns to careers in the arts, journalism, sales and athletics. Copernicus, Harriet Tubman, Mother Teresa, Jay Leno, and Eddie Murphy are famous last borns.

5   Dr. Adler presented his theories as only one of many ways of trying to understand people, and experts continue to both expand upon and question these theories. Birth order is only one of many variables that go into shaping an individual's personality.

Reading as a Believer

1. Adler believes birth order plays a significant role in shaping one's personality. Why might his theory have validity?

2. The author begins each body paragraph with an explanation of the traits associated with a particular birth order. How do these explanations support Adler's theory?

3. The author also includes examples of well-known people. How do these examples support Adler's theory?

4. What in your own experiences supports Adler's theory? In what ways are you like the profile your birth order indicates? Do you have family and friends who fit Adler's birth order profiles?

5. What do you find most convincing or most engaging about Adler's theory?

Now go back and reread the same article as a doubter, looking for ways to question and disbelieve what the writer says. Then answer the following questions.

Reading as a Doubter

1. What questions about Adler and his theory does the introduction raise? Why might you doubt the theory's credibility?

2. What other factors in a person's life might reduce or even negate the influence of birth order?

3. What about Adler's theory seems to suggest stereotyping?

4. What in your own experiences goes against Adler's theory? In what ways are you unlike the profile your birth order indicates? Which friends and/or family members do not fit Adler's birth order profiles?

5. What additional kinds of examples and explanation should the author have included to present Adler's theory more convincingly?

❸ Use the **I D E A S** template to analyze what you read.

MyWritingLab Visit Ch. 2 The Reading Process in MyWritingLab to access the IDEAS videos.

Put **I D E A S** to Work When Reading

Writers try to connect with an **audience**, a group of readers. So, in addition to reading as both a believer and a doubter, you should think about how a writer tries to inform, convince, or entertain readers. Writers who do a good job of connecting with their audience do all three. Good writers provide solid explanations, persuade readers to their point of view, and capture and keep their readers' interest.

When you read, think about the components a writer uses to construct an essay or article. A good way to take apart a piece of writing and to analyze it is to use this five-part comprehensive template **I D E A S**

I nterest

D etails

E xplanation

A udience

S tyle

I nterest

Writers have to grab the reader's attention and keep it. As a reader, you need to judge how well a writer keeps your interest in the subject as you closely read his or her essay. Some common methods writers use to capture and maintain reader interest include the following:

- **Relating personal experiences and anecdotes:** You may have heard the term *human interest*. Writers often engage readers by showing how a subject involves real people. Writers may use their own experiences to establish their authority and show first-hand knowledge of a subject. Writers also appeal to readers' human interest by including **anecdotes**—short, interesting, or amusing incidents about real people.

- **Incorporating surprising facts or statistics:** Writers incorporate **facts**—irrefutable truths—to lend authority and credibility to their writing. Although not as reliable as facts because they can be misinterpreted or manipulated, statistics can also lend strength to an argument or information. The best writers avoid piling facts and statistics together in a dry, boring way. Instead, they look for ways to use this kind of support to capture the readers' interest while providing compelling information.

- **Appealing to or questioning beliefs and assumptions:** Writers try to tap into common beliefs and assumptions as a way to connect with an audience, especially if they are trying to persuade them about something. Some common beliefs in our culture are these: those who work hard will succeed; everyone should have access to public education; our elected officials represent us as citizens; people should vote; and so on. What is interesting and sometimes makes for more thought-provoking writing is when an author takes on commonly held beliefs and shows how they are weak or even wrong. For example, an author could go against the common perception that bottled water is clean and healthy by including examples and studies that show tap water is as clean as—if not cleaner, cheaper, and more environmentally friendly than—bottled water.

D etails

Writers use various types of concrete and specific details to "paint a picture" with words.

- **Concrete details** use the five senses (sight, smell, sound, taste, touch) to present a sensory description of something, such as a Saturday afternoon in June: high-80s temperature, a gentle breeze from the west, the hum of your house's air conditioner, the racket of the neighbor's lawnmower, the green grass of your backyard, the shouts and laughter of kids down the street playing whiffle ball, barking dogs, the aroma of barbeque grills cooking meat, and so on.

- **Specific details** bring descriptive drama and clarity to writing. In contrast, broad or vague generalizations can leave writing bland and uninformative. Here are some examples that show the difference between general and specific details:

General	←			→	Specific
walk		walk slowly			shuffle
fruit	apple		green apple		Granny Smith
haircut		short haircut			mohawk
angry		very angry			outraged
red	dark red	deep dark red			crimson
hot		very hot and humid			sultry
book	college textbook	college writing textbook			*IDEAS & Aims*
team		professional baseball team			Chicago Cubs

E xplanation

Strong **explanation** through good examples, facts, and anecdotes is key to helping readers understand a writer's reasoning or point of view. Developed examples *explain* the reality of situations or problems. In addition, when using specialized terms or working with abstract concepts, a writer must provide explanations, so readers understand them and follow the writer's train of thought. As a reader, you should question whether an author provides enough explanation for you to understand the point of the writing.

Albert Einstein once said, "Example is not the main thing in influencing others. It is the only thing." While Einstein was exaggerating a bit, good **examples** can be informative and persuasive because they explain and show readers what a writer means. A writer trying to convince readers of the dangers of texting and driving might cite examples of serious accidents that occurred because of drivers focused on their cell phones instead of the road. You, as a reader, need to judge how typical, representative, and accurate examples in a piece of writing are. In other words, you need to think, "Do the examples and details provide a strong enough explanation of the writer's point?"

A udience

Good writers use word choice and level of language as well as particular details and examples to best reach their intended audience. They consider what their readers already know and what they need to know about a topic. Writers also project a particular tone or attitude they hope will further appeal to their audience. Look at a typical "Letters to the Editor" page in a local newspaper. You will notice some writers sound angry or frustrated while others come across as polite and cordial. One writer may project a sarcastic or mocking tone while another sounds sympathetic or even sad. When you read, consider how well the writer appeals to the intended audience.

ⓢtyle

Just like we dress differently for different occasions like weddings, job interviews, or athletic events, writers adjust their style of writing based on the writing situation. Style means that writers use various grammatical tools and different types of sentences to further appeal to their audience (see Chapter 14). They play with sentence rhythm by using long, medium, and short sentences. Style also includes the level of formality in a piece of writing. Do the audience and purpose require an informal, formal, or a middle-ground style?

In the next chapter, we will show you how this tool for close reading can also be used for generating ideas for writing. Successful writers use all of these components to inform, convince, and please readers—to make their work interesting, to make people want to read their writing, and to get their ideas and points across to their audience. This ⓘ ⓓ ⓔ ⓐ ⓢ template will serve you well as you read and write in college.

EXERCISE 2.3   Read as a Believer and a Doubter and Use ⓘ ⓓ ⓔ ⓐ ⓢ

Directions: Reading the following essay by Brent Staples entitled "Black Men and Public Space" will help you practice reading actively and critically, working the believing and doubting games, and using the IDEAS tool. After reading the essay, answer the questions related to reading as a believer and as a doubter and using IDEAS to analyze writing. Be sure to read the essay at least twice.

Black Men and Public Space   My**Writing**Lab
by Brent Staples

This essay by Staples first appeared in Ms. Magazine *in 1986, under the title "Just Walk On By." A year later, Staples revised it slightly for publication in* Harper's *magazine under the present title.*

1   My first victim was a woman—white, well dressed, probably in her early twenties. I came upon her late one evening on a deserted street in Hyde Park, a relatively affluent neighborhood in an otherwise mean, impoverished section of Chicago. As I swung onto the avenue behind her, there seemed to be a discreet, uninflammatory distance between us. Not so. She cast back a worried glance. To her, the youngish black man—a broad six feet two inches with a beard and billowing hair, both hands shoved into the pockets of a bulky military jacket—seemed menacingly close. After a few more quick glimpses, she picked up her pace and was soon running in earnest. Within seconds she disappeared into a cross street.

2   That was more than a decade ago, I was twenty-two years old, a graduate student newly arrived at the University of Chicago. It was in the echo of that terrified woman's footfalls that I first began to know the unwieldy inheritance I'd come into—the ability to alter public space in ugly ways. It was clear that she thought herself the quarry of a mugger, a rapist, or worse. Suffering a bout of insomnia, however, I was stalking sleep, not defenseless wayfarers. As a softy who is scarcely able to take a knife to a raw chicken—let alone hold one to a person's throat—I was surprised, embarrassed, and dismayed all at once. Her flight made me feel like an accomplice in tyranny. It also made it clear that I was indistinguishable from the muggers who occasionally seeped into the area from the surrounding ghetto. That first encounter, and those that followed, signified that a vast, unnerving gulf lay between nighttime pedestrians—particularly women—and me. And I soon gathered that being perceived as dangerous is a hazard in itself. I only needed to turn a corner into a dicey situation, or crowd some frightened, armed person in a foyer somewhere, or make an errant move after being pulled over by a policeman. Where fear and weapons meet—and they often do in urban America—there is always the possibility of death.

3   In that first year, my first away from my hometown, I was to become thoroughly familiar with the language of fear. At dark, shadowy intersections, I could cross in front of a car stopped at a traffic light and elicit the *thunk, thunk, thunk* of the driver—black, white, male, or female—hammering down the door locks. On less traveled streets after dark, I grew accustomed to but never comfortable with people crossing to the other side of the street rather than pass me. Then there were the standard unpleasantries with policemen, doormen, bouncers, cabdrivers, and others whose business it is to screen out troublesome individuals *before* there is any nastiness.

4   I moved to New York nearly two years ago and I have remained an avid night walker. In central Manhattan, the near-constant crowd cover minimizes tense one-on-one street encounters. Elsewhere—in SoHo, for example, where sidewalks are narrow and tightly spaced buildings shut out the sky—things can get very taut indeed.

5   After dark, on the warrenlike streets of Brooklyn where I live, I often see women who fear the worst from me. They seem to have set their faces on neutral, and with their purse straps strung across their chests bandolier-style, they

forge ahead as though bracing themselves against being tackled. I understand, of course, that the danger they perceive is not a hallucination. Women are particularly vulnerable to street violence, and young black males are drastically over-represented among the perpetrators of that violence. Yet these truths are no solace against the kind of alienation that comes of being ever the suspect, a fearsome entity with whom pedestrians avoid making eye contact.

6   It is not altogether clear to me how I reached the ripe old age of twenty-two without being conscious of the lethality nighttime pedestrians attributed to me. Perhaps it was because in Chester, Pennsylvania, the small, angry industrial town where I came of age in the 1960s, I was scarcely noticeable against a backdrop of gang warfare, street knifings, and murders. I grew up one of the good boys, had perhaps a half-dozen fistfights. In retrospect, my shyness of combat has clear sources.

7   As a boy, I saw countless tough guys locked away; I have since buried several, too. They were babies, really—a teenage cousin, a brother of twenty-two, a childhood friend in his mid-twenties—all gone down in episodes of bravado played out in the streets. I came to doubt the virtues of intimidation early on. I chose, perhaps unconsciously, to remain a shadow—timid, but a survivor.

8   The fearsomeness mistakenly attributed to me in public places often has a perilous flavor. The most frightening of these confusions occurred in the late 1970s and early 1980s, when I worked as a journalist in Chicago. One day, rushing into the office of a magazine I was writing for with a deadline story in hand, I was mistaken for a burglar. The office manager called security and, with an ad hoc posse, pursued me through the labyrinthine halls, nearly to my editor's door. I had no way of proving who I was. I could only move briskly toward the company of someone who knew me.

9   Another time I was on assignment for a local paper and killing time before an interview. I entered a jewelry store on the city's affluent Near North Side. The proprietor excused herself and returned with an enormous red Doberman pinscher straining at the end of a leash. She stood, the dog extended toward me, silent to my questions, her eyes bulging nearly out of her head. I took a cursory look around, nodded, and bade her good night.

10   Relatively speaking, however, I never fared as badly as another black male journalist. He went to nearby Waukegan, Illinois, a couple of summers ago to work on a story about a murderer who was born there. Mistaking the reporter for the killer, police officers hauled him from his car at gunpoint and but for his press credentials would probably have tried to book him. Such episodes are not uncommon. Black men trade tales like this all the time.

11   Over the years, I learned to smother the rage I felt at so often being taken for a criminal. Not to do so would surely have led to madness. I now take precautions to make myself less threatening. I move about with care, particularly late in the evening. I give a wide berth to nervous people on subway platforms during the wee hours, particularly when I have exchanged business clothes for jeans. If I happen to be entering a building behind some people who appear skittish, I may

walk by, letting them clear the lobby before I return, so as not to seem to be following them. I have been calm and extremely congenial on those rare occasions when I've been pulled over by the police.

12   And on late-evening constitutionals I employ what has proved to be an excellent tension-reducing measure: I whistle melodies from Beethoven and Vivaldi and the more popular classical composers. Even steely New Yorkers hunching toward nighttime destinations seem to relax, and occasionally they even join in the tune. Virtually everybody seems to sense that a mugger wouldn't be warbling bright, sunny selections from Vivaldi's *Four Seasons*. It is my equivalent of the cowbell that hikers wear when they know they are in bear country.

READING "BLACK MEN AND PUBLIC SPACE" AS A BELIEVER

1. Have you or has someone you know ever been misjudged because of appearance? How does having that kind of experience help you better understand Staples' topic?
2. Which of Staples' examples most clearly help you understand his situation?
3. Have you read or heard on the news about other situations similar to those of Staples? Are black men the most likely to suffer from being perceived as "dangerous"?
4. Although Staples does admit to feeling rage, does he also seem reasonable enough to understand why people react to him the way they do—especially women? What evidence in the essay suggests this?

READING "BLACK MEN AND PUBLIC SPACE" AS A DOUBTER

1. Staples gives three examples of his own experiences of "being perceived as dangerous" and one example of a black journalist. Are these examples enough to be convincing? Do you accept his statement that "Black men trade tales like this all the time" as valid? Why or why not?
2. What responsibility does Staples bear for people's reaction to him? Is he justified in feeling "rage" because people can be afraid of him in the situations he describes?
3. Have you ever been in similar circumstances—either as a "victim" or as a menace? If so, was your experience comparable to his?
4. How could Staples have made this essay more appealing to you personally?

DISCOVERING **I D E A S** IN "BLACK MEN AND PUBLIC SPACE"

I nterest

1. How does Staples grab his readers' interest with the opening line of the essay? What word in particular do you think Staples chose to catch readers' attention? Why?

2. In this essay Staples looks at how he is perceived by other people. Why is it important to him that his readers and others understand that he is not a "dangerous" person?

D etails

3. Staples describes his "first victim" as "terrified" as she runs away from him. To describe his own reactions to the encounter, he uses the following adjectives: "surprised," "embarrassed," and "dismayed." How do the later details about his upbringing help the reader to better understand each of his reactions?

4. Staples refers to "the language of fear"—a very abstract idea. What concrete details does he use to help readers understand what he means by this?

E xplanation

5. In addition to the opening example, Staples uses two other personal examples to show how he has "the ability to alter public space in ugly ways." Are these examples enough to convince you of the problem he claims to face? Why or why not?

6. In bear country, hikers wear bells to warn bears of their presence because startling a bear could cause it to attack. Staples describes his whistling classical music as his "equivalent of the cowbell." Explain what he means.

A udience

7. This essay first appeared in *Ms.*—a magazine with a readership primarily composed of white women. What do you think Staples does in this essay to appeal to these female readers? How does he help them understand his situation even as he remains aware that many of them might react as "victims" if they met him on a deserted street?

8. Near the end of the essay, Staples talks about the "rage" he often felt at being mistaken for a criminal. What clues in the essay before this point led you to believe he might be angry about his situation? Why do you think he waited until nearly the end of the essay to state his anger so directly and forcefully?

S tyle

9. What about Staples' writing style indicates that he is an educated individual? Give examples of words and phrases to illustrate your points.

10. Despite his high level of education—a Ph.D. in psychology—Staples still writes in a way that a general audience can follow his ideas. How does he keep his story engaging and his ideas clear?

WRITING ACTIVITIES

1. Drawing from your responses as both a believer and a doubter, write a letter to Brent Staples that presents your reaction to his essay.
2. Staples would whistle classical music in order to create the impression of being educated and nonthreatening. Write a paragraph in which you describe how you would create a positive impression of yourself in a particular situation. For example, as a student, how could you create a positive first impression for a teacher?
3. Staples writes about how during his early life, he saw the negative consequences of violence in the lives of his family and friends. He learned from their mistakes and chose a much different lifestyle. Write a few paragraphs in which you describe how a negative example helped you choose a more positive direction in your life.
4. Write an essay that discusses an incident in your life in which a person's appearance made a big difference in the way he or she was treated, either by you or by others. What did this incident teach you about the importance of appearance? Imagine that this essay will be read by a young (early teens) friend or relative who seems to be too concerned (or perhaps not concerned enough) about his or her appearance.

④ Demonstrate your understanding of a text through summarizing, paraphrasing, and quoting.

Demonstrate Your Understanding of a Text through Summarizing, Paraphrasing, and Quoting

You know that you truly understand another writer's work when you can pull out its most essential information and restate that information *in your own words and writing style*.

Instructors also know that if you can accurately restate the main ideas of written material in your own words, you truly understand what you read. Then you can present your evaluation of the material. This is why in many different courses you will frequently encounter assignments that require you to incorporate outside material through summarizing, paraphrasing, and quoting.

The Essentials of Summarizing

Summarizing is *condensing* all or part of another writer's work to create a much more concise version that focuses on the author's main point(s) *using your own words*. For example, if you summarized Brent Staples' article, you would relate the basic information about his essay in one paragraph or even in one sentence.

A summary must *present the original material accurately in terms of content and tone*. You must not misrepresent or misstate the original author's ideas and information. If the original author takes a negative view of a subject, your summary should not use words that present the subject positively. Of course as a believing and doubting reader, you will both agree and disagree with the author; however, you *must not* do this in the summary itself. Present the original ideas accurately and then respond to them, so your ideas are clearly distinct from those of the original author.

Although you keep the content and tone consistent with the original author's, the words and style of the summary must be your own. A summary that changes only a word or two or flip-flops a few sentences is a form of plagiarism. **Plagiarism** is presenting another's work as though it were your own. Even if you acknowledge that the *ideas* belong to the original author by using a citation or an endnote, a summary is still dishonest if it presents the original author's words and style as though they were your own words and style. If the original author has a term or expression that you cannot put in your own words or style without losing meaning, incorporate it into your summary as a short direct quote. Do this very sparingly.

Here is what you need to do when you summarize:

Guidelines for Summarizing ...

- Begin the summary by providing the name of the author and the title of the work you are summarizing in an introductory phrase (IP).
- Condense what the author says to only the main points that support the thesis. Generally, a summary reduces the original by 50 percent or more.
- Write the summary in your own words and style.
- Place within quotation marks important phrases or terms from the author that you want to keep if you're allowed to quote when summarizing and then properly cite the author's words through in-text citation (see Chapter 13, p. 378, for more details).
- Keep your summary's overall attitude and tone consistent with those of the original author.
- Keep your own comments and opinions separate from the summary.

Sample Summary

An instructor asked his students to read "Black Men and Public Space" and to write a one-paragraph summary of it. He told them that he expected a detailed summary, not one or two sentences, so they needed to provide in-text citations when they paraphrased from the essay.

Here is one student's response to this assignment. Notice how he presents the main points in the same order as Staples and does not include his own ideas and comments. He also uses transitions, so the summary is organized and coherent for readers who may not be familiar with the original essay.

Deondre Johnson
Prof. Kory
Introduction to College Writing
28 November 2016

A Summary of "Black Men in Public Space"

In the article "Black Men and Public Space," Brent Staples describes the impact he has on strangers he encounters in public places. Although people may perceive him as dangerous because of his race, Staples himself is in danger from these misperceptions. Staples begins by describing the impact he has on his "victims," who are the people—especially women—who react with fear and concern when they meet him (39). They avoid eye contact, may hold their purses tighter, cross the street or lock their car doors. While Staples acknowledges that women have good reason to be cautious in public and young black men do commit acts of violence, he says the consistent public judgment against him is discouraging (40). What makes the reactions towards him particularly misguided is that Staples has consistently avoided violent behavior after growing up in a violent area. He saw too many people he knew killed or jailed, so he stayed reserved and quiet in the background (40). Despite his demeanor, Staples knows that his appearance puts him at risk for harm by those, including armed business owners and police officers, who may overreact with violence to the appearance of a large black man (40). But Staples has come to terms with the anger he feels at being mistaken for a violent criminal-type. He tries hard to make himself appear less dangerous, even whistling classical music when he walks alone at night as a way to protect himself from others' perceptions (41).

Works Cited

Staples, Brent. "Black Men and Public Space." *IDEAS & Aims: Paragraphs & Essays*. Tim Taylor and Linda Copeland, Pearson, 2016, pp. 38-41.

Deondre identifies the title, author, and subject of the essay in an introductory phrase (IP) at the start of the summary.

Deondre refers to the author by last name only after having given the full name in his opening sentence.

Because he quotes from the essay, he provides the page number where "victims" appears.

Deondre relates a specific point from the essay, so he cites the page number because he is paraphrasing.

Here is a paraphrase of the specific point Staples makes at the end of his essay.

EXERCISE 2.4   Identify Appropriate Summaries   MyWritingLab

Directions: In the following passage from his essay "'Only Connect. . .': The Goals of a Liberal Education," William Cronon describes the traits of an educated reader. Read the passage, and then analyze each of the following attempts to summarize it. For each summary, determine if it is

(P) plagiarized.

(D) too detailed, containing more than the main ideas.

(G) too general, leaving out key information.

(A) acceptable.

2. They read and they understand.

This too is ridiculously simple to say but very difficult to achieve, since there are so many ways of reading in our world. Educated people can appreciate not only the front page of the *New York Times* but also the arts section, the sports section, the business section, the science section, and the editorials. They can gain insight from not only *The American Scholar* and the *New York Review of Books* but also from *Scientific American,* the *Economist,* the *National Enquirer, Vogue,* and *Reader's Digest.* They can enjoy John Milton and John Grisham. But skilled readers know how to read far more than just words. They are moved by what they see in a great art museum and what they hear in a concert hall. They recognize extraordinary athletic achievements; they are engaged by classic and contemporary works of theater and cinema; they find in television a valuable window on popular culture. When they wander through a forest or a wetland or a desert, they can identify the wildlife and interpret the lay of the land. They can glance at a farmer's field and tell the difference between soy beans and alfalfa. They recognize fine craftsmanship, whether by a cabinetmaker or an auto mechanic. And they can surf the World Wide Web. All of these are ways in which the eyes and the ears are attuned to the wonders that make up the human and the natural worlds. None of us can possibly master all these forms of "reading," but educated people should be competent in many of them and curious about all of them.

▶ **Note to Student:**
Note that when summarizing, paraphrasing, and quoting from a source, a writer has to introduce the where and/or who the information came from. In Chapter 13, these phrases are formally called Introductory Phrases or IPs. See pages 383 and 391 for the five common IP Patterns.

_____ a.   According to Cronon, educated people read and understand what they read, a complex ability with the world's varied texts. Educated people can read newspapers like the *New York Times* from its front page to its more specialized sections on business, science, and sports. They can read magazines like *Scientific American* and the *Economist* as well as more popular general magazines like *Vogue* and *Reader's Digest.* They can read a wide range of authors from classic Milton to contemporary John Grisham. Educated people go far beyond reading only words. They read other "texts," such as works of art, concerts, theater, athletic events and even television programs. When educated people travel through various ecosystems, they know the various kinds of flora and fauna as well as the geographic features. They can identify various crops, such as soy beans and alfalfa. They can also tell whether or not a mechanic or a craftsman has done quality work. Educated people can navigate and read the Internet as well. Whether the text is natural or man-made, educated people can read it success-fully. There are far too many kinds of texts for anyone to learn to the point of being an expert; however, educated people learn as much as they can and always remain open to learning more.

____ b.   Cronon says that educated people understand everything they read. This ability is difficult to achieve because of all the different ways of reading. Educated people read not only scholarly journals, books and newspapers and enjoy authors like John Milton and John Grisham, they read more than just words. They are moved by what they read in great art, concerts, athletic achievements, theater, cinema and television. In different environments, they can identify wildlife and interpret the lay of the land. They can read farmers' fields and rec-ognize craftsmanship by cabinetmakers or mechanics. They can surf the Internet. They can read all these wonders of the human world and the natural world. Although none of us can master all this reading, educated people should be competent in many and curious about all.

____ c.   In his article, Cronon says educated people not only read, but under-stand what they read. Because of all the different ways of reading, this ability is deceptively complex. Educated people can read and enjoy a wide range of materials from scholarly and informative texts to purely enter-taining material. Their ability to read also goes beyond the written word. Educated people respond to great visual art, music, athletic perfor-mances, movies, theatrical performances and even television shows. They can read the natural environment in its varied forms, and can appreciate the achievements of farmers as well as tradesmen. Educated people are technologically literate as well. While no one can be expert in all these natural and man-made texts, Cronon says educated people "should be competent in many of them and curious about all of them" (28).

____ d.   Cronon says it's easier said than done, but educated people should be able to read and understand many different things besides literature, such as art and sports. They should understand nature in all its forms and the achievements of all different careers. Educated people should use computers. They should know a little of everything even though they'll never be masters of anything.

EXERCISE 2.5   **Summarize a Point from Cronon**   MyWritingLab

Directions: Pick one of the remaining nine points in Cronon's "'Only Connect . . .': The Goals of a Liberal Education" (p. 27), and write a summary of that point. Remember, a summary should be a much smaller version of the original passage, it needs to be in your words and style, and you need to introduce the author and title of the work at the start of the summary. For this exercise, try to limit your summary to *one or two sentences*. Refer to the Guidelines for Summarizing on page 44 as necessary.

EXERCISE 2.6   **Summarize "Be an Active Learner"**   MyWritingLab

Directions: In Chapter 1, there's a section called "Be an Active Learner" (p. 2). Reread that section, take notes, and then summarize the whole section, including "Strategies for Active Learning," in one paragraph of 6 to 8 sentences. Refer to the Guidelines for Summarizing on page 44 as necessary.

The Essentials of Paraphrasing

To work at an even closer level than summarizing, you can paraphrase part of an article or essay. You **paraphrase** when you take a specific passage from another writer and present the ideas of that writer entirely *in your own words and style*—without quoting.

Here, the goal is not to condense. A paraphrase is *about the same length* as the original material because it presents the details as well as the major points. But like a summary, a paraphrase restates the original material *in your words and style* while staying consistent with the original author's content and tone. You must also acknowledge where you found the information.

Like summarizing, paraphrasing shows that you truly understand what another writer is saying.

Here is what you have to do when you paraphrase:

Guidelines for Paraphrasing . . .

- Begin the paraphrase by providing the name of the author and the title of the book, article, or other source you are paraphrasing in an introductory phrase (IP).

- Do not use the same words or phrases that are in the original piece of writing. Use your own words and style.

- Make sure the paraphrase is approximately the same length as the original.

- Double-check your words against the author's words in the original passage, to make certain you are not using the author's exact wording.

- Keep the paraphrase's overall attitude and tone consistent with those of the original author.
- Keep your own comments and opinions separate from the paraphrase.
- Properly cite the paraphrase using in-text citation (see p. 378 in Chapter 13).

When paraphrasing, the introductory phrase and the in-text citation at the end of the paraphrase indicate to the reader that you have started (the IP) and then you have stopped paraphrasing (the in-text citation).

Sample Paraphrase

An instructor has assigned readings from David Brooks' essay "Self-Control Is the Key to Success" on page 3 of this text, and she wants to be sure students have understood key points by asking them to paraphrase some passages from the readings. Here is how one student paraphrased a key passage:

Original Passage

The ability to delay gratification, like most skills, correlates with socioeconomic status and parenting styles. Children from poorer homes do much worse on delayed gratification tests than children from middle-class homes. That's probably because children from poorer homes are more likely to have their lives disrupted by marital breakdown, violence, moving, etc.
They think in the short term because there is no predictable long term.

Brooks, "Self-Control
Is the Key to Success," p. 4

Paraphrase

In his essay, Brooks says that homes with higher income levels and parents who create a safe and more loving environment often produce children who are able to take their time to achieve goals and successes. These children are also more future-oriented as a direct result of the positive foundation they find at home. Children from poorer homes, on the other hand, often live in the moment because the present, for them, is so unsettled (4).

EXERCISE 2.7   **Identify Appropriate Paraphrases**   MyWritingLab

Directions: Read and analyze the paraphrases of the following passage, and determine if the paraphrases are

(P) plagiarized.

(G) too general.

(I) inaccurate.

(A) acceptable.

Original Passage

Here is the quotation from Brooks' essay:

"Yet the Mischel experiments, along with everyday experience, tell us that self-control is essential. Young people who can delay gratification can sit through sometimes boring classes to get a degree. They can perform rote tasks in order to, say, master a language. They can avoid drugs and alcohol. For people without self-control skills, however, school is a series of failed ordeals. No wonder they drop out. Life is a parade of foolish decisions: teenage pregnancy, drug use, gambling, truancy and crime" (4).

▶ **Note to Student:**
Note that when summarizing, paraphrasing, and quoting from a source, a writer has to introduce the *where* and/or *who* the information came from. In Chapter 13, these phrases are formally called Introductory Phrases or IPs. See pages 383 and 391 for the five common IP Patterns.

_____ a. According to David Brooks in his essay "Self-Control Is the Key to Success," many young people want everything right now, and if they don't get everything quick enough, they often end up using drugs and alcohol, get pregnant, and fail at just about everything in life. However, those who learn to take their time can have great lives (4).

_____ b. According to David Brooks in his essay "Self-Control Is the Key to Success," if young people are willing to take their time to achieve their goals, their path to success can be full of rewards along the way. These rewards can include everything from a better education to a mastery of skills, which will help them in their future careers and lives. On the other hand, those who are unwilling to move ahead slowly often fail in many ways, including dropping out of school, having problems with substance abuse, and even breaking the law (4).

_____ c. According to David Brooks in his essay "Self-Control Is the Key to Success," all young people who want everything right now end up using drugs and alcohol, usually get pregnant, and even end up with criminal records. So, if young people don't stop to smell the roses along the way, they are going to be in trouble (4).

_____ d. According to David Brooks in his essay "Self-Control Is the Key to Success," self-control is essential for young people. This self-control allows them to sit through boring classes and perform rote tasks in school. They can even master a language if they want to. However, for the students who don't have these skills, life is going to be a series of failed ordeals and a parade of foolish decisions (4).

The Essentials of Quoting

As important as it is to learn to put material in your own words and style, there will be occasions when you will want to quote from a source. Using a **direct quotation** means you have copied the *exact* words from the source and placed them within quotation marks (" "). A direct quote must be properly cited.

When you paraphrase, you give the essential information from a source *in your own words*. In those cases, you are not using a source's exact words, so you do not need quotation marks. Here are examples of an indirect quote or paraphrase and a direct quotation taken from the article "'Only Connect . . . : The Goals of a Liberal Education" on pages 26–30.

Indirect Quote (paraphrase)
According to William Cronon, the goal of a liberal education is to encourage people to develop their talents and then use them for the benefit of all (27).

Direct Quote
William Cronon says that a liberal education "aspires to nurture the growth of human talent in the service of human freedom" (27).

While direct quotations can be effective, you should avoid overusing them. Not only is overusing direct quotes a poor practice in a writing class where your professor wants to read and assess *your* writing, but also it indicates to any professor that you may not have understood the material well enough to paraphrase or summarize it.

Choosing the most suitable material to quote and presenting the material accurately are the keys to using direct quotes effectively. Quote material when the language is particularly striking or memorable. Do not simply quote sentences that contain facts or statistics. Incorporate that kind of material in a summary or paraphrase. If you plan to argue against an author's position, you may also want to quote a key passage that presents that position, so you clearly are not misrepresenting it. Finally, when an author is a notable authority on a topic, you may incorporate some key points as direct quotes.

Because you will introduce those quotes by naming the author and perhaps including a note about the author's authority, the quoted material will have more credibility and impact. In fact, quoted material should always be introduced, whether by naming a specific author or the general source of quoted material. Never simply "dump" quoted material into your writing. When a reader encounters a sentence or passage in quotation marks with no idea where it came from, except perhaps from a citation, that quote loses impact and relevance. *Always introduce direct quotes.*

Guidelines for Using Direct Quotations . . .

Here is what to keep in mind when you use direct quotes:

- **Use direct quotations sparingly.** Situations that require direct quotes rather than summaries or paraphrases include the following:

- The author's words are particularly striking or memorable.
- You plan to refute the author, so it is important that you present his or her position accurately.
- The author is a notable, recognized authority on the topic.
- **Ensure direct quotations are accurate.** Do not change words within the quotation marks.
- **Do not "dump" direct quotations into your paper**, but incorporate them smoothly with verbs like *explains, presents, argues, notes*.
- **Properly cite quotations by using introductory phrases and in-text citation.** (See pp. 378, 383, and 391 in Chapter 13.)

Examples

William Cronon explains, "They can follow an argument, track logical reasoning, detect illogic, hear the emotions that lie behind both the logic and the illogic, and ultimately empathize with the person who is feeling those emotions" (27).

In his article, Cronon argues for the importance of making connections: "More than anything else, being an educated person means being able to see connections that allow one to make sense of the world and act within it in creative ways" (30).

EXERCISE 2.8   Identifying Acceptable Quotes   MyWritingLab

Directions: Evaluate each of the following uses of direct quotes as Acceptable (**A**) or Unacceptable (**U**). Be prepared to explain your decision.

_____ a. According to Brooks, "The children who waited longer went on to get higher SAT scores. They got into better colleges and had, on average, better adult outcomes. The children who rang the bell quickest were more likely to become bullies. They received worse teacher and parental evaluations 10 years later and were more likely to have drug problems at age 32" (4).

_____ b. Scholar and educator William Cronon believes that "skilled readers know how to read far more than just words" (28).

_____ c. "Around 1970, psychologist Walter Mischel launched a classic experiment. He left a succession of 4-year-olds in a room with a bell and a marshmallow" (4).

_____ d. For those unable to delay gratification, Brooks says, "school is a series of failed ordeals" (4).

A Final Note on Documentation

When you use summaries, paraphrases, and direct quotes in your writing, you *must* include acknowledgment that the material comes from an outside source. Typically, in MLA format, this is done through **documenting** the material within your paper with a parenthetical citation and including the source on a Works Cited page at the end of the paper. (APA style also uses parenthetical citations and sources are listed on a References page at the end of the paper.) Not documenting material you have summarized, paraphrased, or quoted is also a form of plagiarism. For more specific guidelines on how to document outside material you incorporate into your papers, see Chapter 13.

CHAPTER AT A GLANCE

Learning Objectives	How they connect to learning, reading, and writing at college . . .
❶ Engage in a conversation with an author through active reading.	When reading in college, use these active reading strategies: • Know the context. • Determine the author's thesis or controlling idea. • Use a dictionary as you read. • Read once for enjoyment and twice for analysis. • Annotate the text as you read. • Take notes. • Make connections.
❷ Read as a believer and as a doubter.	When reading anything, you need to be open minded to and appreciative of the author's ideas and points—*reading as a believer*. You also need to read as a skeptic, looking for weaknesses and problems—*reading as a doubter*.
❸ Put **I D E A S** to work when reading.	You can use the **I D E A S** tool (Interest, Details, Examples and Explanation, Audience, and Style) to analyze other people's writing.

Learning Objectives	How they connect to learning, reading, and writing at college . . .
❹ Demonstrate your understanding of a text through summarizing, paraphrasing, and quoting.	There are three main ways to work with sources:

Summarizing When summarizing, provide the name of the author and the title of the work in an *introductory phrase (IP)*. *Condense* what the author says to only the main points, and do so *in your own words* and style while keeping the attitude and tone consistent with those of the original author.

Paraphrasing When paraphrasing, begin by providing the name of the author and the title of the source in an *introductory phrase (IP)* and use an *in-text citation* at the end of the paraphrase. Use *your own words*, not the same words or phrases in the original piece of writing, so double-check your words against the original passage. The paraphrase should be the *approximately the same length as the original*.

Quoting When quoting a source, use an *introductory phrase (IP)*, *copy the exact words* from the source, place them within *quotation marks* (" "), and use an *in-text citation*.

MyWritingLab Visit **Chapter 2, "The Reading Process,"** in MyWritingLab to test your understanding of the chapter objectives.

Writing and the Process of Writing

3

Like any project that is worth doing, writing demands discipline and a strong work ethic—solid values for any worthwhile effort. Also, effective writing is the result of a smart writing process. What is your current writing process? How can it improve?

Sometimes inexperienced writers think the ability to write effectively is an inborn talent—that some people just have a knack for writing and others do not. However, strong writers did not acquire the ability to write well from genetics. They became effective writers from study, practice, and discipline. Just as athletes, carpenters, welders, hair stylists, and cooks learn new techniques, strategies, and moves, so do writers. Writers must study and practice to write well.

While not always an easy process, learning to write well is certainly worthwhile because it improves your chances for success in life. In college you will find writing is both a way of learning and a means of demonstrating what you have learned. The ability to write well can also enhance your career opportunities because many employers view it as an asset. People who move ahead in workplaces typically have strong communication skills, and writing well is an important part of that package. Even in your personal life, think about the written communication you do on regular basis such as texting your friends, emailing co-workers and friends, crafting cover letters and résumés, or writing messages in social media.

❶ Assess the writing situation—subject, purpose, audience, and genre.

Assess the Writing Situation—Subject, Purpose, Audience, and Genre

If you were to ask successful writers what is important to think about when writing, here are some typical comments you might hear:

- "You have to think about your main point, what you're trying to say, and what details will help you say that."

- "You need to ask yourself, 'Why am I writing this? What do I want to achieve?'"

- "Audience. Audience. Audience. What do readers need to know, and what will make them happy?"

- "Well, what exactly do you have to write? A memo, an informative paper, a report, a review, an email, a persuasive paper? What *kind* of writing will best get the job done?"

Writing is complex because you have to consider many variables. You need to think about your knowledge of the subject and your purpose in writing the document. You have to consider your readers and their expectations. You have to take into account what they may or may not know about the subject, what will interest them, what details are essential, and what kinds of explanation will make your points clear. You also have to consider the best form for presenting this information.

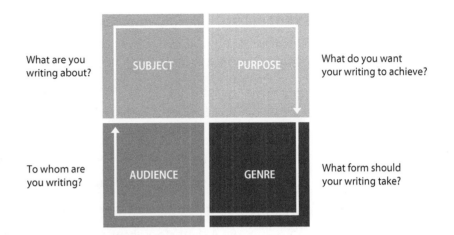

Figure 3-1 **Key Writing Concepts**

Figure 3-1 shows the key concepts that help writers navigate the various writing tasks they undertake: *subject, purpose, audience*, and *genre*.

Subject

"What should I write about?" Some people think the hardest part of writing is finding a topic. However, more often than not, you will have to deal with topics professors or employers assign to you. Sometimes, too, situations in everyday life require you to address a subject in writing. Initially, not all of these topics will engage you. In fact, sometimes you may have to write about topics you dislike. So instead of "What should I write about?" the more frequent question is "How can I make this topic interesting for myself and my readers?"

If you find a topic boring or too hard, your reader will likely have the same reaction to your paper on that topic. Challenge yourself to find your own creative ways of making topics and assignments personally interesting. *Begin by having an open mind about the subject and believing that you have something worthwhile to say about it.* Know, too, that you are more likely to become engaged with a subject after you have listened, read, debated, pondered, and explored beyond the surface.

Purpose

A way to think about purpose is to consider *why* you are writing or what you want a piece of writing to accomplish. The very basic **purposes of writing** are these: *to explain, to convince,* and *to entertain*.

EXERCISE 3.1   Identify Purposes   MyWritingLab

Directions: Identify the main purpose of each of the following pieces of writing: *to explain, to convince,* or *to entertain.* Be prepared to explain your choice.

_____   1. A set of instructions for building a backyard swing set

_____   2. An editorial in the college newspaper calling for a reduction in parking fees

_____   3. A poem that makes fun of a computer spell-checker program

_____   4. A tabloid article about the best and worst beach bodies

_____   5. An advertisement for a cell phone provider

_____   6. A short story about a man who wakes up as a giant bug

_____   7. A set of directions for hooking up a DVD player

_____   8. A letter of reference given to a prospective employer

_____   9. A textbook for an economics course

_____   10. A Composition I essay describing a childhood memory of a fishing trip

As you may have realized by completing Exercise 3.1, some writing, such as a textbook or a set of directions, has a very strong focus on explanation. Writing with a primary purpose to *explain* is sometimes called **expository writing**. Other writing—such as advertisements, editorials, and political speeches—has a strong intent to *persuade* or to *convince* readers to take action or change their way of thinking. A great deal of writing—such as gossip magazines, comics, and fiction—simply *entertains* us.

However, once you start digging more critically into the purposes of those documents, the picture becomes more complicated. While a set of directions can be pretty boring and strictly expository, the authors have carefully chosen a format and organization that they think will make the directions easier to follow. So while the primary purpose may be to provide an explanation, the people who write instructions also think about how to make the format pleasing and simple.

Sure, businesses use advertisements to convince consumers to spend money and buy products. However, advertisements also explain or provide *information* about a product. In addition, some of the best advertisements try to be funny or shocking so people will remember them.

Likewise, while a short story may be entertaining to read, it can also explain people, places, problems, issues, and ideas. Through the way it presents an issue, a story can also convince readers to think about a certain subject or topic in a new way.

In sum, a good piece of writing frequently addresses all three of the purposes: it explains, convinces, and entertains. Keep this in mind as you write papers for this and other college classes. Many of your assignments may seem to have a primarily expository purpose because they will ask you to demonstrate your insights and understanding of a particular topic. However, your writing must also be convincing in that you try to build a good case for readers to accept your points as valid. Finally, you are not going to explain a topic or convince your readers if you cannot keep their attention, so your writing must be pleasing as well.

In later chapters of this textbook you will explore the various methods writers use to achieve their purposes in writing. We refer to these as the **aims of writing**. When you aim for something, you have a goal, something you want to achieve. While your *purpose* is *why* you are writing, the *aim points you toward success* in achieving your purpose. Chapters 6–11 are organized around six common aims of writing you will encounter in college, the workplace, the community, and your personal life:

- Describing (Chapter 6)
- Reflecting (Chapter 7)
- Informing (Chapter 8)
- Analyzing (Chapter 9)
- Evaluating (Chapter 10)
- Persuading (Chapter 11)

Audience

Chapter 1 explains the importance of audience awareness in writing situations (see p. 14). Since you are writing for college courses, you already know that professors do not all have the same requirements for their assignments. A biology professor may want a different style of writing than a history professor does.

There is an old saying from the military that "terrain determines tactics," and this adage proves true with writing. If you think of each person or group of people you are writing to (your audience) as having certain characteristics—values, attitudes, intelligence, and biases—this will take you a long way toward using the right "tactics" to get a good grade, earn a promotion at your job, or influence your community about a certain issue.

EXERCISE 3.2   Write to an Audience   MyWritingLab

Directions: This exercise asks you to think about audience. Below are specific purposes for writing, with two or three distinct readers for each. Given your purpose for writing, explain how you would have to adjust your message or information according to the needs of the specified readers.

1. **Purpose for writing:** Explaining what Twitter is

   Readers: a. an eighty-year-old grandmother who doesn't have a computer

   b. a state legislator who has never used Twitter but wants to restrict its use by students and teachers

2. **Purpose for writing:** Persuading someone to enroll in a local fitness center

   Readers: a. young singles (ages 22–32)

   b. mature adults (50+)

3. **Purpose for writing:** Explaining what you liked about the concert you went to last weekend

   Readers: a. your best friend

   b. readers of a college newspaper column that reviews cultural events

4. **Purpose for writing:** Persuading someone to oppose your community's plans to widen a street in your neighborhood because of safety concerns as the traffic increases

   Readers: a. your local government representative

   b. your local newspaper

   c. your writing instructor who has just assigned a persuasive essay

Overall, you have to think about the purpose of your writing and how that purpose connects to your reader and audience. If you cannot connect to the audience, your writing will be unsuccessful.

Genre—What Type of Writing Is It?

Genre is a fancy way of saying "category" or "type." For example, think about the different genres, or types, of TV shows you watch. There are probably quite a few, such as situational comedies, crime dramas, reality TV shows, news magazines, nightly news broadcasts, sports events, and documentaries.

In writing, genres are defined by their audiences, purposes, and subjects. Writing genres you have probably encountered in daily life, college, and the workplace include the following:

academic essays	newspaper articles	pop-up ads
spam	lab reports	advertisements
résumés	memos	emails
reports	letters	blogs

For the most part, in college you are going to write what are commonly referred to as "papers"—essays often based on a thesis. But in some disciplines, such as those in the sciences or in engineering or business, your writing will include workplace genres like reports, memos, and letters.

❷ Direct your writing with a thesis statement.

Direct Your Writing with a Thesis Statement

The thesis of a paper provides a writer's opinion or point about a subject that is shaped by the audience and expected genre (format) of the document. Overall, a thesis answers this question: "What's the point?" A formal definition of a thesis can be stated this way: A **thesis statement** is a *generalization* written in *precise terms* that presents a *controlling idea* about a subject.

A Thesis Is a *Generalization*

A thesis, first of all, must be a *general statement* because facts or specific statements do not need a whole paper to back them up. Note the difference between the following two statements:

Tuition at my college is $4,000 per semester.

College tuition should be tax deductible.

The first statement, assuming it is true, is a *fact*. Your readers are not going to ask, "Why do you say that?" A **fact** is information that is known to be true because it can be proven through experiment or observation, so it is not open to question. On the other hand, readers could ask you to support the *opinion* that tuition should be tax deductible. **Opinions** are general statements that express personal beliefs and require reasons, facts, and examples to back them up and to demonstrate their validity.

EXERCISE 3.3   **Identify Facts and Opinions**   **MyWritingLab**

Directions: In each of the following sets of items, determine which statements are generalizations that express opinions (**O**) and which are specific statements or facts (**F**).

1. _____ I visited Boston last summer to build homes with Habitat for Humanity.

   _____ A trip to Boston can enhance one's understanding of the Revolutionary War.

   _____ Service projects, like volunteering with Habitat for Humanity, should be a mandatory part of every college program.

   _____ Habitat for Humanity is an organization that builds decent housing for people in need.

2. _____ I go to college, work twenty hours a week, and help with the care of my elderly grandmother.

   _____ My college offers a work/study program.

   _____ Working part-time while attending college has some distinct advantages.

   _____ Time management strategies can help students balance their time in their work, school, and personal lives.

3. _____ Playing video games has taught me strategies I can use in my everyday life.

   _____ I play video games an average of three to four hours every day.

   _____ The current labeling system for video games is misleading and needs to be revised.

   _____ According to the Entertainment Software Association, the average game player is thirty-five years old and has been playing video games for thirteen years.

A Thesis Must Be Written in *Precise Terms*

A thesis is a generalization, so you might ask, "How can a statement be both general and precise?"

    The following two statements are generalizations. Which one would be a more precise thesis?

My friendship with Sam is great.

Even during the toughest times, I can depend upon my friend Sam.

Great is an overused word and does not give much of a clue as to the kind of friend Sam is. The second statement gives a clearer sense of what direction the paper will take and what kinds of support the writer will use. The second statement is written in precise terms.

Since you want your thesis to give your readers a clear sense of what your paper is about as well as the point you want to make about that subject, use clear, precise words. Avoid broad and vague words that leave your reader wondering just what your point is.

EXERCISE 3.4   Identify Precise Thesis Statements   MyWritingLab

Directions: All of the following statements are generalizations. Check the statements that give you the clearest sense of what direction the paper will take and what kinds of support the writer will use to validate his or her opinion.

1. ____ The playground was bad.

   ____ The playground was unsafe.

2. ____ The economics class helped me understand why the U.S. economy is so dependent upon foreign markets.

   ____ The economics class helped me understand many things.

3. ____ Michael Pollan's book *The Omnivore's Dilemma* is interesting.

   ____ Michael Pollan's book *The Omnivore's Dilemma* has changed the way I shop for food.

4. ____ My trip to the Rocky Mountains taught me to appreciate nature's beauty and respect its dangers.

   ____ My trip to the Rocky Mountains was awesome.

5. ____ Eating healthy is a good idea.

   ____ Eating more vegetables and grains is cheaper and more nutritional for us.

A Thesis Presents a *Controlling Idea* about a Subject

A thesis needs to have a *single idea or a set of points that directs the action of a piece of writing*. Without a controlling idea, your paper runs the risk of rambling on about the subject, going in too many different directions, and trying to cover too much. One way to focus your subject with a clear controlling idea is to think of a question you want your paper to answer for your readers. *The thesis will be a single, precise statement that answers that question.*

For example, say you have been asked to write a paper about your experiences so far as a college student. You decide that the question you want your paper to answer is "What did I find most surprising about my first semester as a college student?" After doing some thinking and talking with other students and writing down some thoughts, you come up with the following answer: "During my first semester, I learned that being responsible for my own learning was my biggest challenge." Now you have a thesis with a controlling idea about your subject.

Now imagine a business teacher has asked you to write a memo to a company proposing a particular charity for the company to support as its annual service project. You decide that you will propose that the company support a local food bank. Your memo needs to answer the following question:

"Why should the XYZ Corporation support the community food bank?"

The answer to that question is the thesis that will drive the action of your memo:

"We should support the community food bank because it is a local organization with a proven reputation that meets a growing need in our community."

This controlling idea focuses your memo on the three strongest reasons for supporting the food bank.

Using this approach of deciding what question about the subject you want your paper to answer will help you avoid thesis statements that may produce a "So what?" response from your readers.

The following chart provides boring thesis statements contrasted by thesis statements that answer the question, "So what?"

So What? Thesis	Question I Want My Paper to Answer	Thesis with a *Clear Controlling Idea*
I love all things choco-late. (Why should readers care about my personal preference?)	*Why should I not feel guilty about loving chocolate?*	A lot of my readers also love chocolate and may be interested in knowing it has health benefits.
		Thesis: Even though it seems to be only a delicious treat, chocolate ***has physical and mental benefits.***
My boyfriend is wonderful. (Why should readers care about my relationship?)	*What makes my relation-ship with my boyfriend so successful?*	Many of my readers may be in relationships and looking for ways to make them better.
		Thesis: My boyfriend and I have a success-ful relationship because ***we have learned the importance of compromise.***
Many people have car acci-dents. (Everyone knows this. Can I tell readers something they do not already know?)	*Why do so many of my friends have car accidents?*	Maybe there is a common reason or pattern we can learn from and thus avoid future accidents.
		Thesis: Many car accidents *could be avoided if drivers pay* ***closer attention to the road and other drivers.***

EXERCISE 3.5 Identify Clear Controlling Ideas   MyWritingLab

Directions: In each of the following sets of items, decide which thesis offers a controlling idea—something that points the paper in a clear direction.

_____ 1. a. Young children should eat more nutritious foods and fewer junk foods.

   b. Parents can follow several steps to teach their children healthy eating habits at an early age.

_____ 2. a. You can enjoy using social networking sites like Facebook and Twitter.

   b. Users of social networking sites like Facebook and Twitter should take precautions to prevent unwanted contact with Internet predators.

_____ 3. a. Teachers' PowerPoint™ presentations can be boring for students.

   b. Teachers can make PowerPoint™ presentations more engaging for students by avoiding five common mistakes.

_____ 4. a. College offers far more challenges than high school, but being pre-pared helps.

b. Poor study habits picked up in high school can make the adjustment to college more difficult.

_____ 5. a. As I navigated campus with my broken leg, I found that it was not accommodating for people with disabilities.

b. People with disabilities face many obstacles that the rest of us don't even think about during our daily lives.

EXERCISE 3.6   Write Effective Thesis Statements   MyWritingLab

Directions: Compose an effective thesis statement for each of the following writing assignments. Think of the question you want your essay to answer as you create a thesis statement with a clear controlling idea.

1. An essay that shows the role you play in your family

2. An essay that tells the story of an important lesson you learned outside the classroom

3. An essay that proposes a solution to a dangerous situation that exists in your area

4. An essay that explains the benefits of your favorite pastime or hobby

5. An essay that explains the process you followed in enrolling in your first college classes

❸ Put IDEAS to work.

MyWritingLab Visit Ch. 3 Writing and the Process of Writing in MyWritingLab to access the IDEAS videos.

Put I D E A S to Work: The Essentials of Good Writing

The acronym **I D E A S** stands for **I**nterest, **D**etails, **E**xplanation, **A**udience, and **S**tyle. Successful writers use all of these components to their advantage to inform, persuade, and entertain readers. In Chapter 2, you learned how to use IDEAS to take apart and analyze the work of other writers. As you begin the process of composing your own papers, you can also use the IDEAS template as a way to think about the writing situation as it applies to your particular writing assignment. As you will see in the "Put IDEAS to Work" sections in Chapters 6–11, you can use IDEAS to generate support for your paper as well as to make sure you are thinking about the essentials needed to successfully complete writing assignments.

Developing Content Using the **I D E A S** Tool

Here is a general template for using **I D E A S** as preparation for most kinds of writing. Always remember that most assignments include particular guidelines that you must consider as you generate support for your papers.

I nterest

- How can I capture my readers' interest with a thought-provoking title?
- What introduction strategy will work best with this topic? (see pp. 128–135)
- What about this topic most interests me, and how can I share that interest with readers?
- Why should my readers be interested in this topic? How can I help them see its importance?

D etails

- What strong, specific, concrete, and vivid details can I provide?
- How can I "make this subject real" through good details?
- Do my paragraphs support the controlling idea of my essay?
- Do my details work together to support the controlling ideas of the paragraphs?
- What organizational strategy best suits my topic and purpose?

E xplanation

- Which examples best *show* what I want my readers to understand?
- Can I provide anecdotes and any personal examples?
- Do I use abstract terms or concepts that the reader may need clarified?
- Do I use specialized words or expressions that the readers may not understand? What is the best way to define them for the readers?

A udience

- What do the readers need to know to better understand or appreciate this topic?
- What could bore the readers? If this information is necessary, how can I make it more appealing?
- What attitude or tone is appropriate for the readers?
- What specific words will work best to convey this attitude?
- What level of language will best convey the appropriate attitude to readers?

S tyle

- How can I use sentence variety (different lengths and types of sentences) to make the writing flow effectively from one idea to another?
- What point of view will work best to convey this attitude?
- How will I keep my "voice" as a writer distinct yet appropriate?
- Where can I cut the clutter in my writing?
- What are the kinds of distracting errors I tend to make? How can I avoid them?

❹ Practice writing as a process.

Practice Writing as a Process—Embrace the Messiness and Discoveries Before the Finished Product

As many researchers have learned through the years, the best writing comes from a strong **writing process** through which a writer creates multiple drafts. As readers, we see the finished products of writers: their final drafts. What we do not usually get to see is the messiness of the early efforts or the discoveries that preceded the final product. We do not see the failed attempts at an introduction, the rearranging of paragraphs, the boring thesis the writer began with in the first draft, the cutting of details and examples that did not clarify the topic for the reader, or the mechanical and spelling errors the author did not worry about until the editing stage.

By using a process of writing in several stages or steps, writers discover important points, ideas, and details they had not considered at the beginning of the process. In fact, writers often discover what they know and think through the act of writing.

The Writing Process

Author and former Professor of English, Michael E. Adelstein recommends you think of your paper as "your offspring—to nourish, to cherish, to coddle, to bring up, and finally, to turn over to someone else." He says you will be proud of your paper "only if you have done your best throughout its growth and development." Adelstein recommends that writers spend certain amounts of time on specific aspects of the writing process, as shown in Figure 3-2.

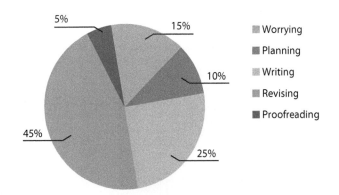

Figure 3-2 **Adelstein's Recommendations: The Writing Process**

EXERCISE 3.7   Thinking about Your Own Writing Process MyWritingLab

Directions: With Adelstein's recommendations in mind, complete and label your own chart that shows what percentage of your time you spend on these five parts of the writing process: *worrying, planning, writing, revising,* and *proofreading*. Then answer the questions that follow.

1. In which parts do you exceed Adelstein's recommended percentages, and where are you below them?

2. At what stage do you spend the most time and why?

3. If you were to spend *more* time on one stage of the writing process above, which stage would it be and why?

4. If you were to spend *less* time on one stage of the writing process above, which stage would it be and why?

5. Where do you question Adelstein's recommended percentages? Which ones seem to include too much time or too little time?

Taking our cue from Adelstein and other scholars who have done research on the writing process, we have provided similar categories for you to think about the writing process. We think worrying happens throughout the whole process, so it is not in our scheme. However, when you worry too much, your writing is likely to suffer. Sometimes you must put pen to paper or type your thoughts and clean up afterward. You have good ideas and you can express them well—just get them down on the page or screen.

To get to a strong finished product, here is a basic writing process that many people use:

Planning and Prewriting	Organizing	Drafting	Revising	Editing
Decide on a topic.	Determine your controlling idea.	Decide upon a specific genre.	Cut irrelevant details.	Correct sentence errors.
Identify your audience and consider your readers' needs.	Eliminate irrelevant ideas.	Get your ideas on paper with a clear beginning, middle, and end.	Develop important details, examples, and explanations.	Cut unnecessary words and repetition.
Determine your purpose.	Arrange ideas in logical order.		Be prepared to change focus or reorder ideas for clarity.	Check for sentence variety.
Think about your topic. Talk to others about it. Read about it.			Insert transitions.	Correct spelling and usage errors.
Generate details, examples, and explanations through prewriting.			Replace weak/vague words.	Format the paper correctly.

Figure 3-3 **The Writing Process**

Keep in mind that every writing situation can be different, so on one paper you may spend more time organizing because you might be working with source material, and on another you may spend much more time brainstorming to understand what you are trying to say about your experience or to come up with the specific and concrete details. Your writing will stumble and sputter along at times, but creating "advance planning" through prewriting and organizing will save you a lot of time in the long run.

Also remember that the writing process is **recursive**, meaning that you can go back at any point at any time to revisit points in the process in order to clarify ideas for your readers. Even if you have written a full rough draft, you can return to the prewriting, organizing, and drafting stages during revision. Overall, though, you need to *embrace the messiness and the discoveries* of the writing process.

To illustrate this process, we will follow student Marcus Adams as he writes an essay. His writing instructor created the following writing situation:

A Best Practice for First-Year College Students

Advisors would like current students to share their experiences with beginning students coming to campus next fall. The advisors are compiling a short booklet entitled "Best Practices for First-Year Students" and would like you to contribute a short essay that describes a "best practice" you have discovered. What have you done as a college student that has helped you succeed in your studies? Use your own experiences and/or those of students you know to explain this practice and to show how it has helped you become a successful college student.

Planning

Marcus begins by identifying the components of the writing situation: *topic*, *audience*, *purpose*, and the *genre* or form the final paper will take. All of these will determine the type of work he will have to do before writing the first draft of his paper. His *topic* is a best practice that has helped him be successful in college. His *audience* is incoming college freshmen. His *purpose* is *to inform* them of a practice that could help them succeed. The *genre* is an essay.

Before writing, Marcus spends some time just thinking about the topic. He talks to some of his classmates and friends who are first-year students to get some of their ideas on possible best practices. Marcus knows he can also go to the campus writing center to talk with tutors about his ideas and to brainstorm the topic.

Eventually, it is time for Marcus to get the words and ideas out of his head and on paper. Many writers—even very good ones—find this first step extremely difficult. The prolific and successful writer of fantasy and horror Stephen King has said, "The scariest moment is always just before you start [writing]. After that, things can only get better." We agree with King. Once you can start to get words and ideas on paper, the process will get better.

During this stage of the writing process, Marcus uses the **I D E A S** template to connect the writing situation to his specific assignment. Exploring the **I** nterest, **D** etails, **E** xplanation, **A** udience, and **S** tyle he will bring to the assignment also helps him to begin prewriting and generate support to use in the paper.

Marcus' IDEAS

Interest: How can I create interest for the reader? I need to think of something a little different—something that will surprise readers who are expecting to hear the same suggestions for success they have heard before. At the same time, I want to give them good advice.
Details: What strong specific, concrete, and vivid details can I provide about my knowledge of how to handle all the responsibilities and work? How can I make the first semester experience real through good details? I need to make sure that my description of the practice is clear enough that those without college experience can follow it.
Explanation: What examples and explanation can I provide to make the best practice clear? Can I provide anecdotes from my own experiences? I should be able to use my friends' experiences to back up what I have

> *learned. Again, these readers may not know some of the college jargon,*
> *so if I use any, I'll have to include short definitions.*
>
> ***Audience:*** *Many of these students are going to be right out of high*
> *school, so I don't want to sound too preachy—like a know-it-all. What*
> *tone is appropriate for this audience while keeping in mind my instructor*
> *is also my audience? Maybe I can use a little humor. I'd really like to tell*
> *these readers something they didn't expect to hear.*
>
> ***Style:*** *How can I use sentence variety (different lengths and types of*
> *sentences) to make the writing flow effectively from one idea to another?*
> *Where can I create strong transitions within paragraphs and from*
> *paragraph to paragraph? I probably need to avoid overusing "I think that"*
> *in the final essay. My instructor has warned us about that wordy*
> *construction. I should use strong action verbs in addition to descriptive*
> *adjectives.*

Prewriting

To get his ideas on paper Marcus uses various methods of prewriting. These methods all share a goal of freeing up his creativity and letting ideas flow on the page. During the prewriting stage of the writing process, Marcus does not worry about getting everything down in a perfectly organized form. He doesn't worry about spelling, grammar, and punctuation. During the prewriting stage, writers like Marcus should follow the advice of another famous author, James Thurber: "Don't get it right, just get it written."

Here are some methods Marcus uses that might work for you. First, Marcus does some general **brainstorming** just to come up with some ideas of best practices. He commits himself to coming up with at least ten to fifteen ideas before stopping.

Brainstorming

Brainstorming involves listing important details or examples or points that you want to make in a piece of writing. For example, if you are writing an argument, you could list possible objections that readers might have and then show how those readers' objections are off base or illogical. If you are writing a descriptive essay about a place that is important to you, you could list specific and concrete details, painting a verbal picture for your readers and making them see, hear, and smell that place so they feel like they are there.

Here is Marcus' brainstorming on the writing process:

Marcus' Brainstorming

regular class attendance	participate in class
take notes	don't be afraid to ask questions
keep up with homework	don't procrastinate
manage time	get to know instructors—visit during office hours
balance work and school	treat school like a job—important investment
study a little every night—no cramming	use the library
learn reading and test-taking strategies	find a boss who understands demands of college work
learn to navigate registration process	don't take on too much
meet deadlines	take advantage of any extra credit opportunities
get to know people in class for study groups	
take advantage of free resources like the writing center	

Marcus looks over his brainstormed list and immediately rules out some of the topics because he thinks that a lot of other students would also think of them, and he wants his essay to stand out. He notices that several of his points have to do with work: managing time, balancing work and school, treating school like a job, and finding a boss who respects a student's work.

From talking with his friends, Marcus knows that many students both work and attend college, as he does. However, he also knows that writing about the importance of managing time to balance work and school will be a pretty common approach, and he wants to do something different. So he does a little **freewriting**.

Freewriting

A method both college and professional writers use is **freewriting**. When freewriting, you should not get caught up in correcting grammar or spelling. Nor should you try to organize or stop to judge the worth of the ideas as you write them down. You just write quickly to get ideas onto the page or screen. You should write non-stop, meaning that whatever is going through your head goes onto the page or screen. If you are thinking, "I don't know what to say," for example, you should literally write, "I don't know what to say" because that is what is in your mind.

This chaotic and messy writing process, in many cases, helps you free up your creativity and discover ideas you might not have discovered if you were carefully crafting a piece of writing. Usually, you should freewrite for anywhere from five to fifteen minutes, and then go back and read what you have written. As you read, underline or circle valid, important, or interesting sections of writing that you might use in your paper. Most of the freewriting may look quite ugly in places, but the point is for you to get ideas out there.

Here is Marcus' freewriting:

Marcus' Freewriting

Working and going to school is hard. Most of us don't have a choice. It's something we have to live with. Is it going to do any good to rehash how hard it is and how we have to learn how to manage both? Will others be taking this same approach? What is a different angle? I like my job. I think besides the pay check I have a lot of other benefits from this job. I remember hearing somewhere that students who work do better than students who just go to school. I guess it depends on how much work. Maybe take the approach that working a reasonable number of hours can actually be beneficial. Working and going to school—hard, hard, hard! Is trying to do both even worth it? I don't have a choice. Need the money for bills and to help with college costs. So the money is an advantage— obvious. What else? Managing time. Having a job forces me to manage time—maybe better than if I didn't have a job. I have to stay organized in both places, so work helps school and school helps work. I think it's the same with communication. I work on a team at work and I do group work at school. Working with people all the time helps me use speaking skills. A lot of what my communications teachers talked about made sense when I thought about work. I was able to write up an accident report at work a little better because of my writing class—at least I wasn't too nervous about it. School helps with work and work helps with school. Well, work didn't help with the algebra test I didn't do so well on. I had studied

	and still didn't do well on that test. I wish I could have done as well as I
	did on the safety first test I took at work. Aced it! Even got a perfor-
	mance raise at work. Take that algebra. Doing well at work kind of helps
	me not feel so bad when I don't do well at school. Working and going to
	school might be hard but has a lot of advantages—maybe more than not
	working at all.

By using freewriting, Marcus gains a better sense of what he wants to write about. Now that he has a topic, Marcus does some more focused brainstorming and freewriting as he tries to think of examples of his own personal experiences, since that's what the assignment called for.

Here is Marcus' focused freewriting and brainstorming:

Marcus' Focused Brainstorming and Freewriting

	<u>*Benefits of working and going to school*</u>
	Get paid—can afford necessities and education costs. Even though this is obvious
	maybe I can use it as a starting point. Financial benefits now and in the future.
	Working gives me job skills I can add to my resume and I'll also make contacts in the
	workplace. Didn't my friend Amy meet someone at her job who got her an interview
	after she finished her degree? So maybe I can move from something most readers
	know to something they haven't thought so much about—better preparation for
	future career—networking and references.
	Learn to budget time—multi-task handle many responsibilities
	Sense of pride in taking care of one's own responsibilities
	Learn about the real world—better connection to what's learned in classes
	Better people skills—bosses/coworkers teachers/classmates
	Builds confidence—capable at work—capable with classes

	What about the hard and soft skills	*Pride and confidence might be something a*
	my business teacher talked about?	*lot of students don't think about. I am proud*
	I'm definitely learning hard skills I can	*that I am working my way through school—*
	use at work in my writing and speaking	*paying my own way. Doing a good job in*

Marcus' Focused Brainstorming and Freewriting (*cont.*)

classes and some in my business class.	both places. This makes me feel I can succeed
But soft skills are really important	in my chosen career which will have all my
to employers, and work and school	focus. I know I can learn and be recognized.
both teach and reinforce these:	Maybe not good at everything I try but I
• showing up on time	know my strengths and capabilities. Not
• following directions	feeling bad about the algebra test because
• working with people	the same week I did so well at work
• meeting deadlines	• good point because it shows how work picked
• handling stress	me up when I'm down
Both work and school reinforce what	• pay my own way
I learn—hard and soft skills.	• recognized for achievements at work and
	school
	• know I'm capable of success

As you can see, Marcus truly embraces the messiness of the writing process as he uses prewriting to find his topic and to generate supporting details and examples.

Once Marcus has generated enough prewriting to have a clear focus and enough support, he moves on to organizing his material. To do this, he must first determine what the point of his essay will be, so he can write a strong **thesis statement** that lets his readers know the **subject** and **controlling idea** of the essay.

One way to compose a thesis is to think of the question you want your paper to answer. The thesis is a clearly stated, one-sentence answer to that question. Here is the question Marcus wants his paper to answer:

Question: What best practice has helped me succeed as a first-year college student?

Answer: Holding a part-time job has helped me succeed in my first year of college.

Now that Marcus has a thesis, he can organize his main points and supporting details and examples.

Organizing

Depending on the way you learn, you might be more open to certain ways of organizing your writing before you get to the drafting stage, so this section will explore various methods of organizing ideas.

Clustering/Idea Mapping

Many people are "visual learners"; they learn better when they can see concepts. For visual learners, the **clustering** or **idea mapping** method of organizing thoughts or points for a paper helps immensely. As you can see in Figure 3-4, using bubbles with basic details in them, Marcus creates sections for his paper while providing specific details for each section. Clustering or idea mapping lets writers space out their ideas and identify relevant and irrelevant support for their thesis.

Formal Outlining

In a **formal outline**, you create a hierarchy of your details and points, organizing your ideas using Roman numerals, letters, and numbers and varying indentations to indicate the importance of each point; the closer to the left margin, the more important the point.

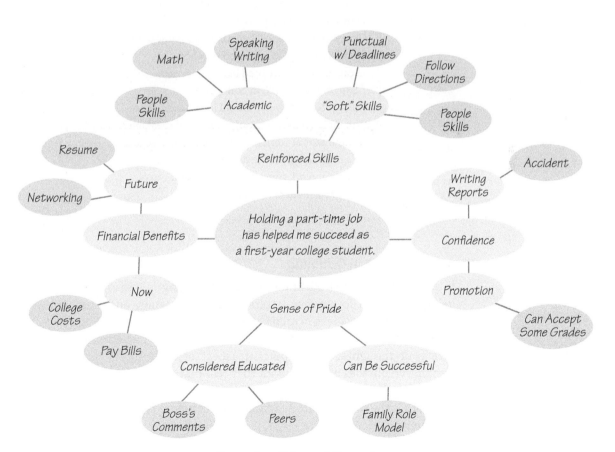

Figure 3-4 **Example of Marcus' Clustering**

Formal outlining is a valuable tool because it encourages you to create your thesis statement and many times write complete sentences. A formal outline also uses numbers and letters to indicate the different levels of support. This approach may also help you generate more ideas and keep you on track. Furthermore, you can experiment with different organizations for your paper in using formal outlines. Since you probably write using a computer, moving your points around using the "cut" and "paste" functions in your word processing program is quite easy.

Here is Marcus' formal outline for his paper, which he wrote on his laptop:

Marcus' Formal Outline

Thesis: Holding a part-time job has helped me succeed as a first-year college student.

I.   Financial benefits are immediate and long-term.
    A.   Now I can cover expenses.
    B.   Work experience will help in future job searches.
II.   Skills are reinforced at work and in school.
    A.   Academic skills are used in both places.
    B.   "Soft" skills are used in both places.
III.   Having a job and going to school builds confidence.
    A.   I'm more confident about writing and speaking at work.
    B.   Promotions at work keep me confident at school.
IV.   There's pride in being able to do it all.
    A.   People at work consider me "educated."
    B.   I'm a role model in my family.

Sketch or Scratch Outlining

In contrast to formal outlining, **sketch outlining** is less rigid. Instead of using upper and lower case letters, Roman numerals, and numbers, you simply sketch your ideas in an order that makes sense to you. You can come back to it and change your organization if you think of a better way to organize your thoughts. The important aspect of outlining is putting down descriptive phrases and thoughts that will make you remember what you want to say in the paper.

Here is the scratch outline Marcus wrote before typing the more formal one above:

Marcus' Scratch Outline

Thesis: *Holding a part-time job has helped me succeed as a first-year college student.*	
Financial	
	Now—cover expenses
	Future—help with job search
Reinforced Skills	
	Academic
	"Soft"
More Confidence	
	Workplace
	Classes
Pride	
	Considered educated at work
	Family role model

First Drafting

Once you have taken the best ideas generated through prewriting and organized them in a logical way to support your thesis or point, it is time to begin drafting. During the drafting stage of the writing process, your ideas began to take the shape of the kind of paper you are writing, whether it is an essay, a single paragraph, a letter, or some other genre. Unlike chaotic prewriting, a draft follows the plan of your outline and has a clear beginning, middle, and end.

When drafting, you should give yourself plenty of time to work, and it helps if you have your pre-writing work in front of you as you compose. Do not worry about grammar and proofreading just yet because the important function of this stage in the writing process is to get a draft done. If you manage your time right, which is always important for successful writing, you can go back and redraft sections of the paper. Depending on how large your writing project is, the first draft stage could take one hour of straight writing or it could involve your writing various sections on several different days.

Following is the first draft of the essay Marcus wrote. As you read the draft, notice the instructor's suggestions for revising the essay.

Marcus' Formal First Draft

Comment [1]: You have a strong thesis. Can you do more in the introduction to generate interest?

Comment [2]: You repeat your thesis here.

Comment [3]: Work on using stronger transitions throughout your paper.

Comment [4]: Look for places in this paragraph that get off track and do not support your controlling idea.

Comment [5]: This is a good example.

Comment [6]: You use good examples here.

Comment [7]: Avoid overemphatic words.

Comment [8]: Can you make the transition more clear?

Comment [9]: Notice how many sentences start with "I." Vary your sentences.

Holding a part-time job has helped me succeed as a first year college student. I work about twenty hours a week at a hardware store. Combining this job with my college work has benefitted me several ways. The job helps me financially, academically, and gives me pride and confidence.

For one thing, there are financial benefits now and in the future. I still live at home, so I am lucky not to have to pay for my living expenses. But I do have to pay for my car and cell phone. Also, helping with college expenses like tuition and books. I was shocked how much my books cost my first semester. The money I can contribute helps out my parents because they have my brother and sister to help through college to. In the future my work experience will pay off by giving me experiences to include in my resume. I am majoring in business and hope to manage a store some day. Maybe even start my own business. I can also do some networking at my job that could get me contacts for a job in the future. I meet all kinds of suppliers and business people almost every day at my job. My friend Andrea met an owner of a graphic arts company while she was working at a coffee shop. Andrea was able to go to work at the company after she graduated.

Second, what I learn at college I can use at work what I learn at work I can use in college. I use my math skills a lot when I help customers decide how much lumber they need for a project. Or how many tiles they need for their kitchen floor. Communication skills are useful to. At work I have to comunicate effectivly, so the speaking and writing skills I learn in my college classes can apply directly to my job. I have had to write an accident report and a suggestion to my manager. I did great on both of those. I even talked to my manager about a promotion idea I got from my business class, and he is going to talk to the store's manager about using it. It helps in my classes to know how I might use what I'm learning in a real job. My business teacher talks about "soft skills" that employers look for, I learn these skills at work and in school. My job has taught me the importance of being on time and following directions. I have to follow directions at work, so I know to read those carefully for all my assignments. I also have to be on time at work and at school. I can lose pay or even my job if I'm late too many times for work. I can also be penalized at school because

I might miss important information at the beginning of class. I have learned to work with supervisors and co-workers. Not to mention customers who occasionally are angry. I also learned how to budget my time carefully having a job and going to school full-time. Unlike some friends who don't.

Comment [10]: You need a stronger transition and a clear topic sentence here.

Third is confidence. One of my friends at work was cut very badly and had to spend time in the hospital. I was with him when the accident occurred so I wrote the report. I would've been nervous about doing that before, but my writing class helped a lot. My boss said I did a great job on the report. I recently earned a merit promotion at work. My supervisors call me dependable and capable and customers ask to work with me. I now I am valued I know I have strengths and skills that arent measured by test scores. This picks me up when I take those classes over subjects that dont come easy for me.

Comment [11]: Your last two body paragraphs are not as well developed with explanation and examples.

Finally, there is a sense of pride having a job and going to school gives me. I know I am capable of managing my time and handling multiple responsibilities now and in the future. I like that my boss calls me "the educated one." They know I'm in college and even when they tease me, I know they respect what I'm doing. At home my parents talk about me to their family and friends. My dad always says, "He's working hard to pay his way through school." I am the first in my family to go to college. I know my aunts and uncles tell my cousins to look at how hard I work. I am proud that I am a role model for them.

Comment [12]: This, too, is an overused transition. Can you do better?

Comment [13]: You need to sound more confident of your ideas.

Comment [14]: Did you cover this in the essay? Avoid bringing up new ideas in the conclusion.

In conclusion, some students think that having to work while going to college will make things hard. I hope I have convinced you that just the opposite is true. I have fewer financial concerns. I learn better because school and work reinforce each other. I have pride and confidence. Just don't work too many hours, and I guarantee school and work can help you be successful too.

Revising and Redrafting

There is an old saying among writing teachers that "Learning to write is really learning how to revise." You may recall that even Adelstein recommends that writers spend most of their writing process revising. Revising and redrafting are *essential* for you to become a better writer.

You should not fall in love with your first draft, and you should not turn in a first draft as though it were your final polished paper. You have to go back and look at your own writing as a skeptic and as a doubter. *True revision* is what you need to shoot for, not simply using a spell checker and turning in a paper after you have drafted it. *True revision* is literally *re-seeing* your work.

Here are three categories of revision to keep in mind:

Deep Revision	Middle Revision	Surface Revision
• Creating new paragraphs	• Reorganizing	• Cutting unnecessary words
• Cutting whole sections	• Adding specific and concrete details to paragraphs	• Combining sentences
• Changing focus		• Varying sentences in length and type
• Adding examples and support	• Modifying a thesis	
• Cutting examples and support	• Addressing the audience more	• Adding needed words
• Changing your thesis or controlling idea for the paper	• Cutting certain details	
• Drafting a new introduction		
• Drafting new support paragraphs		
• Drafting a new conclusion		

As you can see, all three categories of revision involve a great deal of work. But that is writing. Although you may have thought good writers just write quickly and then check for grammar and spelling errors, that is not true. Most of the time you do not get to see the messy drafts and big changes that professional and successful writers had to make to arrive at their final polished writing.

EXERCISE 3.8   Analyze Your Own Revision Process   MyWritingLab

Directions: After looking over the descriptions of the various kinds of revision, answer the following questions about your own writing process.

1. How much of your typical writing process time is spent revising? Has this been enough? Why or why not?

2. Which category of revision do you think most of your revising falls under?

3. If you are not already doing deep revision, what do you need to be doing more of in your current revising?

4. Revision involves cutting, adding, and changing or modifying. Which of these do you find the most difficult to do with your drafts? Why?

5. Notice that editing sentence errors appears in none of the categories of revision. Why do you think it is important not to worry about editing when you are revising?

Revision involves thinking about a document from the reader's perspective. The piece of writing you produce has to connect to the reader. By using questions such as the following, you can determine whether you have made all your points clearly enough.

Questions for Revision

- Do I need to go into more detail at certain points of the paper?
- What is not necessary in this paper?
- How can I appeal to my reader more effectively?
- Is this piece boring? How can I make it more interesting?
- Do I need to be more serious or more informal?
- What does the reader absolutely need to know?

You may know the subject of your paper really well, but the crucial test is whether that subject is clear and entertaining to the reader. That crucial test drives strong revision and redrafting.

Editing and Proofreading

Revision, as you have seen, includes all the ways you can improve the *content* of your writing. In contrast, **editing** focuses on *correcting sentence-level errors*.

While using the spell checker and grammar checker on the computer can be helpful, it is only the beginning of serious and successful editing. Here are some guidelines to follow in the final stage of the writing process: the proofreading and editing stage.

Editing Guidelines

- **Use Effective Time Management**: Giving yourself adequate time to edit is crucial for successful, strong writing. Once you have finished writing a paper, it is a good idea to let the paper rest a while (an hour, four hours, a day) and come back to proofread it later. It is easier to see grammatical and stylistic glitches if the paper is not fresh in your mind. Focus on the style, grammar, and spelling in every single sentence.

- **Beware of the Spell-Check Trap:** If you rely only on spell checkers and grammar checkers, you will probably have many errors in a paper. Spell checkers miss all kinds of usage errors (*they're* vs. *there* vs. *their*, for example) and grammatical problems. These simple errors hurt the readability of an essay by distracting your reader, which in turn damages the paper's credibility.

- **Read the Paper *Out Loud:*** Reading a document aloud is a common technique used by both beginning and professional writers. Reading a paper out loud slowly helps you catch phrases that just do not "sound right" and lets you focus on what is actually on the paper, not what you *meant to say* in the essay.

- **Read the Paper Backwards:** Another helpful technique used by professional writers is reading a paper backwards. You start by proofreading the last sentence, making sure there are no misspellings and mechanical errors. Then you move on to the next-to-last sentence, and so on. Reading a document backwards puts the paper out of context, so you are able to isolate the sentences and their grammatical issues without being distracted by content.

- **Read the Paper Out Loud *and* Backwards:** Use this combined method by incorporating both techniques discussed above.

- **Use the Pencil or Ruler Method:** Some writers use a pencil or ruler as a guide to focus on each individual sentence as they proofread. This technique prevents you from looking ahead and helps you concentrate on the sentence at hand.

An especially helpful editing resource you can use is Chapter 15: Correcting Sentence Errors. This chapter should be your go-to resource when you are nearing the end of the writing process, the time when you are editing to create a strong and polished paper.

EXERCISE 3.9   Edit and Proofread a Paper   MyWritingLab

Directions: Here is the revision of Marcus' rough draft. Use some of the editing techniques described in this chapter to go through this draft and see what sentence errors you can find.

Adams 1

Marcus Adams

Prof. Copeland

Introduction to College Writing

The Benefits Of

Being a Working Student

Those of us who work and take college classes are not alone. According to the 2011 U.S. Census, 72% of undergraduates worked during the year, and 20% worked full-time (Davis 1). I sometimes hear students complain about balancing work, and school. I understand their complaints, because I work twenty hours a week at a hardware store, and I have just begun my second semester as a full-time college student. While working and going to school is not always easy, I have found that holding a part-time job has helped me succeed as a first year college student.

The most obvious benefit of working is financial. I live with my parents, who are helping me pay for college, but I am able to help with some of the expenses. Like the $350 I paid for books my first semester. My job also allows me to pay for my car and cell phone, so I can establish a good credit score, which will pay off in the future. Working now can have future benefits, too. I will be able to use my current work experiences in my resume after I graduate and begin looking for a place to start my career in business. I can also do some networking at my job and maybe find contacts for future work. My friend Andrea, for example, met the owner of a graphic arts company while she was working at a coffee shop. After Andrea graduated, the company owner offers her a job. I meet all kinds of suppliers, contractors, and other business people almost every day at my job. After I graduate, one of them may be the door to my future career.

A real advantage of working and going to school that I didn't expect were how the skills I learn in both places are reinforced. I use

Adams   2

my math skills a lot when I help customers decide how much lumber they need for a project. Or how many tiles they need for their kitchen floor. At work I have to communicate effectively, so the speaking and writing skills I learn in my classes can apply directly to my job. For example, I had to write up an accident report at work. My boss complimented me on how clear and well-written my report was. I even talked to my department manager about a way to promote one of our products based on an idea I got in my business class now she is going to take my idea to the store manager. Then there are what my business teacher calls the "soft skills" that employers look for and professors appreciate too. Showing up on time is important at work and at school. I can loose pay or even my job if I'm late too many times for work. I can also be penalized at school because I might miss important information at the beginning of class. My job has also taught me the importance of following directions, so I know to read and listen to those carefully for all my assignments in my classes. Since working with supervisors, co-workers and customers, I know how important people skills are, I now enjoy the group work I have in my college classes.

Learning all these skills, my confidence at work and school has increased. For instance, before taking a writing class, I would have been really nervous about writing that accident report. I might even have been too unsure of myself about sharing that suggestion for product promotion with my boss. Its probably because I am applying these skills at work and impressing my supervisors that I was given a merit raise. That raise lifted my confidence and showed me I am a valued employee who has strengths and skills that aren't all measured by test scores. This confidence picks me up when I take classes over subjects that don't come easy for me. If I dont do well on a test, I'll try harder, I won't give up.

All the confidence working and going to school has given me makes you proud. I know I am capable of managing my time and handling multiple responsibilities now and will be able to do the same in the future. I feel respected when my boss calls me "the

Adams 3

educated one." They know I'm in college, and even when they tease me, I know they respect what I'm doing. At home my parents talk about my accomplishments to family and friends. Not only am I the first in my family to go to college, I am helping to pay my way. My dad always says, "he's working hard to pay his way through school." I know my aunts and uncles tell my cousins to look at how hard I work. I am proud that I am there role model

Some students complain that they have to work while attending college, but I wouldn't have it any other way. I have fewer financial concerns. My job helps me in my classes and my classes help me at my job. I have confidence in what I can do and pride in my accomplishments. For me, working while going to school is a blessing, not a curse.

Adams 4

Works Cited

Davis, Jessica. "School Enrollment and Work Status: 2011." United States Census Bureau, Oct. 2012, https://www.census.gov/prod/2013pubs/acsbr11-14.pdf.

Extended Analogy Essay: Writing Is Like . . .

Your Task: An **analogy** compares two unlike things. You may have heard the famous analogy from the movie *Forrest Gump*: "Life is like a box of chocolates. You never know what you're gonna get." Looking at the common elements of two very different things can lead to new insights and understanding.

For this assignment you will write an *extended* analogy essay about the writing process. This means you will explain the writing process in some detail by comparing it to a process that is entirely different yet shares some common elements.

A logical strategy in writing is to move your readers from what they know to what they don't know. So following your introduction, in the first part of the essay, explain the process that is like writing—a process your readers should likely be able to readily visualize and understand. In the second part of the essay demonstrate how writing is like the first process, showing how the steps correspond in an imaginative way. Be sure to keep the essay fairly balanced in its explanation of each process. End the essay with a short conclusion that emphasizes a key insight about the nature of writing.

Your Role and Audience: Imagine that this paper will be read by aspiring writers who do not yet know much about the writing process. Therefore, your goal is to both inform them about the writing process and entertain them with the insights of your comparison. Another reader is, of course, your instructor, who will gain some insights about your writing habits and your attitude toward writing. You will also share this paper with your peers in class who will both enjoy and learn from your take on an experience you will all share this semester.

Here are some guidelines for writing a successful extended analogy paper:

A Successful Extended Analogy Paper . . .

- Offers an interest-generating introduction by surprising the reader with an unlikely comparison.
- Provides a clear thesis that reflects the whole essay— "Writing is like . . .."
- Makes the comparison explicit with specific details and examples that lead to an insightful understanding of the writing process.
- Connects ideas through the use of a logical and effective organization with appropriate and effective transitions.

- Has strong paragraph unity—each paragraph has a specific purpose.
- Ends with a clear sense of closure, perhaps leaving the reader with a final thought or insight.
- Exhibits strong sentence variety—varied sentences of different lengths and types.
- Provides a medium level of tone and diction—not too formal but not too informal.
- Does not have editing errors that distract the reader or disrupt the meaning of sentences.

Writing Development Plan Paper

Your Task: Your task is to write a paper detailing a writing development plan that will help you improve as a critical thinker and writer.

Students write a lot in college, whether it is scientific reports, reading journals, essays, PowerPoint™ presentations, or research papers. Based on your experience with writing so far and thinking about what you might want to do after you graduate, what are specific aspects of writing you need to work on and how will you go about addressing them? Here is how to get started:

1. **In the first part of the paper**, its introduction, explain what you feel is essential for effective or quality writing (one or two paragraphs).

2. **In the second part of the paper**, transition to *what you need to do,* essentially relating your goals for this course and how you will go about becoming a stronger writer. You must provide a thesis early on to introduce your writing development plan for the next few years of your life, and then you need to develop the various areas of the plan with details, examples, and explanation in the body of your paper.

3. **To create your writing development plan**, use these questions to aid you in the prewriting, organizing, and initial drafting stages of the writing process:

   - How can I prepare myself to write in college and my potential career?
   - What aspects of writing do I need to work on and why? What will I do to develop them?
   - What components of the writing process do I need to develop more fully? Why, and what are my plans for change?

All of these questions should prepare you to reflect on and support your assertions with specific details and examples.

Your Role and Audience: This paper is assigned to benefit your education, and it should provide direction for your writing in this course, in other classes, and in the future. In addition, the paper serves as a formal document in which you reflect on writing and establish goals in your education.

Here are some guidelines for writing an effective development plan paper:

A Successful Writing Development Plan Paper . . .

- Details what you believe are the components of effective writing, which acts as an introduction before the thesis of the paper.
- Provides a clear thesis that reflects the whole essay—your writing development plan and why those goals are important.
- Presents a clear writing development plan that connects to your academic writing and possible career paths.
- Presents your areas of development as a writer with specific details and examples while relating what you need to do—the tactics and strategies you will use to make yourself a stronger writer.
- Connects ideas through the use of appropriate and effective transitions.
- Has strong paragraph unity—each paragraph has a specific purpose.
- Exhibits effective sentence variety—varied sentences of different lengths and types.
- Provides a medium level of tone and diction—not too formal but not too informal.
- Does not have editing errors that distract the reader or disrupt the meaning of sentences.
- Is relatively free of mechanical and proofreading errors.

USING I D E A S

Here is the I D E A S template as you might adapt it to this particular assignment:

I nterest

- How can I create interest for the reader?
- What does the reader need to know and what could bore him or her?
- Can I remember any good advice about writing that I can relate from experience?
- What have people told me about my writing ability, and what do I already know about writing and the writing process?

D etails

- What strong, specific, concrete, and vivid details can I provide about my knowledge about writing?
- How can I "make it real" through good details about writing in general and, most importantly, my writing development plan that addresses where I need to grow as a writer?
- What writing weaknesses do I need to work on?
- What do I do well in writing, and how can I further enhance those strengths?
- What stages of the writing process do I need to develop more fully?
- What do I need to do to be better prepared to write in my potential career?

E xplanation

- What have I been told about my writing before this course? What did I need to work on, and what did I do well? Who told me this?
- What examples from personal experience (positive and negative) can I provide in the paper?
- How has my writing process proceeded in the past? How should it change and why?
- What techniques and methods detailed in this chapter do I want to try and why?
- What types of writing will I do in the future, and how can I prepare myself to do this writing?

A udience

- What tone is appropriate for the instructor I'm writing for?
- What understanding of writing is my instructor most interested in seeing me demonstrate?

S tyle

- How can I use sentence variety (different lengths and types of sentences) to make the writing flow effectively from one idea to another?
- Where can I create strong transitions within paragraphs and from paragraph to paragraph?
- Am I using strong verbs in my sentences?

CHAPTER AT A GLANCE

Learning Objectives . . .   How they connect to learning, reading, and writing at college . . .

---

❶ Assess the writing situation.

When writing a paper, you need to consider these core components:

- *Subject:* Gain knowledge of, generate content for, and reflect on the topic.
- *Purpose:* Focus your writing by considering the document's purpose.
- *Audience:* Consider what evidence and points will work effectively for the reader.
- *Genre:* Use the correct format the writing situation demands.

---

❷ Direct your writing with a thesis statement.

An effective thesis statement should be a generalization, use precise terms, and have a controlling idea.

---

❸ Put I D E A S to work.

You can use the I D E A S tool (Interest, Details, Explanation, Audience, and Style) to generate content for your papers and to analyze other people's writing.

---

❹ Practice writing as a process.

You should know and be able to work in these stages of the writing process:

Planning

- Considering the subject, purpose, audience, and genre of a paper.
- Using I D E A S to generate content.

Prewriting

- Brainstorming
- Freewriting
- Focused Freewriting and Brainstorming

Organizing

- Clustering/Idea Mapping
- Formal Outlining
- Sketch/Scratch Outlining

First Drafting: Writing a provisional first draft to get the paper started

Revising & Redrafting: Understanding the levels of revision and implementing them into your process

Editing & Proofreading: Using effective editing and proofreading techniques

---

> **MyWritingLab** Visit **Chapter 3, "Writing and the Process of Writing,"** in MyWritingLab to test your understanding of the chapter objectives.

Writing Paragraphs

4

A well-built house is properly planned, has a good foundation, and uses good building materials. Like home construction, papers need to employ sound organization, have solid support, and provide strong cohesion or "flow."

Learning Objectives

In this chapter, you will learn to . . .

❶ Unify your paragraphs with a topic sentence.

❷ Create support in your paragraphs by using details, reasons, examples, and explanations.

❸ Use coherence strategies to connect your support.

❹ Organize support by using patterns of development.

Successful construction projects usually begin with a purpose and a plan. The best builders then gather quality materials and take care to assemble them in a way that assures the final construction is solid. You can usually distinguish the quality work of a craftsman from that of someone who makes do with what is lying around and throws it together willy-nilly. Successful writing is like any successful construction. It begins with a purpose and a plan to assemble quality materials to achieve that purpose.

Building Paragraphs

Strong body paragraphs provide support for the overall purpose of a piece of writing. Successful writing—whether a business memo, a medical report, or an academic paper—must have unified, organized, and fully supported paragraphs. Each paragraph needs a central point supported by specific details, reasons, examples, and explanations that interconnect, so readers are not confused by the paragraphs.

In this chapter you will learn what goes into writing the "body" or core paragraphs of an essay. In Chapter 5 you will focus on more specialized paragraphs—introductions, conclusions, and transitional paragraphs—and you will see how paragraphs work together to build strong essays.

Unify Your Paragraphs with a Topic Sentence

❶ Unify your paragraphs with a topic sentence.

A **unified** paragraph is strong and solid. It has a central point or idea, and every sentence of the paragraph supports that central point with details, reasons, examples, and explanations.

Writers can present a paragraph's central point in a **topic sentence**—a single *general* statement that lets the reader know both the *limited subject* of the paragraph and the *central point* the writer intends to make about it. Some writing teachers refer to this central point as a "**controlling idea**" because it controls or limits what the writer says about the subject. A topic sentence may appear at the beginning, middle, or end of a paragraph.

While a central point may also be **implied**, which means that it is not directly stated in a topic sentence, you will find that well-written, explicit topic sentences will help keep your paragraphs unified by providing guideposts against which to check your supporting details, reasons, and examples. Topic sentences are also useful guides for readers, especially when you are writing about complex subjects.

Recognize Generalizations and Specifics

The first step in writing a topic sentence is recognizing the difference between a *general* statement and a *specific* statement. A **generalization** is a broad statement that covers an entire group or situation. **Specific** statements focus on particular instances, examples, and details. Specifics include facts, statistics, and dates. A well-written paragraph will have far more specific statements than generalizations. After all, you cannot adequately support a general statement with more generalizations.

A paragraph must have a central point that is a generalization—an opinion, an observation—that the rest of the paragraph will then support, explain, or develop with specifics. Here are some examples of generalizations and specific statements:

Generalizations	Specific Statements
• Researchers in Antarctica must face extreme weather conditions.	• In the winter, gale force winds can reach 200 miles per hour, and wind chills can plunge to –148°F. (facts)
• False rumors can hurt or destroy a business.	• One Arab-owned restaurant lost 50 percent of its customers when a false email claimed its employees cheered when they saw the 9/11 attacks on television. (example)
• Consumers should buy organic produce.	• Eating organic produce reduces one's exposure to the toxins in pesticides and chemical fertilizers. (reason)
• Swankee Campgrounds is an ideal place to spend your camping vacation.	• A crystal-clear lake, perfect for swimming or fishing, is only a quarter mile from the campsite. (detail)

EXERCISE 4.1   **Identify General and Specific Statements**   MyWritingLab

Directions: Read each set of statements and determine which statement is a generalization (**G**) and which is a specific (**S**) statement.

1. ____ a. Smaller than a penny, the Alabama Cave Shrimp is found in only two Alabama cave systems.

   ____ b. Cave ecosystems are home to a wide range of unique animals.

2. ____ a. College students should be cautious about overrelying on credit cards.

   ____ b. A student who makes a minimum payment of $40 a month on a $2,000 credit card loan will need eight years to pay off the balance and will have paid $1,994 in interest.

3. ____ a. When he began to lose his eyesight, the French artist Edgar Degas turned to large pastel works and sculpture.

   ____ b. Some of the world's great artists have risen to the challenges of physical disabilities that limit their work.

4. ____ a. Last summer I took my niece to Disney World in Orlando, Florida.

   ____ b. Taking a very young child to Disney World presents a number of challenges.

5. ____ a. Supermarkets employ a number of strategies to encourage shoppers to spend more money.

   ____ b. More expensive products are shelved at eye level on the right on supermarket aisles since that is where consumers' eyes are most likely to rest.

Limit Your Subject

A well-written topic sentence also limits the paragraph's subject. Since a paragraph is a relatively small unit of writing, you should not try to cover a broad subject, or you may find yourself relying on more generalizations rather than specific details and concrete explanation, which readers need to understand your point. Here are some examples of how an overly broad subject can be revised to be more limited:

Overly Broad Paragraph Subject	Limited Paragraph Subject
• Genetic mutations can manifest in many different ways.	• The genetic mutation Delta-32 has positive benefits for its carriers.
• The workplace can be very dangerous.	• Fishermen face daily perils at their job.
• Computers have many benefits, but a lot can go wrong with them as well.	• A computer infected with a virus usually has several symptoms.
• Horror movies say a lot about the time periods in which they appear.	• *Godzilla* has a distinct anti-war message.
• Many courageous men and women helped rescue slaves through the Underground Railroad.	• John Fairfield relied on intricate disguises to lead slaves to freedom through the Underground Railroad.

EXERCISE 4.2   Identify Overly Broad Subjects   MyWritingLab

Directions: Read each set of statements and determine which presents a subject that is probably too broad to cover in a single paragraph.

_____ 1. a. There are many ways to stay healthy.

b. Eating the right foods can help you maintain a healthy immune system.

_____ 2. a. Madame Marie Chouteau defied the marital laws and customs of her time.

b. Madame Chouteau played a big part in early St. Louis history.

_____ 3. a. One reason the local bookstore failed is its location.

b. In today's economy, businesses fail for a variety of reasons.

_____ 4. a. Having diabetes has changed my life.

b. As a diabetic, I must take some extra precautions before going on vacations.

_____ 5. a. Bad calls by officials can cause problems in professional sports.

b. Bad calls by referees plagued the 2010 World Cup finals.

Clearly State Your Controlling Idea

Once you have a subject for your paragraph, you must have a clearly stated controlling idea, so the central point you make about your subject is obvious to the readers. The controlling idea also keeps the development of the paragraph focused.

Notice how many different paragraphs can be written on the subject of attending college. In each case, the *controlling idea* determines which *supporting details* the writer will use.

- Attending college *is expensive.*
- Attending college *can be stressful.*
- Attending college *can benefit one socially, intellectually, and economically.*
- Attending college *opened my mind to new ideas.*
- Attending college *can strain relationships.*
- Attending college *allowed me to meet diverse kinds of people.*

Because the controlling idea plays such a key role in keeping your paragraph focused and unified, always try to state your controlling idea in the clearest terms. Remember, a strong controlling idea points the paragraph in a clear direction. It lets you know exactly the kinds of support you need to use, as shown in the box on page 98.

Vague Controlling Idea	Clearly Stated Controlling Idea
The kappa is an *interesting* creature.	Found in legends and folktales, the kappa is a **dangerous Japanese water creature.**
Being able to listen well is *good.*	Being a good listener has **advantages in the workplace.**
Animals *can do many things.*	Scientists have been astounded by some animals' **ability to make and use tools.**
Rumors can be *bad.*	Rumors can **destroy small businesses.**

EXERCISE 4.3   Recognize Clearly Stated Controlling Ideas   MyWritingLab

Directions: Read each set of statements and determine which presents the controlling idea in the most clearly stated terms.

_____ 1. a. Playstation 3 is awesome.

   b. Playstation 3 offers the most features at the best price.

_____ 2. a. In laboratory experiments, octopuses have demonstrated a surprising ability to learn and to remember.

   b. Octopuses are interesting creatures.

_____ 3. a. Random drug testing of student athletes is a debatable issue.

   b. Random drug testing of student athletes does not effectively deter their drug use.

_____ 4. a. My whitewater rafting trip down the Grand Canyon was a lot of fun.

   b. My whitewater rafting trip down the Grand Canyon tested my physical endurance.

_____ 5. a. In his later life, Beethoven found ways to cope with his hearing loss.

   b. The great composer Beethoven had a hard time in later life.

Check for Paragraph Unity

Once you have a limited subject and a clearly stated controlling idea, you have a way to check whether supporting statements in a paragraph contribute to its unity. Not only must each supporting statement be about the limited subject, but also it must address, support, or prove the controlling idea. For example, you would not support the topic sentence *Attending college opened my mind to new ideas* with an example like "My economics textbook cost $150." Nor would

you support the topic sentence *Attending college is expensive* with a reason like "I now think critically about political issues and do not simply follow the lead of my friends." An important part of revising paragraphs is checking for unity by making sure all the support backs up the topic sentence's controlling idea and removing those sentences that get off track. A paragraph is unified when the details, examples, and explanation work together and provide a united point that makes sense.

EXERCISE 4.4   Eliminate Irrelevant Details   MyWritingLab

Directions: Read the following paragraph and underline the topic sentence. Then cross out any sentences that do not support the controlling idea.

The local bookstore failed because of its location. The owners rented a small retail space on a busy street just outside of the downtown area. Although a large grocery store across the street drew a lot of customers, few risked running across busy lanes of traffic to visit the bookstore. Also, the small strip mall in which the bookstore was located sat too far back from the road for the store to be clearly visible. A larger sign in the window may have helped attract customers. In fact, the owner should have done more to promote the store in the community. The bookstore would have done much better in a central location downtown with more foot traffic. In addition, the building itself was too small. The small space limited the numbers of books for customers to browse, and many left without making a purchase. A bigger space with more books would have made it more likely for customers to find something they liked. Fortunately, the small size made the building easier to sublet when the book store closed. After six months with few sales, it was clear that the small retail space on a busy street was not the ideal location for a bookstore.

❷ Create support in your paragraphs by using details, reasons, examples, and explanations.

Create Support in Your Paragraphs by Using Details, Reasons, Examples, and Explanations

Remember, generalizations do not support generalizations. Nor can a topic sentence be sufficiently supported by statements that are only slightly less general than the topic sentence. Specific statements make up the support that most interests and informs readers.

In the following paragraph, the writer speculates on the reasons for some extreme directions on products. Notice the writer gives three major reasons, each more specific than the topic sentence, and then supports each reason with specific examples (shown in italics) that make this paragraph interesting.

> In this topic sentence, the limited subject is directions manufacturers place on products, and the controlling idea is these directions are outrageous.
>
> First main idea
>
> Specific examples
>
> Second main idea
>
> Specific examples
>
> Final main idea
>
> Specific examples

Because we live in such a litigious society, manufacturers have to be particularly careful. Sometimes, though, **the directions they place on products** seem so completely **outrageous** that you have to wonder what circumstances led to them. Packaging must confuse a lot of people. *For example, how many confused consumers called the company before the directions "Remove wrapper, open mouth, insert muffin, eat" were added to packaging on muffins? Is getting a food product out of its container so confusing that "Remove plastic before eating" had to be added to fruit snacks?* In addition to being confused by packaging, many people must have strange urges to eat the inedible. *A bottle of hair dye warns, "Do not use as an ice cream topping." Even a box of fireworks cautions, "Do not put in mouth."* Perhaps the most extreme directions came about because of tragic mistakes. *Why else would a microwave oven manual include "Do not use for drying pets"? Can you imagine the accident that led to the following label on a Swedish chainsaw: "Do not attempt to stop chain with your hands or genitals"?*

Avoid Support That Is Too General

Sometimes a writer will attempt to develop a paragraph with only main ideas and neglects the more specific support that adds interest and informs readers. The following paragraph shows what happens when a writer tries to support a topic sentence with main ideas that are only slightly more specific than the topic sentence.

There are a lot of benefits to having a small backyard garden. Although our garden is small, it allows us to reduce our negative impact on the environment. Plus, my family doesn't spend as much on groceries. The food we grow also tastes a lot better than what we buy at the store, and it's safer. A big benefit is the family eats healthier. The garden has also brought us closer to others in our community when we share what we've grown. I've even found that working in the garden is as good as any workout at a gym.

The most general statement in this paragraph is the topic sentence: *There are a lot of benefits to having a small backyard garden.* The sentences that follow the topic sentence are a little more specific in that they mention particular benefits; however, they are not specific enough to give readers a clear understanding of those benefits. The writer also attempts to cover too much. If all of the main ideas in this paragraph were fully supported, the paragraph might be a page or more long.

In revising the garden paragraph, the writer should narrow the focus to a single benefit. That first step in revision may look something like this:

> Growing our own fruits and vegetables in a small backyard garden has done much to improve my family's health. We get a lot of fresh air and exercise working in the garden. We don't use pesticides on the food we grow, so it is safer to eat than store-bought food. Most importantly, the family eats more fruits and vegetables, which benefits our overall health.

Now the writer has a topic sentence with a clearly stated controlling idea: *growing fruits and vegetables has improved the health of her family.* The writer also has three main ideas, each one supporting the topic sentence by introducing a healthy benefit: exercise, safer food, and healthier food. The next step is to revise this paragraph by adding *specific* examples and details that support the main ideas and add interest and clarity.

Growing our own fruits and vegetables in a small backyard garden has done much to improve my family's health. One benefit is the exercise we get while working in the garden. *Carrying bags of soil, raking, weeding and watering—all of these physical activities are as strenuous as a workout in a high priced gym. As we improve our stamina and tone our muscles in the fresh air and sunshine, an added benefit is we are growing food for our table.* This food we grow ourselves

Topic sentence

First main idea followed by specific details

Second main idea followed by specific reasons

is also much safer to eat than some store bought food. *We do not use potentially dangerous pesticides or herbicides on our food. In addition we don't have to worry about contamination from improper handling of food in processing plants.* Perhaps the biggest benefit to my family's health is that we now eat more fruits and vegetables. *The fresh produce tastes so good that we enjoy eating the five or more recommended daily servings of fruits and vegetables. Also because they are so proud of having grown the food themselves, my children are more willing to eat zucchini, eggplant, beets, squash, and other vegetables they avoided in the past. This safe and healthy diet strengthens our immune systems and reduces our risks for serious diseases like cancer.*

> Third main idea followed by reasons and details

This paragraph has stronger support because it focuses on a more limited subject and offers interesting and informative details. The following outline will help you see more clearly the levels of generalization that work together to support the paragraph's central point.

Topic sentence: Growing our own fruits and vegetables in a small backyard garden has done much to improve my family's health. *(topic sentence—most general—states controlling idea)*

main idea
I. One benefit is the exercise we get while working in the garden.

specific supporting details
  a. Carrying bags of soil, raking, weeding and watering—all of these physical activities are as strenuous as a workout in a high priced gym.
  b. As we improve our stamina and tone our muscles in the fresh air and sunshine, an added benefit is we are growing food for our table.

main idea
II. This food we grow ourselves is also much safer to eat.

specific supporting reasons
  a. We do not use potentially dangerous pesticides or herbicides on our food.
  b. In addition we don't have to worry about contamination from improper handling of food in processing plants.

main idea
III. Perhaps the biggest benefit to my family's health is that we now eat more fruits and vegetables.

specific supporting reasons and details
  a. The fresh produce tastes so good that it's enjoyable to eat the five or more recommended daily servings of fruits and vegetables.
  b. Also because they are so proud of having grown the food themselves, my children are more willing to eat zucchini, eggplant, beets, squash, and other vegetables they avoided in the past.
  c. This safe and healthy diet strengthens our immune systems and reduces our risks for serious diseases like cancer.

Paragraphs will have different levels of generalization among the supporting sentences, but the most successful paragraphs will have more specific details, reasons, examples, and explanations. For example, if a critic were going to review a new action movie in one paragraph, she is not just going to say it is "good" and it "had some fun chase scenes." She would provide reasons and details about the movie to make readers trust her evaluation of the film such as specifics about a ten-minute-long car chase scene, what makes some of the characters so compelling, and how many plot twists might surprise the reader.

EXERCISE 4.5   Recognize Levels of Generalization   MyWritingLab

Directions: Show that you can recognize the different levels of generalization in the following sets of statements. Identify each statement as a topic sentence (**TS**), a main idea (**MI**), or a specific detail (**S**).

1. ____ a. After the disastrous earthquake in Haiti, search and rescue dogs helped find and save more than seventy victims buried under rubble.

    ____ b. Dogs have a remarkable sense of smell.

    ____ c. Some dogs can smell odors as much as forty feet underground, making them indispensible in rescuing people in collapsed structures.

2. ____ a. Babies who know sign language show less frustration.

    ____ b. A baby will not have to cry for a favorite toy or a bottle but can use signs to let someone know what is needed.

    ____ c. Teaching a baby sign language has several social benefits.

3. ____ a. People could save more money if they did not make some common mistakes.

    ____ b. For example, a man does not really need a $30 electric shaving cream warmer.

    ____ c. Often people buy things they don't need.

4. ____ a. Song writers can find inspiration in just about anything.

    ____ b. Bob Dylan wrote "It Ain't Me, Babe" after breaking up with Joan Baez.

    ____ c. Some songs were inspired by people and events in the song writer's life.

5. ____ a. Some of the most dangerous stretches of ocean are those passages between two land masses.

_____ b. Every second, the Circumpolar Current pushes 140 million tons of water through the Drake Passage, the equivalent of 5000 Amazon Rivers.

_____ c. The Drake Passage between the southern tip of South America and northern tip of Antarctica has been described as the roughest stretch of water in the world.

EXERCISE 4.6   Write Supporting Sentences   MyWritingLab

Directions: Practice composing specific reasons, examples, and details that could be used to support each of the following general statements.

1. My car is not very dependable.

2. Sometimes my workplace obligations can interfere with my school obligations.

3. Clearly, the boss was angry.

4. The apartment was not a safe place for children.

5. Camping can be comfortable.

❸ Use coherence strategies to connect your support.

Use Coherence Strategies to Connect Your Support

Coherence refers to the ways a writer *connects* the ideas in a piece of writing. In the best writing—the writing that *flows*—paragraphs are unified around controlling ideas, and the supporting details, reasons, and examples have logical and stylistic connections. Clear connections help readers follow and understand ideas.

Because coherence is so important to readers' enjoyment and understanding, writers have developed a number of ways to make clear connections in their writing. Here are some of the most common methods of achieving coherence:

* Following basic organization strategies
* Using transitional words and phrases
* Repeating key words and phrases or using synonyms
* Creating connections with pronoun reference

Follow Basic Organization Strategies

The following strategies are logical and conventional ways of organizing ideas. While there are certainly other strategies for organizing ideas, these are used most frequently. Most readers are already familiar with these basic strategies and should be able to follow them:

- Chronological organization
- Spatial organization
- Emphatic (or least important/most important) organization

Chronological

Chronological or **time** organization means the writer presents supporting details, events, or reasons as they occur in time. This strategy is used most often when telling a story, giving directions, or explaining how something happened. The following paragraph uses chronological order to explain how immigrants arriving at Ellis Island were processed.

> *[Topic sentence. The subject is a "process," which calls for a time organization.]*
>
> In 1892, the first year it opened, the Ellis Island Immigration Station processed nearly 450,000 immigrants. The process that commissioners developed to handle this volume of immigrants was efficient, though perhaps impersonal.
>
> *[The first step in the process]*
>
> After arriving in New York, first and second class passengers were allowed to disembark and pass quickly through customs. Officials believed the more affluent immigrants were less likely to be ill and more able to support themselves once in the United States.
>
> *[Second step in the process]*
>
> Those passengers in steerage, however, were taken by barge to Ellis Island for medical and legal inspections. Entering the huge registry room, immigrants were quickly scanned by medical personnel. Those immigrants who had apparent illnesses or disabilities were

> labeled with a chalk mark on their shoulders and sent off for closer scrutiny.
>
> *[Third step in the process]*
>
> Those passing the medical inspection then underwent the legal inspection. In a matter of minutes, immigrants had to show they had money and to prove they
>
> *[Final step in the process]*
>
> had a safe place to stay upon leaving Ellis Island. Those who passed were taken by barge to Battery Park on Manhattan. From New York, the immigrants dispersed to cities and farmlands across the country. Today, nearly 40 percent of U.S. citizens are descendents of immigrants who passed through Ellis Island.

MyWritingLab Visit
Ch. 4 Writing Paragraphs
in MyWritingLab to access
the IDEAS videos.

I D E A S for Your Own Writing   **MyWritingLab**

Step-by-Step

Write a paragraph that describes a process you have gone though. For example, what steps did you go through to enroll in college, try out for a sports team, or apply for a job? Use a chronological organization.

Spatial

Spatial organization is typically used in descriptive writing. Using this strategy, the writer presents details according to their physical position in space. It is important that this organization follow a logical movement through space such as front to back, right to left, top to bottom. The following paragraph describes the famous study where Mark Twain composed some of his greatest works.

> Where were Huckleberry Finn and Tom Sawyer born? Mark Twain brought them to life in a small octagonal study his sister-in-law, Susan Crane, had built for him at Quarry Farm in Elmira, New York, where Twain and his family spent their summers. Each morning after breakfast, Twain would cross the lawn and climb the stone steps leading up the hill to the study. The outer design of the study seemed to recall the riverboat pilot houses of Twain's younger years. It had a peaked roof, and each side held a spacious window looking out over the Chemung River valley, a view Twain called a "foretaste of heaven." Twain described the inside as a "cozy nest," a perfect place where he could write and smoke his cigars. Against one wall was a small fireplace. A writing table and a wicker chair stood in front of the fireplace. Along another wall was a cot that could easily provide a resting place for a quiet nap. And, of course, the study was equipped with a cat door for Twain's beloved cats that roamed the farm.

This sentence introduces the topic of the paragraph.

The writer begins by moving towards the study.

Next, the writer describes the outer features of the study.

Finally, the writer describes the inside of the study.

> ## I D E A S for Your Own Writing   MyWritingLab
>
> **My Ideal Workspace**
> Mark Twain's study at Quarry Farm was his ideal workspace where he produced some of his best literary works. Write a paragraph that describes your ideal workspace. This might be the place where you do your schoolwork, or your job, or even your favorite hobby. Be specific and detailed in your description, using a spatial organization.

Emphatic (Most Important/Least Important)

An **emphatic** organization presents support from least to most important. Readers typically expect a writer to build up to the main point, so placing the most important detail, example, or reason at the end gives it more importance or emphasis. In the following paragraph, the writer gives examples of problems caused by starlings, an invasive species introduced into the United States a little over a hundred years ago. Notice how the problems described become increasingly serious.

Topic sentence

In 1890, Eugene Schieffelin released sixty European starlings in New York's Central Park as part of his program to introduce into North America all the birds mentioned in Shakespeare's plays. Today we are still paying a costly price for Schieffelin's tampering with nature. Starlings have become one of the most prolific birds in North America to the detriment of native species.

First problem

Because the more aggressive starlings compete with woodpeckers, bluebirds, and swallows for nest cavities in trees, those species have declined while starlings thrive.

The second more serious problem

And the many millions of starlings now living in North America are voracious eaters, willing to eat just about anything. Starlings plague farmers by devouring vast quantities of fruits and grains. They even raid livestock feed lots, eating the high protein supplements added to the animals' feed.

The third and even more serious problem

In urban areas, large noisy flocks can spread disease through their droppings. Among the most serious of these diseases are histoplasmosis, a fungal lung disease and toxoplasmosis, a parasitic disease especially harmful to pregnant women.

The most serious problem

Flocks of starlings are particularly dangerous near airports where they can threaten aircraft. In 1960 a plane taking off from a Boston airport crashed after colliding with a flock of starlings, killing sixty-two people.

I D E A S for Your Own Writing   MyWritingLab

Consequences

Write a paragraph that describes several consequences resulting from
something you did. For example, perhaps you did a favor for a friend, and
there were a number of very positive outcomes. Or maybe you took a
chance on a new job and experienced outcomes you had not anticipated.
Organize the consequences you describe from least to most important.

You will find that these basic organization strategies infuse the patterns of development discussed on pages 114–123 in this chapter. As a
writer, you have to decide which strategies and patterns work best to help
your readers follow and understand your ideas.

Use Transitional Words and Phrases

Successful writing makes the reading experience easy by presenting ideas
clearly and guiding readers to important information. **Transitional words
and phrases** guide readers by signaling where a piece of writing is going.
For example, the common transition "In contrast" lets the reader know the
writer is showing some type of difference between two items. The phrase
lets the reader know something important is coming, almost implying,
"Hey you, listen up! This is an important difference."

There are many transitions to choose from. It is important to vary the
types of transitions you use in order to avoid boring repetition within your
paragraphs. Avoid using transitions to the point that they become distracting and call unnecessary attention to themselves.

Here is a list of common transitions you can use within your paragraphs. They are organized by function; that is, they are organized by what
they do in sentences (contrast, show time, examine cause or effect, etc.).
These words and phrases can be useful in creating paragraphs that are
coherent and lead readers where you want them to go. You can find more
discussion about transitions in Chapter 5.

Function	Examples
To Add	*additionally, again, also, and, as well as, first, furthermore, in addition, last, moreover, next, too*
To Compare	*also, in a similar manner, in the same way, just as, likewise, similarly*

Function	Examples
To Contrast	*although, but, but at the same time, despite, even so, even though, however, in contrast, in spite of, in the same way, nevertheless, on the contrary, on the other hand, regardless, still, though, yet*
To Emphasize	*another key point, indeed, in fact, in particular, most importantly, of course*
To Indicate Cause or Effect	*accordingly, as a result, because, consequently, for this purpose, otherwise, since, then, therefore, thus, to this end*
To Indicate Time	*after, after a while, afterward, as long as, as soon as, at last, at that time, before, earlier, formerly, immediately, in the meantime, in the past, lately, later, meanwhile, now, presently, shortly, since, so far, soon, then, thereafter, until, when*
To Indicate Place	*above, below, beyond, elsewhere, farther on, here, near, nearby, next to, on the other side, opposite to, there, throughout, under*
To Repeat	*as has been stated, in other words, in simpler terms, that is, to put it differently*
To Show or Illustrate	*for example, for instance, to illustrate the point*
To Summarize or Conclude	*all in all, altogether, in brief, in conclusion, in other words, in short, in summary, on the whole, therefore, to summarize*

While this list shows the most common transitions, you should not limit yourself to them. Transitions are any words or phrases that lead readers from one idea to another. As you see by the chart above, certain words have specific roles. You would not use "in short" the same way you would use "first" or "for example" or "on the other hand" in a paragraph. As you read the paragraphs in this chapter section, you will see the common transitions used as well as more varied transitions that fit the particular needs of individual paragraphs.

EXERCISE 4.7   Choose Transitions   MyWritingLab

Directions: Read the following paragraph and identify how the writer has organized his ideas. Then decide what transitions you would add to this paragraph, using the list of common transitions. Add the transitions to the paragraph, making any necessary changes in punctuation and capitalization.

School districts have some good reasons for turning toward structured recess for elementary age children. Organized games with adult monitors allow all the children to participate without fear of being bullied. One school reported that discipline problems during recess dropped by three-quarters after a structured recess program was introduced. A program of structured recess can improve students' social skills. With so many students playing video games in isolation, they often don't know how to play, how to interact with others. Participation in an organized program teaches them how to follow the rules of a game, to take turns and to be part of a team. Structured recess is a way to address the growing trend of childhood obesity. Some children just sit around and talk during their recess period, and others are cut out of games because of bullying and peer squabbles. With structured recess, a coach or other facilitator engages all the children in a variety of games that keep children engaged and exerting energy. A well-run structured recess program can reduce playground aggression, teach students important social skills, and improve their physical fitness.

Repeat Key Words and Phrases or Use Synonyms

Writers will often repeat key words throughout a paragraph to remind the reader of the subject or the main idea. When used effectively, repetition creates coherence in a piece of writing and enhances its overall unity. In the paragraph on structured recess in Exercise 4.7, for example, notice the repetition of the words *structured recess*, *children*, and *program*. This repetition keeps a clear focus on the subject and key points in the paragraph.

EXERCISE 4.8   Find Repeated Key Words   MyWritingLab

Directions: Read the following paragraph and circle words the writer repeats.
How does this repetition keep the paragraph unified and coherent?

As you visit colleges to choose the one that's right for you, be sure to visit
one of the most important resources on any campus: the library. As you
walk around the building, imagine yourself going there to study. Is the
atmosphere warm and welcoming? Are there enough quiet and comfortable places to study? Look to see if there are areas where you can socialize,
perhaps even small rooms where you can collaborate with peers on special
projects. Next, check out how easy it is to find information in the library.
Have some topics in mind and see how quickly you can find information
on those topics in the books and periodicals. This will introduce you to
the library's website and all of the digital resources as well. As you walk
around the library and browse its computers, you will undoubtedly have
questions. Take this opportunity to meet the staff. Are the librarians and
other staff members polite and helpful? Do they provide an orientation?
The library is going to play an important role in your college career, so
take what you learn from this visit and make it a crucial part of your decision in determining which college to attend.

Just as writers can overuse transitions, they can overdo repetition.
One way to avoid distracting and ineffective repetition is to use
synonyms—words that have the same or nearly the same meaning as the
key words you are using—to emphasize a main idea. Be cautious when
using synonyms, though, because words that have the same literal meaning
or **denotation** may have different emotional meanings or suggestions
called **connotations**. You have to use synonyms that have the same connotations as the key words you repeat.

EXERCISE 4.9   Use Synonyms   MyWritingLab

Directions: The following sentences contain synonyms. In which sentences are the synonyms effective and in which sentences do different connotations change the writer's presentation of the topic? In each sentence circle the synonyms and revise those that are ineffective. Be prepared to explain the reasons for your revisions.

1. The **fans** poured into the stadium to watch their favorite team. Some **enthusiasts** wore their team's colors. A couple of **fanatics** behind me waved signs with their favorite players' names.

2. Many people are bothered by the **odor** from a cat's litter box. Clean Cat Litter absorbs the **fragrance** of the cat's waste. If you switch to Clean Cat litter, no one will notice the **smell** again.

3. For my birthday, my family treated me to a **delicious** meal at my favorite restaurant. Everything from the main course to the dessert was simply **scrumptious**. The only thing better than the **tasty** food was the wonderful company.

4. A variety of exercises can tighten the **stomach** muscles. A lot of people with big **guts** try to reduce them with sit ups. Actually, standing up straight will make a **belly** look smaller.

5. In order to earn a degree, I must take a number of **required** courses. History and psychology are among the **obligatory** classes. Math and English are also **compulsory**.

Use Pronouns to Create Connections

Pronouns are words that can take the place of nouns. Writers use pronouns—*it, he, she, they, we, you, its, his, her, their, our,* and *your*—to avoid unnecessary repetition in a paper. Pronouns improve coherence by *linking* sentences, as in the following example.

noun   *pronoun*

Paul is an outstanding student. **He** is always an active participant in class.

The pronoun *he* in the second sentence refers back to *Paul* in the first sentence. Clear pronoun reference links sentences, making the writing more coherent. See the Handbook page 471 for ways to avoid references that are vague or unclear.

EXERCISE 4.10   Eliminate Unnecessary Repetition   MyWritingLab

Directions: How would you use synonyms and pronouns to cut the boring repetition in the following paragraph? Are there other ways you could improve this paragraph?

I would like to recommend Paul Franklin for the position of photographer at Memories Portrait Studio. Over the past two semesters, Paul has taken three of my photography courses here at Metro Community College. Through my experience with Paul, I have found him to be trustworthy and hardworking. Because Paul could be so trustworthy in handling expensive lab equipment, I appointed Paul director of the photography lab, a job that required Paul to manage all of our equipment and to make sure the lab was secure at the end of each day. I had no problems during the semesters that Paul managed the lab. I also found Paul to be very hardworking. Paul always did more than was required to make his portfolio of work outstanding. Paul also showed his hardworking nature when he ran the lab. Paul kept the lab clean and organized and managed all the equipment while maintaining good grades in his classes. Paul would make an outstanding addition to your business.

When you edit and proofread your papers, look for places to create good repetition and to cut boring repetition by using effective synonyms and clear pronoun reference.

❹ Organize support by using patterns of development.

Organize Support by Using Patterns of Development

If you take a strong academic essay or business report and examine it closely, you are likely to find that each paragraph has a specific purpose. For example, a paragraph may focus on describing a work environment, narrating a conversation, discussing the effects of a certain policy, or walking the reader through the process of performing a task. In other words, *each paragraph has a certain role*—such as comparing, presenting causes, or defining—within a larger piece of writing. The guiding principles behind these roles are called **patterns of development**. These patterns are ways to develop ideas as well as to organize them. In fact, some writers and texts refer to them as "patterns of organization" or even "rhetorical modes."

What follows are brief descriptions and examples of the important patterns for paragraphs. All of the examples deal with a common subject: *cyberbullying*. Notice how each pattern both organizes and develops the common subject in a distinct way.

Description

When a paragraph focuses on **description**, the author takes the time to richly portray a person, place, event, or thing with specific and concrete details (see Chapter 2, p. 36). Often people say that strong descriptive writing "paints a picture with words" because of its strong details. In this example, the writer describes the scene of a grieving father speaking about the dangers of cyberbullying before an audience of high school students.

Description Paragraph

The writer presents the descriptions of the young man in **chronological order**; the words in bold show this organization strategy. The writer uses descriptive details to paint a picture with words.

Standing on the stage before the high school assembly as pictures of his young son scrolled on the wall behind him, the father recounted the short life of his son. Pictures of a **smiling toddler** opening Christmas gifts and a gangly young boy playing sports dissolved into more pensive photos of a **young teen**. The boy still smiled, but his eyes had lost their shine. The bullying had started just at the time when a young person's ego is particularly fragile, and the pain was already starting to show in those eyes. The father's voice trembled as he told of how hard he tried to reassure his son that the trials of **junior high** were survivable. He promised his son there would be friends—even girlfriends—who would see the same kind and loving boy who brought such joy to his family. The father's voice cracked as he described **the horrible day he found his son dead**. Total stillness filled the auditorium as the last picture—the picture of a flower-strewn grave—filled the screen. **Only after his son was buried** did the father learn what led to the suicide. Going through his son's computer, the grieving father found the taunting IMs, the pages of ridicule and vicious rumors—all more than a sensitive boy already struggling with depression could handle. Some in the audience nodded in quiet understanding while others struggled to hold back tears.

I D E A S for Your Own Writing   **MyWritingLab**

An Emotional Moment

In a paragraph, describe a scene that you have experienced or witnessed that conveys a strong emotion such as nervousness, joy, excitement, or disappointment. Do not explicitly tell your readers what the emotion is. Let the descriptive details convey the emotion of that moment.

Narration

Narrative writing is much like descriptive writing because there is a strong emphasis on specific and concrete details. However, in a narrative paragraph, there is usually more focus on an event that happened, a story. So when narrating, you become a storyteller. The following paragraph tells the story of "Star Wars Kid," perhaps the most famous victim of cyberbullying.

Narration Paragraph

Although this paragraph does not have an explicit topic sentence, all the support focuses on this one story.

Descriptive details make narratives more engaging by helping readers see the characters and action.

Notice the transitions in bold that indicate the passage of time.

In November 2002 a young Canadian *Star Wars* fan made a video of himself using a golf ball retriever as a light saber. Jumping and spinning, the heavy-set teen made his own sound effects as he battled an unseen foe. Unfortunately, the video fell into the hands of classmates who posted it on the web in 2003. **Within weeks**, the file had been downloaded several million times. **In the years that followed**, over one billion people have watched the young boy engage in what he thought was private fun. The fame was both unwelcome and destructive. "I want my life back," the boy told one newspaper reporter. Unable to deal with the ridicule, "Star Wars Kid," as he came to be known, dropped out of school and spent some time in a psychiatric ward for treatment of depression. **Later** he and his parents sued and reached a settlement with the families of the classmates who posted the video. **Today**, "Star Wars Kid" has been able to move past his unwanted fame. He is in college studying law.

Examples/Illustration

Another word for *example* is *illustration*. Most often we think of illustrations as pictures. Like pictures, good **examples** *show* what you mean. Often in academic writing, you will be asked to provide examples to support what you mean by using personal experience, others' experiences, or research. When you can provide multiple examples to support the aim of your piece of writing, your paper is going to be more persuasive. The following paragraph gives examples of legislation that has come about because of high profile cases of cyberbullying.

Example/Illustration Paragraph

> The topic sentence is supported with three examples. Note the transitions in bold that indicate emphatic order.

> First example

> Notice how the year serves as a transition.

> Second example with supporting details

> Third example with supporting details

Out of the tragedies of cyberbullying has come some important legislation. **For example**, John Halligan, whose son Ryan committed suicide after years of being bullied at school and online, was instrumental in the Vermont Bully Prevention bill, signed into law in May 2004. **In 2008** the Florida State Legislature passed the Jeffrey Johnston Stand Up for All Students Act in memory of Jeffrey Johnston, a talented and handsome middle grade honors student, who committed suicide after being relentlessly bullied online by a fellow classmate. The Florida law requires schools to implement anti-bullying policies and imposes strict fines for non-compliance. **Perhaps the case that drew the most attention** to the need for laws to address cyberbullying was that of Megan Meier from Dardenne Prairie, Missouri. Megan had been befriended on MySpace by Josh Evans, a teenage boy fabricated by a former friend's mother. After winning the emotionally fragile Megan's trust and affection, "Josh" turned on her, taunting her and saying the world would be better off without her. After Megan's suicide, people were outraged that no criminal charges could be brought against the woman behind "Josh." Later, both houses of the Missouri legislature voted to criminalize cyber harassment laws. Also inspired by this case, federal legislation, the Megan Meier Cyberbullying Prevention Act, is currently pending.

I D E A S for Your Own Writing   MyWritingLab

So Far, So Good

Write a paragraph that gives three or four examples of ways your writing has improved since beginning this course. Consider everything from the way you approach the writing process to your sentence skills.

Causes and/or Effects

To look at **causes** is to ask, "Why?" To look at **effects** is to ask, "What happened?" Regardless of which basic question you ask, you should be prepared to delve into the causes and/or effects of an event or action in great detail. In fact, in some papers, you may have a number of paragraphs devoted to the various effects of a problem you are researching. For example, you could research the effects on people in a large city who commute to work in cars: getting less exercise, having less free time, eating lots of fast food, experiencing high stress levels because of traffic, and so on. Likewise, causes can become quite complex when you examine why people take certain actions, such as binge drinking, buying a house that is too expensive, or procrastinating. The following paragraph explores some of the effects of cyberbullying on young teens.

Cause and Effect Paragraph

> The topic sentence states the paragraph will discuss the effects of cyberbullying. The following sentences explain what those effects can be.

Cyberbullying can have a wide range of effects on its victims. Just like those who are bullied on the schoolyard, victims of cyberbullying can become anxious and depressed as their self-esteem is devastated. They may look for excuses to avoid going to school and isolate themselves from friends. Victims even lose the sense of comfort and safety in their own homes since the bullying follows them there. Fear of ridicule and harassment can lead them to withdraw from online sites they had enjoyed like Facebook. Grades can suffer and health may decline as the victims have trouble eating and sleeping properly. They may act out in anger and frustration. In seeking revenge on cyberbullies, some victims may engage in similar behavior, thus becoming bullies themselves. In extreme cases, feeling alone and helpless, victims of cyberbullying have turned to suicide.

> ## I D E A S for Your Own Writing   MyWritingLab
>
> **Why Are You Here?**
>
> Think about the various reasons why you have chosen to pursue higher education. Choose the top three or four reasons and explain them in a paragraph. Use emphatic organization (see page 107) to organize these reasons—or causes—that led you to college.

Comparison or Contrast

When **comparing** two subjects, you focus on similarities; when **contrasting**, you focus on differences. A paragraph will typically focus on one or the other. Since you can explore the similarities or differences of almost any subject, it is important that you have a good reason—a clear point—for making the comparison. What new understanding or insight do you want your readers to gain?

Comparison/contrast paragraphs also require some special organization considerations. Do you want to move back and forth between the two subjects—sometimes called the point-by-point organization? Or do you want to discuss one subject completely before moving on to the next—sometimes called the block pattern?

Point-by-Point Pattern	Block Pattern
I. Point 1	I. Subject A
Subject A	Point 1
Subject B	Point 2
II. Point 2	Point 3
Subject A	II. Subject B
Subject B	Point 1
III. Point 3	Point 2
Subject A	Point 3
Subject B	

In the following example, the writer compares the cyberbully to the more traditional schoolyard bully to make the point that cyberbullying can be more extreme in its scope and intensity. First, here is the paragraph written with a point-by-point organization.

Comparison and Contrast Paragraph: Point-by-Point

In this paragraph, the writer discusses each point as it relates to both traditional and cyber bullies by comparing and contrasting them.

Cyberbullying is more extreme than traditional bullying. Traditional bullies threaten and insult their victims at school, but at the end of the school day, victims retreat to the safety of home and family. The cyberbully, however, can torment victims in their own homes at any time, day or night. The cyberbully also commands a much larger audience than the traditional bully who may have only a few eye witnesses and rely on word of mouth to spread hateful messages. The speed and extensiveness of the Internet allow the cyberbully to harass victims on a worldwide stage. The hateful rumors and embarrassing photos can remain on the Web indefinitely with a growing audience watching or even joining in the ridicule. Perhaps cyberbullying is even greater in its cruelty because it lacks the face-to-face confrontation of traditional bullying. The traditional bully can see the tears and pain on a victim's face and perhaps back off from the torment. Because the cyberbully is so removed from the impact of the cruelty on the victim, there is less chance for feelings of remorse or empathy. Furthermore, those cyberbullies who feel safe cloaked in the anonymity of the Internet can release unrestrained cruelty toward their victims without fear of reprisal.

Now here is the same topic organized in a block pattern.

Comparison and Contrast Paragraph: Block Pattern

Notice the writer starts by discussing traditional bullies.

Cyberbullying is more extreme than traditional bullying. Traditional bullies threaten and insult their victims at school, but victims find relief at the end of the school day in the safety of home and family. The traditional bully has an audience limited to eye witnesses, and it takes a while for news of the bullying to spread throughout a school. Although traditional bullying can be physically and emotionally hurtful, the face-to-face nature of the confrontation between bully and victim often tempers the cruelty. Seeing the tears and pain on a victim's face, the traditional bully may back off from the torment. The concern about eye witness reports getting back to authorities would also give the traditional bully some pause.

Now the writer transitions to discussing cyberbullying.

Enter the new cyberbully, and the scope and intensity of bullying changes dramatically. Not confined to the schoolyard, the cyberbully can torment victims in their own homes at any time, day or night. The speed and extensiveness of the Internet allows the cyberbully to harass victims on a worldwide stage. Hateful rumors and embarrassing photos can remain on the web indefinitely with a growing audience watching or even joining in the ridicule. Without a face-to-face confrontation, the cyberbully is so removed from the impact of the cruelty on the victim, there is less chance for feelings of remorse or empathy. Furthermore, those cyberbullies who feel safe cloaked in the anonymity of the Internet can release unrestrained cruelty toward their victims without fear of reprisal.

The following chart shows the differences in the two organizational strategies in relation to the sample paragraphs:

Point-by-Point Pattern	Block Pattern
I. Scope of Bullying	I. Traditional Bully
• Traditional Bully	• Scope of Bullying
• Cyberbully	• Witnesses to Bullying
II. Witnesses to Bullying	• Intensity of Bullying
• Traditional Bully	II. Cyberbully
• Cyberbully	• Scope of Bullying
III. Intensity of Bullying	• Witnesses to Bullying
• Traditional Bully	• Intensity of Bullying
• Cyberbully	

I D E A S for Your Own Writing   MyWritingLab

Which One Is Best?

Compare two different brands of a single product you have used—such as two brands of cell phones, frozen pizza, tennis shoes, or cold medicine. The point of this paragraph is to tell your reader which of the two you recommend. Use a clear organization: point-by-point or block.

Process

If you have ever cooked something based on a recipe, you have read a process by which the author of the cookbook tells you the steps—in order—that you have to follow to create a successful dish. So **process** paragraphs lead the reader from beginning to end, describing the way something happens or instructing on how it should be done. The following paragraph describes the steps a victim of cyberbullying should take to protect himself or herself.

Process Paragraph

If you encounter a cyberbully, you can protect yourself and end the abuse by following these steps. **First,** it is very important when you encounter an abusive message or posting, not to retaliate in anger. Getting upset and losing your

> The first step in the process followed by reasons

temper only affirms the bully's power over you. Also, your angry message could be turned around and used as evidence that *you* are a cyberbully. **Once you have calmed down**, you should download and save all the abusive messages and postings as possible evidence. **Then** you can decide if you can handle the cyberbully yourself. You may choose to ignore the bully, blocking future messages and avoiding online groups where you might encounter him or her. Or you may send the cyberbully a calm but clear message to stop the harassment. **If, however, the cyberbullying does not stop or escalates in ways that threaten you, it's time to seek outside help.** You can file a complaint with the website or service the bully uses. Many sites have policies that prohibit bullying and will remove the damaging material. You might **also** consider contacting an attorney. **If the cyberbullying involves threats of violence or extortion, you should contact the police.** Many states have enacted laws that have criminalized such online behavior, and the cyberbully will be held accountable.

> The second step in this process

> The third step in this process

> This sentence works as a transition to the fourth step in the process.

> The final step in the process and the conditions that call for it

---

I D E A S for Your Own Writing   MyWritingLab

How I Did It

In a paragraph describe the steps you took to solve a problem you faced. Be sure to use a chronological organization.

Classification

Classification involves taking a group of items and dividing it into different categories based on a ruling principle. Biologists, for example, classify animals into different phyla based on physical characteristics. Books can be classified according to subject (mystery, romance, biography, and so on) and movies by genre (horror, romantic comedy, action, sci-fi, etc.). Classification is an important way to manage a lot of information because it breaks the information down into more manageable groups.

The following paragraph classifies cyberbullies into different groups or categories based on what motivates their behavior.

Classification Paragraph

Depending upon their motivation, cyberbullies can fall into one of four basic types. The Power-Hungry Cyberbullies are most like the traditional schoolyard bully who uses fear and intimidation to gain power over others. Power-Hungry

> The topic sentence introduces the topic—cyberbullies—and the ruling principle—their motivation.

Cyberbullies use their high-tech abilities to scare others online or even to damage computers. Mean Girl Cyberbullies, while not always girls, are groups that set out to have fun by ridiculing and embarrassing someone. They usually consider themselves the "cool" kids and want their victims to feel excluded and humiliated. The third group, Vengeful Angel Cyberbullies, do not see themselves as bullies but as good guys trying to protect others by attacking online bullies. Similarly, the Inadvertent Cyberbullies do not see themselves as bullies as they try to protect themselves. Vengeful Angels and Inadvertent Cyberbullies have a "two wrongs make a right" mentality, so they become cyberbullies themselves in retaliation for something done to others or to themselves.

I D E A S for Your Own Writing   **MyWritingLab**

Classroom Types

Write a paragraph that classifies the kinds of students you have noticed in your classes based on the degree of active learning they demonstrate. (See what is meant by an "active learner" on page 2 of Chapter 1.)

Definition

When you **define** something, you explain what it is and what is important about that term, phrase, concept, idea, or object. When you write papers, professors might ask you to "define your terms," meaning that you have to define exactly what you mean, which could entail a whole paragraph that defines terms you use such as "biodiversity," "return on investment," "cognitive dissonance," or "pornography."

Writing definitions can become difficult when you try to define concepts like "freedom," "poverty," or "friend." More complex definitions may call for you to incorporate a variety of developmental patterns. Describing, giving examples, and showing causes and effects can all be part of defining. In addition, you often can define something by explaining what it *is* and what it *is not*—that is, by showing contrasts. The following paragraph defines what is meant by the term *cyberbully*.

The typical cyberbully is an older teen, as likely to be male as female, who wants to exert power over others. Caught up in their need for attention and domination, most cyberbullies accept no responsibility for their actions and have no sympathy for their victims. Cyberbullies' weapons of choice are cell

Here the writer shows a cause for the cyberbully's behavior.

The writer uses examples of how cyberbullies harass their victims.

phones and the Internet, and they often consider themselves quite proficient with technology. Using digital technology, they humiliate, torment, and threaten victims with email, IM's or texts. Victims may also find ugly messages posted on Facebook or other social networking sites. Some cyberbullies have even set up special blogs or web pages designed to humiliate a victim with posts of unflattering pictures and cruel or lewd comments. This attachment to technology with a fear of losing computer privileges may be one of the few outward signs of a cyberbully. Cyberbullies often seem to be model students with good relationships with their teachers; however, they use computers excessively and often secretly, closing the screens when others are around. They may become angry or anxious when they cannot use the computer, but they avoid talking about what they do online.

Here the writer uses comparison/contrast.

I D E A S for Your Own Writing   **MyWritingLab**

Success

Write a paragraph that presents your definition of success by describing a successful person you know personally or a famous person. Your main purpose is to leave your readers with a clear idea of what you mean when you say someone is a success.

As you can see, there are many different ways you can develop or organize a subject. The pattern or patterns you use will depend on your readers and your purpose. Choose the approach that best leads your readers to the understanding you want them to have about the subject.

Analyze Paragraphs for Coherence

One of the ways you can learn to make your own writing more coherent is to analyze the techniques used by other writers. Good writers will use most—and sometimes all—of the various methods to achieve coherence.

Notice the various methods used in this paragraph about elephants:

What key words do you notice repeated in this paragraph?

Observing elephants in the wild, researchers have determined that elephants have a complex communication system. One way elephants communicate is through smell. The elephant's sensitive trunk is almost always in motion, picking up odors given off by other herd members. From odors in saliva, urine, feces and other bodily secretions, elephants can determine the health, dominance and sexual availability of other elephants. Elephants also communicate

This is a common transition. What other common transition do you notice?

through their sense of touch. Here again, the trunk is important. Mother elephants will use their trunks to caress and reassure their young. Elephants intertwine trunks as part of courtship or use trunks to slap during shows of aggression. In addition, elephants have been found to use more than 150 visual signals to communicate. For example, an elephant may show its dominance by spreading its ears, jerking its head and tossing its trunk forward. A frightened elephant may raise its chin and tail. Most of all, elephants communicate vocally. In fact, elephants use a wide variety of different sounds to converse. For instance, a loud trumpet like blast is usually a warning while low growls and deep rumbles are used to communicate among friends and family members. Even more surprising, researchers have discovered that elephants make low rumbles below the level of human hearing that can travel over miles. Thus, elephants can call for help or relocate lost herd members that are miles away.

> This transition suggests the writer has used an emphatic organization strategy. What pattern of development has the writer used?

> *Converse* is a synonym for what key word?

EXERCISE 4.11   Analyzing Coherence   MyWritingLab

Directions: Read and annotate the following paragraph carefully, noting the ways the writer achieves coherence. Then answer the questions that follow.

Becoming a successful competitive eater takes extensive preparation and, ultimately, a strong mind and stomach. Once you decide to become a competitive eater, your first step is to visit your doctor. After your doctor has ruled out any problems that could put you at risk during a competition, you can begin researching the various competitions. A number of organizations such as the International Federation of Competitive Eating and the Association of Competitive Eaters have websites you can check for upcoming events. Experts recommend that beginners look for competitions of short duration—no more than eight minutes—and involving soft food like pancakes, ice cream, or pasta. In the weeks leading up to the competition, you should exercise to build up your stamina and to avoid gaining weight. Practice breathing through your nose because you cannot mouth breathe while eating. You will also need a strong jaw, so chew lots of gum to strengthen your jaw muscles. A short time before the actual contest, practice eating the food to familiarize yourself with how it feels and the best and fastest ways to eat it. You may find that for most food, dipping it in water will make it faster to chew and swallow. Also, work on your hand-eye coordination, so you can devour the food as quickly as possible. During the days right before the contest, you should eat regular meals, so your stomach does not shrink. Drinking lots of water may also help to stretch your stomach. When the big day arrives, eat very little if anything beforehand. Try to put yourself into a calm and relaxed state to avoid panic and rushing, which could cause you to choke or vomit—either of which would disqualify you. Now you're prepared and calm, so ready . . . set . . . eat!

1. Which organization strategy does the writer use in this paragraph—chronological, spatial, or emphatic?

2. Which pattern of organization does the writer use—cause and effect, classification, comparison/contrast, definition, description, narrative, or process?

3. What transitional words and phrases does the writer use?

4. What key words does the writer repeat?

5. What synonyms does the writer use?

CHAPTER AT A GLANCE

Learning Objectives	How they connect to writing at college . . .
❶ Unify your paragraphs with topic sentences.	A *topic sentence* is a general statement that lets the reader know both the limited subject and the controlling idea—or central point—the writer wants to make about the subject. A clearly stated controlling idea helps the writer keep the development of a paragraph focused and unified.
❷ Create support in your paragraphs by using details, reasons, examples, and explanations.	*Generalizations*—broad statements that cover an entire group or situation—do not support topic sentences. *Specific* details, reasons, examples, and explanations make up the support that interests and informs readers.

Learning Objectives	How they connect to writing at college . . .
❸ Use coherence strategies to connect your support.	*Coherence* refers to the ways a writer connects ideas in a piece of writing. The most common methods of achieving coherence are . . .

- Follow basic organization strategies
  - Chronological organization
  - Spatial organization
  - Emphatic organization
- Use transitional words and phrases
- Repeat key words and phrases or use synonyms
- Use pronouns to create connections

❹ Organize support by using patterns of development.	Each paragraph has a specific purpose—such as comparing, presenting causes, or defining—within a larger piece of writing. The guiding principles behind these roles are called *patterns of development*, which are ways to develop and organize ideas. These patterns include *description, narration, example or illustration, cause and effect, comparison/contrast, process, classification*, and *definition*.

> **MyWritingLab** Visit **Chapter 4, "Writing Paragraphs,"** in MyWritingLab to test your understanding of the chapter objectives.

Paragraphs Working Together: The Essay

Learning Objectives

In this chapter you will learn how to . . .

❶ Write effective introduction paragraphs.

❷ Create conclusion paragraphs that leave a lasting impression.

❸ Identify the various strategies for constructing paragraphs and using transitions.

Just as cogs have to work together in order for the gears in cars, drills, or heavy machinery to function well, paragraphs must work together. Good papers generate interest, use appropriate details, provide explanation, consider audience, and have style.

127

Since most of the essays you will write for your college courses demand multiple paragraphs, it is important to know how paragraphs should work together—how they have to be connected and how they should flow.

Body paragraphs make up the largest part of the academic essays you will write in college. Unified, supported, and coherent body paragraphs present the material that supports the aim and thesis of your papers. The number of paragraphs in the body of a paper varies and depends on the complexity of the topic and restrictions on length.

While Chapter 4 covers the patterns writers use in constructing body paragraphs, Chapter 5 focuses on specialized paragraphs and the various strategies writers use to create introduction, conclusion, and transitional paragraphs. This chapter emphasizes how paragraphs work together to create strong, fully supported essays.

❶ Write effective introduction paragraphs.

Write Effective Introduction Paragraphs

In general, **introductions** have two main functions: They spark the readers' interest and they present the thesis—that is, the subject and controlling idea—of a paper.

There is no rule about how many paragraphs can make up an introduction. Books, for example, can have introductions that comprise many paragraphs and go on for many pages. A short memo's introduction paragraph may be only one or two sentences long. The overall length of a piece of writing plays the biggest part in determining the extent of an introduction. In a typical composition course, you will often be writing short essays, so introductions will usually be one or two paragraphs. This is a guideline to consider when you write—*not* a rule. Remember, the introduction sets the stage. It should not dominate or overpower the body of a paper.

Strategies for Writing Introduction Paragraphs

You can begin a paper in a variety of ways, but you need to keep in mind that you want to capture your readers' attention. After reading a good introduction, readers want to go on. They are curious and engaged, and they know what they can expect to find in the essay since its subject and controlling idea are clearly presented.

Say you want to write a paper about competitive eating contests. The following examples show some of the ways you can begin your paper. In addition to noting the ways each introduction generates readers' interest, observe how the thesis in each introduction presents the essay's subject and controlling idea.

Begin with a Paragraph That Follows a Pattern of Development

Many of the patterns of development explained and illustrated on pages 114–123 can be used to begin a paper as the following examples show.

Cause and Effect. This type of introduction sets the stage by outlining the causes and/or effects of an event or an action. Writers often use this strategy to show causes or consequences in an effort to make the issue, information, or concept "real" to readers.

In the following example, the introduction draws reader interest by presenting some of the harmful effects of competitive eating. It could be used to begin an essay intending to persuade readers that such competitions are dangerous and should be stopped.

> On July 4, 2013 Joey Chestnut won Nathan's Famous Fourth of July International Hot Dog Eating Contest by eating 69 hotdogs in ten minutes. That's more than 27,000 calories, over 1,250 grams of fat and more than 59,000 milligrams of sodium—hardly a healthy meal. Competitive eaters run the risk of becoming morbidly obese. They may also develop acid reflux disease, diabetes, and gastroparesis—the inability of the stomach to empty itself. Even during the competitions themselves, speed eaters run the risk of vomiting and choking or perforating their stomachs if they have undiagnosed ulcers. If these physical risks to participants were not bad enough, competitive eating celebrates unrestrained consumption to a nation of people already at risk for obesity and health problems related to poor diets. **For these reasons, competitive eating contests should be outlawed in the United States.**

Comparison/Contrast Another strategy is to show how the topic is different from or comparable to another subject. Especially if the topic is unfamiliar, comparison/contrast can be an effective move to connect to what readers might already know.

In this example, the writer compares competitive eating to other sporting events, and the unlikely comparison is the key to capturing reader interest. This introduction could begin a persuasive paper.

Most would agree that a sport involves physical exertion and skill. Participants in a sport follow rules and usually compete for prizes and recognition. Competitive eating certainly involves physical exertion and skill. Like other athletes, competitive eaters often begin training months in advance of a competition to prepare physically by stretching their stomachs and strengthening their jaws, and mentally by learning to stay focused and to ignore the gag reflex. Competitive eating competitions also have strict rules laid out by such governing bodies as the International Federation of Competitive Eating. Judges enforce these rules at each sanctioned contest. Although the competition is not between teams, competitive eaters face not only their fellow gurgitators but the food itself. Fiery jalapeños, chicken wings, hot dogs, and even sticks of butter can be worthy adversaries. Prizes for conquering foes and food can range from mere titles to the $10,000 and Mustard Yellow Belt awarded to the winner of Nathan's Famous Fourth of July International Hot Dog Eating Contest. **Add to all of this the drama and excitement of a competitive eating match, and one can see no reason not to make this activity an official sport.**

Definition. Writers sometimes create introductions that define a topic in order to offer core information about the topic and to make sure readers understand it. Often they will use experts, sources, and concise examples to support the definition.

The following introduction uses definition to give some necessary information before beginning an essay that aims to persuade.

In competitive eating, sometimes called speed eating, participants compete to consume the most food in a designated time period, usually fifteen minutes or less. The International Federation of Competitive Eating hosts many of these organized professional eating contests, which can offer substantial cash prices to the  winners. Competitive eaters, known as "gurgitators," often undergo rigorous training and preparation and must win regional qualifying contests before being allowed to compete in major events such as Nathan's Famous Fourth of July International Hot Dog Eating Contest or the Chinook Winds World Rib Eating Championship. The IFOCE keeps track of world records and ranks the top eaters, among whom are Tim "Eater X" Janus, Crazy Legs Conti, Sonya "The Black Widow" Thomas, and Joey "Jaws" Chestnut. **All of this makes competitive eating sound a lot like a sport, and perhaps it is time to give competitive eating the sports status it deserves.**

Description. One way to immerse readers in a topic is to describe a situation or place with specific and concrete details. A descriptive introduction sets readers into a scene or situation like a good story does.

After sparking reader interest with the following vivid description, the writer could go on to inform readers about competitive eating competitions.

> On a brutally hot July 4th, the crowd of 40,000 keeps up a steady cheer and beat Pepto-Bismol clap sticks. The spectators have been whipped into frenzy by the pregame show of magicians and martial artists, rock bands, and giant dancing hot dogs. Now the focus is on the stage where men and women smash hot dogs and soggy buns into their gaping mouths. Television cameras roll as the MC urges on the gurgitators who sweat and grunt and gag as they eat their way through plate after plate of hot dogs and buns. More than a million home viewers join the Coney Island spectators in cheering on their favorites: face-painted "Eater X," petite Sonya "The Black Widow" Thomas, and past champion Joey "Jaws" Chestnut. It's all-American fun. It's the thrill of competition. **It's the world of competitive eating.**

Narrative (a short story or anecdote). Similar to descriptive introductions, a narrative tells a story, which can invite readers into the topic. The story sets the stage for a thesis and the important information about the topic.

This introduction might be used to write a paper that informs the readers about U.S. competitive eating contests. Readers will want to know more about the technique that changed competitive eating.

> On a foggy July 4, 2001, a crowd of 150 fans gathered around a stage to witness Nathan's Famous Fourth of July International Hot Dog Eating Contest at Coney Island. Cheering on the massive four hundred plus pound giants Ed "Cookie" Jarvis and Eric "Badlands" Booker, the crowd took little note of the slight Japanese man who also took his place on the stage. At the sound of the gun, the competitive eaters were off, each eager to win and perhaps to break

the previous year's record of 25-1/8 hot dogs in twelve minutes. Soon the crowd and the competitive eaters themselves stared in amazement as the newcomer devoured hot dogs in a way no one had seen before. At the rate of about one every ten seconds, he broke each dog in half, shoved it in his mouth and swallowed it whole. At the same time, he dipped each bun in a glass of water to soften it before sending it down his gullet with the meaty dogs. **In twelve minutes Takeru Kobayashi devoured 50 hotdogs, shattered the hot-dog-eating record, and brought competitive eating to the attention of U.S. audiences.**

Begin with Background or an Historical Overview of the Topic

In academic writing, this strategy is sometimes called presenting the "academic conversation" about a topic, meaning that writers relate what experts have to say about a subject. Or writers can relate important history or relevant background information related to a topic.

The following introduction could be used to begin a paper that analyzes the various components of this particular contest to see why it remains the most popular in the growing field of competitive eating.

> On July 14, 1916, Nathan's Famous held its first hot dog eating contest when four immigrants competed to see who was the most patriotic. Fast forward to 2001 when Takeru Kobayashi, a competitive eater from Japan, devoured 50 hot dogs, breaking the previous record of 25 and winning the prized mustard-yellow belt. For six long years Kobayashi dominated this Super Bowl of competitive eating, but in 2007, he was finally defeated by Joey Chestnut, who ate 66 hot dogs to Kobayashi's 63. Chestnut has since held on to his title and belt. In 2013 in front of a crowd of 40,000 and an ESPN audience of 1.5 million, Chestnut set a world record of 69 hot dogs in ten minutes. **In the world of competitive eating, Nathan's Famous Fourth of July International Hot Dog Eating Contest at Coney Island has set the standard for this kind of event.**

Begin with a Surprising Fact or Statistic

One way writers try to grab readers' interest is by beginning with something that is surprising. Strong writing uses facts and statistics relevant to the topic.

This introduction sets up an essay that aims to inform the readers about the process of preparing for competitive eating contests. It generates interest by showing the astounding eating records of some famous competitors.

Don Lerman ate 6 pounds of baked beans in under two minutes and 7 quarter-pound sticks of salted butter in five minutes. Japanese competitive-eating great Takeru Kobayashi devoured 58 Johnsonville Brats in ten minutes and holds the record for eating the most cow brains—over 17 pounds in fifteen minutes. Sonya Thomas, who can outeat men twice her size, scarfed down 80 chicken nuggets in five minutes and 11 pounds of cheesecake in less than ten minutes. Joey Chestnut, ranked number one by the International Federation of Competitive Eating, holds numerous records, including eating 103 Krystal Burgers in eight minutes, 380 shrimp wontons in eight minutes and 69 Nathan's Famous Hot Dogs in ten minutes. **Being a contender in the world of competitive eating takes dedication, training, and the right state of mind.**

Begin with a Quotation

Beginning a paper with an important and relevant quotation is a common strategy used by writers. The key, though, is making sure the quotation connects with the topic of the paper.

This introduction might begin an essay that analyzes why many Americans are fascinated by eating competitions.

George Bernard Shaw once said, "There is no sincerer love than the love of food." That love of food seems more apparent today than ever before. Consider that the sale of cookbooks continues to rise while the overall publishing industry languishes. While there have always been cooking shows on television, now there are more shows about food and eating than ever before such as *Food Wars*, *Hell's Kitchen*, *Man vs Food*, and *Iron Chef*. Chefs like Emeril Lagasse, Rachael Ray, Paula Dean, and Jamie Oliver have reached celebrity status. **But it is America's growing fascination with competitive eating that is taking our love affair with food to new—and sometimes stomach busting—heights.**

Begin with a Question

Beginning with a question can be an effective strategy in an introduction. The key is posing a question that is detailed enough and connects to the core of the paper. Do not ask questions that you are not going to answer in your paper.

Note how this introduction could lure readers into an essay that informs or persuades. It frames the discussion with a question at the *end* of the paragraph.

An international governing body sponsors and promotes its competitions. Judges enforce strict rules for fairness and safety. It draws thousands of spectators and is covered on ESPN. Fans cheer for the superstars—"Deep Dish," "Black Widow," "Crazy Legs," "The Tsunami," and "Jaws." Many of these competitors train rigorously before competitions and are willing to risk physical injury in order to win. The physical exertion and skill needed to compete are beyond the range of average people. Winners earn trophies, thousands of dollars, endorsements, and the adoration of their fans. **Who says competitive eating isn't a sport?**

Avoid Common Mistakes in Introduction Paragraphs

Avoid making the following common mistakes when writing introduction paragraphs.

1. **Do Not Begin with an Announcement.**

   "In this essay, I will explain why competitive eating contests have become so popular."

   An announcement indicates only the subject of an essay, not the point or controlling idea. Announcements may also give the impression you are insecure as a writer and feel you have to spell out exactly what you are doing, or the readers will not understand.

2. **Do Not Apologize for What You Do Not Know.**

   "While I haven't been able to find a lot of current research on the subject, there seem to be some obvious reasons why competitive eating is so popular."

   The first rule is *do not* write about what you do not know. The second rule is if you must write about what you do not know, do not call attention to your ignorance.

3. **Do Not Start with a Dictionary Definition.**

   "According to *Webster's Dictionary*, a competition is a contest among rivals. Who could have imagined that one of the hottest kinds of competitions today involves eating unbelievable amounts of food?"

   Beginning with a dictionary definition is an overused device that is more likely to bore readers than interest them.

4. **Do Not Begin with a Broad Statement About Something Nearly Everybody Already Knows.**

"Everybody eats food. Some people eat more food than others. What makes competitive eating so fascinating is that people eat so much food."

You do not want the first statement of your paper to make the reader think, "Duh!" If your opening statement is something painfully obvious or even a cliché that most readers are likely to have heard, do not use it.

5. **Do Not Begin with an Unclear Question or a Question That Could Annoy Readers.**

"Did you ever think about eating food fast? Some people eat food more quickly than others. What makes competitive eating so fascinating is that people eat so much food."

You do not want the first sentence of your paper to make the reader think, "*Why* are you asking me a question like that?" If you begin with a question that does not relate fully to the topic at hand, then the first sentence of your paper could annoy the reader, which is not a good way to start.

In addition to avoiding these techniques, do not begin with an introduction that is too long or too short. A very long introduction may include some of the supporting material that really belongs in the body paragraphs. Also, a visually intimidating paragraph at the beginning may turn off some readers. On the other hand, a very short introduction, such as simply stating the paper's thesis, is not likely to generate interest in your topic.

Your introduction should show evidence of the time and effort you have put into the paper, so take special care when writing it. Remember, too, there is nothing in the writing process that demands you write the introduction first. Often you can write the best introduction after you have written the rest of the paper.

EXERCISE 5.1   Find and Present Sample Introduction Paragraphs

Directions: Find three different essays in this textbook from Chapters 6–11. Determine the strategies that the authors have chosen to use. In your opinion, which is the strongest introduction and why? Present your ideas to the class with specific details and explanations.

❷ Create conclusion paragraphs that leave a lasting impression.

Create Conclusion Paragraphs that Leave a Lasting Impression

How you conclude your paper is just as important as how you begin it. While the introduction makes the readers decide whether they want to keep reading, the conclusion offers that final thought readers are most likely to take away with them. The best conclusions create positive lasting impressions about a paper.

Like introductions, conclusions can range in length from a single paragraph to multiple paragraphs, depending upon the length of the essays they wrap up. In a short essay of five pages or less, a conclusion is typically a paragraph in length.

Strategies for Writing Conclusion Paragraphs

The following examples show some of the ways a writer could end a short essay on competitive eating.

End with a Reference Back to the Introduction

Writers sometimes call this strategy "circling back." They mention an example, quotation, or detail from the introduction and wrap up the paper by bringing the reader's attention back to how the paper began.

This conclusion refers back to the introduction on page 134 that begins with a question. Notice how the writer deliberately uses a series of sentence fragments here. Sometimes a writer will intentionally break a grammar rule for stylistic reasons.

> Who says competitive eating isn't a sport? Only those who do not acknowledge its governing body, enforcing safety standards and regulations. Only those who are not willing to give credit to the training and endurance of its star competitors. Only those who have not been caught up in the pageantry and excitement of a competitive eating event. Whoever says competitive eating isn't a sport, doesn't know much about competitive eating.

End with a Reflective Statement

Ending with reflection is a strategy in which you conclude the paper with the "big picture." This type of conclusion makes readers see the topic with a questioning and contemplative attitude.

This conclusion refers back to the introduction on page 133 that begins with a quotation. In this conclusion the writer offers some final thoughts on the popularity of competitive eating.

> Perhaps this fascination with competitive eating is just another manifestation of our love of food. Maybe it is more than our love of competition and colorful characters. Maybe we just love watching people break every food taboo from our childhood as competitive eaters gobble everything in sight, chew with their mouths open, belch, and gag. Whatever the reason, competitive eating seems here to stay.

End with a Call to Action (Best in Persuasive Essays)

Writers often use this strategy when they are discussing contested issues or problems. Questions writers have to consider include: Is my solution or stance practical? Will it work? Is it likely to create change? What exactly do I want readers to do?

This paragraph could end a paper that explores the harmful effects of competitive eating contests. Having convinced readers of the dangers of competitive eating, the writer urges them to take action to end the practice.

> Competitive eating contests simply have no redeeming features. Not only have there already been deaths during competitions, but medical researchers have called the behavior "potentially self-destructive" for all the participants. The competitions glamorize behaviors that under other circumstances would be labeled eating disorders. Glamorizing these events, calling the participants athletes, and even offering a video version of competitive eating for kids—have we reached a new all-time low in entertainment? Let's stop this madness and outlaw competitive eating.

End with a Summary of Key Points (Best in Longer Papers)

Ending with a summary of what you stated in a paper is a conventional way to conclude your writing. It works especially well in longer papers, but we do not recommend it in shorter to medium-size papers because it can be boring for readers.

This paragraph could end a paper that analyzes the popularity of Nathan's Hot Dog Eating Contest. In it, the writer presents a concise restatement of each of the essay's major points.

It's no wonder that Nathan's Famous Fourth of July International Hot Dog Eating Contest is the premier competitive eating event. No other eating contest has such a long history. Its July 4th date appeals to our sense of patriotism. It has extreme pageantry and showmanship to stir up the competitive spirit of contestants and spectators alike. And perhaps, most importantly, it involves an exceptionally good all-American food—the hot dog. We have the World Series. We have the Super Bowl. And now we have Nathan's.

▶ Joey Chestnut ate 69 hot dogs to win the 2013 Nathan's Famous Hot Dog Eating Contest at Coney Island on July 4, 2013 in the Brooklyn Borough of New York City.

Avoid Common Mistakes in Conclusion Paragraphs

Effective conclusions take careful reflection and often require multiple revisions. You should also avoid some of these common mistakes in conclusion paragraphs:

1. **Do Not Simply Run Out of Steam.**

   Some writers seem to be so relieved to be finished with a paper that they just stick anything at the end, usually prefaced by "In conclusion." Often these kinds of conclusions simply repeat the thesis statement or some other part of the introduction. Instead of being left with an impressive ending, the readers are left yawning.

2. **Do Not End with an Announcement.**

   Avoid announcements anywhere in your papers. You do not want readers to think you are unsure of your ability to get your points across.

3. **Do Not End with an Apology or a "Hope" That You Did Your Job.**

   Avoid apologizing for what you do not know in any part of your paper. Likewise, do not end with "So I hope I have shown you. . . ." That, too, makes you sound like a pretty insecure writer. Sound confident even when you are not.

4. **Do Not Bring Up New Ideas.**

A conclusion should wrap up what you have covered in the paper. Bringing up something not covered in the paper may leave the readers confused or distracted by the topic you did not cover.

5. **Do Not Summarize the Points of a Very Short Essay.**

While summarizing can be an effective way to end a longer paper on a complex subject, a summary of a short paper simply comes across as repetitive.

EXERCISE 5.2 Find and Present Sample Conclusion Paragraphs
Directions: Find three different essays in this textbook from Chapters 6–11. Identify the conclusion strategies the authors have chosen to use. In your opinion, which is the strongest conclusion and why? Present your ideas to the class with strong details and explanations.

❸ Identify the various strategies for constructing paragraphs and using transitions.

Identify the Various Strategies for Constructing Paragraphs and Using Transitions

Chapter 4 discusses the different patterns of development for paragraphs (pp. 114–123) and how transitional words and phrases can be used at the beginning of paragraphs to link them together (pp. 108–110).

Sometimes in longer papers, writers will use an entire paragraph to indicate a major shift in a paper's focus. These transitional paragraphs are generally short, since their function is to connect ideas and not to support a generalization. The following sample essay contains examples of transitional paragraphs as well as the various kinds of paragraphs discussed in this chapter and in Chapter 4.

Paragraphs Working Together: The Essay

Tyrus Jones' instructor assigned the following paper:

STUDENT WRITER AT WORK

Topic: Today's high schools must deal with a number of problems, and you can offer valuable insights toward solutions to some of these problems. For this essay, you will propose a solution to a problem you have personally encountered or know exists in our local high schools. In this paper you should identify the problem and show that it is serious. You will then propose a solution or plan of action that will alleviate the problem or eliminate it altogether. Your solution should be both practical and affordable.

Audience: Your readers for this proposal will be members of the high school community: students, parents, teachers, and administrators who are eager to solve the problem.

Special Guidelines:

- Write an introduction that will grab the readers' attention. Be sure that your introduction also includes a clear statement of the paper's subject and focus—a thesis statement.
- Use an emphatic organization in your paper. Build up to your strongest points, your most convincing arguments. Clearly connect your ideas.
- Your conclusion should re-emphasize your paper's point but should not simply repeat it.

Tyrus Jones' essay follows. As you read it, notice the various patterns of development in the body paragraphs as well as the strategies Tyrus uses in the introduction and conclusion. Pay particular attention to the transitions used to connect body paragraphs.

Tyrus Jones
Professor Taylor
Introduction to College Writing
5 May 2014

Stop the Cyberbully

Standing on the stage before the high school assembly as pictures of his young son scrolled on the wall behind him, the father recounted the short life of his son. Pictures of a smiling toddler opening Christmas gifts and a gangly young boy playing sports dissolved into photos of a young teen. The boy still smiled, but his eyes had lost their shine. The bullying had started, and the pain was already showing in his eyes. The father told of how he tried to reassure his son that the trials of junior high were survivable. He promised his son there would be friends—even girlfriends—who

> The writer uses vivid description of the pain caused by cyberbullying to capture reader interest.

would see the same kind and loving boy who brought such joy to his family. The father's voice broke as he described the horrible day he found his son dead. Total stillness filled the auditorium as the last picture—the picture of a flower-strewn grave—filled the screen. Only after his son was buried did the father learn what led to his suicide. Going through his son's computer, the grieving father found the taunting IMs, the pages of ridicule and vicious rumors—all more than a sensitive boy already struggling with depression could handle. Some in the audience nodded in quiet understanding while others struggled to hold back tears.

Sadly, there have been several high profile cases of suicide in reaction to cyberbullying in the United States. While most victims of

Jones 2

cyberbullying will not take such extreme measures, many will suffer and carry the emotional scars of being abused. In 2008, the Cyberbullying Research Center surveyed 2,000 middle grade students in a large school district and found that 43% had experienced some form of cyberbullying. An AP-MTV survey of over a thousand young people ranging in age from fourteen to twenty-four reported that 50% had experienced cyberbullying. With so many young people at risk, steps must be taken by school authorities, parents, and students themselves to prevent this problem.

> Jones presents the thesis of the essay and sets up the organization strategy for presenting the solution.

Stopping cyberbullying must begin with an understanding of both the bullies and the victims because the lines between the two sometimes become blurred. Once there is a clear understanding of the problem, a collaborative approach can be taken to solve it.

> Here he explains the problem in a transitional paragraph.

The typical cyberbully is an older teen, male or female, who wants to exert power over others. Most cyberbullies accept no responsibility for their actions and have no sympathy for their victims. Cyberbullies' weapon of choice is the Internet, and they often consider themselves quite proficient with the technology they use to humiliate, torment, and threaten victims. Victims may find ugly messages posted on Facebook or other social networking sites. Some cyberbullies have even set up special blogs or web pages designed to humiliate a victim with posts of unflattering pictures and cruel comments. This attachment to technology with a fear of losing computer privileges may be one of the few outward signs of a cyberbully. Cyberbullies often seem to be model students with good relationships with their teachers; however, they use computers excessively and often secretly, closing the screens when others are around. They may become angry or anxious when they cannot use the computer, but they avoid talking about what they do online.

> This paragraph is unified by focusing on defining the cyberbully.

In many ways **cyberbullying** is more extreme than traditional bullying. Traditional bullies threaten and insult their victims at school, but at the end of the school day, victims retreat to the safety of home and family. The cyberbully, however, can torment victims in their own homes at any time, day or night. The cyberbully also commands a much larger audience than the traditional bully who

> He provides an explicit topic sentence in this paragraph.

Jones 3

may have had only a few eyewitnesses and relies on word of mouth to spread hateful messages. The speed and extensiveness of the Internet allow the cyberbully to harass victims on a worldwide stage.

> This paragraph uses a point-by-point comparison/contrast pattern.

The hateful rumors and embarrassing photos can remain on the web indefinitely with a growing audience watching or even joining in the ridicule. Perhaps cyberbullying is even greater in its cruelty because it lacks the face-to-face confrontation of traditional bullying. The traditional bully can see the tears and pain on a victim's face and perhaps back off from the torment. Because the cyberbully is so removed from the victim, there is less chance for feelings of remorse or empathy.

> This transitional phrase links what will come with what has gone before.

Furthermore, those cyberbullies who feel safe cloaked in the anonymity of the Internet can release unrestrained cruelty toward their victims without fear of reprisals.

Although their methods are similar, not all cyberbullies are alike. Depending upon their motivation, cyberbullies can fall into one of four basic types. The Power-Hungry Cyberbullies are most like the traditional schoolyard bully who uses fear and intimidation to gain power over others. Power-Hungry Cyberbullies use their high-tech abilities to scare others online or even to damage computers. Mean Girl Cyberbullies, while not always girls, are groups who set out to have fun by ridiculing and embarrassing someone. They usually consider themselves the "cool" kids and want their

> The writer uses both classification and definition in this paragraph.

victims to feel excluded and humiliated. The third group, Vengeful Angel Cyberbullies, do not see themselves as bullies but as good guys trying to protect others by attacking online bullies. Similarly, the Inadvertent Cyberbullies do not see themselves as bullies as they try to protect themselves. Vengeful Angels and Inadvertent Cyberbullies have a "two wrongs make a right" mentality, so they become cyberbullies themselves in retaliation for something done to them.

> The writer uses the word *motivation* as a transition from the previous paragraph.

Whatever its motivation, cyberbullying can have a wide range of effects on its victims. Just like those who are bullied on the schoolyard, victims of cyberbullying can become anxious and depressed as their self-esteem is devastated. They may look for excuses to avoid going to school and isolate themselves from friends. Victims even lose the sense of comfort and safety in their own homes

Jones 4

since the bullying follows them there. Fear of ridicule and harassment can lead them to withdraw from online sites they had enjoyed like Facebook and chat rooms. Grades can suffer and health may decline as the victims have trouble eating and sleeping properly. They may act out in anger and frustration. In seeking revenge on cyberbullies, victims may engage in similar behavior thus becoming Inadvertent Cyberbullies. In extreme cases, feeling alone and helpless, victims of cyberbullying have turned to suicide.

> This paragraph uses a cause/effect pattern of organization.

Given the complexity and seriousness of cyberbullying, schools, parents and young people should first educate themselves about cyberbullying and its consequences. They must then work together to identify instances of cyberbullying and to respond to them in ways that go beyond mere discipline. Each group can take specific steps to support this community effort.

> Jones introduces the solution section of the essay with a second transition paragraph.

Across the United States, state legislatures are giving schools the responsibility and the power to crack down on bullies, including cyberbullies. **In fact**, many states have passed laws requiring schools to specifically create anti-cyberbullying policies. School administrators should involve the entire school community—teachers, students and parents—in designing and implementing a policy for appropriate and safe Internet use. **As part of developing this policy**, schools could sponsor workshops to educate teachers, students, and parents about the dangers of cyberbullying, including how to recognize both bullies and victims. **The final policy** should be distributed throughout the school community, so everyone is aware of the rules and the consequences for breaking them. Each year the policy should be reviewed and updated if necessary. Schools can **also** implement a "Netiquette" program to show students how to use technology in positive and safe ways. Computers on campus should be closely monitored by teachers in the classroom and through filtering and tracking software. If **despite these precautions** cyberbullying should still occur, schools should provide easy ways for students to report these incidents, including ways to do so anonymously online or in a specially designated drop box. Reports of cyberbullying—on and off campus—should be investigated promptly and if valid,

> This paragraph uses a chronological pattern of organization and a number of transitions.

Jones 5

should be handled according to the school policy. **In addition**, both victims and cyberbullies should be offered support services from counselors to determine the causes of the behavior and ways to prevent it from reoccurring.

Parents can support **these school efforts** by participating in the workshops to learn about cyberbullying and by staying current in the technology their children use. **They** need to familiarize themselves with the school's anti-cyberbullying policy and discuss it with their children. Parents should **also** make clear expectations for ethical and responsible behavior. **They** should encourage their children to immediately report any instances of cyberbullying or any other inappropriate online behavior. **Once they have made sure their children know the rules and expectations**, parents should monitor their children's online activities by, **first of all**, keeping the home computer where it can be easily seen such as in a family room. Parents may also install special filtering software and monitoring programs. They should know the online names and passwords their children use to access social networking sites. Children are entitled to privacy, but if parents have safety concerns, they should not hesitate to review all their children's online communication. Parents who find that their children are being bullied online should block future contacts from the bully, save all evidence of the bullying and insist that there be no online retaliation. Parents **should then** notify the school and the cyberbully's parents, presenting the proof of cyberbullying. If the cyberbullying does not stop, parents should consider contacting an attorney or the police to determine if the cyberbullying involves criminal behavior.

Finally, the students themselves must take steps to prevent cyberbullying. They have to be open-minded about the school policies and be willing to participate in the workshops designed to teach them responsible online behavior and Internet safety. Through workshops and role-playing activities, students can learn not to be cyberbullies of any kind. Students should not retaliate in response to hurtful messages and postings, but should inform their teachers and parents of the situation. Students must **also** learn that they cannot

Referencing "school efforts" and repeating the pronoun "they" creates coherence.

This paragraph blends chronological and emphatic order, repeats key words—*cyberbullying* and *parents*—and includes transitional words and phrases.

Jones 6

simply stand by and witness others being cyberbullied. **In both of these circumstances**, they are not "snitching" or "narcing" when they tell adults about situations that can cause serious harm. An easy formula for students to remember if they receive a cruel or threatening message is Stop, Block, and Tell: stop corresponding with anyone who is mean or threatening, block the bully from email or IM, and tell an adult about what has happened. **By taking these steps**, students can prevent themselves and others from being victims.

> The author ends with a call to action.

Bullies of any kind can thrive only when a culture remains indifferent to cruelty and disrespect. That kind of culture must not be allowed in our schools, in our homes or online. Let us work together to bring civility to students' lives in cyberspace and beyond.

EXERCISE 5.3   Identify Paragraph Strategies   MyWritingLab

Directions: Read the following essay, answering the questions about the various strategies the writer uses.

Season of the Zombie

> 1. What does the author do to generate **interest** in the topic?

We are in the midst of a zombie invasion. Movies such as *Zombieland, Shaun of the Dead*, and *Dawn of the Dead* are box office hits. The mid-season finale of AMC's series *The Walking Dead* drew over six million viewers, making it the most watched basic cable series of all time. Max Brooks's novel *World War Z* was on the *New York Times* best-seller list, and Seth Grahame-Smith's mashup novel *Pride and Prejudice and Zombies* has spawned a literary trend that includes zombies in Oz and Wonderland and on Huckleberry Finn's raft. Zombie walks draw thousands of participants in cities around the world. Occupy Wall Street protestors donned zombie make-up and carried signs saying, "Don't be a Zombie!" Even the

> 2. What introduction strategies does the author use?

Centers for Disease Control includes a plan for dealing with a zombie apocalypse on its website. Why have zombies become the darlings of popular culture?

ZOMBIES AHEAD

3. This paragraph has an implied topic sentence. What pattern of development keeps the paragraph unified?

4. What overall organization strategy does the author use to achieve coherence?

5. What transitions help you identify this strategy?

6. This paragraph uses the classification pattern of development. What does it classify?

7. What transition indicates an emphatic organization strategy?

8. Which words in the topic sentence indicate the controlling idea of this paragraph?

9. What pattern of development does this paragraph use?

10. Give examples of specific details that support the controlling idea.

Our fascination with zombies actually began back in 1929 with the publication of *The Magic Island*, William Seabrook's account of Voodoo in Haiti, Seabrook introduced the word *zombie* into U.S. speech. According to Haitian Voodoo lore, a zombie is one who has fallen under a spell or potion administered by a *bokor* or sorcerer. The zombie exists in a trancelike state, unable to reason or exercise free will and completely under the *bokor's* control. In 1968, George Romero's *Night of the Living Dead* redefined the Voodoo zombie. Romero's zombies are corpses reanimated by radiation from a crashed spacecraft. Lacking all human consciousness, Romero's zombies plod relentlessly after the living, turning them into zombies with a bite or devouring them altogether. In more recent movies, such as *28 Days Later* and *Zombieland,* the zombies are not reanimated corpses but humans transformed by a virus or parasitic infection. While showing no signs of human reasoning or emotion, these zombies are often fast moving predators driven by a craving to devour anything within reach and infecting others with their bites. Zombie purists, however, argue that only those who have died and been reanimated can be technically called zombies.

Although the zombie has been around for a long time, nowadays the horror genre has embraced the gruesome zombies because they evoke such a variety of fears. First, there is the fear of losing what makes us most human: our free will. Zombies have lost all human capacity to think, to reason and to feel emotions. They are driven only by the most primal need to feed, and it doesn't matter if the "food" is a loved one. Zombies also appeal to our fear of our own mortality. In zombie movies death is not sanitized with ritual and the comforting display of the groomed and make-up covered deceased at rest in a satin-lined casket. The gruesome features of dead and decaying human bodies mock our efforts to ignore the gruesome realities of death. Perhaps zombies most evoke our fear of apocalyptic destruction. Just as Godzilla and the other radioactive monsters of the 1950's reflected a fear of nuclear annihilation brought on by the cold war, the zombie apocalypse reflects our fear of an unstoppable pandemic, perhaps caused by AIDS, mad cow disease, or a genetically engineered bird flu virus. The zombie apocalypse shows the complete breakdown of civilization through the spread of an uncontrolled contagion.

Above everything else, zombies appeal to us because they tap into our basic fears of death and decay. They typically have evidence of the bite that led to their transformation—sometimes a bite-sized chunk out of a cheek or the side of the neck or entire missing limbs. Dark and sunken zombie eyes are understandably "vacant," sometimes completely white. Often one eye swings from its socket as the oblivious-to-pain zombie staggers along. Zombies wear the clothes of their pre-zombie lives and occupations, but the clothes are torn and bloodied. Hair, too, is most often matted with blood. While most authors of zombie fiction make do with having characters gag over the smell of decay when they encounter zombies—sort of the eau d'zombie one would expect—some can be particularly creative in trying to capture in words the scent of a zombie. Author and video game expert Dan Birlew described the probable smell of a zombie as being "like unflushed wet feces stirred into old hamburger that's been sitting out for a week."

Wrap up this gruesome, foul-smelling creature with the sounds of its guttural moan as it catches sight of a potential victim, and you have the classic zombie.

> 11. Which sentence is the topic sentence of this paragraph?

Interestingly, zombies seem to have surpassed in popularity their fellow undead horror icon: the vampire. Although the zombie and vampire share some similarity in that their bites are infectious, turning victims into the undead, the differences between the two groups are striking. Zombies may be known for eating brains, but they use their own for little more than finding food and eating. Their communication is usually limited to moaning. Vampires, however, retain their intelligence after death and, in fact, may accumulate knowledge through centuries of unliving. They not only speak but can be quite sophisticated and seductive in their conversations. Most zombies shuffle along slowly, and their mobility decreases as their bodies decay whereas vampires can move faster than the human eye can follow and are even able to fly. The not very bright or fast zombies must stumble upon victims, catching them unaware or overwhelming them with sheer numbers. Zombies' unquenchable hunger then leads them to devour any and all parts of their victims. Vampires typically work alone, sometimes surprising but often seducing victims. The vampire's meal of choice is blood. Both can be difficult to kill, but zombies have no sense of self-preservation, and drop like rocks when their brains are destroyed. The clever vampire must be trapped or tricked into a vulnerable state and then dispatched with a stake through the heart or exposure to sunlight.

> 12. Which organization strategy does it use—a block or point-by-point comparison/contrast pattern?

Despite their association with the supernatural, zombies are not simply dismissed by the scientific community. Medical professionals use the idea of a zombie apocalypse to draw attention to real world health issues, such as a pandemic, while scientists point out zombie-like conditions caused by drugs, diseases, and parasites.

> 13. What function does this paragraph serve in this essay?

In his 1985 book *The Serpent and the Rainbow*, anthropologist Wade Davis claimed that Haitian *bokors* created zombies by giving their victims a concoction of neurotoxins, such as those found in the pufferfish and some toads. These drugs produced a deep coma, resembling death. The *bokor* would dig up the victim after burial and keep him in a trancelike state through other drugs. A well-documented case of this type of zombification is that of Clairvius Narcisse. On April 30, 1962, Narcisse checked into the Albert Schweitzer Hospital in Haiti. Feverish and achy, he was coughing up blood. Over the next two days his conditioned worsened. On May 2, two physicians pronounced Narcisse dead, and he was buried the next day. Eighteen years later, his sister was walking through the village when she was approached by a man claiming to be Narcisse. After careful questioning by his family, Narcisse was found to be the same man who had been buried those many years ago. He told a fantastic tale of being aware though unable to move or speak as he was put into his coffin and buried. He was dug up by a *bokor*, who forced him to work on a sugar plantation. After two years of working in a dream-like state, he was able to escape and return to his village.

> 14. What is the primary pattern of development used in this paragraph?

In addition, some scientists have speculated that the type of brain deterioration necessary for zombies could be caused by a type of infectious protein called a prion. Prions are responsible for mad cow disease and Creutzfeldt-Jakob disease in humans. In his fictitious account of a scientist sent to study a zombie plague, *The Zombie*

Autopsies, Harvard psychiatrist Steven C. Schlozman attributes zombiism to an airborne prionlike virus, which he calls Ataxic Neurodegenerative Satiety Deficiency Syndrome. The novel presents the progression of this brain-degenerating disease. When first infected with this virus—most often from a bite by an infected person—the victim becomes feverish and feels the first hunger pangs. During the next twenty-four hours, the fever increases as cognition declines and hunger increases. At this stage the victim also begins to lose a sense of balance, staggering with outstretched arms. The third stage brings rapid deterioration of cognitive and neurological functions and intensified aggressive behavior as the victim tries to sate uncontrollable hunger. By the final stage the victim has lost all human cognitive abilities and is driven by only the most primal instinct to feed.

While Schlozman's book is science fiction, scientists have actually found parasites that can create zombie-like conditions in their hosts. A carpenter ant, for example, can become infected by a parasitic fungus that takes over its brain and compels the ant to bite into the vein running down the underside of a leaf—something the ant would not normally do. Tightly anchored to the leaf, the ant dies, but the fungus thrives and grows a stalk out of the ant's body that releases spores to continue the cycle. The pill bug can also be compelled to behave in an unnatural manner when infected by a parasitic worm. Because the worm cannot reproduce inside the pill bug, it takes over the bug's brain, making the bug leave its protective hiding place and crawl out into the open where it is devoured by a bird. Once inside the bird, the parasitic worm can reproduce and continue its life cycle. Even more striking is the behavior of a crab that has been infected by Sacculina carcini—a type of barnacle. The barnacle attaches itself to the crab and implants tendrils throughout the crab's body, taking total control of the crab's behavior. The crab lives only to eat and nourish the parasite even foregoing its instinct to mate. An infected female or male crab will instead treat the barnacle's larva as its own offspring. With these examples in nature, is it surprising that some speculate that a parasite could take over human brains and cause zombielike behaviors?

Perhaps the notion of a zombie apocalypse is so popular because it intrigues us even as it horrifies us. Part of the appeal of the zombie apocalypse is that it levels the playing field. Wealth and power in the pre-apocalyptic world mean nothing once a zombie horde is on the move. With some degree of luck, cunning, and a willingness to use available weapons, the average Joe who stays calm can survive with all the available resources left behind by a significantly depleted human race. Unlike the total annihilation brought on by a nuclear war or an earth-shattering meteor strike, a zombie apocalypse gives survivors a fighting chance. And who doesn't wonder if he or she has what it takes to survive?

With a global recession, wars, fears of terrorism, the rise of AIDS, and nuclear proliferation among unstable nations—is it any wonder that we turn to zombies for a little distraction from life's problems? Whether we simply like being frightened or imagining the challenge of testing our mettle against fearsome odds, zombies have hordes of fans. The walking dead truly have become the new pop stars of horror.

---

15. What is the primary pattern of development in this paragraph? What transitions help organize this pattern?

16. What pattern of development does this paragraph use?

17. What pattern of development does this paragraph use?

18. What strategy does the author use in this conclusion?

19. The introduction used a question at the end of the first paragraph to orient the paper. Did the author effectively answer that question?

EXERCISE 5.4   Planning Development Strategies for an Essay

Directions: Working with a group of peers, determine what kinds of development you would use to support the following thesis statements. How would you organize that support into paragraphs? How would you organize the paragraphs into an essay? Pick one thesis and write a scratch outline (see page 78) that shows how you would develop and organize paragraphs to support the thesis.

EXAMPLE   A paper that argues for a college course on zombies.

> *Introduction: Descriptive narrative of a boring class. The right subject can both interest and inform.*
>
> *Thesis: Zombies are a suitable subject for a college-level interdisciplinary studies course.*
>
> *Cause and Effect: Why zombies are so popular among young people.*
>
> *Definition: What makes a good interdisciplinary class? Engages students and has applications in several disciplines.*
>
> *Division: How the study of zombies can be carried throughout the curriculum:*
> - *zombies in history*
> - *science—zombies in nature, pandemics*
> - *psychology—fear, behavior during a crisis*
> - *business/economics—impact of zombie walk on local economy*
> - *literature—mashup novels*
>
> *Process: Getting an interdisciplinary course on zombies into the curriculum.*

1. The Centers for Disease Control (CDC) should (or should not) use zombies to inform the public about disaster preparedness.

2. Schools have an obligation to protect students from bullying.

3. Colleges should enforce a strict policy of no electronic devices in the classroom.

4. Having a better understanding of college codes can help students be more successful.

5. Social networking sites can both help and hurt a job applicant.

6. It is no surprise that _____ has been so successful. (Pick your own narrowed topic to fill in the blank.)

**EXERCISE 5.5 Compose an Introduction and   MyWritingLab
Conclusion**

Directions: Using the strategies presented in this chapter, write an introduction and a conclusion paragraph that might be used in the essay you planned in Exercise 5.4.

CHAPTER AT A GLANCE

Learning Objectives . . .   How they connect to writing at college

❶ Write effective introduction paragraphs.

Introductions serve two main purposes: to engage readers' interest and to present the thesis.

Writers can craft effective introductions in the following ways:

- Use a pattern of development.
- Provide a background or historical overview.
- Start with a surprising fact or statistic.
- Begin with a quotation.
- Ask an important and relevant question.

To avoid common mistakes in introductions, writers should not do the following:

- Begin with an announcement.
- Apologize.
- Provide a dictionary definition.
- Start with a broad statement.
- Begin with an unclear question.

❷ Create conclusion paragraphs that leave a lasting impression.

Conclusions should leave readers with a positive lasting impression of a paper. Writers can use the following strategies for memorable conclusions:

- Refer back to the introduction.
- Provide reflection on the topic.
- Offer a call to action.
- Summarize key points.

Learning Objectives ...   How they connect to writing at college

To avoid common mistakes in conclusions, writers should not do the following:

- Run out of steam and simply repeat the thesis.
- End with an announcement.
- Apologize.
- Introduce a new idea not covered in the essay.
- Summarize key points of a very short essay.

❸ Identify the various strategies for constructing paragraphs and using transitions.

Writers can use the various patterns of development to organize body paragraphs and provide support for their points.

Transitions serve three primary roles in essays: They connect ideas within paragraphs, connect paragraphs within essays, and, in the form of short transitional paragraphs, may be used to introduce major sections of an essay.

> **MyWritingLab** Visit **Chapter 5, "Paragraphs Working Together: The Essay,"** in MyWritingLab to test your understanding of the chapter objectives.

Descriptive Writing

Learning Objectives

In this chapter you will learn and practice how to …

❶ Create a dominant impression.

❷ Use concrete, specific, and inviting details.

❸ Use descriptive verbs.

❹ Put **I D E A S** to work in descriptive writing.

Here a detective writes a report that describes a crime scene. Providing specific details about the scene is essential if the police want to catch the perpetrator. Besides this example, there are many other times writers have to use description. When have you had to use descriptive writing? For whom, when, and what kind?

Imagine communication without descriptive details. How could you begin to share a favorite childhood memory? How could a police officer report an accident or a crime without using descriptive details? Stories without description would be pretty dull. Even a set of instructions for assembling a swing set requires some description of the parts and how they fit together. How effective would a travel brochure be without descriptive details to entice visitors to faraway locations? What if patients could not describe their symptoms to doctors?

Communication without description lacks important information, and it neglects the lively features of our language that add interest and excitement to what we say and write. Whether a person is a scientist describing chemical reactions in a laboratory or a sales representative trying to convince a family to buy a new minivan, descriptive details matter.

Besides the everyday reasons why careful description is important, descriptive writing can be fun both to read and to write. By focusing on insightful details, a writer can reveal interesting facts and features of a subject that might otherwise be dull. Since strong descriptive writing uses the senses sight, sound, touch, smell, and taste—readers can become so immersed in an author's description that they are transported to another place, or they can see the person or situation being described in their mind's eye. The details lift the subject from the page and make it real.

When thinking about the **I D E A S** (see pp. 66–68) that will go into a piece of writing, a writer selects the specific and concrete details along with reflection and information that will connect to readers. The writer's goal is to spark readers' interest, inform and entertain them about the topic, and keep them reading to the end.

MyWritingLab Visit Ch. 6 Descriptive Writing in MyWritingLab to access the IDEAS videos.

❶ Create a dominant impression.

Create a Dominant Impression—Make It Real for Your Readers

You want to be sure your descriptive writing gives readers a **dominant impression**—an overall feeling the details work together to create. One of the best compliments a writer can get is a statement along the lines of "You really took me there" or "You helped me see it" or "You painted a picture for me" or "It is clear what you are writing about."

Suppose, for example, you had to write a description of a diner where locals hang out. Ideally, you would go to the diner and begin taking notes on all the concrete details around you: the sights and sounds of all the customers, the smell of the food wafting through the air, the taste of the food, and the details about the diner's appearance. Now, including all of those details in a paper could create a sensory overload in your readers, who could be left wondering, "What's the point?" A better approach is to decide on the *dominant impression* of the diner you want your details to convey. Is the diner family friendly—a fun place to eat? Is it romantic? Is it a greasy spoon where workers gather to complain about their jobs?

Once you have a dominant impression, you can omit the details that are not relevant and focus on making clearer those details that do convey the impression.

EXERCISE 6.1   Create a Dominant Impression   MyWritingLab

Directions: Look carefully at each of the following pictures of very different kinds of restaurants. Write a brief description of each, using details that capture a dominant impression.

EXERCISE 6.2   Describe Your Class   MyWritingLab

Directions: Imagine you have arranged for a guest speaker to visit your writing class. In order to help the person feel more at ease, write a short but vivid description of the class. What happens in the classroom? What does the room look like? What kinds of students will the speaker be addressing? Choose details that create a clear dominant impression of the classroom.

Use Concrete, Specific, and Inviting Details

❷ Use concrete, specific, and inviting details.

When most people think of description, they tend to think only about the way something looks, which is fine. However, people are affected by much more than what something looks like, so it is important to work with all of the senses when you can. Stronger writers also incorporate into their descriptions the other four senses—*sound, touch, smell,* and *taste.* These four senses combined with sight make up what are called **concrete details** in writing.

If you were to describe your bedroom, for example, it would be easy to focus on the color of the walls, the furniture, the way the room is configured, and what you have on your walls. But to create a descriptive piece of writing that grabs readers' attention and places them there, why not describe the music you are playing, what's on the TV, the smell of dirty laundry piled in the corner, the sounds that creep in from outside the windows, or the softness of your bed?

What you want your readers to learn or to better understand about your subject determines the details you select. You are in control. You determine the dominant impression you want the description to make, and you choose the details that best develop and present that impression to your readers.

As we also explained in Chapter 2, there are significant differences between general description and specific details (see page 37). The famous American author Mark Twain once said, "The difference between the right word and the almost right word is the difference between lightning and a lightning bug." By using specific word choices such as *crimson*, *Mohawk*, and *waddle*, writers create lightning in their writing; they bring it vividly to life. In contrast, general word choices like *red*, *haircut*, and *walk* act as lightning bugs; they create only a brief flicker of interest. For example, look at the different meanings of the following words. The general words like *walk* and *talk* are not descriptive; however, the others provide vivid description for readers:

General	Specific and Descriptive Words
walk	strut, waddle, march, lurch, limp, hustle, creep
talk	shout, whisper, drone, holler, mumble, chatter

EXERCISE 6.3   Generating Concrete Details   MyWritingLab

Directions: As a consumer, you often call upon your senses when deciding on a purchase. Think about how you would use your senses if you were test driving a car in order to determine whether to purchase it. Brainstorm the sensory details in answer to each of the following questions.

- What would you notice about how the car looks?
- What sounds would you listen for during the test drive?
- What smells could warn you of potential problems?
- How might your sense of touch come into play as you drive the car?

It is not likely that your sense of taste would come into play as you make your decision about purchasing the car, but using all of your other four senses during your test drive would help you make a more informed decision.

Now imagine examining a product that does call upon your sense of taste. Suppose you have gone to the bakery to order a special cake—perhaps for a wedding, a graduation, or some other special occasion. Brainstorm some of the sensory details you might use to describe the samples of cake the bakery provides to help you make your decision.

- What would you look for in the appearance of the cake?
- What kinds of texture would you want the cake to have?
- What kinds of smells would be acceptable?
- How would you like the cake to taste?

Unless you smack your lips with satisfaction, sound would probably not enter into this decision.

EXERCISE 6.4   Lightning or Lightning Bug?   MyWritingLab

Directions: In *Life on the Mississippi,* Mark Twain wrote about his training to become a riverboat pilot. In this famous passage from the book, he talks about what he both lost and gained through his acquired knowledge of the river. To see if you can tell lightning from a lightning bug, circle the words you think Mark Twain used from the choices provided within parentheses.

Now when I had (**discovered, learned, mastered**) the language of this water and had come to know every (**trifling, small, diminutive**) feature that bordered the great river as familiarly as I knew the letters of the alphabet, I had made a (**great discovery, valuable acquisition, important find**). But I had lost something, too. I had lost something which could never be restored to me while I lived. All the grace, the beauty, the poetry had gone out of the (**great, majestic, amazing**) river! I still keep in mind a certain wonderful sunset which I (**saw, witnessed, watched**) when steamboating was new to me. A (**huge, broad, great**) expanse of the river was turned to (**blood, crimson, red**); in the middle distance the red hue (**turned, changed, brightened**) into gold, through which a (**single, lone, solitary**) log came floating, black and (**conspicuous, obvious, noticeable**); in one place a long, slanting mark lay (**shining, sparkling, glimmering**) upon the water; in another the surface was broken by boiling, tumbling rings, that were as many-tinted as (**an opal, a rainbow, a diamond**); where the (**reddish, ruddy, rosy**) flush was faintest, was a smooth spot that was covered with graceful circles and radiating lines, ever so (**delicately, gently, softly**) traced; the shore on our left was (**heavily, densely, thickly**) wooded, and the (**dark, somber, gloomy**)

shadow that fell from this forest was broken in one place by a long, (**ruffled, winding, curving**) trail that shone like (**sunlight, gold, silver**); and high above the forest wall a clean-stemmed dead tree waved a single leafy bough that glowed like a flame in the (**unblocked, wide-open, unobstructed**)(**light, splendor, brilliance**) that was flowing from the sun. There were (**beautiful, graceful, elegant**) curves, reflected images, woody heights, soft distances; and over the whole scene, far and near, the dissolving lights (**drifted, moved, passed**) steadily, (**improving, enriching, enhancing**) it, every passing moment, with new (**spectacles, wonders, marvels**) of coloring.

❸ Use descriptive verbs.

Use Descriptive Verbs

When writing a description, you should remember to make good use of your most important—yet often overlooked—tool: the verb. **Linking verbs** indicate a state of being (*is, was, have been*), or they provide a state of action. (See a list of linking verbs on pages 417 and 448 of Chapter 14.) Most verbs are **action verbs** because they show how someone or something is performing an action. For example, the action verbs in the sentences below are underlined.

- The dog <u>raced</u> across the backyard.
- Stephanie quickly <u>consumed</u> her dinner.
- The gymnast <u>straddled</u> the beam.

Using Active Verbs

Verbs are the driving force behind strong description and observation. Because verbs are so important, many professional writers look specifically at their verb choices when they revise their writing. They typically try to take out the versions of the "to be" verbs (*is, was, were*, etc.) and replace them with more descriptive and interesting action verbs.

For example, look at how a writer edited the following sentences to make the verbs (and some other words) more descriptive and interesting:

BLAND SENTENCE	I *was going* to the airport's ticket counter.
SENTENCE WITH A DESCRIPTIVE VERB	I <u>rushed</u> to the airport's ticket counter.
BLAND SENTENCE	The ducks *were* on the pond.
DESCRIPTIVE SENTENCE	Twenty mallards <u>stationed</u> themselves on the pond.
BLAND, GENERAL SENTENCE	*That guy was trying* to sell me the *used car.*
DESCRIPTIVE SENTENCE	**The car dealer** <u>attempted</u> to sell me the **beat-up Ford Escort.**

All writers should use this method, especially if they are writing descriptive and observational writing.

EXERCISE 6.5   Replace Weak Verbs with Active Verbs   MyWritingLab

Directions: In each of the following sentences, replace the weak—and often wordy—linking verb constructions with stronger action verbs.

EXAMPLE   The store is~~going to close~~ next Tuesday.

(closes)

1. Alex is hoping to start college in the fall.

2. My car is in need of a new muffler.

3. As Carrie was exploring the library, I was surfing the Internet.

4. Michael is approaching his problems too cautiously.

5. The leaves were whirling in the wind.

Using Descriptive Verbs

On page 156 we provided the specific verb choice of *waddle* versus the more general verb *walk.* How are these different? If you envisioned a duck or a portly gentleman crossing a street when you read the word *waddle*, the verb did its job. *Walk*, in contrast, is lifeless and boring. It does not provide an interesting image at all. Choose verbs that create a vivid depiction for readers—verbs that convey the dominant impression you want readers to gain from your description.

EXERCISE 6.6 Compose Descriptive Verbs MyWritingLab

Directions: Think about your own specific word choices to move the reader beyond "walk." Here are some sentences about people walking. Use some more vivid alternatives to *walk* that help the reader visualize a lively image of the action.

1. The tired factory worker _____ home after a long day.

2. The beauty queen _____ down the runway.

3. The two-year-old _____ across the room to his mother's arms.

4. The proud football player _____ across the stage to receive his award.

5. The burglar _____ around the bushes to the patio door.

When writing dialogue, a writer may overuse the verb *said*. For each of the dialogue sentences below, fill in the blank with a strong action verb that indicates *how* something was said. Choose a word that helps the reader truly hear how the sentence was spoken.

6. "I can't believe my tire is flat," Carlos _____.

7. "There will be a test next Monday," the teacher _____.

8. "But I don't want to go to bed," the child _____.

9. "You'll do this job my way, or you'll hit the highway," the boss _____.

10. "I'd like *you* to hit the highway," the employee _____, slinking away.

❹ Put **I D E A S** to work in descriptive writing.

MyWritingLab Visit Ch. 6 Descriptive Writing in MyWritingLab to access the IDEAS videos.

Put **I D E A S** to Work in Descriptive Writing

How do I begin my paper? What should I lead with? Should I mix up the senses as I write? What should the writing focus on more to create a dominant impression? What is my point? How can I convey emotions and frame how a reader might view the subject? Can my readers see it?

Writers ask themselves questions such as these when they brainstorm before drafting a descriptive piece of writing. Often writers find their focus through the act of writing. So, as many writing teachers will tell you, you should not fall in love with your first draft. Getting your description onto the page or screen will help you organize it. Once you get something in writing, tinkering with the flow of the details is *crucial*. And you will need to focus on specific details and descriptive verbs.

As you think through which details are most important, keep in mind **IDEAS**:

I nterest

D etails

E xplanation

A udience

S tyle

How will you create interest? What explanation is needed? How can you paint a picture with words for your readers through word choice and, specifically, active verbs? How can you make the paper read with style? What details will you provide, and how will you develop them?

STUDENT WRITER AT WORK

Harrison Duncan's writing teacher wanted the class to practice a different genre: letter writing. The full assignment is on page 183 of this chapter, but here is the general topic.

Problem in Your Community Letter

Your Task

Write a one- or two-page letter that describes and discusses a particular problem at your college or in your community (your neighborhood or city or suburb). Describe your subject, demonstrate its existence through strong details, and explain why it is a pressing problem that citizens need to address. Through strong description based on personal experience, others' experiences, and reflection, you should persuade readers that the issue is important. Consider what your readers already know about the subject and how your essay might add to what they know. Also consider why this problem or issue is important to you and why others should care about it.

Harrison has decided to write a descriptive letter about a problem in his local community: the poor condition of the roads. Using **I D E A S** as a strategy to think through his letter, he considered the following questions:

	Interest: *How can I help the reader see this is more than my problem? What are some ways I can show how poor roadways negatively impact the whole community?*
	Details: *What details will show my dominant impression—how dangerous the roads have become? What concrete details can I use to describe the size and depth of the potholes and the damage they do to cars? As I move from description of the problem to its consequences, how should I organize my details? Safety seems the most important issue, but economic concerns need to be emphasized, too.*
	Explanation: *Should I include the experience I had taking my friends downtown? Will showing the negative impact the roads have on visitors' impression of our town be an effective way to reinforce the seriousness of the problem? I've witnessed cars damaged by potholes. Which of these examples should I include? Which examples best show the serious nature of the problem? How can I connect the condition of the roads to the economic consequences within our community in addition to safety issues?*
	Audience: *I don't want to come across as just a complainer. What can I include to show I am proud of our city and concerned about its reputation? How can I explain that I know the city budget is tight, but these repairs are still necessary?*
	Style: *How can I mix paragraphs up so my letter is not a listing of details, but a variety of details and my explanation of the problem? This is a letter, so the paragraphs should not be too long. While I want to share some of my specific experiences, I want to also emphasize this is a community issue. Can I blend the use of "I" and "we" effectively?*

Another useful strategy Harrison could employ would be to simply sit and observe Main Street and take detailed notes of what he sees. His notes could include specific colors, sounds, smells, sights, and textures that work together to convey the dominant impression he wants his description to convey.

Harrison's Letter

The following letter is Harrison's response to the "Description of a Problem Letter" assignment. Notice how he follows the format conventions of a letter. Notice, too, his strong use of specific and descriptive details.

Author's address and the date the letter was written.

2313 Mockingbird Drive
Pine Rapids, IA 50614
May 21, 2014

Name and address of the person to whom the letter is sent.

Mr. John Smith, Director of Streets
City Hall
724 Scenic Drive
Pine Rapids, IA 50614

In a formal letter, the salutation is followed by a colon. Unless you know how a person wants to be addressed (e.g., Dr. or Mrs.), the safest tactic is using Mr. or Ms.

Dear Mr. Smith:

As you know, the brutal Iowa weather devastates our roads every winter, but usually city crews begin extensive repairs on the roads during the first warm days of spring. This spring, however, repairs consisted of a few shovels of gravel tossed in only the deepest holes. Now in addition to losing hub caps and wearing out shocks as their cars rumble and bounce through cavernous holes, drivers must contend with cracks in their windshields from the flying gravel. I

Placing the main point, purpose, and possibly what needs to be done in the first paragraph is crucial, so a writer does not waste a reader's time. A thesis, or bottom line, is expected early on.

realize that in these tough economic times, the city—like many of its households—must cut back on services. However, the poor condition of our roads, especially Main Street, requires immediate attention since the state of the roads hurts the appeal of the shopping district and, more importantly, serious accidents could occur.

Notice the specific details Harrison uses to develop this example.

Main Street is particularly bad as I discovered when I took some out of town friends down town for lunch. When I first turned onto Main Street from University Avenue, I encountered a series of buckles in the road that nearly shook my car apart as it rattled my and my passengers' teeth. As we continued down the street, I weaved my car as much as traffic would allow, avoiding the gaping holes. At one point the driver in front of me had to slam on her brakes to avoid a particularly nasty crevice that filled almost half a lane. The chunks of asphalt around this virtual sinkhole made it particularly dangerous. The holes in the street in the downtown area are not as deep, but there are more of them. And with all the spring rain we've had lately, these holes were filled with water. Cars could not help but drive through them, spraying water on the nearby pedestrians who were trying to enjoy a leisurely stroll as they shopped. Needless to say, my friends' view of our downtown area was negatively impacted by the bumpy and even dangerous drive.

Here Harrison appeals to his reader's sense of civic pride and describes how the poor streets hurt the economy.

We in Pine Rapids are proud of our community and particularly proud of our downtown area. What a blemish on our community it is to have these torn up roads. Visitors are not likely to return to our highly promoted shopping district if they risk damaging their cars and being drenched by passing vehicles when they walk along our streets. The city has found money for the flower baskets that hang from the street lamps and beautify downtown. However, I think the money could have been better spent on repairing the streets.

Notice how Harrison ends the letter with the important issue of public safety, which directly connects to the bottom line at the end of the first paragraph.

I am even more concerned about the safety issues raised by this problem. Some of the holes are so deep that drivers unfamiliar with the area could easily lose control of their cars if they hit one, even when they are driving the speed limit. Drivers who try to avoid these holes risk side-swiping another vehicle because the lanes on Main Street are so narrow. I recently witnessed a smaller car hit the bottom of a large hole so hard that it lost a muffler and damaged a tire. The damage was so bad the driver had to limp over to the side of the road and call a tow truck. Something must be done before people, and not just cars, are injured.

Here Harrison repeats his point that the streets must be repaired and shows that he expects to get feedback from Mr. Smith.

I hope the city is taking some steps to resolve this problem. These streets are the key to our livelihood, our economy and our safety. Let's not put off those repairs any longer. I look forward to hearing from you about this important matter.

Sincerely,

Harrison Duncan

Harrison Duncan

MyWritingLab Visit
Ch. 6 Descriptive Writing
in MyWritingLab to access
the IDEAS videos.

I D E A S in Action

In the first reading, commentary using the **I D E A S** template is provided to show how close, analytical, and critical reading is important when
reading descriptive writing.

SELECTION 1   MyWritingLab

Dandelion: A Virtuous Weed

Craig Holdrege

*In this selection, Craig Holdrege provides a different take
on what some homeowners see as a problem. As the subtitle of his essay relates, he thinks the dandelion is a "virtuous weed." So, through focused description and details,
Holdrege attempts to persuade his readers to view the
dandelion not as a plant we should despise, but a flower
we should respect.*

PRE-READING PROMPT

1. Why are some plants and flowers cared for and cultivated and others
   called "weeds" are pulled and poisoned? Who decides what is a
   flower and what is a weed?
2. Are weeds really so bad? What might be some positive traits of a
   lowly weed?

Interest: The quotation connects
to what Holdrege wants to express
in his article: his admiration of the
dandelion.

Details: Notice how specific word
choices paint pictures.

Style: This short sentence presents
the **dominant impression** about
the "weed": admirable and
unstoppable.

Explanation: He uses the example
of one weed to explain its
complexity.

Interest and Audience: Rejecting
conventional thinking about the
dandelion, Holdrege shows his
respect and admiration for the
weed.

1   As Emerson said, "a weed is a plant whose virtues have not been discovered."
The virtues of the dandelion are many. Prolific and hardy, its bursting yellow flower
heads, rising above a rosette of sharply toothed leaves, can be found almost everywhere in the urban environment. The dandelion-sea of yellow in yet unmowed parks
and lawns provides a feast for the winter weary eye. Thrusting its way up between
cracks in the expanses of concrete and asphalt, a single dandelion can remind us of
the power of life in a seemingly barren world. Dandelions won't be held back.

2   When you look closely at its flower, you'll discover many (one to two hundred)
yellow ribbons. You might think that they are petals, like those of a rose or tulip. But
no, each one is a complete tiny flower, so that the dandelion blossom as a whole is
in fact a bouquet of tiny flowers! This development of a superflower made of individual flowers represents the pinnacle of flower differentiation in the plant kingdom.

3   When the sun shines, dandelion flower heads open in the morning and close again in the afternoon. When clouds shield them from the sun they close up, as if they were saying: we are of the sun and for the sun. Dandelion flowers attract bees and nearly a hundred species of other insects that enjoy their nectar. This is a true gift of plant to animal, since—remarkably—their seeds can develop without fertilization. One day the flower head opens as a white feathery globe. The parachute-bearing seeds drift off to some new place just waiting for a dandelion to take root.

> **Audience and Style:** Reinforcing his theme of being "unstoppable," the author describes the planting process.

QUESTIONS FOR DISCUSSION

1. What new insights about the dandelion has this selection given you?
2. Do you think Holdrege has convinced most people not to pull up or poison the dandelions in their yards? If you were to revise this essay, what would you add to persuade readers not to worry about dandelions in their yards? What details, examples, and explanations would you provide, and why?

I D E A S for Your Own Writing   My**Writing**Lab

Complexity Thesis Essay

Holdrege's short essay is an example of what people who study writing call a "complexity thesis." The author has taken a topic that most readers would think is really simple ("Dandelions are a nuisance and should not be tolerated.") and, through describing the weed, tries to make readers see the dandelion in a very different light. He tries to change minds through description.

In a short essay, take an object, idea, or event and go against conventional wisdom. If most people look at that subject in a negative or positive way, take the other side and describe how that subject is positive or negative. Use strong, specific, concrete, and vivid details to show how the topic is positive or negative.

Save It with Details Essay

Imagine one of your cherished possessions is on the chopping block. Perhaps your parent or spouse wants to throw out your favorite t-shirt. Maybe there is talk of getting rid of a couch or easy chair where you enjoyed many hours of TV. Or—heaven forbid!—someone wants to get rid of a pet whose charms are still obvious to you. Write a description of this possession that convinces others it is worth keeping.

SELECTION 2   MyWritingLab

The Trail Winds . . .

Jane Braxton Little

This passage comes from an article published in Audubon Magazine, *the journal of the environmental organization, the Audubon Society. The article, "A Rare Jewel" by Jane Braxton Little,*

describes the adventure of self-described "phib freaks"—people who study and care about amphibians and the environment—who explore an old-growth forest in Oregon. This paragraph chronicles part of the group's hike.

PRE-READING PROMPT

1. What kind of attitude toward nature would an environmentalist convey in a description of a forest?
2. Besides the fact that they study and care about amphibians, what does the name "phib freaks" suggest about these people?

The trail winds past fern-cloaked spring and puddles yellow with pollen. A winter wren follows us from the safety of the deep woods. We sally off the trail at every amphibian-promising seep as the walk draws us ever deeper into the emerald-green magic of the forest. Lichens cling to our clothes as we brush past them. Fawn lilies beckon us with shy beauty. By the time we arrive at the cabins of the Ancient Forest Center compound, we have left behind homework, deadlines, and the detritus of our workaday worlds. Under the canopy of trees that began life before Christopher Columbus, we are learning to sense which streams likely harbor coastal tail frogs, which decaying logs might hide clouded salamanders. We are becoming phib freaks.

QUESTIONS FOR DISCUSSION

1. What verb does Little use instead of *walk*? What type of walking does this verb describe?
2. What does Little mean by "every amphibian-promising seep"? What is a seep?
3. The hikers leave behind "homework, deadlines, and the detritus of our workaday worlds." What is *detritus*? Why do you think Little uses this word instead of a more common synonym?
4. Little could have written "we are learning to sense which streams likely *contain* coastal tail frogs." Why is *harbor* a better word choice? How does it suggest more than simply a stream that *contains* frogs?

5. *Personification* is a type of figurative language that writers use. It involves assigning human traits and behaviors to nonhumans. What are some examples of personification in this passage?
6. What is Little's dominant impression in this description? What words work together to convey that impression?
7. What does it mean to become a "phib freak"?

SELECTION 3   MyWritingLab

Clog Dancing at the Illinois State Fair

David Foster Wallace

This essay is from the writer David Foster Wallace, who describes his experience of watching a dance competition at the Illinois State Fair. The article was published in 1994 in Harper's *magazine, a journal whose readers are typically well educated and usually come from urban areas.*

PRE-READING PROMPT

1. What do you know about clog dancing? What kind of people do you expect would clog dance at a state fair?
2. Since most people do not know what clog dancing is, nor do they have an interest in it, what would a writer have to do to generate curiosity about such a topic?
3. What do you think is a writer's biggest challenge in trying to describe something as intricate as a dance?

1   I'm on a teetery stool watching the Illinois Prairie Cloggers competition in a structure called the Twilight Ballroom that's packed with ag-folks and well over 1000 degrees. I'd nipped in here only to get a bottle of soda pop on my way to the Truck and Tractor Pull. By now the pull's got to be nearly over, and in half an hour the big U.S.A.C. dirt-track auto race starts. But I cannot tear myself away from the scene in here. I'd imagined goony Jed Clampett types in tattered hats and hobnail boots, a-stompin' and a-whoopin', etc. I guess clogging, Scotch-Irish in origin and the dance of choice in Appalachia, did used to involve actual clogs and boots and slow stomps. But clogging has now **miscegenated** with square dancing and honky-tonk boogie to become a kind of intricately synchronized, absolutely kick-ass country tap dance.

miscegenated: Literally means married or living with someone of another race; here it is used to indicate a "marriage" between very different types of music.

2   There are teams from Pekin, Le Roy, Rantoul, Cairo, Morton. They each do three numbers. The music is up-tempo country or dance-pop. Each team has anywhere from four to ten dancers. Few of the women are under thirty-five, fewer still under 175 pounds. They are country mothers, red-cheeked gals with bad dye jobs and big pretty legs. They wear western-wear tops and midiskirts with multiple ruffled slips underneath; and every once in a while they grab handfuls of cloth and flip the skirts up like cancan dancers. When they do this, they either yip or whoop, as the spirit moves them. The men all have thinning hair and cheesy rural faces, and their skinny legs are rubberized blurs. The men's western shirts have piping on the chest and shoulders. The teams are all color-coordinated—blue and white, black and red. The white shoes all the dancers wear look like golf shoes with metal taps clamped on.

3   Their numbers are everything from Waylon and Tammy to Aretha, Miami Sound Machine, Neil Diamond's "America." The routines have some standard tap-dance moves—sweep, flare, chorus-line kicking. But it is fast and sustained and choreographed down to the last wristflick. And square dancing's genes can be seen in the upright, square-shouldered postures on the floor, and there's a kind of florally enfolding tendency to the choreography, some of which uses high-speed **promenades**. But it is methedrine-paced and exhausting to watch because your own feet move; and it is erotic in a way that MTV looks lame. The cloggers' feet are too fast to be seen, really, but they all tap out the exact same rhythm. A typical routine is something like: *ta*tatatat*a*tatatat*a*tata. The variations around the basic rhythm are **baroque**. When they kick or spin, the two-beat absence of tap **complexifies** the pattern.

4   The audience is packed in right to the edge of the portable hardwood flooring. The teams are mostly married couples. The men are either rail-thin or have hanging guts. A couple of the men on a blue-and-white team are great fluid Astaire-like dancers, but mostly it is the women who compel. The men have constant smiles, but the women look orgasmic; they're the really serious ones, transported. Their yips and whoops are involuntary, pure exclamation. They are arousing. The audience claps **savvily** on the backbeat and whoops when the women do. It is almost all folks from the ag and livestock shows—the flannel shirts, khaki pants, seed caps and freckles. The spectators are soaked in sweat and extremely happy. I think this is the ag-community's special treat, a chance here to cut loose a little while their animals sleep in the heat. The transactions between cloggers and crowd seem **synecdochic** of the fair as a whole: a culture talking to itself, presenting credentials for its own inspection, bean farmers and herbicide brokers and 4-H sponsors and people who drive pickup trucks because they really need them. They eat non-fair food from insulated hampers and drink beer and pop and stomp in perfect time and put their hands on neighbors' shoulders to shout in their ears while the cloggers whirl and fling sweat in the crowd.

promenades: Dancers moving together in a square dance

baroque: extravagant, ornate

complexifies: makes more difficult or complex

savvily: in a wise or perceptive way

synecdochic: representative

⁵   There are no black people in the Twilight Ballroom, and the awakened looks on the younger ag-kids' faces have this astonished aspect, like they didn't realize their race could dance like this. Three married couples from Rantoul, wearing full western bodysuits the color of raw coal, weave an incredible filigree of high-speed tap around Aretha's "R-E-S-P-E-C-T," and there's no hint of racial irony in the room; the song has been made this people's own, emphatically. This Nineties version of clogging does have something sort of **pugnaciously** white about it, a kind of performative nose-thumbing at M.C. Hammer. There's an atmosphere in the room—not racist, but aggressively white. It's hard to describe—the atmosphere is the same at a lot of rural Midwest events. It is not like a black person who came in would be ill treated; it's more like it would just never occur to a black person to come here.

> **pugnaciously:**   aggressively

⁶   I can barely hold the table still to scribble journalistic impressions, the floor is rumbling under so many boots and sneakers. The record player is old-fashioned, the loudspeakers are shitty, and it sounds fantastic. Two of the dancing Rantoul wives are fat, but with great legs. Who could practice this kind of tapping as much as they must and stay fat? I think maybe rural Midwestern women are just congenitally big. But these people clogging get down. And they do it as a troupe, a collective, with none of the narcissistic look-at-me grandstanding of great dancers in rock clubs. They hold hands and whirl each other around and in and out, tapping like mad, their torsos upright and almost formal, as if only incidentally attached to the blur of legs below. It goes on and on. I'm rooted to my stool.

QUESTIONS FOR DISCUSSION

Interest

1. The author was not initially interested in clog dancing. What does he tell us in the introduction to spark the readers' curiosity and make us want to read on?

Details

2. Do you think Wallace meets the challenge of describing a dance? Which details work best to create a dominant impression of the clog dancers?
3. If the clog dancers read Wallace's essay, which details would they find flattering? Which might they find offensive? Again, why do you think Wallace has chosen such a blend of diverse details?
4. Which details suggest Wallace's admiration of the clog dancers?

Explanation

5. Which descriptive examples stand out to you as a reader? Why are they important, and why do you think Wallace chose to spend so much time describing them? What is the point of these examples?

6. Wallace describes the scene as "a culture talking to itself." As an outsider, is Wallace fair in his description of this culture? Why or why not? Which examples support that statement? Does he need to explain that idea more?

7. What is the distinction Wallace tries to make between being racist versus being "aggressively white"? Is his explanation clear? Why or why not?

Audience

8. What seems to be Wallace's attitude toward the clog dancers? Do his details primarily suggest admiration or ridicule or something else? Support your observation with specific examples.

Style

9. Think about the fast-moving dance and the excitement Wallace describes. How does he use sentence structure to try to mimic the fast-paced rhythm of the dancers? (Hint: Look at his use of series, the word *and*, and dashes.)

10. Writers are often told to keep their writing consistent in style and level of language. However, in his first paragraph Wallace uses words that are not usually found in the same piece—i.e., *goony*, *a-whoopin'*, *miscegenated*, *intricately synchronized*, and *kick-ass*. What are some other examples of this blend of levels of language in this essay? Why do you think Wallace uses this approach?

I D E A S for Your Own Writing   My**Writing**Lab

Observing and Describing a Dance

The philosopher Friedrich Nietzsche said, "Dancing in all its forms cannot be excluded from the curriculum of all noble education; dancing with the feet, with ideas, with words, and, need I add that one must also be able to dance with the pen?"

Let's try dancing with our pens—or computers—by writing a descriptive essay about dancing. Observe a dance and then describe it in a way that engages readers and makes the subject "real" as Wallace does in his essay on clog dancing. The Internet is full of videos showing a variety of dancing styles. Here are some kinds of dances you might observe:

ballet	belly	flamenco	hip hop	jitterbug	swing	salsa
ballroom	country	western	folk	polka	square	tap

Or you could simply find an interesting video of a person dancing from the heart and not following any particular style.

Once you have found a video of a dance that captures your interest, watch it several times and write down impressions and images the visuals evoke. Like Wallace, you can make your own emotions and reactions a part of the description. As you begin to write your paper, think of the **dominant impression** you want to make about this kind of dancing and use your details to shape this impression for the readers. If possible, show your classmates the video of the dance you chose and follow it with a reading of your description.

This assignment began with a quote. Sometimes writers can effectively use quotations to begin a piece of writing because they choose a quote that connects to the point the writing will make. Here are some quotes about dance that you might use to begin this essay. Choose one that best fits your description's dominant impression.

Dancing is the poetry of the foot.   —*John Dryden*

We're fools whether we dance or not, so we might as well dance.
                                                      —*Japanese Proverb*

Nobody cares if you can't dance well. Just get up and dance.
                                                      —*Dave Barry*

Dancing is like dreaming with your feet!
                                                      —*Constanze*

The truest expression of a people is in its dance and in its music.
Bodies never lie.   —*Agnes de Mille*

Kids: they dance before they learn there is anything that isn't music.
                                                      —*William Stafford*

To dance is to be out of yourself. Larger, more beautiful, more powerful.
                                                      —*Agnes de Mille*

It is of course possible to dance a prayer.   —*Glade Byron Addams*

There is a bit of insanity in dancing that does everybody a great deal of good.   —*Edwin Denby*

To watch us dance is to hear our hearts speak.   —*Hopi Indian Saying*

And those who were seen dancing were thought to be insane by those who could not hear the music.   —*Friedrich Nietzsche*

Dance, even if you have nowhere to do it but your living room.
                                                      —*Kurt Vonnegut*

SELECTION 4   MyWritingLab

The Knife

Richard Selzer

Drawing from the experiences of his medical career as a surgeon and professor of surgery at Yale University, Richard Selzer has written extensively about the humanity of both doctor and patient. In the following selection from Mortal Lessons: Notes on the Art of Surgery *(1974), Selzer takes readers into a doctor's mind during the course of a surgery.*

PRE-READING PROMPT

1. What do you imagine goes through a doctor's mind during surgery? Do you think a surgeon feels confident? Nervous? A little of both?
2. How would you imagine a surgeon reacts when he or she finds that a patient has a serious, even fatal, condition?
3. We may think of surgery, of cutting into a living human being, as being bloody and somewhat gruesome. How can it also be beautiful?

1   One holds the knife as one holds the bow of a cello or a tulip—by the stem. Not palmed nor gripped nor grasped, but lightly, with the tips of the fingers. The knife is not for pressing. It is for drawing across the field of skin. Like a slender fish, it waits, at the ready, then, go! It darts, followed by a fine wake of red. The flesh parts, falling away to yellow globules of fat. Even now, after so many times, I still marvel at its power—cold, gleaming, silent. More, I am still struck with a kind of dread that it is I in whose hand the blade travels, that my hand is its vehicle, that yet again this terrible steel-bellied thing and I have conspired for a most unnatural purpose, the laying open of the body of a human being.

2   A stillness settles in my heart and is carried to my hand. It is the quietude of resolve layered over fear. And it is this resolve that lowers us, my knife and me, deeper and deeper into the person beneath. It is an entry into the body that is nothing like a caress; still, it is among the gentlest of acts. Then stroke and stroke again, and we are joined by other instruments, hemostats and forceps, until the wound blooms with strange flowers whose looped handles fall to the sides in steely array.

3   There is sound, the tight click of clamps fixing teeth into severed blood vessels, the snuffle and gargle of the suction machine clearing the field of blood for the next stroke, the litany of monosyllables with which one prays his way down and in: clamp, sponge, suture, tie, cut. And there is color. The green of the cloth, the white of the sponges, the red and yellow of the body. Beneath the fat lies the fascia, the tough fibrous sheet encasing the muscles. It must be sliced and the red beef of the muscles separated. Now there are retractors to hold apart the

wound. Hands move together, part, weave. We are fully engaged, like children absorbed in a game or the craftsmen of some place like Damascus.

4   Deeper still. The peritoneum, pink and gleaming and membranous, bulges into the wound. It is grasped with forceps, and opened. For the first time we can see into the cavity of the abdomen. Such a primitive place. One expects to find drawings of buffalo on the walls. The sense of trespassing is keener now, heightened by the world's light illuminating the organs, their secret colors revealed—maroon and salmon and yellow. The vista is sweetly vulnerable at this moment, a kind of welcoming. An arc of the liver shines high and on the right, like a dark sun. It laps over the pink sweep of the stomach, from whose lower border the gauzy omentum is draped, and through which veil one sees, sinuous, slow as just-fed snakes, the indolent coils of the intestine.

5   You turn aside to wash your gloves. It is a ritual cleansing. One enters this temple doubly washed. Here is man as microcosm, representing in all his parts the earth, perhaps the universe.

6   I must confess that the priestliness of my profession has ever been impressed on me. In the beginning there are vows, taken with all solemnity. Then there is the endless harsh novitiate of training, much fatigue, much sacrifice. At last one emerges as celebrant, standing close to the truth lying curtained in the Ark of the body. Not surplice and cassock but mask and gown are your regalia. You hold no chalice, but a knife. There is no wine, no water. There are only the facts of blood and flesh.

7   And if the surgeon is like a poet, then the scars you have made on countless bodies are like verses into the fashioning of which you have poured your soul. I think that if years later I were to see the trace from an old incision of mine, I should know it at once, as one recognizes his pet expressions.

8   But mostly you are a traveler in a dangerous country, advancing into the moist and jungly cleft your hands have made. Eyes and ears are shuttered from the land you left behind; mind empties itself of all other thought. You are the root of groping fingers. It is a fine hour for the fingers, their sense of touch so enhanced. The blind must know this feeling. Oh, there is risk everywhere. One goes lightly. The spleen. No! No! Do not touch the spleen that lurks below the left leaf of the diaphragm, a manta ray in a coral cave, its bloody tongue protruding. One poke and it might rupture, exploding with sudden hemorrhage. The filmy omentum must not be torn, the intestine scraped or denuded. The hand finds the liver, palms it, fingers running along its sharp lower edge, admiring. Here are the twin mounds of the kidneys, the apron of the omentum hanging in front of the intestinal coils. One lifts it aside and the fingers dip among the loops, searching, mapping territory, establishing boundaries. Deeper still, and the womb is touched, then held like a small muscular bottle—the womb and its earlike appendages, the ovaries. How they do nestle in the cup of a man's hand, their power all dormant. They are frailty itself.

9   There is a hush in the room. Speech stops. The hands of the others, assistants and nurses, are still. Only the voice of the patient's respiration remains. It is the rhythm of a quiet sea, the sound of waiting. Then you speak, slowly, the terse entries of a Himalayan climber reporting back.

10   "The stomach is okay. Greater curvature clean. No sign of ulcer. Pylorus, duodenum fine. Now comes the gallbladder. No stones. Right kidney, left, all right. Liver . . . uh-oh."

11   Your speech lowers to a whisper, falters, stops for a long, long moment, then picks up again at the end of a sigh that comes through your mask like a last exhalation.

12   "Three big hard ones in the left lobe, one on the right. Metastatic deposits. Bad, bad. Where's the primary? Got to be coming from somewhere."

13   The arm shifts direction and the fingers drop lower and lower into the pelvis—the body impaled now upon the arm of the surgeon to the hilt of the elbow.

14   "Here it is."

15   The voice goes flat, all business now.

16   "Tumor in the sigmoid colon, wrapped all around it, pretty tight. We'll take out a sleeve of the bowel. No colostomy. Not that, anyway. But, God, there's a lot of it down there. Here, you take a feel."

17   You step back from the table, and lean into a sterile basin of water, resting on stiff arms, while the others locate the cancer . . . .

18   What is it, then, this thing, the knife, whose shape is virtually the same as it was three thousand years ago, but now with its head grown detachable? Before steel, it was bronze. Before bronze, stone—then back into unremembered time. Did man invent it or did the knife precede him here, hidden under ages of vegetation and hoof prints, lying in wait to be discovered, picked up, used?

19   The scalpel is in two parts, the handle and the blade. Joined, it is six inches from tip to tip. At one end of the handle is a narrow notched prong upon which the blade is slid, then snapped into place. Without the blade, the handle has a blind, decapitated look. It is helpless as a trussed maniac. But slide on the blade, click it home, and the knife springs instantly to life. It is headed now, edgy, leaping to mount the fingers for the gallop to its feast.

20   Now is the moment from which you have turned aside, from which you have averted your gaze, yet toward which you have been hastened. Now the scalpel sings along the flesh again, its brute run unimpeded by germs or other frictions. It is a slick slide home, a barracuda spurt, a rip of embedded talon. One listens, and almost hears the whine—nasal, high, delivered through that gleaming metallic snout. The flesh splits with its own kind of moan. It is like the penetration of rape.

21   The breasts of women are cut off, arms and legs sliced to the bone to make ready for the saw, eyes freed from sockets, intestines lopped. The hand of the surgeon rebels. Tension boils through his pores, like sweat. The flesh of the patient retaliates with hemorrhage, and the blood chases the knife wherever it is withdrawn.

22   Within the belly a tumor squats, toadish, fungoid. A gray mother and her brood. The only thing it does not do is croak. It too is hacked from its bed as the carnivore knife lips the blood, turning in it in a kind of ecstasy of plenty, a gluttony after the long fast. It is just for this that the knife was created, tempered, heated, its violence beaten into paper-thin force.

23   At last a little thread is passed into the wound and tied. The monstrous booming fury is stilled by a tiny thread. The tempest is silenced. The operation is over. On the table, the knife lies spent, on its side, the bloody meal smear-dried upon its flanks. The knife rests.

24   And waits.

QUESTIONS FOR DISCUSSION

I nterest

1. Why do you think Selzer begins and ends this essay by focusing on the knife? Why is the knife given as much—or even more—attention than the human characters, the doctor and the patient?

2. After getting this vivid look inside the mind of a surgeon, how was this description what you might have expected? What most surprised you?

D etails

3. Because they are abstract, emotions are often very difficult for writers to convey. Selzer describes a range of emotions he feels as he carries out the surgery; some he states explicitly and others he implies through his details. What are some of these emotions? Which of them are unexpected?

4. How does the dominant impression of the knife in action change from the first half of the essay to the second half? Why do you think the imagery and the "character" of the knife is so different in these two parts of the essay?

E xplanation

5. What is the doctor's reaction to finding the cancerous tumor? Why do you think Selzer keeps this part of the essay so brief?

6. How does Selzer keep his explanation of a surgery clear and understandable for those without medical expertise?

A udience

7. One might expect a doctor to be very objective, especially during a surgery. Does Selzer seem objective in his description? Explain why or why not.

8. Selzer describes the surgeon as a "priest," a "poet," and a "traveler." How does he convey the reverence of a priest, the insights of a poet, and the sense of discovery in a traveler?

Style

9. Selzer frequently uses figurative language in this piece, especially similes and metaphors. Give five examples of imagery or figurative language that you found particularly vivid.
10. Selzer also uses very clinical language, the surgeon's "code." Give examples of words that indicate the author is indeed a surgeon.
11. Sometimes Selzer uses "you"—as though the reader were the surgeon. Do you think this is an accidental slip in his use of first person, or does this seem deliberate? Explain.
12. Selzer ends the essay with a very short, very stark sentence about the knife: "And waits." Is this an effective conclusion? Why or why not?

I D E A S for Your Own Writing   MyWritingLab

Thinking Through the Job

Describe an activity that you perform regularly. It may be part of your work, like checking groceries or waiting on tables. Or it may be a household chore or yard work or an activity that is part of a hobby. As you describe the activity, describe the thoughts and emotions you feel as you undertake it. Like Selzer, unify your thoughts and actions with descriptive imagery that enhances the readers' understanding of both what you do and your feelings about this activity.

Through the Patient's Eyes

Selzer describes a medical procedure through the eyes of the surgeon. Describe a procedure you have undergone in the same way. You might, perhaps, describe getting stitches or having a broken bone set or even getting a filling in your tooth. Like Selzer, make the description of the procedure itself vivid and expressive, and at the same time incorporate your thoughts and feelings as a patient. Just as Selzer helps patients understand the mind of their surgeon, your essay may help medical professionals better understand the thoughts and feelings of their patients.

Bring a Tool to Life

Selzer describes the surgeon's knife in a way that makes it seem almost alive. Describe a tool that you use regularly in a similar way. For example, the tool can be one you use in gardening or when working on a car or woodworking. It can be a pair of scissors, a paintbrush, or even a pen. Your goal is to make your readers see the tool in a vivid and imaginative way that makes them better appreciate its function.

SELECTION 5   MyWritingLab

Just Off Main Street

Elmaz Abinader

In the next essay, the author, poet, performance artist, and activist Elmaz Abinader draws from her experience growing up Arab American in an all-white Appalachian coal mining community. Her books, Children of the Roojme: A Family's Journey from Lebanon, *and* In the Country of My Dreams. . . ., *and her play,* Country of Origin *chronicle the experiences of Arabs and Arab Americans. In the following article, taken from the U.S. Department of State publication,* Writers on America, *Abinader describes her journey toward embracing her cultural identity.*

PRE-READING PROMPT

1. How important is your cultural heritage to you and your family? Do you feel comfortable sharing that heritage with others outside of your family? Why or why not?
2. What kinds of situations might cause people in the United States to hide their cultural heritage and to simply try to "blend in"? What might make this difficult?
3. Today in the United States do you think it is easier or more difficult to publically embrace one's cultural heritage than it was in the past? Why or why not?

1   When I was young, my house had a magic door. Outside that door was the small Pennsylvania town where I grew up. Main Street ran in front of our house bearing the standard downtown features: a bank, a newsstand, the hardware store, the auto parts supply, and other retail businesses. Families strolled the streets, particularly on weekends looking at the displays of furniture in Kaufman's giant window, the posters for movies hanging behind the glass at the Rex Theatre, and the mannequins, missing hands or fingers, sporting the latest fashions in the windows of my aunt's clothing store. In those days, the early 1960s, the small businesses in a town like Masontown fed the community's needs for food, clothing, and shelter.

2   My family's shops took their positions on Main Street as well: Nader's Shoe Store, Nader's Department Store, and the Modernnaire Restaurant. From the face of it, our businesses looked like any others and we gratefully satisfied the local mother trying to buy church-worthy shoes for the children, the father in for a good cigar and the newspaper, and the after-school crowd, who jittered near the juke box on the restaurant tiles. My father and my uncle stood in the doorways of their establishments, perfectly dressed in gray suits and white shirts, ties, and glossy polished shoes.

3   At that moment, frozen in second grade, at the threshold of the store, I saw no difference between my father, uncle, and the people who passed by. Many of them too sent their children to Mrs. Duffy for piano lessons, shopped at the A & P, and bar-b-qued in the backyard on the Fourth of July. Many of my dad's customers had their children in All Saints School with me. Their daughters had shiny bikes with streamers flowing from the handlebars. The popular girls, Jeannie and Renee, wore freshly polished Mary Jane shoes every day, and discussed quite vocally their ever growing collection of Barbie doll paraphernalia. I listened with fascination to the descriptions of a house for Barbie, her car, and her wardrobe. Jeannie wrapped her finger around her blond pony tail as she described Barbie's ball gown. Renee pulled her spit curl into a C as she showed us pictures of her trip to Virginia Beach.

4   In these moments of social exchange, the illusion of similarity between me and the girls in my class floated away, bubble light. Despite sharing the same school uniform, being in the Brownies, singing soprano in the choir, and being a good speller, my life and theirs were separated by the magic door. And although my classmates didn't know what was behind that portal, they circled me in the playground and shouted "darkie" at my braids trying to explode into a kinky mop, or "ape" at my arms bearing mahogany hair against my olive pale skin. It was dizzying and my stomach squirrel-squealed in loneliness.

5   I dragged myself home to our gray-shingled house on Main Street feeling the weight of my book bag and the heaviness of the differences between me and the girls jumping rope just across the street. As I pulled on the silver aluminum handle of the screen door that led to the hallway of our house, the rust crumbled against my thumb. Nothing was particularly enchanting about this door, but when I entered, the context of the world changed.

6   Drawing me from the entrance, down the hall, to the dining room, was one of my favorite smells. It was Wednesday, the day of the week when my mother covered the table for eight with newspaper, dragged two large blue cans from the pantry, and lined up the cookie sheets. By the time I arrived home from school in the afternoon, the house smelled of Arabic bread and loaves and loaves of the round puffy disks leaned against each other in rows on the table. She made triangles of spinach pies, cinnamon rolls, and fruit pies filled with pears from the trees growing on our land. Before greeting me, she looked up, her face flour-smudged, and said, "There are 68 loaves. You can have one."

7   By now, my sisters have joined me at one end of the table where we pass the apple butter to each other to slather on the warm bread. When Arabic bread comes out of the oven, it is filled with air and looks like a little pillow; as it cools, the bread flattens to what Americans recognize as "pita" bread. Other bread was rarely eaten in our house; even when we put hot dogs on the grill, they were dropped into a half of "cohbs," then covered with ketchup.

8   The smell was hypnotic and mitigated the melancholy I carried home with my lessons to do that night. The revelry ended soon after we finished our treat.

Each child of the six of us had after-school duties. My three brothers reported to the store to clean and manage the inventory, and we three girls shared the demands of house and garden. In the summer, we weeded, watered, and picked the vegetables; in the fall, we reported to the basement where we canned fruits, beans, jams, and pickles. Between these seasons were endless piles of laundry, ironing, and cleaning to maintain the nine people who filled our little house. Barbies, coloring books, after-school sports were other children's worlds, not ours.

9   Behind the magic door, the language shifted as well. Mother-to-daughter orders were delivered in Arabic—homework, conversations, and the rosary, in the most precise English possible. Three things dominated our lives: devotion to God, obedience to our parents, and good grades in school. A sliver of an error in any of these areas was punished with swiftness and severity. The reputation of our family relied on our perfection and my parents had no idea that their struggling-to-be-perfect daughters digested unsavory ridicule from their peers.

10   Our social interactions on the other side of the door had little weight inside the house. We had a different community who gathered on weekends and during the summer. Relatives from towns around Pennsylvania and Ohio filled our living room and dining room, circling the table crowded with my mother's fabulous array of Arabic dishes: *hummus*, chick bean dip, *baba ghanouj*, eggplant with sesame, stuffed grape leaves, shish kebob, *kibbee*, raw or fried lamb and bulgur wheat patties, a leg of lamb, a turkey stuffed with rice and raisins and platter after platter of side dishes. The famous Arabic bread sat skyscraper high on plates at either end.

11   My uncle, the priest, blessed the table, and the chatter of Arabic began as cousins dipped their bread, scooped up the tabouleh salad, and daintily bit the sweet baklava pastry. As the end of the meal approached, we pushed slightly away from the table, as my father told a story of the old days, or someone read a letter from Lebanon; or a political argument snarled across the empty dishes.

12   We girls cleared the table and Arabic music wound its way out of the record player. Before we knew it, someone started a line dance and others linked arms, and stomping and kicking and clapping shook the house. As children and as worker bees, we were busy, both cleaning dishes and bringing the adults anything they wanted, as well as standing up to having our cheeks pinched and our bodies lifted into the air.

13   My family scenes filled me with joy and belonging, but I knew none of it could be shared on the other side of that door. The chant of schoolyard slurs would intensify. Looking different was enough; having a father with a heavy accent already marked me, dancing in circles would bury me as a social outcast.

QUESTIONS FOR DISCUSSION

I nterest

1. How does Abinader try to create interest for the reader? Where is she successful and where could she have done a better job? Explain with specific details.

2. Do the opening descriptions prepare you for the burst of cruelty as Abinader describes her classmates' taunting? Why is it particularly ironic or surprising that the cruelty takes place at this particular school?

Details

3. What details in the first three paragraphs help you picture Masontown, Pennsylvania, where Abinader grew up? Does the town she describes seem very different from small towns today? Why or why not?
4. What are some of the vivid descriptive details Abinader uses to describe the food prepared in her family's home? Why do you think she goes into such detail about food?

Explanation

5. What do you think were some of the reasons Abinader kept her family life secret and apart from her life outside the family home? What parts of the essay explain this?
6. Which of the details about life behind the "magic" door reveal this family's distinct culture? Which of the details could describe almost any American home?

Audience

7. How does Abinader convey her dominant impression—sense of "joy and belonging"—she felt with her family?
8. What do you think Abinader most wants her readers to understand about her Arab culture?

Style

9. How does Abinader use the images of doors to unify her essay? Is this an effective device? Why or why not?
10. Find the sentences in which Abinader uses a colon (:). What kinds of key points do these sentence constructions emphasize?

I D E A S for Your Own Writing   MyWritingLab

We Are What We Eat

Describe a meal that your family enjoys and that brings you all together. Perhaps the meal represents your cultural heritage or region or perhaps it is simply a tradition of your family alone. Make your description of the meal vivid with lots of concrete details, so your readers can see, taste, and smell the meal. Imagine that this descriptive piece will be part of a feature article in a food magazine entitled "Special Meals That Bring Families Together."

Descriptive writing provides an opportunity to observe, analyze, and reflect on a specific place and your experience(s) there.

Descriptive Place-Based Paragraph or Essay

Your Task: This assignment asks you to observe your subject closely and then present your observations in a way that *informs and engages your audience*. The reader should walk away from your paragraph or essay with a great sense—a visual impression—of what this place is like (through varying levels of detail) and why it is important or interesting. Essentially, your paragraph or essay should present a **dominant impression** of the place. Use description, observation, and dialogue if appropriate to get your main point across. You have two options for this paper:

Option A: Describe a place that is personally important to you. Provide concrete and specific details so the reader can easily visualize this place and understand why it is so important. The "place" you describe must be focused. For example, you would not want to describe your grandparents' entire farm (way too broad), but you could detail the kitchen in your grandparents' house (focused).

Option B: Describe a place in your community or neighborhood that you find unique or interesting. Through the details you provide, the paragraph's or essay's dominant impression should demonstrate why others should recognize this place's value. Give an account of the action (or inaction) that typically occurs there, making sure to describe the place in vivid detail. *Note:* You cannot use a place that is commonly known or is a tourist attraction. The place you describe must be focused. For example, you would not want to describe an entire city park (way too broad), but you could detail a specific playground area in that park (focused). You would not describe all of a shopping district (way too broad), but you could detail a unique shop within the district (focused).

A Successful Descriptive Place-Based Paragraph or Essay . . .

- Is entertaining, easy to read, and thought provoking.
- Leads the reader to recognize a dominant impression about this place.
- Relates specific, concrete, and vivid details about this place.

- Has clearly connected ideas and varied sentences.
- Provides a medium level of tone and diction—not too formal, but not too informal.
- Is free of mechanical and proofreading errors.

Problem in Your Community Letter

Descriptive writing can be very effective when you write letters to different audiences (newspapers, city officials, or college staff) in order to alert them to problems and/or suggest solutions to problems.

Your Task: Write a one- or two-page letter that describes and discusses a particular problem at your college or in your community (your neighborhood or city or suburb). Describe your subject, demonstrate its existence through strong details, and explain why it is a pressing problem that citizens need to address. Consider what your readers already know about the subject and how your essay might expand their knowledge. Also consider why this problem or issue is important to you and why others should care about it.

Your Audience: Address your letter to an individual or a group of people who have decision-making power at your college or in your community. In the letter, you need to provide your address, the date, and the name of the person and his or her address at the top, above "Dear Mr. or Ms. _____:"; then describe the problem in the body of the document.

A Successful Problem in Your Community Letter . . .

- Needs to have clear points with detailed description about one problem in your college or community.
- Provides a recognizable thesis or organizing idea (what the problem is and why is it important) by the end of the second paragraph at the latest.
- Uses detailed, specific, and concrete details to inform the reader about the problem and argue why it is important.
- Employs personal experience and examples from others' experiences to show why the issue is a problem.
- Does not venture into whining, but details the problem with specifics.
- Uses a letter format to convey the message (proper information at the top, single-spaced paragraphs, and double-spacing in between paragraphs).

- Uses clear transitions and other linking devices, so the sentences work together.
- Provides a medium level of tone and diction—not too formal, but not too informal.
- Is free of mechanical and proofreading errors.

Real Estate Description: Describing to Make the Sale

Clear, vivid descriptive language is vital to any sales-related writing.

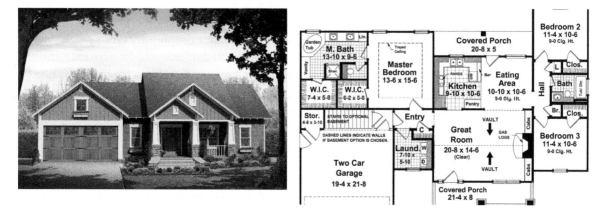

Your Role: Howard and Sweeney Realtors, a real estate firm in the Chicago area, has recently hired you as an advertising copywriter. Howard and Sweeney show homes throughout the Chicago metro area, but they tend to work mostly in the northwestern and northern suburbs. Your first assignment is to write a description of this home in Palatine, Illinois, which will be featured in a high-end real estate magazine that comes out every month.

Your Writing Task: This will be a feature article of several paragraphs. Make your details specific and vivid, so they will entice prospective buyers. Also, be accurate and realistic. Houses do not typically come furnished, for example, so do not spend time describing sofas and fish tanks. Focus on the architectural elements and other features that would be of interest to potential homebuyers.

Working with the picture and layout map of the home is essential, but here are some background details that should help you craft your article. Palatine is known to have a good school district—Illinois school district 211. Since homebuyers like this school district, this is sought-after property. The new homes in this subdivision tend to not have basements. However, this house has an unfinished basement.

The subdivision in which this home is located is a new development that partly took out older homes and built new ones on existing property, so there are mature trees and still some woods left throughout the subdivision. Many families have moved into this neighborhood over the past few years.

Your Readers: This home is in a new, upscale neighborhood of single-family homes. Your target audience is young families.

A Successful Real Estate Description . . .

- Provides concise, relevant, and sufficient details that work together to create a positive dominant impression.
- Moves readers through the house in a logical manner by taking them on an imaginary walk through the home.
- Keeps in mind that potential buyers are looking for a house in a quiet neighborhood in a good school district.
- Uses clear transitions and other linking devices, so the sentences work together.
- Provides a medium level of tone and diction—not too formal, but not too informal.
- Is free of mechanical and proofreading errors.

CHAPTER AT A GLANCE

Learning Objectives	How they connect to writing at college . . .
❶ Create a dominant impression.	A *strong dominant impression* is the crucial point of the description, the overall feeling it creates. It makes the writing "real" to your reader.
❷ Use concrete, specific, and inviting details.	• *Concrete details* refer to descriptions in writing that appeal to the five senses: sight, sound, touch, taste, and smell. • *Specific details* bring writing to life; they are "lightning," not "lightning bugs."

Learning Objectives	How they connect to writing at college . . .
❸ Use descriptive verbs.	Strong writers avoid weak linking verbs—like *is, are, was, were, have, has*—and instead use strong action verbs that add interest and description—verbs like *waddle, groaned, soared,* and *hissed*.
❹ Put **I D E A S** to work in descriptive writing.	*To put* **I D E A S** *to work in descriptive writing,* ask and answer the following questions. How will you create interest? Which details will you provide, and how will you develop them? What explanation is needed? How can you "make it real" for your audience through word choice and, specifically, active verbs? How can you make the paper read with style? Analyzing the techniques successful writers use as you read their work and applying them as you write will improve your writing.

> **MyWritingLab** Visit **Chapter 6, "Descriptive Writing,"** in MyWritingLab to test your understanding of the chapter objectives.

Reflective Writing 7

The stereotypical look of reflection is someone staring off into the distance. This pose captures the idea that reflection is when we think deeply. Likewise, reflective writing presents one person's point of view in an intriguing way and is supposed to make people think beyond the obvious.

Reflective writing helps people examine their lives, grow intellectually, and generate ideas for their academic work as well as for their jobs. John C. Bean, a professor of writing at Seattle University, describes reflective writing as the "thinking-on-paper writing we do to discover, develop, and clarify our own ideas" (97).

The person who possibly started this type of writing—the reflective essay—is Michel de Montaigne, an aristocratic Frenchman who lived in the 17th century. In the French language, *essay* can be translated as "attempt"—a try at getting to the heart of the matter, an attempt to understand or to make sense of one's experience.

Today, people write personal journals, they have their own blogs, they write short notes on Facebook, and they tweet. In fact, with the strong influence of blogs and social networking sites, there is probably a lot more reflective writing than there used to be. Reflective writing helps people explore who they are: their backgrounds, influences on their lives, ideas that interest them, issues or problems that trouble them, and feelings they simply want to vent.

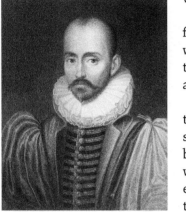
▲ Michel de Montaigne

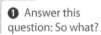
❶ Answer this question: So what?

MyWritingLab Visit Ch. 7 Reflective Writing in MyWritingLab to access the IDEAS videos.

Answer This Question: So What?

Like other aims of writing, reflective writing should have a point. In addition, unless it is for a personal journal or a diary, reflective writing will fail if you do not consider your readers.

Strong reflective writing moves readers beyond the obvious. When polished and ready for readers, a reflective essay makes something new or interesting. It captures and holds readers' imaginations and attention. This is the **I** in the **I D E A S** template.

Interpretation for the Reader—What Does It All Mean?

In a great deal of reflective writing, you will grapple with personal experiences, anecdotes, and various examples from your own or others' lives and then present them to readers for a *reason*, for a purpose. Through the act of reflective writing, you discover what you think or feel, but when you move to writing for an audience, you need to help readers see what you see or feel what you feel. You must sift through the ideas, examples, and evidence and lead readers to a new or interesting way of thinking about a subject.

The "So-What Factor"

James C. Raymond, Professor Emeritus at the University of Alabama, describes a writer's ability to move beyond the obvious as avoiding the "so-what factor." After reading your essay, readers should not think, "So what?" Instead, Professor Raymond says your interpretation of the subject should inform, interest, or surprise readers. You want them to think, "Wow, that's interesting! I hadn't thought about it that way before."

Move a Thesis from "So What?" to "That's Interesting!"

A "So what?" thesis typically states an obvious point—something most people already know. A "That's interesting!" thesis offers a point or an insight that grabs the readers' attention. Look at the following revisions of thesis statements for reflective essays.

So what?   Being in a car accident was a frightening experience.

Revised   Wrapping my car around a telephone pole taught me what is most important in life.

So what?   My boyfriend is a great guy.

Revised   My boyfriend has shown me that compromise is the key to a successful relationship.

So what?   It is hard to go to work and school.

Revised   Working my way through college has brought balance to my life.

So what?   My trip to the beach was a lot of fun.

Revised   My trip to Huntington Beach helped me appreciate the fragility of our environment.

Remember, your thesis plays an important role. It is the director that keeps your essay focused on the important insight you want your readers to understand after reading your reflections.

EXERCISE 7.1   Turn "So What?" into "That's Interesting."   MyWritingLab

Directions: Try your hand at revising some "So what?" thesis statements by making them more focused and directed toward an insight that will interest readers.

1. Music is important to me.

2. It is fun to hang out in my back yard.

3. Losing a loved one can be hard.

4. Helping others makes me feel good.

5. Everybody needs friends.

6. Holidays are great family times.

7. Attending college is challenging.

8. Peer pressure is bad.

9. I like going to movies.

10. Being sick or injured is no fun.

❷ Employ examples, anecdotes, and evidence for support.

Employ Examples, Anecdotes, and Evidence for Support

Once you have arrived at the point of your reflection, you must develop and support that point in a way that will continue to engage your readers and make them want to keep reading. As you read in Chapter 2 (pages 36–37), writers can use a variety of support in their writing such as examples, personal experiences or anecdotes, and evidence such as facts, statistics, and quotes.

Adrian, for example, was assigned the "Reflecting on a Current Event Essay" on page 216, which starts like this:

> Every day we are bombarded with current issues on television and radio and in newspapers and magazines. Sometimes these are issues on which we must take a stand, voicing our opinions in voting booths. Often our reactions to these issues or the stands we take for or against them have been shaped by the personal experiences in our lives. For this essay, you will write about how an experience in your life has shaped your view toward a current issue.

Adrian decided to write about unemployment. He used his own family's experiences since his father had been laid off for four months. He gave specific

▲ What current events—social, economic, political—have affected you and/or your friends and family?

examples of how his family had to dramatically cut expenses, including giving up cable television and family cell phone plans. He described how meatless pasta dinners became the norm in his family. Adrian told how hard it was for his mother to sell her car because the family could not afford the insurance and needed the money for basic bills. He also related how difficult it was for his father, a proud man, to apply for unemployment.

In addition to using examples and experiences from his own life, Adrian found a quote from Harry Truman that he thought summed up his family's experiences: "It's a recession when your neighbor loses his job; it's a depression when you lose yours." While his family went through a period of hard times, they were fortunate that his father did find another job. But Adrian realized other families are not so fortunate. He read in the *New York Times* that the average unemployed person in America spends more than nine months looking for work, and he included that sobering statistic in his paper.

As Adrian reflected on the experiences that shaped his opinions about the unemployment problem, he made those experiences vivid and real for his readers, and he chose evidence that further supported his thoughts and feelings about the issue.

EXERCISE 7.2   Identify Support in an Essay   MyWritingLab

Directions: One prime example of a reflective essay is Brent Staples' "Black Men and Public Space" in Chapter 2 (p. 38). In that essay, Staples uses short anecdotes, dialogue, description, narration, and medium-size and longer examples to guide the reader to think about how black men are depicted, perceived, and treated in American society.

Read that essay again and make a list of how many and what types of support Staples uses. Here are some basic categories for your list:

- anecdotes (a blend of very short, medium-size, and longer examples of personal experiences)
- what others say (sources)
- facts/statistics, and questions to make the reader think

After you have tallied up the results, make an outline of the organization of his supporting details. Then answer these questions:

- How would the essay have had a much different feel with a different organization?
- If you were asked to organize it differently, what would you do? Explain your reasons for your choices.

There are also cases where reflective essays use just one example or experience as a diving board from which to jump into thinking about certain ideas or particular topics. While, like Adrian, you can create an essay that uses a variety of support, another strategy is to play with one experience or example as a way to make the reader understand a concept or see something differently. In this chapter you will see in the essay "Why the Best Kids Books Are Written in Blood" that author Sherman Alexie uses multiple examples to make his point. On the other hand, in "Two Bad Bricks," Ajahn Brahm uses a single story or experience to make readers think.

EXERCISE 7.3   Exemplify a Thesis Statement   MyWritingLab

Directions: Take one of the thesis statements you revised in the previous practice and show how you might support it using each of the following types of support: *a short anecdote, dialogue, description, narration, a medium-size example*, and *a longer example.*

---

❸ Use concrete, specific, and inviting details.

Use Concrete, Specific, and Inviting Details

The sensory images you create with words frame what you want your audience to feel and think, so it is especially important to paint a picture for readers when relating personal experiences, examples, and anecdotes. In "The Day I Met Bruce Lee," Bonnie Devet selects words or phrases to make the reader feel a certain way or to evoke images. Examples include "staid, bespeckled, middle age college instructor," "weather worn stone," "prodded along," "standing like a sentinel," "patiently pronouncing," "short spiked hair like tiny Matterhorn peaks," and "a brief tenuous moment on a hilltop in a Seattle cemetery."

What makes her reflection memorable are the details, the ways in which she makes us see and hear her own experience. She makes it real for readers, so they can experience what she experienced. Like Devet, you have to make it real. Just as in descriptive writing, you will use imagery along with specific and concrete details to convey a message or a scene or recount an experience. The specific details often come from your own reflection and remembrances—what you choose to relate and to focus on for the benefit of the reader.

▲ How do you come up with concrete details that create vivid images or emotions in your readers?

EXERCISE 7.4   Expand an Example   MyWritingLab

Directions: Take the anecdote or one of the examples you came up with in the previous exercise and expand and develop it with details that paint a picture for your readers and reveal your attitude toward the subject.

❹ Put **I D E A S**
to work in reflective
writing.

MyWritingLab Visit
Ch. 7 Reflective Writing in
MyWritingLab to access
the IDEAS videos.

Put **I D E A S** to Work in Reflective Writing

When you write a reflective essay, you may find it helpful to use the clustering/ idea mapping detailed in Chapter 3 (p. 77) or another strategy for organizing and planning. You also have to consider whether you want to insert a thesis, a controlling idea, early on to orient the reader. Many writers who do reflective writing do not state the thesis in the beginning. Instead, they lead toward one in the conclusion (**delayed thesis**) or leave it up to the reader to draw connections or ideas from the essay (**implied thesis**). Even if you choose to write a reflective essay with a delayed or implied-thesis organization, you still need to think about these questions: "So what?" and "What's my point?"

Whether you are working with a number of personal experiences or one or two really important ones, generate specific details to make the experiences vivid and memorable. As you think through what details are most important, keep in mind **I D E A S**, which stands for **I**nterest, **D**etails, **E**xplanation, **A**udience, and **S**tyle. How will you create interest? What details will you provide, and how will you develop them? Which examples or experiences will you develop? How can you avoid a "so what?" reaction from your readers? How can you make the essay read with style?

Sam Johnston's teacher asked students to read "Why the Best Kids Books Are Written in Blood" (see p. 194), a reflective essay by Sherman Alexie. He then asked students to write on the following topic:

A "Seeing the Sides" Essay

Alexie uses a critic's comments about young adult literature as an opportunity to write his reflective article, but the essay leans heavily toward just his perspective. For this assignment, you need to use personal experience to look at an issue that has perplexed you. However, unlike Alexie, you must make sure you show that you can see and understand both or all of the sides of an issue. The subject you write about might be a personal or family issue—perhaps seeing why parents sometimes enforce strict curfews—or it might be a larger social issue, such as laws requiring helmets for motorcycle riders or a even a policy at your workplace. Write your essay for readers who may not always understand that some issues are more complicated than they seem at first glance.

Active Reading

Sam read Alexie's essay, and made notes in the margin. He paid careful attention to **I D E A S**, so he could learn techniques he could include in his own reflective essay.

Why the Best Kids Books Are Written in Blood   MyWritingLab

Sherman Alexie

This essay is by Sherman Alexie, a well-known author, whose novel The Absolutely True Diary of a Part-Time Indian *has created controversy and even been banned in some high schools. The essay appeared on a blog associated with* The Wall Street Journal. *Alexie responds to a critic's claims by reflecting on his experience with students and his own experience growing up on the Spokane Indian Reservation.*

PRE-READING PROMPT

1. Think about what you read when you were younger. Did you ever read anything that was violent or had sexually graphic images in it? Did these books or stories affect you in any way? How? And do those texts affect you still?

2. What should teenagers read? Are there any reading materials—books, magazines, online sites—you think teenagers *should not read*? Why not? If teenagers should not read these materials, at what age would they be appropriate?

¹ Recently, I was the surprise commencement speaker at the promotion ceremony for a Seattle alternative high school. I spoke to sixty students, who'd come from sixteen different districts, and had survived depression, attempted suicide, gang warfare, sexual and physical abuse, absentee parents, poverty, racism, and learning disabilities in order to graduate.

Interest and Details: Alexie presents extreme situations to get readers' attention.

² These students had read my young adult novel, *The Absolutely True Diary of a Part-Time Indian*, and had been inspired by my autobiographical story of a poor reservation Indian boy and his desperate and humorous attempts to find a better life.

Explanation: The author explains why he's there.

³ I spoke about resilience—about my personal struggles with addiction and mental illness—but it was the student speakers who told the most important stories about survival.

Style: Alexie uses a one-sentence paragraph as a transition.

Explanation: The author uses an example of how people underestimate others.

4   A young woman recalled the terrible moment when indifferent school administrators told her that she couldn't possibly be a teen mother and finish high school. So they suggested she get a General Education Degree (GED) and move on with her life. But, after taking a practice test, she realized that the GED was far too easy for her, so she transferred to that alternative high school, and is now the mother of a three-year-old and a high school graduate soon to attend college.

5   After the ceremony, many of the graduates shook my hand, hugged me, took photos with me, and asked me questions about my book and my life. Other students hovered on the edges and eyed me with suspicion and/or shyness.

Audience: It's interesting how Alexie doesn't seem angry here. There's a calm, maybe even weary, tone here that may work with his readers.

6   It was a beautiful and painful ceremony. But it was not unique. I have visited dozens of high schools—rich and poor, private and public, integrated and segregated, absolutely safe and fearfully dangerous—and have heard hundreds of stories that are individually tragic and collectively agonizing.

7   Almost every day, my mailbox is filled with handwritten letters from students—teens and pre-teens—who have read my YA [young adult] book and loved it. I have yet to receive a letter from a child somehow debilitated by the domestic violence, drug abuse, racism, poverty, sexuality, and murder contained in my book. To the contrary, kids as young as ten have sent me autobiographical letters written in crayon, complete with drawings inspired by my book, that are just as dark, terrifying, and redemptive as anything I've ever read.

Details: The details here connect with the ones he uses in the first paragraph.

8   And, often, kids have told me that my YA novel is the only book they've ever read in its entirety.

9   So when I read Meghan Cox Gurdon's complaints about the "depravity" and "hideously distorted portrayals" of contemporary young adult literature, I laughed at her condescension.

Style: Anger comes out in this sentence, and he ends the paragraph with "condescension" for a reason.

10   Does Ms. Gurdon honestly believe that a sexually explicit YA novel might somehow traumatize a teen mother? Does she believe that a YA novel about murder and rape will somehow shock a teenager whose life has been damaged by murder and rape? Does she believe a dystopian novel will frighten a kid who already lives in hell?

Explanation: Alexie uses detailed questions to show how Gurdon's position is incorrect.

11   When I think of the poverty-stricken, sexually and physically abused, self-loathing Native American teenager that I was, I can only wish, immodestly, that I'd been given the opportunity to read *The Absolutely True Diary of a Part-Time Indian*. Or Laurie Halse Anderson's *Speak*. Or Chris Lynch's *Inexusable*. Or any of the books that Ms. Gurdon believes to be irredeemable. I can't speak for other writers, but I think I wrote my YA novel as a way of speaking to my younger, irredeemable self.

12   Of course, all during my childhood, would-be saviors tried to rescue my fellow tribal members. They wanted to rescue me. But, even then, I could only laugh at their platitudes. In those days, the cultural conservatives thought that KISS and Black Sabbath were going to impede my moral development. They

> **Details:** Alexie uses contrasts to show the silliness of people's concerns.

wanted to protect me from sex when I had already been raped. They wanted to protect me from evil though a future serial killer had already abused me. They wanted me to profess my love for God without considering that I was the child and grandchild of men and women who'd been sexually and physically abused by generations of clergy.

13   What was my immature, childish response to those would-be saviors?

14   "Wow, you are way, way too late."

> **Audience:** He starts out calm to keep readers on his side but turns to sarcasm here.

15   And now, as an adult looking back, I wonder why those saviors tried to warn me about the crimes that were already being committed against me.

16   When some cultural critics fret about the "ever-more-appalling" YA books, they aren't trying to protect African-American teens forced to walk through metal detectors on their way into school. Or Mexican-American teens enduring the culturally schizophrenic life of being American citizens and the children of illegal immigrants. Or Native American teens growing up on Third World reservations. Or poor white kids trying to survive the meth-hazed trailer parks. They aren't trying to protect the poor from poverty. Or victims from rapists.

> **Style:** The use of "Or" at the start of these sentences makes it seem like he could go on and on.

17   No, they are simply trying to protect their privileged notions of what literature is and should be. They are trying to protect privileged children. Or the seemingly privileged.

18   Two years ago, I met a young man attending one of the most elite private high schools in the country. He quietly spoke to me of his agony. What kind of pain could a millionaire's child be suffering? He hadn't been physically or sexually abused. He hadn't ever been hungry. He'd never seen one person strike another in anger. He'd never even been to a funeral.

19   So what was his problem?

20   "I want to be a writer," he said. "But my father won't let me. He wants me to be a soldier. Like he was."

> **Details:** Here Alexie uses another longer example to go with the one earlier in the essay.

21   He was seventeen and destined to join the military. Yes, he was old enough to die and kill for his country. And old enough to experience the infinite horrors of war. But according to Ms. Gurdon, he might be too young to read a YA novel that vividly portrays those very same horrors.

22   "I don't want to be like my father," that young man said. "I want to be myself. Just like in your book."

23   I felt powerless in that moment. I could offer that young man nothing but my empathy and the promise of more books about teenagers rescuing themselves from the adults who seek to control and diminish him.

24   Teenagers read millions of books every year. They read for entertainment and for education. They read because of school assignments and pop culture fads.

> **Interest:** He argues the exact opposite of his opponents.

25   And there are millions of teens who read because they are sad and lonely and enraged. They read because they live in an often-terrible world. They read because they believe, despite the callow protestations of certain adults, that books—especially the dark and dangerous ones—will save them.

Explanation: Alexie draws comparisons between what he read and what he dealt with in life.

26   As a child, I read because books—violent and not, blasphemous and not, terrifying and not—were the most loving and trustworthy things in my life. I read widely, and loved plenty of the classics so, yes, I recognized the domestic terrors faced by Louisa May Alcott's March sisters. But I became the kid chased by werewolves, vampires, and evil clowns in Stephen King's books. I read books about monsters and monstrous things, often written with monstrous language, because they taught me how to battle the real monsters in my life.

27   And now I write books for teenagers because I vividly remember what it felt like to be a teen facing everyday and epic dangers. I don't write to protect them. It's far too late for that. I write to give them weapons—in the form of words and ideas—that will help them fight their monsters. I write in blood because I remember what it felt like to bleed.

Style: He uses a strong word choice, "blood," to make his point.

Planning

Sam is planning to be a teacher, so he decided to write about an issue that both students and teachers struggle with: Should late assignments be penalized? Sam has had his own experiences with turning in late work, so he knows the student side pretty well. He thought about the reasons teachers might have for penalizing late work, and then he arranged to talk to an aunt who was a high school teacher. She gave him some additional understanding of the teacher's side in this issue.

Sam then used the **I D E A S** template as a way to brainstorm ideas for his paper. He asked these questions and had these thoughts about his topic:

	Interest: What do I want to lead with to get the reader's attention? I could use my own experience with working too much and being tired, but is that a typical example and will readers relate to it? Or should I begin with a basic discussion of how some students think late penalties on late work are unfair at times? But maybe that's just whining? What do I want my reader to see in this reflective essay that is supposed to fairly present the student and teacher sides of the issue? How do I answer, "So what?" Why should readers care?

Details: I wonder how many examples are necessary. When presenting the student side, what are the typical and realistic reasons why stuff is turned in late: working and going to school, not being good with time management, bad planning, too much partying, procrastination, what else? I guess I could use my own examples. But what about other people's situations? What are the reasons why teachers have these policies? Are they trying to make college like the workplace? I have to make sure I represent both sides equally.

Explanation: I think I'll use the car accident example since that makes me look good. I had that car accident that messed things up. But aren't there bad reasons why students don't get stuff in on time though? If I were a professor who taught four sections of a course, would I have a late policy and why? Are there any examples of how late work would make a professor's job tough? Where do they draw the line?

Audience: I could write this in an angry tone because in that one class my grade dropped from a B to C because of her late work policy, but the assignment says, "you must make sure you show that you can see and understand both or all of the sides of an issue." So maybe do I just relate the facts since the professor is reading it? With that reader, reasons why are important. He's always talking about details and development.

Style: He's written a few times that I need to switch up the types of sentences I use since I seem to use a lot of compound sentences. I need to try to include more complex sentence constructions. Also, he's talked about how I need transitions in my writing since the last paper had so few.

When Sam went to the Writing Center with a draft of his paper two days before it was due, the tutor there asked these questions and made these comments:

- Could you provide some more details and specific examples that show what you mean? Right now in paragraph two, you only have one. You probably need more than that because there are all kinds of reasons why students turn in late work. Also, can you further detail the reasons why professors have late policies? What other reasons are there?

- Instead of just relating some of these experiences, what experiences could you detail with dialogue? Could you provide a statement from a teacher or a quote from a professor's course policy that shows their perspectives? What did your aunt say?

- Make sure to pay attention to paragraph unity. You have one huge paragraph that works with the student and professor perspectives all at once. Why not split them apart and develop your ideas more in each? Could you even provide more perspectives? How do people look at this issue differently?

- With the way you've set up the paper, there probably needs to be some kind of transition in the middle of the paper when you move from the student view to the professor view. Can you think of a way to create a transitional paragraph?

◄ Before you begin reading Sam's essay, think about the reasons each side might have for being for or against a late-work policy.

Now read the paper Sam turned in after considering the tutor's suggestions.

Sam's "Seeing the Sides" Essay

Johnston 1

Sam Johnston

Prof. Copeland

Introduction to College Writing

15 May 2014

> Sam offers a thoughtful title that previews what the essay will cover.

"Sorry It's Late"—Seeing Both Sides of an
Age-old Homework Dilemma

> Sam begins this paper with a personal anecdote that many of his readers will be able to relate to and understand.

I was overwhelmed. I had a paper due in English class, and an algebra test coming up on the same day as an oral history report. What might have been a full night of homework vanished when my boss called, begging me to come in and cover for a sick checker at the grocery store. Getting home at 10:00 p.m. with a screaming headache, I decided to skip finishing the paper. It's only the second time I had been late, and I thought surely the teacher would understand. But when I got back the graded paper, I found the teacher had subtracted 10%. Why can't teachers understand that students sometimes can't meet deadlines? I have thought a lot about this and have come to realize that, surprisingly, teachers often understand why students turn in work late, and perhaps students should understand why late work is still penalized.

> This statement presents the **thesis** of the essay. Readers can clearly see the two sides whose points of view will be considered.

> Sam uses specific examples to *show* the reader what he means by "good reasons."

Students like myself have some very good reasons to justify not meeting assignment deadlines. When taking several classes, students may have multiple assignments coming due at once, and sometimes even the best time management is not enough to get them all completed. Occasionally, assignments may be more difficult and time-consuming than anticipated. A student who has budgeted two hours to finish revising a paper for a composition class may suffer from a severe case of writer's block and give up at midnight because of an early morning algebra class that he or she can't afford to miss by oversleeping. Sometimes students may have the time and ability to get all their work completed, but unforeseen circumstances keep them from turning it in on time. For example, a sudden stomach virus keeps them housebound. For other students, a sick child or another family emergency keeps them from turning in work they

Johnston 2

stayed up late to complete on time. Once I had an unfortunate fender bender on the way to school and missed a history quiz that I could not make up. All of these excuses are good ones, so why do teachers still penalize late work or sometimes not accept it at all?

Teachers were once students themselves, and memories of their own struggles to meet the demands of classes do not disappear with graduation. In fact, there are some teachers who continue to take graduate classes after they have started their teaching careers and face the same tough assignment deadlines their students face. You would think this would make teachers more tolerant of late work, but that seldom seems to be the case. There is an old saying that before you criticize someone, you should walk a mile in his shoes. So I am going to slip on some teacher shoes and try to understand.

> The author uses a comparison/contrast pattern of organization in this paragraph to create a transition between the two halves of the essay.

Teachers have their reasons for imposing deadlines and deducting points from late assignments. One reason is to discourage late assignments. A composition teacher, for example, who may teach four or five classes with as many as a hundred students, needs deadlines to keep grading manageable. Staggering assignment deadlines for different classes allows the teacher to grade and return papers in a timely manner. Too many late papers can leave a teacher struggling to keep up with grading in addition to regular class preparation. Penalizing late assignments is also a way to recognize those students who do meet deadlines. A student who takes an extra weekend or even an extra week to write a paper has an unfair advantage over a student who turns the assignment in on time. A late penalty cancels out that advantage. And while teachers realize some reasons for turning in late work deserve more sympathy than others, few want to have to play Solomon, deciding which excuses are true and reasonable. A teacher who decides to judge each late assignment on a case by case basis runs the risk of being overwhelmed by the sheer number and variety of excuses and being accused of bias when deciding some excuses are better than others. A straightforward, no exceptions policy keeps the process simple and as fair as possible. Finally, some teachers see a no-tolerance policy as

> Here Sam gives two specific reasons why teachers have penalties for late work.

> The teacher's perspective is provided.

Johnston 3

> Sam uses emphatic organization to present his final point as the most important. Do you agree that this is the most important reason?

reflective of the "real world." A job seeker who misses an application deadline will not get the job. Few bosses accept excuses for missing workplace deadlines, so learning the importance of deadlines is as important as other skills students learn in college.

I would like to think my teacher at least sympathized with me even as she deducted that 10%. I am going to try to understand her rationale even as I feel frustrated by the lower grade on a paper I worked hard on. It's not a perfect system, but understanding both sides of the late homework dilemma might make students and teachers more respectful of each other's side.

MyWritingLab Visit
Ch. 7 Reflective Writing
in MyWritingLab to
access the IDEA videos.

I D E A S in Action

In the first reading, commentary using the **IDEAS** template is provided to
show how close, analytical, and critical reading is important when reading
reflective writing.

SELECTION 1   **My**WritingLab

The Day I Met Bruce Lee

Bonnie Devet

*Bonnie Devet is the Director of the Writing Lab at the College of Charleston.
In this extended essay, she details her experience visiting the grave of the
famous martial arts star Bruce Lee, she reflects on that experience, and she
interprets it for her audience.*

PRE-READING PROMPT

1. What do you know about Bruce Lee? (If you have never heard of him,
   do a quick search on the Internet to learn something about him.)
2. In what kinds of ways can celebrities—living and dead—inspire people?

Details and Explanation: Devet
begins with examples of what most
moviegoers remember about Lee.

1   He taught actors Steve McQueen and James Coburn how to fight. He kicked
so rapidly Hollywood slowed down his fight scenes so audiences could see his
speedy delivery. He defeated enemies through finger punches called chi sao (or
"sticking hands"). He numchaked (from numchaku or "two wooden sticks joined
by a cord") his opponents. And, like most moviegoers, back in 1973, I had seen
him at his best in the American release of *Enter the Dragon*. Little did I expect that
one day I would meet the true Bruce Lee.

Interest: Here the author creates
interest with a statement that
might puzzle people since Bruce
Lee is dead.

2   The conference where I had delivered a paper as a staid, bespeckled, middle-
aged college instructor had ended. With the flight home still a half-day off, I
decided to seek out something novel in the conference city of Seattle, Washington,
and visit a lesser-known site: the grave of martial arts master Bruce Lee.

Explanation: Here Devet explains
one of her reasons for visiting the
grave.

3   Though he's been dead for over thirty years, all my students know Lee. His
posters decorate their dorm rooms. If I could report I had seen The Master's last
resting place (as if the energetic Lee could ever rest), my classes would more than
likely think I was pretty hip (do students use "hip" any more?). My students—
especially the freshmen—might even see me as "cool" or "very cool" or that
highest of teenage adjectives . . . "awesome."

4   I bravely surrendered myself to the Seattle metro system, hoping I had the right bus numbers to reach the Lake View Cemetery on Capitol Hill. Two hours later, in a scorching, simmering, so-hot-that-even-eggs-refuse-to-fry day, I arrived at the cemetery, following the directions of my trusty guidebook. At the same time, like doves to a rooftop, a car showed up with a couple half my age, the girl dressed in the classic summer uniform of what my generation, unfortunately, labels as "Punk Rock": short, spiked hair like tiny Matterhorn peaks, tank top with spaghetti straps, and, of course, a pierced nose. Her driver boyfriend looked like a Sumu wrestler who had lost a bit of weight yet was still a lumberingly solid Paul Bunyan.

Style: This single sentence acts as a transition to the drama in the next few paragraphs—how Devet befriended the couple and they travel together.

5   One does not mess with this couple.

6   They did, however, want to talk to me. I had directions to locate Lee's grave among the hundreds and hundreds interred in Lake View, so they asked me to ride around with them as we scouted for the site.

7   Getting into a car with total strangers? Didn't my mother always warn against such foolishness? Yet I did, answering the little mother voice inside my head with, "But these are fans, too, Mom, and, besides, they are driving such a conservative car the Chevy Malibu, so how dangerous can they be?" Logical? No, but in the heat of the hunt for the grave of Lee, who could stop to be rational or careful. The Punk Rockers and I were as one, weren't we? Already, Lee was working some kind of magic . . . different strangers engaged in the same enterprise.

Details: This and the following two paragraphs narrate her trip to the gravesite and describe the grave with concrete details.

8   The hunt was successful. Around a bend and on top of a hill sat the garnet stone (red for good luck in Chinese lore?) with a Hollywood photo of a young Lee and his name inscribed in both Chinese and English. Standing like a sentinel, the stone carried an inscription, "May Your Inspiration Guide Us Toward Our Personal Liberation."

9   The Punk Rockers and I were not alone. Coming up the cemetery hill was a grandfathery Chinese man with his two middle-school-aged grandchildren dressed in the latest khaki shorts and skin-tight t-shirts straight from Old Navy.

10   The three groups—the conservative professor, the Punk Rockers, and the Chinese family—converged at Lee's side.

Style and Explanation: This transition sentence sets up three types of people who are attracted to Lee.

11   The Chinese grandfather was reverently silent at the grave for different reasons, I suspect, than were the Punk Rockers. To this elderly man, Lee symbolized the triumph of East over West. Lee's movies simplistically but graphically displayed the power of Eastern thought and movement in a fighting style called jeet kune do ("the art of the intercepting fist"). Using his art, Lee—the classic underdog—always triumphed over oppressors, be they Japanese or Westerners. Being victorious wasn't enough, though. Embodying contradictions, Lee was a dancer (a noted cha cha champion of Hong Kong) as well as a fighter (learning kung fu to protect himself from street gangs). He balanced two worlds, surely not unlike how the elderly Chinese grandfather must do as he lives in a western culture.

Details and Explanation: Devet speculates as to what Lee represents to Chinese-Americans through details about his life's story and how he continues to represent the struggle of the immigrant experience.

12   When Lee finally broke into mainstream Hollywood with his $100-million-grossing blockbuster *Enter the Dragon*, he had, at last, achieved his own personal

victory—recognition by the West. But, ironically, this conquest arrived after he had died at age 32 from an acute cerebral edema (swelling of the brain), probably induced by an ingredient in the prescription painkiller Equagesic.

13   In one sense, Lee's heritage lives on. Without him, could we, today, have *House of Flying Daggers*, Jet Li (in the recent movie hit *Hero*), Michelle Yeogh (co-star with Pierce Brosnan in the 1997 James Bond thriller *Tomorrow Never Dies*), *Crouching Tiger, Hidden Dragon*, a Texas Ranger (Chuck Norris was a pupil of Lee's), *The Matrix*, the hugely popular video game *Mortal Kombat*, or even the comic version of martial arts successfully represented by Jackie Chan?

14   In its list of the most famous heroes and icons of the 20th century, *Time* also attributes to Lee the oddest of influences: the rise of Arnold Schwarzenegger. Through rigorous training (maybe even too much), Lee ascended from street thug to iconic star, becoming a lightening-fast fighter with a taut physique that, at his death, had virtually no body fat. He set the stage for others like Arnold to arrive in Hollywood with the same agenda of taking charge of one's body and career. Sure, Lee was merely a Hong Kong martial arts movie star. To many, though, he represented transformation, opportunity, respect.

15   The Chinese kids didn't see any of that. Looking at the grave with its silk flowers, notes of thanks from well-wishers, and coins for Lee's travels through the underground, the kids asked their grandfather, "What does the tombstone say?" Patiently pronouncing the Chinese inscription, the grandfather translated, "It's just Bruce Lee's name in Chinese." The teenagers' response reminded me of tourists ogling the walk of fame stars embedded on Hollywood Boulevard, squealing delightedly when spying a name they knew: "Oh, yeah. I've heard of him." To them, Lee was not a *Fists of Fury* symbol but only a dead movie star.

16   Lee had strived to bring East and West together, but these kids—the latest examples of the American-Chinese world—couldn't connect with a part of their culture or language.

17   And the Punk Rockers? As many New Yorkers have never visited the Statue of Liberty, they had not seen their own hometown's tourist spots. "We just doing some sightseeing," they explained.

18   I suspected, though, there was more to their visit than merely dropping by a local attraction. The Punk Rocker girl, pushing up her spaghetti strap slipping under the sweaty sun, sat down oh-so-carefully on the backless concrete bench in front of Lee's grave, a bench provided by Lee's widow Linda so visitors could do like the Punk Rocker, contemplate the site.

19   She gingerly ran her finger over the inscription as if by touching it she could reach Lee. Then, she read each of the mementos left by adorning fans for the anniversary of his death—July 20, 1973.

20   "He was cursed, you know." She spoke, as if to no one but to herself and possibly Lee. "He was not supposed to reveal ancient fighting skills to non-Chinese."

21   More than likely, Lee was merely another street kid trying to get ahead by teaching his version of martial arts. By coalescing various fighting styles into a

Interest, Details, and Explanation: Devet fully addresses the "So what?" question by detailing the "heritage" he started.

Explanation: This detailed anecdote introduces a sense of loss about how some may not understand Lee's importance.

Details: This short paragraph amplifies the sense of loss.

Details and Explanation: The example of the Punk Rock Girl creates another transition for Devet to reflect on the urban mythology about Lee and how he was revolutionary.

new form, however, he symbolized the skill to re-shape one's self and the world in spite of odds ... not unlike what the Punk Rockers want to do.

22   The Punk Rockers were there, too, because like Lee, they see themselves as struggling to be acknowledged; in Lee's case, he battled his way through life, getting into countless skirmishes at his Hong Kong high school so that, finally, his family sent him away to America to finish his education. In the hit tv show *Green Hornet* (1966-67 on ABC), he played only the second lead of the faithful servant Kato, masked, no less, so that he was rarely recognized. He also resented not getting the title role in the tv show *Kung Fu* (with the lead going to that most non-Chinese of men David Carradine). Lee (and the Punk Rockers) desired to be seen, heard, accepted for their philosophy and their own selves.

23   The Chinese kids soon grew bored and walked away, becoming more interested in the grave of an unnamed Nineteenth century Irishman who possessed the most unfortunate luck to have Lee buried next to him ... or perhaps it was good luck ... because everyone visiting Lee stops to read his weather-worn stone, too. The grandfather prodded along after the Chinese kids, paying attention not to step on Lee's grave.

24   As I turned to leave, the Punk Rockers remained behind, glad the rest of us were finally departing. They could pay their own homage, now.

25   And the staid, middle-aged, bespeckled English professor? This little jaunt to Lee's grave had been designed ostensibly to fill time before a flight home and to gain bragging rights before my freshman students. I could also claim that I was being professional, looking for elements in pop culture to illustrate for my classes the universality of literary classics. Wouldn't Lee be a swell example of A. E. Housman's poem "To An Athlete Dying Young"? Or I could maintain I was interested in seeing the grave of the man who, ultimately, made it possible for a movie like *House of Flying Daggers* to become a hit in the US. These reasons were, really, mere excuses, as rationalizations often are. Something more powerful was at work.

26   We are told we live in a multi-cultural world. We are told to celebrate differences. It is all true, and yet ... it's also beneficial to celebrate union and the ability to bring together. Lee did just that on a sweltering summer day. For a brief, tenuous moment on a hilltop in a Seattle cemetery, I feel I had met the true Lee—someone with the power to unite the disparate, the desperate, the divergent, and the dissimilar ... the real heritage and influence of this martial arts star.

Interest and Explanation: Devet directly compares Lee to the Punk Rock movement and shows the obstacles he faced.

Details: Not stepping on the grave highlights the respect some people show toward Lee.

Interest, Details, and Explanation: Here the author reflects on why she visited Lee's grave and ends with what she wants the reader to take away from the essay.

Attitude and Interest: The conclusion invites the reader to think about the significance of Lee and what he represents.

QUESTIONS FOR DISCUSSION

1. If you know little or nothing about Bruce Lee, is this introduction enough to spark your interest? Why or why not?
2. What examples does Devet use to explain the heritage or influence of Bruce Lee? Do you think most readers will be familiar with these examples? Why or why not?

3. Devet reflects upon the similarities between Lee and the Punk Rockers. Do you think the Rockers themselves see these similarities and that's why they are drawn to the grave? Why or why not?
4. What details does Devet include to show the respect the visitors to the grave hold for Lee?
5. Devet gives examples of ways she could use this visit in class with her students. What do you think her students might be most interested in hearing about the experience?
6. Can you name any other celebrities who seem to have the ability to bring together very different kinds of people? Explain what their appeal might be.

I D E A S for Your Own Writing   MyWritingLab

What's the Appeal? Essay

As Devet relates in her essay, Bruce Lee has a broad appeal that extends across cultures and generations. Think of another famous figure—movie star, sports star, politician, or other celebrity—who has that sort of appeal. Write an essay in which you reflect on what qualities the person has that give him or her the same magical ability as Bruce Lee to bring dissimilar kinds of people together. Your goal is to help your readers see this celebrity in a way they may not have considered before.

Reflecting Upon a Memorial

Bruce Lee's memorial—a red stone with his Hollywood photo and the inscription "May Your Inspiration Guide Us Toward Our Personal Liberation" with a bench placed nearby where visitors could sit and reflect—is a fitting tribute to the man, no doubt carefully designed by his loved ones. All around us, along highways, in schools and in cemeteries are memorials to individuals set up by their loved ones. Some people may even have more private memorials—perhaps a place in a backyard garden or a yearly ritual that honors a special memory of a person. Tell of a memorial that you played a part in setting up. You might describe an effort at your school to put up a memorial to a fellow student or maybe your work with family and friends to honor a special loved one with a scholarship or other donation to a charity. Reflect on how the memorial honors the memory of the person and how it comforts those dealing with the loss.

SELECTION 2   MyWritingLab

Country Hams

John Egerton

The next example comes from an essay called "The Pleasures of the Smokehouse" by John Egerton. This excerpt is the final four paragraphs of the essay in which the author discusses "country ham," which leads him to reflect about what is being lost.

PRE-READING PROMPT

1. Think about some of your favorite dishes or most memorable meals from your childhood. What makes them so unforgettable?
2. What kinds of food traditions are in your family? For example, do you always have certain dishes for a particular holiday or special occasion? What are they?
3. What can cause traditions to be lost or forgotten?

1   From the time I was seven or eight or so, I knew what an extraordinary culinary combination that was: to take a boiled or baked country ham—coated with my grandmother's special crust of bread crumbs, brown sugar, and black pepper—and slice it paper-thin so that you got a cross section with red ham meat, a little strip of fat, and finally the brown coating. That ham on a beaten biscuit is just about as near to a perfect comestible as I have ever tasted.

2   I've been eating country ham and beaten biscuits for at least fifty-five years. Tradition means a lot to me. It means almost as much as the flavor does. So I still go back to Cadiz, back to Trigg County, Kentucky, every year, to get my hams. There aren't many people who cure hams the old-fashioned way anymore.

3   But the tradition is not dying out on its own. It is being strangled to death by United States Department of Agriculture regulations that say unless you can document the temperature of the meat and other factors at every step along the way, the meat is unsafe. It is dangerous. Never mind that these hams have been made this way for a couple hundred years, and as far as anyone knows, no one has ever died of food poisoning from eating a traditionally cured ham. The USDA has decreed that these hams are dangerous. And dangerous means that you can't send them through the mail, but if somebody wants to drive to your house and pick one up, that's okay. That won't make you sick.

4   There are a lot of mysteries in life. And that's one I've never been able to figure out. But it saddens me to know that something as old and rich and vital as this—a true culinary art, like winemaking—may soon be lost forever.

1. What details in the first paragraph does Egerton use that appeal to the senses?
2. How does Egerton's memory of his grandmother's ham become a "diving board" to his thoughts on tradition?
3. *Tradition* is an abstract term. How does Egerton use concrete details to make it real?
4. What words in the third paragraph best reveal Egerton's attitude toward the actions of the USDA?
5. Why do you think Egerton repeats the word *dangerous*? What does that repetition add to his tone?
6. What words in the final paragraph best reveal Egerton's attitude toward country ham?
7. Does Egerton manage to convince you that the USDA's regulations are unfair? Why or why not?

I D E A S for Your Own Writing   MyWritingLab

Defending Tradition Paragraph(s)

In a paragraph or in a few paragraphs, defend a threatened tradition in your family or community by reflecting on what the tradition means or represents in your family or community. This document needs to be written with a specific reader or audience in mind, whether it is a letter or an email to certain members of your family or a letter to the editor of the local paper.

Reflect and Respond

Write a short response that might be read by John Egerton, explaining why you agree or disagree with his position that the USDA is "strangling" a beloved Southern tradition.

SELECTION 3   MyWritingLab

I Dream of Egypt Even When I Dream in English

Soha Youssef

This short reflective piece of writing is by Soha Youssef, a Ph.D. student at Bowling Green State University in Ohio. Youssef grew up in Cairo, Egypt, which is one of the largest cities in the world.

1. Think of an important place in your life. Why is it important?
2. What people, sights, smells, sounds, and tastes do you associate with that place?

[1]   The year was 2009. That was when I made a life changing decision that opened up some doors for me and shut others. The decision brought me a sense of self-accomplishment and perpetual nostalgia. Before I collected the courage to apply for a student visa and book a one-way ticket to the United States, I had had what most fellow Egyptians would call a dream job. With the poor socioeconomic statuses that most Caireans inherit from one generation to the next, that dream job typically fulfills a specific category: pays more than L.E. 2,500 or what was then equivalent to a little less than $500 per month. I quit my two-year old "dream" teaching job at a private university to follow my other dream of studying abroad, which came with the price of missing the smells, sights, and sounds of Cairo.

[2]   Although I now live in the US, I vividly remember walking into our family home and being swept away by the aroma of garlic and cumin from my mom's kitchen. I still recall that sense of pure, youthful, innocent joy of having fish and shrimp for dinner, which was almost always accompanied with a spicy, garlicky tahini sauce for extra kick. "You should never cook fish with white rice. Only brown rice with caramelized onions," my mom would emphasize to my sister and me each time our dad brought back home his favorite, freshly caught Nile seafood for her to prepare. As my siblings and I grew up, my mom was quite particular about our nutrition as well as about filling our house with a different aroma each day—from Koshari to Moussaka to Molokhia.

[3]   If I manage to replicate my mom's recipes and fill my current Ohio home with what I call "Egypt's smell," I can never replicate the sights of Cairean streets or perfectly conjure them to my memory. There is always something missing. It is surprising how what seemed to be narrow, run-down alleys only six years ago now seem like a far-fetched wish. I do remember the distinct smells of those streets as my friends and I strolled at night down the streets of a city that's always alive. I yearn for a walk by the banks of the Nile while enjoying some grilled corn on the cob that street vendors always served in husks. To me, the mixed smell of the river Nile and grilled corn is the smell of nightlife. On breezy nights, the typical destination would be Khan El Khalili bazaar, which is lined by tiny shops, diners, and coffee shops. As my friends and I walked by shops, customers chattered as they haggled for lower prices, and the sound of clinking tea glasses over tin-topped tables announced our final destination, El Fishawy coffee shop. There we would sit for hours to enjoy a few glasses of mint tea followed by obsidian-black Turkish coffee.

4   I miss the sounds of Cairo's streets. During hot, summer days, street vendors sold chilled licorice drinks and sugarcane juice; others sold semit bread along with hardboiled eggs and cheese. The latter were blessed with hoarse voices that would wake me up from my late afternoon nap. They would screech, "Semit, eggs, and cheese," while scrap metal vendors yelled out for buyers. They infuriated me when they disrupted my sleep, but I yearn for those voices now. Also, it always fascinated me that the sound of the adhan or call to prayers was as loud as the church bells. The sheikh of each mosque would start the adhan by saying, "Allah is the greatest." However, the sound of the adhan and the clanging of church bells were so orchestrated that they never overlapped. All these sounds echo in my mind.

5   Six years ago, I followed my dream of being a valued member of the US academic world, and every day my dreams are closer to fruition. Those dreams are invaluable, and the price is not in bank currency. Rather, the price is perpetually reminiscing about the smells, the sights, and the sounds of Cairo. I still dream of Egypt even when I mostly dream in English.

QUESTIONS FOR DISCUSSION

1. What details surprised you and why? Did they spark your interest?
2. Where did the author use effective concrete and specific details?
3. Where did you want more details about Cairo?
4. How does Youssef address the "so-what factor"?
5. What types of support does she use in her short essay? Which details and examples stand out the most and why?

I D E A S for Your Own Writing   MyWritingLab

Place Shapes Heritage

John Egerton's love of country-cured ham is largely the result of his having grown up around Cadiz, Kentucky, and Soha Youssef's nostalgia stems from growing up in Cairo, Egypt. Think about how your "place"— where you grew up or where you live now—has shaped a particular part of your character. It may be a like or dislike of a particular food or sport. Or perhaps your "place" has led to your fondness of a hobby or a pastime. Explain the connection between your place and your character for your classmates in a way that allows them to fully understand both, along with the connection between them. Because this is not a subject that may initially interest them, try, as did Egerton and Youssef, to draw your readers in with engaging concrete, sensory, and specific details.

SELECTION 4   **My**WritingLab

Two Bad Bricks

Ajahn Brahm

The next selection is an essay from Ajahn Brahm's book, Who Ordered This Truckload of Dung?: Inspiring Stories for Welcoming Life's Difficulties. *Brahm, who is a Buddhist monk, uses a story to make readers think about their own mindsets, how they might fall into thinking about "two bad bricks" way too often.*

PRE-READING PROMPT

1. Have you ever tried to learn a new skill—something you had never tried before? What was the experience like? How long did it take you to become competent at the skill? What kinds of mistakes did you make along the way?

2. What do you think people tend to most reflect on—their successes or their failures? Their strengths or their weaknesses? Why?

1   After we purchased the land of our monastery in 1983, we were broke. We were in debt. There were no buildings on the land, not even a shed. Those first few weeks we slept not on beds but on old doors we had bought cheaply from the salvage yard; we raised them on bricks at each corner to lift them off the ground. (There were no mattresses, of course—we were forest monks.)

2   The abbot had the best door, the flat one. My door was ribbed with a sizeable hole in the center where the doorknob would have been. I joked that now I wouldn't need to get out of bed to go to the toilet! The cold truth was, however, that the wind would come up through that hole. I didn't sleep much those nights.

3   We were poor monks who needed buildings. We couldn't afford to employ a builder—the materials were expensive enough. So I had to learn how to build: how to prepare the foundations, lay concrete and bricks, erect the roof, put in the plumbing—the whole lot. I had been a theoretical physicist and high-school teacher in lay life, not used to working with my hands. After a few years, I became quite skilled at building, even calling my crew the BBC ("Buddhist Building Company"). But when I started it was very difficult.

4   It may look easy to lay a brick: a dollop of mortar underneath, a little tap here, a little tap there. But when I began laying bricks, I'd tap one corner down to make it level and another corner would go up. So I'd tap that corner down then the brick would move out of line. After I'd nudged it back into line, the first corner would be too high again. Hey, you try it!

5   Being a monk, I had patience and as much time as I needed. I made sure every single brick was perfect, no matter how long it took. Eventually, I

completed my first brick wall and stood back to admire it. It was only then that I noticed–*oh no!*–I'd missed two bricks. All the other bricks were nicely in line, but these two were inclined at an angle. They looked terrible. They spoiled the whole wall. They ruined it.

6   By then, the cement mortar was too hard for the bricks to be taken out, so I asked the abbot if I could knock the wall down and start over again—or, even better, perhaps blow it up. I'd made a mess of it and I was very embarrassed. The abbot said no, the wall had to stay.

7   When I showed our first visitors around our fledging monastery, I always tried to avoid taking them past my brick wall. I hated anyone seeing it. Then one day, some three or four months after I finished it, I was walking with a visitor and he saw the wall.

8   "That's a nice wall," he casually remarked.

9   "Sir," I replied in surprise, "have you left your glasses in your car? Are you visually impaired? Can't you see those *two bad bricks* which spoil the whole wall?"

10   What he said next changed my whole view of that wall, of myself, and of many other aspects of life. He said, "Yes. I can see those two bad bricks. But I can see the 998 good bricks as well."

11   I was stunned. For the first time in over three months, I could see other bricks in that wall apart from the two mistakes. Above, below, to the left and to the right of the bad bricks were good bricks, perfect bricks. Moreover, the perfect bricks were many, many more than the two bad bricks. Before, my eyes would focus exclusively on my two mistakes; I was blind to everything else. That was why I couldn't bear looking at that wall, or having others see it. That was why I wanted to destroy it. Now that I could see the good bricks, the wall didn't look so bad after all. It was, as the visitor had said, "a nice brick wall." It's still there now, twenty years later, but I've forgotten exactly where those bad bricks are. I literally cannot see those mistakes any more.

12   How many people end a relationship or get divorced because all they can see in their partner are "two bad bricks"? How many of us become depressed or even contemplate suicide because all we can see in ourselves are "two bad bricks"? In truth, there are many, many more good bricks, perfect bricks—above, below, to the left and to the right of the faults—but at times we just can't see them. Instead, every time we look, our eyes focus exclusively on the mistakes. The mistakes are all we see, they're all we think are there—and so we want to destroy them. And sometimes, sadly, we do destroy a "very nice wall."

13   We've all got our two bad bricks, but the perfect bricks in each one of us are much, much more than the mistakes. Once we see this, things aren't so bad. Not only can we live at peace with ourselves, inclusive of our faults, but we can also enjoy living with a partner. This is bad news for divorce lawyers, but good news for you.

14   I have told this anecdote many times. After one occasion, a builder came up to me and told me a professional secret. "We builders always make mistakes," he said,

"But we tell our clients that is 'an original feature' with no other house in the neighborhood like it. And then we charge them a couple of thousand dollars extra!"

15   So the "unique features" in your house probably started out as mistakes. In the same way, what you might take to be mistakes in yourself, in your partner, or in life in general, can become "unique features," enriching your time here—once you stop focusing on them exclusively.

QUESTIONS FOR DISCUSSION

I nterest

1. Why do you think Brahm begins his story by talking about how poor the monastery was and how the monks slept on doors? How does that information prepare you for what follows?

2. Did you expect Brahm to be such a perfectionist about laying bricks? Why or why not?

D etails

3. Which details in the first four short paragraphs tell you something about Brahm's character? Does he sound like someone you would expect to be a Buddhist monk? Why or why not?

4. How does Brahm describe the process he went through in building the wall? How does that process paragraph lead to something important?

E xplanation

5. Why do you think the abbot insisted that the wall stay even though Brahm had the time and willingness to tear it down and rebuild it without flaws? Why does Brahm choose to explain that?

6. Brahm includes two specific examples of outsiders' responses to his wall. What does he learn from their reactions? How are these examples important to answering the "So what?" question?

7. What does Brahm mean by "the two bad bricks" we sometimes see in ourselves and others?

A udience

8. In this essay Brahm tries very hard to connect with his readers in order to teach them a lesson he learned through his experience with building a brick wall. At what points in the passage do you most notice him trying to reach out to his readers, to connect with them personally? What specific words, phrases, or sentences does he use to overtly connect to readers? Do you find this effective or ineffective?

9. Sometimes writing that tries to teach a lesson or moral can come across as preachy. Does Brahm avoid this trap? Why or why not?

S tyle

10. Look for short sentences in the essay that seem important. How does Brahm use short sentences as signposts, guides, and transitions?

I D E A S for Your Own Writing

MyWritingLab

Your Bricks and Walls Essay

Using "Two Bad Bricks" as your context, in a reflective essay, discuss how you might connect to Brahm's experience with the wall, especially in regard to education or other parts of your life. How has a "two bad bricks" mindset limited you or made you limit yourself? You can use one large example like Brahm does, or choose multiple and varied examples, anecdotes, and personal experiences to show what you mean. What does your experience tell us about human beings?

Lessons from Life

From his simple experience of building a wall with two bad bricks, Brahm learned an important lesson that could be applied to other areas of his life. Think about an experience in your own life in which you learned something that gave you a fresh insight into your own or other people's behavior. Using Brahm's short essay as a model, describe the experience and then explain the lesson you took from the experience and applied to other areas in your life.

Reflecting on a Culinary Tradition Paragraphs

Your Task: Families, ethnic groups, and communities have culinary traditions. In this assignment, you need to identify a food-related tradition that relates to your family, ethnic background, or neighborhood or city. Describe the tradition with examples, anecdotes, and strong specific, concrete, and vivid details in one paragraph, and then in the second (and possibly third) paragraph you need to reflect on what this culinary tradition explains about your family, ethnicity, or community.

Your Audience: As part of a "Food Culture" project sponsored by the culinary arts program on your campus, a committee is collecting short pieces of writing that could be published on the program's website. This reflective piece of writing needs to inform and hold the interest of readers through the use of personal experiences, examples, and reflection. Consider what readers might already know about your culinary tradition and how your writing might add to what they know or complicate what they think they know.

A Successful Reflecting on a Culinary Tradition Document . . .

- Is entertaining, easy to read, and thought provoking.
- Helps the reader to understand, from your point of view, what this tradition *means*—what it makes us understand about human nature and culture.
- Has focused and unified paragraphs that relate specific, concrete, and vivid details about this culinary tradition.
- Exhibits strong concision, cohesion, transitions, and sentence variety in length and type.
- Provides a medium level of tone and diction—not too formal but not too informal.
- Is free of mechanical and proofreading errors.

Reflecting on a Current Event Essay

Your Task: Every day we are bombarded with current issues on television and radio and in newspapers and magazines. Sometimes these are issues on which we must take a stand, voicing our opinions in voting booths. Often our reactions to these issues or the stands we take for or against them have been shaped by the personal experiences in our lives. For this essay, you will write about how an experience in your life has shaped your view toward a current issue.

Think about how some of the authors of the essays you have read view certain issues based on their experiences. Think of how John Egerton's childhood experiences with his grandmother's country ham shaped his attitude toward the USDA. Sherman Alexie's childhood contributed to his sympathy for poor and abused children. Perhaps in your own life, you had a relative saved by an innovative medical procedure, so you are against the limitations that have been put on stem cell research. Maybe a loved one is suffering or has died from lung cancer caused by smoking, so you are in favor of even higher taxes or more restrictions on tobacco use. You might want to write about how your own workplace experience has shaped your views on unions, strikes, or unemployment benefits.

By examining how your life experiences have shaped your attitudes and opinions, you will better understand the connections between your personal life and the world around you. You might also better understand how people whose opinions differ from yours have been shaped by their experiences as well. The topic you choose to write about should be one that is meaningful for you, but do keep in mind that what you write will be shared with other people in class.

Your Audience: Address your paper to peer-scholars who might be captivated by your subject and could be interested in your analysis and/or findings. Your purpose is to inform and hold the interest of your readers through the use of personal experience, examples, and reflection. Consider what your readers already know about the subject and how your essay might add to what they know.

A Successful Reflection Essay . . .

- Captures the readers' interest with a strong introduction.
- Has engaging and logically organized descriptive and narrative components, including dialogue when appropriate, to give the reader a sense of sharing the event.
- Uses a subjective style (first person "I"), including reflective comments about the event.
- Pulls the ideas together and may point to their implications in the conclusion.
- Demonstrates a clear grasp of grammar, punctuation, and mechanics while presenting ideas in varied sentence styles.

Case Study: Marketing Ideas Memo

You and Your Role: You are a marketing specialist for Tucker Motor Company, a new automobile manufacturer that is known for producing fuel-efficient vehicles. You work at the company's headquarters in Livonia, Michigan, but you have been working extensively with the manufacturing plant in Flint where the company has begun building its newest vehicle called the "Ecowagon," which is set to debut next year. As is standard procedure before the company rolls out a new vehicle, you, along with eleven other marketing specialists, are assigned to write a memo that offers strong and specific ideas on how to advertise the Ecowagon.

Your Reader: Your immediate audience is the Head Supervisor of the Ecowagon project, Logan Wilson, an experienced engineer who has ascended the ranks of Tucker Motors since the company was founded in 2008.

Details about the Ecowagon and Your Writing Task: The company is expanding its product line with this mid-sized station wagon, a vehicle that will have a zero-emission vehicle rating with a 60 city/51 highway miles-per-gallon average. The company is hoping to capitalize on its best-selling compact vehicle called the E-Car that is a plug-in electric vehicle. That car has sold well, and the company wants to target a larger market with the Ecowagon: families with kids.

In the memo, you need to consider the target market for this vehicle (families with kids) and offer three possible marketing strategies, sales pitches, and ideas on how to "sell" this vehicle to consumers. Mr. Wilson has told the twelve marketing specialists that he wants each of you to write a memo that offers ideas on how to market this product through three types of media: (1) an ad in *Redbook* magazine (2) a radio ad that will air in various markets, and (3) a nationwide commercial. This memo is to serve as a type of exploratory writing that your department does all the time in order to brainstorm so that the best advertising ideas can get recognized and implemented.

For each category (magazine ad, radio ad, and commercial), you need to describe and detail how you think Tucker Motors can attract consumers with its Ecowagon. For each one, you need to offer strong specific and vivid details and offer "copy" (the writing or narration of an ad) that can be used in the magazine, radio, and television advertisements. So for each category, you have to explain the details of the ad—the setting, the music used, the writing, the arrangement of the ad, and the flow of the presentation.

If you come up with good marketing ideas that Tucker can use, this could be your step up the corporate ladder.

A Successful Marketing Ideas Memo . . .

- Asserts a strong bottom line (thesis) in the first paragraph by offering a concise context about the Ecowagon and then a statement about your general ideas of how to market this vehicle that introduces your marketing ideas.
- Offers three separate paragraphs that provide details about your ideas for the magazine, radio, and TV ads.
- Provides specific, vivid, and concrete details about your marketing ideas.
- Has focused and unified paragraphs that are highly developed and connect to the bottom line in the first paragraph.
- Is free of irrelevant details.
- Follows the proper format of a memorandum.
- Exhibits strong concision, cohesion, transitions, and sentence variety in length and type.
- Provides a medium level of tone and diction—not too formal but not too informal.
- Is free of mechanical and proofreading errors.

CHAPTER AT A GLANCE

Learning Objectives	How they connect to reading and writing at college . . .
❶ Answer this question: So what?	Writers must move beyond the obvious and present reflections that are informative, interesting, and surprising.
	Writers find the meaning or point of their reflection through interpretation—and then help readers see what they see and feel what they feel.
	A "That's interesting!" thesis presents a point that grabs the readers' attention by offering new insights or understanding.
❷ Employ examples, anecdotes, and evidence for support.	Support must engage the readers and make them want to keep on reading.

Learning Objectives	How they connect to writing at college . . .
❸ Use concrete, specific, and inviting details.	It is important to paint a picture for readers when relating personal experiences, examples, and anecdotes.
❹ Put **I D E A S** to work in reflective writing.	Consider these crucial factors when brainstorming, drafting, and revising your descriptive writing: • **I** nterest • **D** etails • **E** xplanation • **A** udience • **S** tyle

> **MyWritingLab** Visit **Chapter 7, "Reflective Writing,"** in MyWritingLab to test your understanding of the chapter objectives.

Informative Writing

Learning Objectives

In this chapter you will learn how to …

❶ Get your facts straight.

❷ Make the information interesting.

❸ Organize information appropriately.

❹ Put **I D E A S** to work in informative writing.

This woman is reading instructions as she constructs a crib. What do you think is most important for creating effective informative writing?

Informative writing is everywhere in our lives, and we encounter it nearly every day. We read sets of instructions to put new products together. We read newspaper articles on the Web. We write grocery lists. We read textbooks. Informative writing can be dry and not very exciting, or it can be quite interesting. Either way, the purpose of informative writing remains the same: it must clearly and accurately relate essential information.

While some informative writing is purely personal, such as letting Facebook friends or Twitter followers know what is going in your life, this chapter will focus on more formal informative writing designed for specific audiences.

MyWritingLab Visit Ch. 8 Informative Writing in MyWritingLab to access the IDEAS videos.

The best informative writing presents accurate and essential information while keeping the readers interested and engaged. When thinking about the types of support (the *Details* and *Explanation* of **I D E A S**) that go into informative writing, a writer selects examples, personal experiences, specific and concrete details, facts, statistics, anecdotes, and beliefs/assumptions that will connect to the readers. All of that support is often guided by a thesis, a controlling idea of the paper. As in all writing, the writer's goal is to spark the readers' interest and keep them reading to the end.

Get Your Facts Straight

❶ Get your facts straight.

If you wrote that the Declaration of Independence was written in 1781, your reader would doubt the reliability of the information throughout your paper. Simple mistakes, like using a wrong date or not knowing your facts, can seriously hurt your message and your credibility. A glaring weakness disrupts reading and makes readers look at your writing more skeptically. In turn, they will not trust you.

When working with sources, when paraphrasing, when using examples, or when relating details, you have to be accurate and precise. Accurate details matter whether you are writing a memo to your boss, composing a history paper, or filling out a medical chart for a patient.

EXERCISE 8.1   Writing Specific Statements   MyWritingLab

Directions: What specific details and explanations would make the following statements more informative and enhance the writer's credibility?

EXAMPLE: They say the government should do something to improve the economy.

The writer should tell who "they" are and explain what "something" is.

The Nonpartisan Economic Watchdog Group (*they*) said Congress should work in unison to improve the economy through additional stimulus spending for infrastructure repair, job retraining for displaced workers, and development of renewable energy. (*something*)

1. Everybody knows that creek has dangerous pollutants that are probably making people who come into contact with the water sick.

2. I heard things that make me think that politician should not be trusted.

3. No one needs to have bad skin. My brother took some stuff he saw on TV that cleared his acne up fast.

4. I heard on the radio that the public employees' unions will soon bankrupt our state.

5. I read that people hate the new changes to that computer's operating system.

❷ Make the information interesting.

Make the Information Interesting

All of us have read boring writing. You can probably think back to some high school textbooks that were pretty dry; they did not spark interest in what you needed to learn. But think about what made them boring:

- Did the text assume you knew information that you did not know?
- Were there no examples that you could connect to?
- Did the author talk down to you?
- Was the text too small to be read effectively?
- Was it all just too confusing?

Good writers spark their readers' interest through memorable quotations, compelling examples, vivid details, strong explanations, and interesting word choices. Details, examples, explanations, and clear language make informative writing "go." They are crucial to keeping readers interested. In addition, a smart, interesting thesis directs the action of a piece of writing, and details and explanation must also be provided to support that thesis.

EXERCISE 8.2   Analyzing Details in Informative Writing   MyWritingLab

Directions: The following passage gives some basic information about medical treatments during a particular era in American history.

During the period of 1780 to 1850, known as the "Age of Heroic Medicine," patients were as likely to die from their treatment as they were from disease. Many reputable doctors at this time believed most illnesses could be cured by removing toxins from the body through bloodletting, purging, and blistering. Sometimes patients, already weakened from disease, died when too much blood was taken. Others suffered serious side effects from the poisons used to clean out their intestines. Few wanted the additional pain from acidic materials applied to the skin to cause blisters that were then pierced and drained. Given the misery these dangerous treatments induced, the patients truly were the "heroes" of this age.

Now read the same passage after it has been expanded with details and examples. After you have finished reading, answer the questions that follow.

During the "Age of Heroic Medicine" from 1780 to 1850, many reputable doctors believed they could cure illnesses by removing toxins from the body. Unfortunately, patients, even wealthy and highly esteemed ones like George Washington, were likely to suffer as much from their treatment as they were from their illness. When the retired President developed a severe sore throat after riding around his estate on horseback during a snow storm, three prominent physicians were called to his aid. A doctor typically began treatment with bloodletting, a remedy for everything from fever to toothaches to mental illness. The doctor removed "stagnant" blood by applying leeches to the patient or by cutting open a vein. Over the course of nine to ten hours, Washington's physicians bled him multiple times. They eventually drained about four pints of his blood—almost half the blood in his body. Doctors also removed toxins by purging the intestines with powerful, often dangerous, chemicals, such as calomel or mercurous chloride. Those who survived often suffered from serious side effects, such as losing teeth or having their jawbones deteriorate. Washington received multiple doses of calomel. Along with being bled and poisoned, a patient might undergo blistering, a painful procedure in which the doctor would apply a "blister," an acidic substance, to the patient's skin, resulting in a second degree burn and blisters. The theory behind blistering was that the body's toxins would be drained along with the blood and pus. Washington's physicians initially applied to his throat a blister made from a mixture of dried beetles. As his condition worsened, doctors applied additional blisters to his extremities. Further weakened by his treatment, Washington died that evening, unable to overcome the septic sore throat and possibly pneumonia. Given the misery these dangerous treatments caused, the patients truly were the "heroes" of this age of medicine.

1. Which details in the second paragraph make it both more informative and more interesting to you?

2. How does including the example of George Washington help you better understand what medical treatment was like during the "Age of Heroic Medicine"?

❸ Organize information appropriately.

Organize Information Appropriately

Informative writing can be confusing and even boring if readers get lost in the details. Writers who keep their readers' needs in mind know that organization is key. We will emphasize that point again: *Organization is key.*

Move from Old to New Information

There is an old saying that goes something like this: "To catch a fish, you have to think like a fish." With that adage in mind, be aware that when you are trying to inform readers, you have to think about what they already know and what they need to know in order to catch and keep their attention. You have to hook and hold them on the line. You do not want the readers to get away.

For example, a human resources director writing to employees at a company about changes in health insurance plans will probably start with what the old plan offered and then transition to what the new plan provides for employees. An employee of that company talking about this health plan to her husband will probably start with a general context ("You remember Bill, the guy in accounting?"); she will establish particulars about the situation ("Last quarter, the company had some really nice profits—we were up ten percent in sales."); and then she will offer the new information ("Now, he wants to increase our co-pays because he says the health insurance plan is way too expensive.").

Many times as speakers and writers, we move from known to new unconsciously because it is a strategy we have used for years when communicating. But more importantly, when writers think about how to generate interest in a topic, they have to think about the details, examples, and explanations needed to make the new information come alive for the reader.

EXERCISE 8.3   Organize Informative Essays   MyWritingLab

Directions: In the following examples, two writers have brainstormed ideas and support for their informative papers. Each writer has generated some points to include in the paper and is ready to begin organizing.

As you read each list, think about which points are the most important and how the writers could organize them. First, cross out those points that do not seem relevant for the writer's audience and purpose. Next, add any points that would make the paper more interesting and informative. Finally, suggest how the writer should organize these points in a scratch outline. Be prepared to explain why you recommend a particular organization. Also keep in mind that the writers should move from known to new information.

1. Each spring Sandra suffers from seasonal allergies that make it difficult to focus. She plans to write a paper that presents information about pollen allergies and how they may impact a student's performance. Here is what she has brainstormed so far.

Seasonal Allergies
worst times of year for allergies
different kinds of allergies in my family—food, bee stings
how they differ from colds
how drowsy allergy medications make me
other allergies that could make studying difficult
what might be making pollen counts rise
allergy symptoms
dangers—overmedication and trigger asthma
treatments—medication and non-medication
what causes these allergies
how I did poorly on final exams because my allergies were so bad

2. Drew is an avid comic book collector and wants to share information about his hobby with his fellow students. He wants to show that collectors are not "nerds," and the hobby can be enjoyable and profitable. Here is what he has brainstormed so far.

Collecting Comic Books
buying and selling
protecting
why collect comic books

how I got started collecting
famous comic book artists
which comics are the most desirable
Comic Book Collecting Association (CBCA)
The history of comic books
grading scale for condition of books
my favorite series
where to find comic books
stereotypes of comic book collectors
conventions
examples of valuable comics

❹ Put **I D E A S** to work in informative writing.

Put **I D E A S** to Work in Informative Writing

What essential information does my audience need to know? Which details are important? How can I make this subject interesting to my readers? What is the focus? What is my point here?

MyWritingLab Visit Ch. 8 Informative Writing in MyWritingLab to access the IDEAS videos.

You should ask yourself these questions as you prepare to draft informative writing. As you think through which details are most important, keep in mind **I D E A S**, which stands for **I**nterest, **D**etails, **E**xplanation, **A**udience, and **S**tyle.

STUDENT WRITER AT WORK

In Collin Seibert's Introduction to College Writing class, the professor gave the following assignment. (See the full assignment on p. 248.)

Historical/Cultural Marker:
Informing About a Place in Your Community

Writing Task

Drawing on your knowledge of your neighborhood, city, community, or metro area, locate a place that is significant to your community or a special group of which you are a member. You need to find a landmark and inform a general reader about it. Your aim is to provide a text (one to four paragraphs) that describes and offers reasons why this place is important. Ideally, if funds are available, your informative prose would be printed on a historical/cultural marker at that place.

Collin thought about his high school's home field, where up until this year he played left tackle. It is named after a former coach and teacher at his high school, but he realized there was no marker nor any information at the stadium to inform fans as to why it was named after Ken Pickerell.

Using the **I D E A S** template, Collin asked these questions about his Historical/Cultural Marker paper:

**Interest:** How can I get the reader's attention? After the info about where it's located, what do readers need to know about Coach Pick that will show how he's such a great guy? How has he been such a positive influence for me and others? I assume that's why they named the stadium after him.

**Details:** I wonder how much I will have to detail. I could provide the various titles he's had since that'll show why they named the stadium after him. But what else? The way he coached people? When did he start at Oswego?

**Explanation:** Since I only have so much space, I can't really provide detailed examples. From looking at other markers that our professor showed us, it seems to be "just the facts." But I don't want it to be boring. What about describing the situation with his wife?

**Audience:** I can't assume that someone looking at the marker will know much about Coach Pick since he retired in the 80s. We all know him because he's around, but I want to make sure I show respect for what he stands for. My audience needs to get that positive vibe.

**Style:** It's a historical marker, and from the ones I've seen, they don't usually have a lot of long sentences. You gotta get right to the point. My professor, he keeps talking about how I need to vary the lengths of my sentences though.

When Collin visited the Writing Center with a draft of his paper, the tutor made these comments:

- Your paper starts a bit abruptly. On some markers I've seen, they start with a quotation related to the battle, the building, or the person. Is there anything he said often that people remember him by? You could start the whole text part with a quote that really tells a lot about him.
- You don't have enough information in the location section. All you have right now is that it's in front of the stadium.
- Is there anything else he's known for other than coaching? Was he a booster after he retired? What other important info might you want to add into the second paragraph? It's kind of light right now.

After revising his historical/cultural marker after visiting the Writing Center, Collin turned in the following paper for his college writing class.

Collin's Historical Marker

Seibert 1

Collin Seibert

Professor Taylor

English 1000

19 March 2014

Coach Pick

Location

Seibert explains where the marker will be and provides a reason why it needs to be there.

This historical marker will be placed at the entrance of the main gate leading into the football stadium. This spot is the ideal spot because at Oswego High School the football stadium is already named after Ken Pickerill, but no historical markers are present.

Text

He took the tutor's advice and begins with a quotation.

"I just enjoy being there with the kids."

He was the first to arrive at the field and the last one to leave. He was a coach, manager, groundskeeper, and sports fan. Ken Pickerill served as a teacher, athletic director, board member, and a

The last two sentences serve as a thesis.

coach for longer than five decades at Oswego School District 308. Coach Pick served as a football, wrestling, and baseball coach at Oswego H.S. since 1956.

In addition to his duties in the athletic department, Coach Pick is responsible for creating the Oswego Booster Club, which helps raise money for all of the athletic teams at Oswego H.S. He donated and helped raise money to help fund projects on the grounds of Oswego High School, including Jackie's Field of Dreams, which is named after his wife who lost her battle with cancer in March 2001. His dedication to Oswego's student-athletes was seen daily even after he retired in the early 1980s. Either in the dugout of the ball field or on the sidelines of a football game, he was always around in a positive way. He would encourage athletes to do their best and work harder than others not only on the field but also in life. He always told the athletes he coached that there is always something you can do to get better.

> Seibert provides details about the coach's character.

Coach Pick was so valuable to the thousands of student-athletes who have been a part of Oswego High School's athletic programs. Ken Pickerill was not only a coach but also an inspiring person to the many people's lives he has touched, and as a community we grew to love the guy.

> He concludes by explaining why the stadium is named after the coach.

I D E A S in Action

MyWritingLab Visit Ch. 8 Informative Writing in MyWritingLab to access the IDEAS videos.

In the first reading, commentary using the **I D E A S** template is provided to show how a close, analytical, critical reading is important when reading informative writing.

SELECTION 1   MyWritingLab

The Apple, Alcohol, & "Johnny Appleseed"

Michael Pollan

This passage is from The Botany of Desire: A Plant's Eye View of the World *by Michael Pollan. In this section of the book, Pollan discusses Americans' love affair with apples, and he specifically informs readers about the relationship of apples to alcohol during the history of America.*

PRE-READING PROMPT

1. Who was Johnny Appleseed? What do you know about this character from American history and folklore? If you have never heard of him, look up the name on the Internet and briefly tell what you have learned about him.
2. What are the ways people today typically consume apples? What products typically contain apples?
3. Why do you think early pioneers in America might have avoided drinking water? What might their alternative beverages have been?

1   The sweetest fruit makes the strongest drink, and in the north, where grapes didn't do well, that was usually the apple. Up until Prohibition, an apple grown in America was far less likely to be eaten than to wind up in a barrel of cider. "Hard cider" is a twentieth-century term, redundant before then since virtually all cider was hard until modern refrigeration allowed people to keep sweet cider sweet.

2   Corn liquor, or "white lightning," preceded cider on the frontier by a few years, but after the apple trees began to bear fruit, cider—being safer, tastier, and much easier to make—became the

Comment: **Details:** Pollan provides a fact that might surprise readers.

Comment: This sentence functions as a general **thesis.**

Comment: **Explanation:** Pollan provides a historical context.

alcoholic drink of choice. Just about the only reason to plant an orchard of the sort of seedling apples John Chapman had for sale would have been its intoxicating harvest of drink, available to anyone with a press and a barrel. Allowed to ferment for a few weeks, pressed apple juice yields a mildly alcoholic beverage with about half the strength of wine. For something stronger, the cider can then be distilled into brandy or simply frozen; the intensely alcoholic liquid that refuses to ice is called applejack. Hard cider frozen to thirty degrees below zero yields an applejack of 66 proof.

> Comment: **Details and Explanation:** Pollan points out important differences among cider, brandy, and applejack.

3   Virtually every homestead in America had an orchard from which thousands of gallons of cider were made every year. In rural areas cider took the place not only of wine and beer but of coffee and tea, juice, and even water. Indeed, in many places cider was consumed more freely than water, even by children, since it was arguably the healthier, because more sanitary, beverage. Cider became so indispensable to rural life that even those who railed against the evils of alcohol made an exception for cider, and the early prohibitionists succeeded mainly in switching drinkers over from grain to apple spirits. Eventually they would attack cider directly and launch a campaign to chop down apple trees, but up until the end of the nineteenth century cider continued to enjoy the theological exemption the Puritans had contrived for it.

> Comment: **Details:** Pollan offers new information—a description about how widespread and popular cider was and how it was healthier to drink on the frontier.

> Comment: **Explanation:** Pollan provides another historical context by discussing early attempts to ban alcohol.

4   It wasn't until the twentieth century that the apple acquired its reputation for wholesomeness—"an apple a day keeps the doctor away" was a marketing slogan dreamed up by growers concerned that temperance would cut into sales. In 1900 the horticulturalist Liberty Hyde Bailey noted that "the eating of the apple (rather than the drinking of it) has come to be paramount," but for the two centuries before that, whenever an American extolled the virtues of the apple, whether it was John Winthrop or Thomas Jefferson, Henry Ward Beecher or John Chapman, their contemporaries would probably have smiled knowingly, hearing in the words a distinct Dionysian echo that we are apt to miss. When Emerson, for instance, wrote that "man would be more solitary, less friended, less supported, if the land yielded only the useful maize and potato, [and] withheld this ornamental and social fruit," his readers understood it was the support and sociability of alcohol he had in mind. Part of reason John Chapman was welcome in every cabin in Ohio was because he was bringing the gift of drink. Since Prohibition we've been taught to think of Johnny Appleseed as a Walt Disney character, harmless and saccharine, when in fact the man was an American Dionysus.

> Comment: **Explanation:** This quote provides a transition from the temperance movement in America (banning of alcohol) to the apple's new reputation.

> Comment: **Audience and Style:** This allusion refers to Dionysus, the Greek god of fertility and wine.

> Comment: **Explanation:** Another allusion refers to John Chapman or "Johnny Appleseed," who is credited with creating apple orchards across America.

QUESTIONS FOR DISCUSSION

1. In summary, how has the perception of the apple changed from what it was two hundred years ago to what it is today?
2. In order to understand why apple growers began to market the fruit as a wholesome, healthy treat, you have to know what is meant by the temperance movement and Prohibition. Look these up on the

Internet. In your own words explain why Prohibition threatened the apple industry.

3. Why do you think the Puritans, who were among those who "railed against the evils of alcohol," were willing to make an exemption for apple cider?

4. Often writers use *allusions*—references to characters or events from literature, history, or popular culture. Twice Pollan alludes to a Greek god—"Dionysian echo" and "American Dionysus." Look up Dionysus. Why is "American Dionysus" an appropriate label for John Chapman?

I D E A S for Your Own Writing   MyWritingLab

Explore a Change

Pollan shows how apples went from being thought of as the main ingredient of a popular alcoholic beverage to being a "wholesome" fruit. In a short set of paragraphs or a longer essay, explain how our perception of something has changed with time. For example, cigarettes were once used in movies to suggest sophistication and sensuality. What is the perception of smokers today? Having a cell phone once meant a person was wealthy and probably a high-power businessperson. Who has cell phones today? Other possible topics include the following:

the role of either parent	fast food
exercise	eating every supper with one's family
rap/hip hop music	recycling
kindergarten	

As part of your research for this paper, you may want talk to older friends or family members to learn what they remember about how the topic was viewed twenty years ago or more. They can work as sources for your paper.

SELECTION 2   MyWritingLab

from The Cave of Bats

Richard Conniff

The next passage comes from a chapter in Richard Conniff's book Every Creeping Thing. *Conniff is an accomplished award-winning author of books and articles on human and animal behavior. In this excerpt, he explains a significant difference between two flying creatures—bats and birds.*

1. Before you begin reading, what are some of the obvious differences between bats and birds that you already know?
2. If you knew your readers already understood the basic differences between mammals and birds, what kinds of details would you look for to make a comparison more interesting and engaging?

Birds lay eggs and spare themselves from having to fly around with all that extra weight. But a bat gives birth to a single offspring weighing a quarter of her normal body weight, or sometimes to twins. (To ease birth with the help of gravity, she may hang upside down and catch her newborn in the wing membrane between her legs.) Her young may then latch on to a nipple and cling to her in flight for several days afterward. Birds can gather food and **regurgitate** it for their young back at the nest; bats can't. The mother must continue to eat for two, nursing her offspring until it is capable of taking flight to **forage** for its own food. Since a young bat starts to fly when it reaches 80 to 90 percent of its adult weight, this is the equivalent of nursing a teenager.

> **regurgitate:** vomit

> **forage:** gather

QUESTIONS FOR DISCUSSION

1. Conniff discusses some basic differences between bats and birds, but makes the information new and interesting for his readers. How does he do this? What details make these basic differences more interesting?
2. At the end of this passage, Conniff makes a surprising shift in his comparison. What is he comparing bats to in this final sentence?
3. Besides simply showing readers the difference between bats and birds, what insight about bats do you think he is trying to give his readers? What do you think is his reason for sharing this insight?

Ⓘ Ⓓ Ⓔ Ⓐ Ⓢ for Your Own Writing   MyWritingLab

A Fresh Look at the Obvious

Taking your cue from Richard Conniff, write a paragraph in which you present in a new and engaging way an obvious difference between two subjects. Just as Conniff wants his readers to better understand and appreciate the bat, your comparison should help readers better appreciate one of the subjects by looking more closely at differences they take for granted. Possible topics include the following:

comparing a modern-day bathroom to the outhouse of the past

comparing a fast food hamburger to a burger hot off the grill

buying an apple from the store compared to picking one off a tree

reading an ebook compared to reading a paper text

housebreaking a puppy compared to potty-training a baby

wearing dress shoes compared to wearing sneakers or flip-flops

SELECTION 3   MyWritingLab

A Night of Lynching, a Life of Remembering

Sharon Cohen

In the first longer reading selection of the chapter, Sharon Cohen profiles James Cameron who, as a young man, narrowly escaped a lynching. In his later years, he turned the terror of that night into America's Black Holocaust Museum.

PRE-READING PROMPT

1. What kinds of situations might cause people to take the law into their own hands? Do you think this is ever justified?
2. Why do you think it's important for us to remember the mistakes and injustices of the past?
3. Having an experience that puts one seconds away from death can be life changing. What kinds of changes do you think it can bring about in a person?

1   He remembers every detail about that long-ago night: the pearl-white glow of the moon, the roar of the frenzied mob, the fists and clubs beating him—then the rough hands forcing his head into a noose. And, of course, he remembers the rope. It left a burn mark on his neck.

2   He is an old man now, a great-grandfather with a cane and a cap of frosty silver hair. It has been more than 70 years since two of his friends were **lynched** one horrible August night—and he was supposed to be next. James Cameron turned his near-death experience into his life's work, telling his story of Aug. 7, 1930, hundreds of times over the years and creating America's Black Holocaust Museum—dedicated to the suffering that blacks have endured throughout the nation's history.

3   Cameron, about to turn 89 and frail from heart surgery and cancer, is determined to keep the flame burning and ensure that his small, struggling

lynched: hanged by a mob without a trial

15-year-old museum survives after he is gone. "It's the most important thing in the world to me to carry on this fight, to explain the history that's been hidden. I wonder if God saved me for this mission?" He paused, then answered his question: "It had to be. And I thank him for that."

4   When Cameron talks about the night he was almost killed, his words flow like those of an actor with a keen sense for the dramatic pause, the telling detail, the precise moment to raise or lower his raspy voice.

5   Always, the memory brings tears to his eyes.

6   Cameron, then 16 and living in Marion, Ind., had finished playing horseshoes and accepted a ride from his friend, Thomas Shipp. Soon they picked up Abe Smith. As they coasted along in the 1926 Ford roadster, he says, one of the other teens suggested holding up someone to get money. Cameron says he told them he wasn't interested, but they all drove to a lover's lane.

7   One of his companions, he says, handed him a .38-caliber revolver and, calling him by his nickname, said: "Apples (Cameron's mother had an apple orchard), you take the gun and hold the people up." Cameron approached a car and pointed the gun at a man—who was with a woman—but realized it was one of his regular shoeshine customers. So, he says, he gave the gun to Shipp, told him that he wouldn't rob anyone, then ran down the road.

8   A few moments later, he heard gunshots.

9   The man in the car had been shot to death. Rumors spread that the woman was raped. Both were white. The three black teens were quickly rounded up and taken to jail, where thousands of people, including women and children, gathered with gas cans, iron bars and sledgehammers, crashing through bricks and pounding down the door. The mob rushed past law enforcement officers to grab the youths. Marion actually had fairly good race relations for the time, says James Madison, an Indiana University history professor who wrote about the incident in "A Lynching in the Heartland: Race and Memory in America." He says the town had an NAACP branch and two black police officers.

10   None of that mattered that night.

11   Shipp and Smith were brutally beaten, then lynched on a tree in the courthouse square. Cameron was next. "They began to chant for me like a football player: 'We want Cameron, we want Cameron,'" he recalled, clasping his hands tight. "I could feel the blood in my body just freezing up."

12   Cameron, who says he was beaten into signing a false confession, was hit in the head with a pick handle; pummeled with fists, clubs and rocks; bitten and spat on as the mob dragged him out of the jail, shouting racial slurs. "The miracle is I didn't go unconscious," he said. They pulled him toward the tree, where he saw the dangling, bloody bodies of his friends.

13   "They put the rope around my neck and threw it over the limb," Cameron said. "They were getting ready to hang me up when I said, 'Lord, have mercy, forgive me my sins.' My mother always told us children, 'Before you do anything,

always pray.'" So he prayed. "Then," he said, "I gave up hope." Then suddenly, he said, came a heavenly voice with an order: "Take this boy back. He had nothing to with any raping or killing." The crowd parted, he says, as he stumbled back into the jail. Cameron has asked others who were there that night, but no one else heard that voice. But there apparently was a protest.

14   One man stood atop a car and shouted that Cameron was innocent and should be freed, according to documents unearthed by Madison, who said a few others also tried to calm the crowd. The lynching scene was captured in a photo—reproduced and sold for 50 cents—that became an enduring symbol of racial terror in America. It shows a milling crowd, people smiling or staring calmly into the camera, women in summer dresses, men in fedoras and ties, one pointing up to the mutilated bodies. Two men were charged with **inciting** the mob, but they were **acquitted**, according to Madison. Cameron was convicted of being an **accessory before the fact** to voluntary manslaughter. He spent four years in prison, was freed at age 21, and attended technical high school and college.

15   He and his wife, Virginia, reared five children, and Cameron supported them as a truck driver, laundry man, record store owner, waiter, junk man and mainte-nance engineer. He was a strict father, instilling pride in his children, says his 59-year-old son, Virgil, who recalls how the family resisted the segregation poli-cies at movie theaters in Indiana. "We sat wherever we wanted," he said. "We were the Camerons. He had that type of strength. He would not tolerate racism."

16   Cameron was always determined to tell his story. In 1946, he sent a letter to his idol, poet-writer Langston Hughes, seeking advice. He received an answer (framed on his museum wall) but no publisher. Decades passed and, in 1979, he and his wife visited Israel and Yad Vashem, the Holocaust memorial, where he was moved by exhibits of Jewish persecution and the inscription: "To remember is salvation. To forget is exile." Turning to his wife, he said, "Honey, we need a museum like that in America to show what happened to black people."

17   The big civil rights museums were still years away, and Cameron's interests were in the horrors of slavery and lynching—atrocities he believed were neglected by white historians. When he began soliciting help for his museum, he said, "People thought I was crazy. They thought everything should be buried and not dug up." He forged ahead and published his memoirs in 1982, mortgaging his house to print 5,000 copies of "A Time of Terror." The book was later reprinted by Black Classic Press.

18   For his museum, Cameron visited the Library of Congress; he haunted rummage sales and bought books, lynching photos, and Ku Klux Klan robes and hoods. In 1988, he opened his museum in a small storefront room, then six years later moved to an abandoned 12,000-square-foot gym that the city of Milwaukee sold him for $1. About that time, he met Daniel Bader, who offered a generous check. "He's somehow able to put you in his skin and let you see the world through his eyes," said Bader, presi-dent of the Helen Bader Foundation, which remains a financial supporter.

---

inciting: causing

acquitted: declared not guilty

accessory before the fact: person involved before a crime, but not in the crime itself

19   On a whim, Cameron says he wrote a letter to the governor of Indiana in 1991 seeking a pardon. Two years later, it was granted. A week later, Cameron, decked out in a black tuxedo, returned to Marion to receive the key to the city that, an accompanying letter said, should serve to "lock out any denial of the abuses of that ugly time." The letter is displayed at the museum, but another piece of Marion's past is locked up for safekeeping—a thumb-size hunk of yellow rope given to him several years ago that was purported to have been used in the lynchings.

20   Over the years, Cameron's museum has featured the works of black photographers and artifacts from the Henrietta Marie, a slave ship found off the Florida coast. But times have been tough and the museum operates on a shoestring budget, says Jessie Leonard, the interim director. She says she's still looking for financing for a permanent exhibit on Cameron's life—from his days as a young man helping to form three NAACP chapters to his protest at a Klan rally a few months ago, in a wheelchair.

21   Leonard calls Cameron "a quiet soldier" but "not so quiet he cannot be heard." Cameron vows to continue talking—and protesting—as long as he can: "Something inside me just keeps urging me on."

QUESTIONS FOR DISCUSSION

I nterest

1. One of the simplest ways to grab a reader's attention is by having a strong title. In what ways does the title of this article attract readers, and how might the title make someone not want to read further?

2. The essay profiles James Cameron and the museum he created. In writing an informative profile of a person and/or place, what should a writer focus on and emphasize in order to keep a reader's interest? In what ways does the author keep your interest? How does she do this? Are there any parts of the article that didn't seem necessary? Which ones, and why do you think so?

D etails

3. Which details give you a sense of the kind of person Cameron was before the incident that nearly cost him his life?

4. Which details show that Cameron has become "a quiet soldier" whose voice is still heard?

5. Which details about the museum connect to Cameron's determination and spirit?

6. The author uses statements from people who know Cameron. How do these quotations provide interesting and new information in the essay? How do the statements by Cameron function in the same way?

E xplanation

7. Cameron was convicted of accessory before the fact to voluntary manslaughter and sentenced to four years in prison. Was this a fair

sentence? Why or why not? Why does the writer choose not to address this question?

8. What might be some of the reasons that the men who allegedly incited the riot were acquitted? How does the author address this issue?

9. Cohen describes the photo taken of the lynching: "It shows a milling crowd, people smiling or staring calmly into the camera, women in summer dresses, men in fedoras and ties, one pointing up to the mutilated bodies." What about this image makes it especially fitting as an "enduring symbol of racial terror in America"? Do you agree with the author on this point? Why or why not?

Audience

10. How would you describe the writer's attitude toward her subject? Does her approach to the topic of her article invite her readers to listen, or does it alienate them?

Style

11. This is a newspaper article, and newspaper articles tend to have short sentences and paragraphs. Look at all of the one-sentence paragraphs. Which ones work as transitional paragraphs and paragraphs that relate important quotations?

I D E A S for Your Own Writing   MyWritingLab

Profile of an Event and a Person

Taking your cue from Cohen's article, profile a person in your community and relate an important event in his or her life. In the essay, you need to inform readers about the significance of this event without being preachy or angry or sappy. Like Cohen does in her essay, relate the facts of the event and its effect on the person without trying to persuade a reader about something. Make sure the essay is interesting for readers.

Informing about Your Community

Your new boss just relocated to your local area. During the course of your conversation with her, she asks you, "Since I don't know much about this area, are there any events or places I need to check out?" In your conversation, you suggest a few you can think of off the top of your head. But when you get home later that night, you remember more, so you decide to email your boss. In two to three paragraphs in an email format, inform your new boss about the event or place she should "check out." Provide details, examples, and explanation in your email.

SELECTION 4

Seven Sustainable Wonders

Alan Thein Durning

The second essay of this chapter is by the environmental activist, Alan Thein Durning. The author founded the Sightline Institute, and his most famous book is How Much is Enough?: The Consumer Society and the Future of the Earth *(1992). "Seven Sustainable Wonders" makes readers look at simple but important innovations that he deems are "sustainable."*

PRE-READING PROMPT

1. What are some inventions that have made an important impact on people's lives? Which have made the greatest impact on your own life?
2. Think about inventions that do not involve electronics or other sophisticated forms of technology. Which of these do you think have been the most significant?
3. Of the inventions you have thought about so far, which have had the most destructive impact on our environment?

[1]   I've never seen any of the Seven Wonders of the World, and to tell you the truth I wouldn't really want to. To me, the real wonders are all the little things— little things that work, especially when they do it without hurting the earth. Here's my list of simple things that, though we take them for granted, are absolute wonders. These **implements** solve every day problems so elegantly that everyone in the world today—and everyone who is likely to live in it in the next century— could make use of them without Mother Nature's being any the worse for wear.

> **implements:** tools

1. The Bicycle

> **thermodynamically:** energy, in the sense of power to work.

[2]   The most **thermodynamically** efficient transportation device ever created and the most widely used private vehicle in the world, the bicycle lets you travel three times as far on a plate full of calories as you could walking. And they're 53 times more energy efficient—comparing food calories with gasoline calories—

than the typical car. Not to mention the fact they don't pollute the air, lead to oil spills (and oil wars), change the climate, send cities sprawling over the country-side, lock up half of urban space in roads and parking lots, or kill a quarter million people in traffic accidents each year.

[3]   The world doesn't yet have enough bikes for everybody to ride, but it's getting

there quickly: Best estimates put the world's expanding fleet of two-wheelers at 850 million—double the number of autos. We Americans have no excuses on this count: We have more bikes per person than China, where they are the principal vehicle. We just don't ride them much.

2. The Ceiling Fan

4   Appropriate technology's answer to air conditioning, ceiling fans cool tens of millions of people in Asia and Africa. A fan over your bed brings relief in sweltering **climes**, as I've had plenty of time to reflect on during episodes of digestive turmoil in cheap tropical hotels.

climes: environments

5   Air conditioning, found in two-thirds of U.S. homes, is a juice hog and the bane of the stratospheric ozone layer because of its CFC coolants. Ceiling fans, on the other hand, are simple, durable, and repairable and take little energy to run.

3. The Clothesline

6   A few years ago, I read about an engineering laboratory that claimed it had all but perfected a microwave clothes dryer. The dryer, the story went, would get the moisture out of the wash with one-third the energy of a conventional unit and cause less wear and tear on the fabric. I don't know if they ever got it on the market, but it struck me at the time that if simple wonders had a PR agent, there might have been a news story instead about the perfection of a solar clothes dryer. It takes few materials to manufacture, is safe for kids, requires absolutely no electricity or fuel, and even gets people outdoors where they can talk to their neighbors.

4. The Telephone

7   The greatest innovation in human communications since Gutenberg's printing press, telephone systems are the only entry on my wonders list invented in this century, and—hype of the information age not-with-standing—I'll wager that they never lose ground to other communications technologies. Unlike fax machines, personal computers and computer networks, television, VCRs and camcorders, CD-ROMs, and all the other **flotsam and jetsam** of the information age, telephones are a simple extension of the most time-tested means of human communication: speech.

flotsam and jetsam: wreckage, ruins

5. The Public Library

8   Public libraries are the most democratic institutions yet invented. Think of it! Equal access to information for any citizen who comes inside. A lifetime of learning, all free. Libraries foster community, too, by bringing people of different classes, races, and ages together in that endangered form of human habitat: noncommercial public space.

9   Although conceived without any ecological intention whatsoever, libraries are waste reduction at its best. Each library saves a forest full of trees by making thousands of personal copies of books and periodicals unnecessary. All that paper savings means huge reductions in energy use and water and air pollution, too. In

principle, the library concept could be applied to other things—cameras and cam-corders, tapes and CD's, cleaning equipment and extra dining chairs—further reducing the number of things our society needs without reducing people's access to them. The town of Takoma Park, Maryland, for example, has a tool library where people can check out a lawn mower, a ratchet set, or a sledgehammer.

6. The Interdepartmental Envelope

[10]   I don't know what they're really called: those old-fashioned slotted manila envelopes bound with a string and covered with lines for routing papers to one person after another. Whatever they're called, they put modern recycling to shame.

7. The Condom

[11]   It's a remarkable little device: highly effective, inexpensive, and portable. A few purists Greens might complain about disposability and excess packaging, but these are trivial considering the work the condom has to do—battling the scourge of AIDS and stabilizing the human population at a level the earth can comfortably support.

QUESTIONS FOR DISCUSSION

I nterest

1. Which parts of the first paragraph make an audience want to read more? Which parts of the paragraph might not grab readers' attention?
2. What criteria does Durning use to determine which "wonders" go on his list?
3. Why do you think Durning chose to inform readers about "simple" wonders?

D etails

4. Which items does Durning do the strongest job of detailing why they are wonders and how they have benefitted humankind? Why do you think he chose them?
5. Which details and reasons provided for any of the wonders are the most surprising to you, and why? What is the most important new information to you? What doesn't seem new?
6. What are common details among the wonders that the author informs readers about? Are there any features shared among some of them, and if so, what are they?

E xplanation

7. In the last sentence of the first paragraph, Durning explains the reasons he has noted these particular wonders: "These implements solve everyday problems so elegantly that everyone in the world today—and everyone who is likely to live in it in the next century—could make use of them without Mother Nature's being any the

worse for wear." Which of the seven wonders is the most detailed in connecting with this description? Why do you think so? Which one is the least detailed? Why do you think so?

8. If you had to reduce his list of wonders by two items, which would you remove? Why?

9. If Durning had to expand his list of wonders by two items, what would you suggest he add? Why?

Audience

10. Durning's title has the word "sustainable" in it. What kind of attitude toward the world does that word choice show?

Style

11. Describe the style of this essay. Is it formal, in the middle, or informal in its approach to the reader? Or does it mix the levels of formality? How and why?

I D E A S for Your Own Writing   MyWritingLab

Two Unsustainable Wonders

Durning describes inventions that have benefitted humankind without hurting the environment. Take a different approach and describe what you think are two inventions that have *least* benefitted humankind and have most hurt our environment by informing readers about the effects of these inventions. Like Durning, you need to describe and explain each of your selections.

Informing about Your Own Wonder

Write an essay that informs readers about a type of technology or a service that is free or reasonably priced and beneficial to many people in American society. In this short essay, you need to use strong examples and provide detailed explanations to show how it is a "wonder."

SELECTION 5   MyWritingLab

Soup

The New Yorker

The final reading selection of the chapter is "Soup," an unsigned essay that first appeared in the "Talk of the Town" section of New Yorker *magazine in January of 1989. Albert Yeganeh, the subject of this article, also inspired the "Soup Nazi" episode on the television series* Seinfeld.

1. Given the competition in today's market, what does it take to be a successful business owner?
2. How do you think a successful business owner should treat customers?
3. When you visit a restaurant, which is more important to you—the food or the service? Why?

1   When Albert Yeganeh says "Soup is my lifeblood," he means it. And when he says "I am extremely hard to please," he means that too. Working like a demon **alchemist** in a tiny storefront kitchen at 259-A West Fifty-fifth Street, Mr. Yeganeh creates anywhere from eight to seventeen soups every weekday. His **concoctions** are so popular that a wait of half an hour at the lunchtime peak is not uncommon, although there are strict rules of conduct inline. But more on that later.

alchemist: early scientists who conducted chemical experiments in the search for mixtures with magical properties

concoctions: mixtures

2   "I am psychologically kind of a health freak," Mr. Yeganeh said the other day in a lisping staccato of Armenian origin. "And I know that soup is the greatest meal in the world. It's very good for your digestive system. And I use only the best, the freshest ingredients. I am a perfectionist. When I make a clam soup, I use three different kinds of clams. Every other place uses canned clams. I'm called crazy. I am not crazy. People don't realize why I get so upset. It's because if the soup is not perfect and I'm still selling it, it's a torture. It's my soup, and that's why I'm so upset. First you clean and then you cook. I don't believe that ninety-nine per cent of the restaurants in New York know how to clean a tomato. I tell my crew to wash the parsley eight times. If they wash it five or six times, I scare them. I tell them they'll go to jail if there is sand in the parsley. One time, I found a mushroom on the floor, and I fired the guy who left it there." He spread his arms, and added, "This place is the only one like it in . . . in . . . the whole earth! One day, I hope to learn something from the other places, but so far I haven't. For example the other day I went to a very fancy restaurant and had **borscht**. I had to send it back. It was junk. I could see all the chemicals in it. I never use chemicals. Last weekend, I had lobster bisque in Brooklyn, a very well-known place. It was junk. When I make a lobster bisque, I use a whole lobster. You know, I never advertise, I don't have to. All the big-shot chefs and the kings of the hotels come here to see what I'm doing."

borscht: an Eastern European beet soup

3   As you approach Mr. Yeganeh's Soup Kitchen International from a distance, the first thing you notice about it is the awning, which proclaims "Homemade Hot, Cold, Diet Soups." The second thing you notice is an aroma so delicious that it makes you want to take a bite out of the air. The third thing you notice, in front of the kitchen, is an electric signboard that flashes, say "Today's Soups . . . Chicken Vegetable . . . Mexican Beef Chili . . . Cream of Watercress . . . Italian Sausage . . . Clam Bisque . . . Beef Barley . . . Due to Cold Weather . . . For Most Efficient and Fastest Service the Line Must . . . Be Kept Moving . . . Please . . . Have Your Money . . . Ready . . . Pick the Soup of Your Choice . . . Move to Your Extreme . . . Left After Ordering."

4   "I am not prejudiced against color or religion," Mr. Yeganeh told us, and he jabbed an index finger at the flashing sign. "Whoever follows that I treat very well. My regular customers don't say anything. They are very intelligent and well educated. They know I'm just trying to move the line. The New York cop is very smart—he sees everything but says nothing. But the young girl who wants to stop and tell you how nice you look and hold everyone up—yah!" He made a **guillotining motion with his hand**. "I tell you, I hate to work with the public. They treat me like a slave. My philosophy is: The customer is always wrong and I'm always right. I raised my prices to try and get rid of some of these people, but it didn't work."

guillotining motion with his hand: pretends to cut his head off

5   The other day, Mr. Yeganeh was dressed in chefs' whites with orange smears across his chest, which may have been some of the carrot soup cooking in a huge pot on a little stove in one corner. A three-foot-long hand-held mixer from France sat in the sink, looking like an overgrown gardening tool. Mr. Yeganeh spoke to two young helpers in a twisted Armenian-Spanish **barrage**, then said

barrage: outpouring, a rush of words

to us, "I have no overhead, no trained waitresses, and I have the cashier here." He pointed to himself theatrically. Beside the doorway, a glass case with fresh green celery, red and yellow peppers, and purple eggplant was topped by five big gray soup urns. According to a piece of cardboard taped to the door, you can buy Mr. Yeganeh's soups in three sizes, costing from four to fifteen dollars. The order of any well-behaved customer is accompanied by little waxpaper packets of bread, fresh vegetables (such as scallions and radishes), fresh fruit (such as cherries or an orange), a chocolate mint, and a plastic spoon. No coffee, tea, or other drinks are served.

6   "I get my recipes from books and theories and my own taste," Mr. Yeganeh said. "At home, I have several hundreds of books. When I do research, I find that I don't know anything. Like cabbage is a cancer fighter, and some fish is good for your heart but some is bad. Every day, I should have one sweet, one spicy, one cream, one vegetable soup—and they must change, they should always taste a

repertoire: collection, portfolio

little different." He added that he wasn't sure how extensive his **repertoire** was, but that it probably includes at least eighty soups, among them African peanut butter, Greek moussaka, hamburger, Reuben, B.L.T., asparagus and caviar, Japanese shrimp miso, chicken chili, Irish corned beef and cabbage, Swiss chocolate, French calf's brain, Korean beef ball, Italian shrimp and eggplant Parmesan, buffalo, ham and egg, short rib, Russian beef Stroganoff, turkey cacciatore, and Indian mulligatawny. "The chicken and the seafood are an addiction, and when I have French garlic soup, I let people have only one small container each," he said. "The doctors and nurses love that one."

7   A lunch line of thirty people stretched down the block of Mr. Yeganeh's doorway. Behind a construction worker was a man in expensive leather, who was in front of a woman in a fur hat. Few people spoke. Most had their money out and their orders ready.

8   At the front of the line, a woman in a brown coat couldn't decide which soup to get and started to complain about the prices.

9   "You talk too much, dear," Mr. Yeganeh said, and motioned to her to move to the left. "Next!"

10   "Just don't talk. Do what he says," a man huddled in a blue parka warned.

11   "He's downright rude," said a blond woman in a coat. "Even abusive. But you can't deny it, his soup is the best."

QUESTIONS FOR DISCUSSION

I nterest

1. Analyze the attention-getting quality of the first paragraph. How does the author reach out to the audience, and what aspects of the paragraph would make a reader want to read further? Why?

2. Of all of the direct quotations from Yeganeh, which one sticks out the most to you and why? What is the writer trying to inform his readers about through this article about Yeganeh, his philosophy, his business, and his personality?

D etails

3. What dominant personality trait of Yeganeh is emphasized in this article? Is he someone you would want to work for? Why or why not?

4. The author uses specific details throughout the essay. Which details help you picture the workplace? Which details help you envision Mr. Yeganeh and understand his personality? Which details help you to understand the product—Mr. Yeganeh's soups? Which details reveal the types of customers who come for this soup?

E xplanation

5. Why do so many customers tolerate Mr. Yeganeh's strict rules and rude behavior? What examples in the article support their tolerance for his attitude?

6. What explanation of his methods does the author provide through direct quotations? Why do you think the author chose to not take a side or comment extensively on the way Mr. Yeganeh acts in this article?

7. How do customers' statements provide an explanation for the popularity of his restaurant?

A udience

8. Do you think the author's approach and tone in the essay is successful? Why or why not?

S tyle

9. In the final part of the essay, the author details the lunch line and Yeganeh's attitude toward customers who don't follow the rules. Look at the quotations and how the author describes the action, but focus specifically on the verbs used. How does the author create a mood with his verbs?

10. Most of the essay has long paragraphs that provide long quotations from the chef. Why would a writer choose to use such long paragraphs that provide direct quotations from Yeganeh?

I D E A S for Your Own Writing   MyWritingLab

Preparing for a Job Interview: Informing about Your Work Ethic

The *American Heritage Dictionary* defines the term *work ethic* in this way: "A set of values based on the moral virtues of hard work and diligence." In "Soup," the author informs readers, in part, about the work ethic and cooking/business philosophy of Albert Yeganeh. In a short essay, prepare for future job interviews where an interviewer may ask a question such as this: "How would you describe your work ethic?" Inform your reader/future employer about your personal work ethic.

Informing about the Characteristics of a Successful Business

Based on your experience as a consumer, explain the characteristics of one kind of successful business. What, for example, makes a grocery store, gas station, hair salon, or bookstore a good place to shop? What qualities does a good business have to have, and why? Use details, examples, and thoughtful explanations to inform a reader about what you know are essential characteristics for a certain kind of business or shop.

Historical/Cultural Marker: Informing about a Place in Your Community

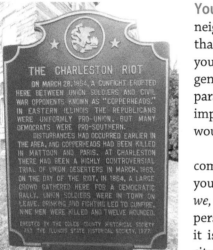

Your Writing Task: Drawing upon your knowledge of your neighborhood, city, community, or metro area, locate a place that is significant to your community or a special group of which you are a member. Your task is to find a landmark and inform a general reader about it. Your aim is to provide a text (one to four paragraphs) that describes and offers reasons why this place is important. Ideally, if funds are available, your informative prose would be printed on a historical/cultural marker at that place.

Since you are writing for a wide audience (anyone who might come along and read this historical marker at a certain spot in your community), your writing cannot use first person (*I, mine, we, us*) or second person (*you, your*). The marker must use third person when relating details about this place and explaining why it is a significant and important place in your neighborhood, city, community, or metro area.

Your Audience: Keep in mind that the person reading this marker will be standing exactly in front of the place that you are writing about. So think about how your text can complement and inform a general reader about that landmark.

Format: Before you offer the full text for the historical/cultural marker, you should indicate under the heading of "Location" in one or two sentences where exactly this marker would be placed. The informative prose for the marker (one to four paragraphs) should be placed under the heading of "Text," and the text should be single-spaced with double-spacing between paragraphs.

A Successful Historical Marker . . .

- Is entertaining, easy to read, and thought provoking.
- Provides a strong background and context about this place at the beginning of the text.
- Relates specific and concrete details about this place that are important and significant to your community or special group.
- Presents these details clearly and concisely.
- Has focused and unified paragraphs.

- Uses transitions and a variety of sentence types.
- Provides a medium level of tone and diction—not too formal, but not too informal.
- Is free of mechanical and proofreading errors.
  See page 229 for Collin Seibert's response to this assignment.

Career Profile Assignment

Your Writing Task: Write an informative essay about a career in which you have an interest, ideally a career you hope to have some day. You will present information about this career by highlighting the experiences—perhaps a typical day on the job—of an individual currently engaged in this career. Some possible subjects for this essay include a doctor, a small business owner, a teacher, a gardener, a parole officer. While any career profile will include a discussion of the work itself and the workplace environment, you should present these elements through the individual's perspective. The essay "Soup" is a good example of a workplace profile that presents the restaurant business through the experiences of one individual—Mr. Yeganeh.

You will gather material for this paper by observing, interviewing, and notetaking; thus, you will practice firsthand research techniques (see Chapter 12, p. 356 for tips on preparing for interviews). Once you have compiled sufficient information, you will organize it into an informative profile.

NOTE: **It is best to avoid profiling an immediate family member. You will not gain meaningful experience in interviewing, notetaking, and research by talking to Mom or Dad over the supper table. However, if you want to interview a distant family member who has a profession you are interested in, please discuss the matter with your instructor.

Your Audience: Imagine that the counselors have asked for your career profile to be kept as a resource in the Career Center to be read by students interested in that career. Your profile will be an important resource because it is more than just dry facts about a career. It is a lively, entertaining account that highlights your individual attitude and point of view while presenting important information.

Special Considerations

- **Determine a *dominant impression* that you want your profile to convey**. A profile of a particular career professional might stress the necessary leadership skills or perhaps the person's ability to communicate well. Having a dominant impression to convey will help you to focus your details, so the essay communicates a specific point about the subject to the readers.

- **Make your essay *informative, interesting,* and *well organized*.** Inform your readers by including facts and relevant information about the career. Remember, "memorable quotations, compelling examples, vivid details, and interesting word choices" will interest and engage your readers. Finally, you may also find using the writing strategy of narration a good approach for your topic. A dramatic narrative of your topic in a story form is an effective way to capture your readers' interest while presenting information.

- **Give careful consideration to *your role* in this profile.** Do you want to be a visible part of the discussion? In other words, will the profile be a first person narrative? (i.e., "After being held spellbound by his thrilling highwire act, I asked the Great Fernando how he got involved in circus work.") You may also choose to not be a visible part of the narrative, to write it in third person as was the approach of the author of "Soup." Either approach can be successful.

Rejection Letter

Your Role and Position: You are a regional director of Missouri Health Matters, a non-profit health promotion organization that works in urban, suburban, and rural communities within the state of Missouri to encourage exercise and healthy eating habits to young children, tweens, and teenagers. Your official title is Regional Director of Health Programs, and your territory is the western, northwestern, southwestern, and some central parts of the state.

The Rhetorical Situation: Context, Audience, Purpose, and Genre: Your organization has a need for more health program specialists, employees who give presentations and workshops about topics such as these: the need to eat more grains, vegetables, and fruits; the crucial need for young adults to exercise more often; the perils of obesity; and the negative health effects of junk food. The Executive Director of MO Health Matters gave you clearance to hire one new health program specialist because the organization is expanding. You conducted interviews, you've offered the job to a candidate, and that person has now formally accepted the job offer. During the process of finding these new hires, you interviewed five other very qualified individuals.

You have to write a rejection letter that will go to the five people who didn't get the position as health program specialist. Since you're incredibly busy as a Regional Director of MO Health Matters, you cannot personalize these five letters. That's a shame because the people you interviewed were very qualified and would have been great at the job. However, the person you hired—someone right out of college with a community health degree and substantial internship experience—was the best candidate.

You have to create a one-page form letter for the five candidates who did not get a job. All of them were very well qualified, had substantial work or internship experience, and held degrees that cohere with what MO Health Matters wanted. They just didn't get the job because of the strong competition.

A Successful Rejection Letter . . .

- Provides a respectful and appropriate buffer before relating the bad news.
- Explains the situation with poise, honesty, and thoughtfulness.
- Offers a tone that is respectful and appropriate.
- Provides a closing paragraph that offers goodwill and positive closure.
- Has focused and unified paragraphs.
- Is free of irrelevant details.
- Follows the proper format of a professional letter.
- Exhibits strong concision, cohesion, transitions, and sentence variety in length and type.
- Provides a medium level of tone and diction—not too formal, but not too informal.
- Is free of mechanical and proofreading errors.

CHAPTER AT A GLANCE

Learning Objectives	How they connect to writing at college . . .
❶ Get your facts straight.	Presenting inaccurate information can create distrust in readers.
	Present information accurately and truthfully.
❷ Make the information interesting.	Spark readers' interest through memorable quotations, compelling examples, vivid details, strong explanations, and interesting word choices.
❸ Organize information appropriately.	Organization is key to keeping readers interested and informed.
	Think about what the readers already know and what the readers need to know in order to catch and keep their attention.

Learning Objectives	How they connect to writing at college . . .

❹ Put **I D E A S** to work in informative writing.

Consider these crucial factors when brainstorming, drafting, and revising your informative writing:

- Interest
- Details
- Explanation
- Audience
- Style

MyWritingLab Visit **Chapter 8, "Informative Writing,"** in MyWritingLab to test your understanding of the chapter objectives.

Analytical Writing 9

Learning Objectives
In this chapter you will learn how to . . .

1 Analyze a subject by breaking it down and building it back up.

2 Support your analysis (and your thesis) with details, examples, and explanation.

3 Be a critical thinker when analyzing.

4 Put **I D E A S** to work in analytical writing.

This woman is doing her weekly grocery shopping. After seeing what food was already on hand at home, planning possible meals for the week, and checking store flyers for sales, she wrote out a list and headed off to the store. How do you use analysis in your everyday life?

People often associate the word *analysis* with something complicated or scientific, such as an astronomer *analyzing* the data sent back by a space probe. However, analytical thinking is very much a part of our everyday lives. Each of the following examples shows analytical thinking at work:

- As they prepare to vote before an election, thoughtful voters study the candidates' stands on various issues in order to support the candidate whose views most closely match their own.

- Before launching a new product, a company examines consumer trends and marketing strategies as well as manufacturing and sales costs. On the basis of these studies, the company will decide where and how to market the product.

- Students gather in groups in a writing class to review each other's papers. They look at how each paper organizes and supports its points while keeping readers engaged and interested. They also look at grammar and style issues in order to suggest ways the writer can improve the paper during revision.

So, to **analyze** you must look closely at something. You examine it to see how it works (or does not). You take apart an object, an idea, a situation, or a text—its structure, its organization, its parts—in order to better understand it.

The primary purpose of analytical writing is to arrive at a better understanding of a subject or a situation. Analysis, however, is often used as the basis, the support, for other aims of writing. When evaluating, you have to analyze your subject to determine how well it meets a set of standards. For example, only after analyzing all the features of several cell phones can you decide which one is best for you. When persuading, you have to provide a thorough and accurate analysis of an issue to give credibility to your argument. For instance, if a group of citizens wants a traffic light installed at a dangerous intersection, they might first look at what causes the frequent accidents at that intersection and explore how a light could prevent these accidents. A thorough and accurate analysis gives credibility to their proposal. Strong analytical skills are crucial to your success as a citizen, an employee, and a college student.

▼ Sometimes when people analyze, they look for causes and effects. What are some more realistic consequences of dumping chemicals in water?

"Have we been dumping chemicals in the swamp?"

❶ Analyze a subject by breaking it down and building it back up.

Analyze a Subject by Breaking It Down and Building It Back Up

When **analyzing**, you break down an idea, a situation, or an opportunity. You separate something into its parts so that you can better understand how it works as a whole.

The first step in writing an analysis is to identify your purpose. Why do you need to examine this subject more closely? For example, imagine you are a doctor meeting with a new patient—a four-year-old boy who has trouble breathing. Your purpose for analysis in this situation is to figure out why the boy has trouble breathing and how to help him.

Once you have identified your analytical purpose, you need to figure out what parts of your subject you need to look at more closely to achieve that purpose. In this case, you are going to break down the state of the child's health by asking the right questions and making careful observations. You might ask whether there are pets in the home. Or you might ask about the patient's general physical activity and diet. Then you are likely to move on to a physical exam: looking in his mouth, listening to his heartbeat and breathing. Based on your findings, you will order different tests and then analyze the results. Eventually, you will narrow the possible causes to a specific diagnosis and suggest treatments. You have looked at the parts of the child's life to better understand the whole picture of his health.

Analysis is a process of discovery. It is only after you have broken down your subject and looked closely at all its parts that you can begin to understand how the parts work together and can answer such questions as: "What does this mean?" "Is this the best option?" "How can this be done?" "What caused this?" "What might be the consequences?" "Why is this important?" In other words, you analyze to reach a conclusion.

For example, if a supervisor on a construction site finds a building is running behind schedule, he is going to seek solutions. He will examine blueprints and schedules, check over the site, talk to the people responsible, and come to an understanding of what is going wrong. He will break down the problem and then use this information to figure out a solution.

EXERCISE 9.1   Identify Elements for Analysis

Directions: On your own or in a small group, use your understanding of analysis to explain which parts might be examined in each of the following analytical situations and what might be learned from the analysis.

EXAMPLE   A potential home buyer has an inspector examine/analyze the house she is interested in buying.

An inspector will go through all the parts of the house to see if the home is up to code. The inspector will look at the roof, foundation, basement, wiring, hot water heater, central air unit, carpeting, flooring, toilets, pipes, etc. and examine the quality of these components. The inspector fills out an extensive form to provide analysis about these parts and then provides an overall analysis of the house's quality.

1. A student must decide whether to live in the dormitory on campus or to rent an apartment.

2. A family must choose a nursing home for an elderly grandmother.

3. A personal trainer works with a client to determine a fitness plan.

4. A fast food restaurant chain analyzes the cost effectiveness of opening a new franchise in a small town.

❷ Support your analysis (and your thesis) with details, examples, and explanation.

Support Your Analysis (and Your Thesis) with Details, Examples, and Explanation

Whether you are explaining, interpreting, or problem solving in analytical writing, you must provide **support**. You have to clearly express how all the parts connect to the conclusion you have reached about them. Use details, examples, and explanation to show readers how you reached your point, your **thesis**.

When analyzing a film, a movie critic looks closely at all the elements. She considers the plot, the acting, the soundtrack, the special effects, and the musical score. She breaks down all of a film's components in order to evaluate the overall quality of the film. As she watches the film, her notes may include references to specific lines of dialogue and the way one scene shifts to another. When she sits down to write a review, she uses all of these observations as details, examples, and explanation to support her analysis of the film.

EXERCISE 9.2   Analyze a Cover Letter   MyWritingLab

Directions: A friend of yours, Shirley Able—a recent high-school graduate with very little work experience—has written a cover letter to send with her résumé to an employment agency and has asked for your opinion of her letter. Read the letter, and then on your own or in a small group, analyze the letter by breaking it down into the following components.

1. **Appeal to audience:** Has Shirley chosen the best reasons and examples to make an employer want to hire her?

2. **Supporting evidence:** Does Shirley give sufficient and well-chosen details and examples to show she has the workplace qualities she claims to have?

3. **Organization:** Does Shirley have a clear thesis that connects to her support? Has she built up to her most important quality—that is, has she organized her points emphatically?

4. **Form and style:** Has Shirley avoided sentence errors that might distract readers or even create a negative impression of her abilities? Has she used appropriate language for the audience and purpose of this writing situation?

Dear Ms. Jones:

I am a recent high school graduate who is looking forward to applying my abilities and talents to an entry level position that offers opportunity for advancement. My experiences in high school and in my previous job have allowed me to develop skills that will appeal to employers.

    First of all, I have strong communication skills. In high school I took Communications 1 and 2 and did very well in these courses. I was also one of ten seniors picked to be conflict mediators for other students who where having conflicts with there peers or sometimes even there teachers. I am also dependable and trustworthy. At my previous job at Swankee Country Club, I have been given the responsibility of locking up the golf cart barn after all the employees have left. They gave me a key and the alarm code. I am also dependable cause I show up to work and on time every day. Most importantly, I am a good leader. I was elected class president my junior and senior years. This showed me how to take charge and get things done on time and the right way. During my senior year, I had the awesome opportunity to be head captain of the girls varsity basketball team. Being captain made me step up and take charge when there where team conflicts or when one of the girls where having a hard time. I was head of the homecoming committee my senior year and had many responsibilities, such as ordering the food, getting the D.J., selling tickets and decorating the gym.

(continued)

As a responsible communicator with strong leadership skills, I will be an asset to any company. I hope you are able to help me share my abilities soon.

Sincerely,

Shirley Able

Shirley Able

Now, write a letter to Shirley, suggesting what she might do to improve her letter to the employment agency. Include the reasons behind your suggestions and give sufficient examples and explanation to justify the changes you suggest. Also, keep in mind that although Shirley very much wants this job, she is sensitive to criticism.

❸ Be a critical thinker when analyzing.

Be a Critical Thinker When Analyzing

While you may have a great deal of support—details, examples, and explanation—when you analyze something, college professors insist that students look at both the obvious details and **beyond the obvious**. Then they expect students to use that information to make an informed decision or to offer a relevant insight. In other words, they expect students to be critical thinkers.

Outside of college, people look beyond the obvious all the time. For example, imagine you are shopping for a car and the sales representative offers you a low monthly payment that seems too good to be true. As an analytical and critical thinker, you would not accept the deal at face value; you would look more closely at the details and the sales rep's explanation. Do the parts of the offer (length of the loan, the financing rate, etc.) add up to a good deal?

Similarly, critical thinkers recognize that just because something is written does not mean it is true. Think of all the advertisements for weight-loss products that claim to be supported by doctors and medical researchers, when in fact most objective doctors will tell you that reducing calories combined with regular exercise is the best way to lose weight and become more healthy.

Critical thinkers question **assumptions** (ideas people take for granted), **biases** (a preference for certain points of view that blocks out alternative ideas), and **authorities** (the quality of the sources of the information). People's experiences and background influence the way they look at issues and problems. They might make assumptions that you or others may not agree with. Or they could have biases that make it difficult for them to see your perspective. Or like in the weight-loss ads, their sources may lack quality and reliability. (See Chapter 1 for more on critical thinking.)

EXERCISE 9.3   Analysis in Your Life   MyWritingLab

Directions: Based on your own experience, describe a time when you have done analysis that has "looked beyond the obvious." Specifically, what did you have to notice and examine in order to analyze effectively? How did those details contribute to your interpretation of the situation or subject?

EXERCISE 9.4   Using Critical Thinking and Analysis   MyWritingLab

Directions: Imagine that you are a manager of a hardware store and one of your employees—Louis—is up for promotion. Before you make a decision, you must analyze various recommendations based upon Louis' character and job performance. Thinking critically, how would you assess the quality of the following recommendations?

- Louis has not missed a day of work in two years and often fills in when other employees call in sick.
- His supervisor says Louis meets all deadlines for reports.
- Louis has completed several college courses and is currently enrolled in another evening course as he works toward his degree.
- Other employees frequently turn to Louis if they have questions about the store's merchandise.
- Louis plays on the company softball team, and the coach says Louis is the best fielder on the team.
- A disgruntled customer complained when Louis would not accept a return of defective merchandise.

What additional information would you want to know before deciding whether to promote Louis?

❹ Put **IDEAS** to work in analytical writing.

MyWritingLab Visit Ch. 9 Analytical Writing in MyWritingLab to access the IDEAS videos.

Put **IDEAS** to Work in Analytical Writing

Which parts should I spend the most time analyzing? How do all these parts work together? Which details are important? How can I make this interesting to the reader? What's my point here?

Writers ask themselves these types of questions as they prepare to draft an analytical piece of writing. As you think through which details are most important, keep in mind **IDEAS**, which stands for **I**nterest, **D**etails, **E**xplanation, **A**udience, and **S**tyle.

STUDENT WRITER AT WORK

Janet Lopez was assigned the following "Analyze an Ad Paper" assignment. (See the full assignment on page 280.)

Analyzing an Ad

Write an essay that analyzes a print advertisement from a magazine. The paper needs to describe the ad in detail so a reader can easily visualize it, but the main focus of the paper is analysis/critique. In addition to analyzing how the ad tries to persuade consumers, you need to discuss what the ad says about our American culture.

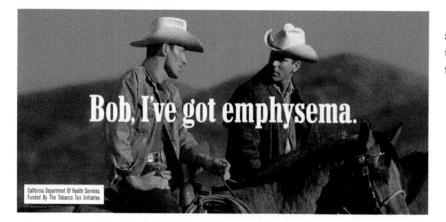

Janet chose an anti-smoking advertisement and used **IDEAS** as a strategy to think through her essay:

Planning

Interest: Should my readers know something about California's Tobacco Control Program since it is the ad's sponsor? Will my readers know the Marlboro cowboy advertisement? Maybe I should provide a context for readers before I get to specifics as I analyze the ad.

Details: Since readers won't have the ad in front of them, I need to describe it in detail in a way that emphasizes how healthy and rugged the men look because this shows the contrast with the words, which are so prominent.

Explanation: Readers need to know something about how tobacco advertisements typically appeal to consumers in order to see how this ad uses those same tactics to send an anti-smoking message. I should probably begin with these explanations, but I need to keep them fairly short. This is background information and not the focus of the paper. Since I need an assertive opinion about what the ad suggests about our culture, I'd have to say it shows we place importance on health.

Audience: I need to sound objective in the paper—no use of first person "I." I'll have to be careful not to let my own anti-smoking views make this paper sound biased.

Style: I'll probably use a spatial organization to describe the ad itself. I need to be sure my sentences—especially the beginnings—are varied, so this description doesn't read like a list.

In addition to using **I D E A S** to generate ideas for the essay, Janet showed this ad to her friends and got their reactions to it. She asked questions such as these:

- What do you notice first and why?
- What do you like?
- What works for you?
- How does this ad make you feel?
- What does the ad make you think about?

After she brainstormed ideas for the paper, she wrote a draft and then took it to the writing center at her college a day before her paper was due. During her conference, the writing tutor, Kendel, noticed that she didn't have a thesis statement, so they worked together to create one for the end of the first paragraph. Also, Janet had related information from two sources but had not cited them correctly within the paper. She and Kendel worked together to make sure she was citing her sources accurately and correctly. They finished the conference by developing more specific details in the third paragraph and re-drafting a stronger conclusion.

Janet's Advertisement Analysis Essay

Lopez 1

Janet Lopez
Professor Taylor
Introduction to College Writing
3 December 2014

The Real Marlboro Man

Since 1989, the California Tobacco Control Program (CTCP) has worked to prevent illness and death from the use of tobacco products. Funded by a 25-cent tax on each pack of cigarettes sold in California, the program uses radio, print and television advertisements to get its anti-smoking message out to the public ("About California"). One of the most memorable of these advertisements twists the well-known image of the Marlboro Man into a simple yet strong statement about the dangers of smoking.

> Janet begins with background about the ad's sponsor, including an in-text citation for paraphrase.

> The author provides a clear thesis about the advertisement. She states that it is "simple yet strong."

In the 1950s the Philip Morris Company was looking for a way to increase the sales of its Marlboro cigarettes. The Marlboro brand was Philip Morris's first filtered cigarette and had been marketed to women with the slogan "mild as May" (Madison). The company not only wanted to increase sales among men but had to deal with the growing concerns over smoking's link to cancer and other diseases. A Chicago advertising agency came up with the image that would save Marlboro: the cowboy (Madison). In the early 1960s, images of handsome, rugged cowboys living a healthy outdoor life in "Marlboro Country" appeared in magazines and ran on television. By 1972, Marlboro was the world's leading tobacco brand. Although cigarette advertisements are no longer allowed on television, and Philip Morris

Lopez 2

stopped using the Marlboro Man on billboards and magazine covers in 1998, *USA Today* still named the Marlboro Man on its 2008 list of the 101 most influential people who never lived (Madison).

> Janet paints a picture for the reader with specific details.

The CTCP advertisement includes two typical Marlboro Men on horseback shown against a backdrop of blue sky and mountains. The men are obviously cowboys, wearing blue jean jackets and white cowboy hats—the "good guys." The cowboy in the forefront has a rope on his horse to suggest he is on the range taking care of cattle. Both men are tan and appear healthy. They seem to be in their late

> A transitional sentence notes the difference in this ad from Marlboro's typical ones.

thirties and engaged in a conversation. So far, this has all the marks of a typical Marlboro Man advertisement. The difference is in the written text. The typical Marlboro advertisement has prominent white text proclaiming, "Come to Marlboro Country" or simply "Marlboro." This advertisement, however, has part of the dialogue between these two cowboys. The statement is frank and bleak: "Bob, I've got emphysema." This bold statement is prominently displayed across the middle of the advertisement. If that statement were not enough of a clue that this is no ordinary Marlboro advertisement, in the left corner, instead of the Surgeon General's warning, there is a white box containing the name of the sponsor of the advertisement—California Department of Health Services—and notice that the advertisement was funded by the Tobacco Tax Initiative.

Cigarette advertisers promote their product by associating smoking with positive qualities, especially qualities that suggest health and well-being. The cowboys in this eye-catching advertisement are good-looking men who appear capable of handling the demands of riding the range. No one would suspect from their appearance that one has a serious and incurable lung condition, most often caused by smoking: emphysema. The advertisement reminds us that appearances can be deceiving. Of course, many smokers appear attractive and healthy, but the frequent reality is that smoking is destroying their health on the inside. Even more importantly, the

> Janet uses her critical thinking skills to uncover what the real message is.

advertisement reminds us that advertisements themselves are deceiving. By leading consumers to associate handsome healthy people leading adventurous lives with smoking, cigarette companies try to make us forget the real dangers of smoking.

Lopez 3

Janet summarizes her main points.

The California Department of Health Services uses the cigarette industry's most recognizable figure to call attention to the dangers of smoking and the deceptiveness of advertising. While some anti-smoking campaigns use images of people suffering from disease to warn consumers of the dangers of smoking, this advertisement is effective without using hard-hitting images to stir up fear or pity in viewers. Its message is a simple and blunt wake-up call to the reality of smoking.

Works Cited

"About California's Tobacco Control Program." *Tobacco Education Clearinghouse of California*, 2015, tobaccofreeca.com/ about-us/.

"Bob, I've Got Emphysema." *Tobacco Education Clearinghouse of California*, 2006-15, http://www.tobaccofreecatalog.org/ productdetails.aspx?id=1&itemno=A119.

Madison, Cathy. "The Marlboro Man: A Real Smoking Cowboy Lassos Top Billing in Imagination and Memorability." *North American Hunter*, www.scout.com/outdoors/hunting/story/ 1441065-the-real-marlboro-man-clarence-hailey-long?

MyWritingLab Visit Ch. 9 Analytical Writing in MyWritingLab to access the IDEAS videos.

I D E A S in Action

In the first reading, commentary using the I D E A S template is provided to show how close, analytical, critical reading is important.

SELECTION 1

Bundle of Trouble: Kids are Supposed to Bring Joy So Why are Parents So Unhappy?

Robin W. Simon

In this article, published originally in Contexts, *a journal of the American Sociological Association, and later published in* Utne *magazine, the author analyzes the effects of parenting on people's well-being and the possible ways parents' lives can be less stressful and more fulfilling.*

PRE-READING PROMPT

1. If you are a parent or plan to be a parent, what do you feel are the challenges and joys of being a parent?
2. What do you think are some unrealistic demands that parents have to deal with?

1   Americans harbor a widespread, deeply held belief that no adult can be happy without becoming a parent. Parenthood, we think, is pivotal for developing and maintaining emotional well-being, and children are an essential ingredient for a life filled with happiness, joy, excitement, satisfaction, and pride.

Audience & Explanation: The author begins with how many people think about parenthood.

2   That's not exactly the case. Although studies indicate parents derive more purpose and meaning from life than nonparents, as a group, moms and dads in the United States also experience depression, emotional distress, and negative emotions (such as fear, anxiety, worry, and anger) far more than their child-free peers. What's more, parents of grown children report no greater well-being than adults who never had children.

Interest & Details: Simon then presents compelling details that contradict those assumptions about parenthood.

3   Such facts fly in the face of cultural dogma that proclaims it impossible for people to have an emotionally fulfilling life unless they become parents. And yet: Why doesn't parenthood have the positive emotional effects on adults that our cultural beliefs suggest?

Style: The author poses a question that he then answers in the subsequent paragraphs.

4   Children provide parents with an important social identity. They help them forge emotional connections to extended family members and their communities. Children fulfill basic human desires, including having someone to love and nurture, carrying on family traditions, and allowing us to become grandparents.

265

Watching children grow is enjoyable, and parents often feel comforted by the perception that they won't be alone in old age.

5   The disconnect lies in the social conditions in which Americans now parent; they're far from ideal for allowing parents to reap the emotional benefits of having children. Parents cope with stressors that cancel out and often exceed the emotional rewards of having children. Making matters worse, parents and others perceive the strain as a private matter and a reflection of their inability to cope with the "normal" demands of parenthood.

6   A significant source of parental stress simply comes from the high financial cost of raising a child to adulthood. Even the basics such as food, clothing, and (for those who have it) health care are expensive, not to mention extracurricular activities and the astronomical cost of college education. Demographers estimate that 70 percent of children in the United States are raised in households in which all adults work outside the home—and there's a fundamental incompatibility between employment as we know it and raising children.

> **Details & Explanation:** Simon provides statistics and reasons why stress negates the benefits of parenthood.

7   Sociologist Arlie Hochschild was the first to document how the lack of flexible work schedules, high-quality and affordable child care for preschool-age children, and after-school care for elementary-age children all contribute to stress from what's now commonly referred to as the "second shift" for employed parents, who leave their jobs at five o'clock only to start another job caring for children at home.

8   There are few policies or programs to alleviate this stress. In the end, the collective response to stressed out employed parents is that they need to become better organized.

9   Although financial stress and the strain of the "second shift" subside as children become more independent, the majority of parents continue to be involved in the lives of their adult offspring. Among other things, parents worry about their grown children's financial well-being, social relationships, happiness, and mental and physical health.

10   Our culture also places high expectations on parents for the way children "turn out." Irrespective of their children's age, we question parents' child-rearing skills when kids have problems. In fact, the way children turn out seems to be the only measure our culture offers for assessing whether men and women are good parents.

> **Explanation:** The author provides another cause of stress for parents—high expectations.

11   Yet unlike other societies, ours offers comparatively little preparation for parenthood, and most parents raise their children in relative social isolation with little assistance from extended family members, friends, neighbors, and the larger community. We lack institutional supports that would help ease the social and economic burdens—and subsequent stress and social disadvantages—associated with parenthood. Instituting better tax credits, developing more and better day care and after-school options, as well as offering flexible work schedules for employed mothers and fathers would go far toward alleviating some of the difficulty of raising children.

12   Of equal importance is the need to take stock of and reevaluate existing cultural beliefs that children improve the emotional health and well-being of

adults. These cultural beliefs—and our expectation that children guarantee a life filled with happiness, joy, excitement, contentment, satisfaction, and pride—are an additional, though hidden, source of stress for all parents. The feelings of depression and emotional distress that parents experience can cause them to question what they're doing wrong.

13   These negative emotions can also lead parents to perceive themselves as inadequate, since their feelings clearly aren't consistent with the cultural ideal.

14   Reducing the enormous and unrealistic cultural expectations we have for parenthood is as important as greater cultural recognition of the unrelenting challenges and difficulties associated with having children. Hallmark stores stock baby cards filled with happy wishes for new parents, celebrating their precious bundles of joy. Perhaps the selection should also include cards to acknowledge the difficult emotions that often accompany parenthood.

QUESTIONS FOR DISCUSSION

1. Simon provides some services and changes that would make parenthood less stressful. Which of those services would benefit the most people? If you could argue for only one of the services or changes, which one would you choose and why?

2. If you are a parent or if you want to think about the people who raised you as a child, what are some specific details and examples the author could have added from your life to really show the stresses and joys of parenting?

I D E A S for Your Own Writing   MyWritingLab

Analyzing an Ideal

Simon analyzes the cultural ideal of parenthood in "Bundle of Trouble," and there are a number of ideals we have in our society. In an essay, present how an ideal people have is both positive and negative by analyzing how it affects people's perceptions, attitudes, and activities.

SELECTION 2

The School Smarts Effect

Kirsten Weir

This passage comes from an article in Current Health *magazine. By looking at different research, the author, Kirsten Weir, analyzes the benefits of regular exercise for children and young adults. In this excerpt, we have included the introduction and only one of the benefits she details in the article.*

▲ Do you think recess is an important part of the day for elementary school children? Why or why not?

1. Most people think immediately of the physical benefits of exercise. What are some benefits other than improving physical well being?
2. Do you think physical fitness programs are emphasized enough by schools—especially grade schools? Why or why not?

1   Being active can help a person maintain a healthy body weight and ward off health problems such as obesity, heart disease, and diabetes. But a growing number of studies are proving that exercise is also important for keeping the brain healthy. So what are the good reasons?

2   Regular exercise can help kids do better in school. Young people who are physically fit may have better memories than kids who aren't active on a regular basis. Kids who have time for physical activity during the school day score better on tests, according to a study by the California Department of Education. Physically fit kids also have faster reaction times and make fewer mistakes when performing a computer task, according to Castelli. "Running one more lap won't make you smarter," she says. "But if you work toward [being physically fit], you have a tendency to do better in school."

QUESTIONS FOR DISCUSSION

1. What seems to be Weir's strategy for generating reader interest in the short opening paragraph?
2. Weir cites a study by the California Department of Education and includes a quote from Castelli. What additional information about these sources would you like to know before accepting the validity of the information they provide?
3. Would the information in this short passage be enough to convince you to include more exercise in your weekly routines? Why or why not?

I D E A S for Your Own Writing   My**Writing**Lab

Another Effect of Exercise Paragraph

Write a paragraph or two that analyzes how exercise benefits you. The benefit you choose, however, has to be *non-physical*. In this paragraph be sure to show what you mean by using personal experience, details, strong explanation, and examples.

Using Analysis to Convince

Imagine that your child's middle school is going to eliminate its physical education program as part of a cost-saving effort. Using information from Weir's essay and your own experiences, write a letter that argues for maintaining the program because of its physical and mental benefits for children.

SELECTION 3

Space Invaders

Richard Stengel

Richard Stengel is a long-time writer and editor of Time *magazine and managing editor since 2006. Stengel has written for* The New Yorker, The New Republic, *and the* New York Times *and has been a frequent television commentator on* CNN *and* MSNBC. *In the following essay, originally published in* The New Yorker, *he offers an analysis of what he sees as the growing lack of respect for personal space.*

PRE-READING PROMPT

1. Looking at the title of the essay, what do you expect it will be about?
2. Are you familiar with the expression "personal space"? What is your definition of the term?
3. Have you ever been made uncomfortable by someone intruding into your "personal space"? Give examples of when this typically happens.

▲ What is the etiquette, the proper manners, for sharing crowded spaces like this subway platform? What is the proper amount of personal space? How do you know?

1   At my bank the other day, I was standing in a line snaking around some tired velvet ropes when a man in a sweatsuit started inching toward me in his eagerness to deposit his Social Security check. As he did so, I minutely advanced toward the woman reading the *Wall Street Journal* in front of me, who, in mild annoyance, began to **sidle** up to the man scribbling a check in front of her, who absent-mindedly shuffled toward the white-haired lady ahead of him, until we were all **hugger-mugger** against each other, the original lazy line having collapsed in on itself like a Slinky.

2   I estimate that my personal space extends eighteen inches in front of my face, one foot to each side, and about ten inches in back—though it is nearly impossible to measure exactly how far behind you someone is standing. The phrase "personal space" has a quaint seventies ring to it ("You're invading my space, man"), but it is one of those gratifying expressions that are intuitively understood by all human beings. Like the twelve-mile limit around our national

sidle: inched toward

hugger-mugger: jumbled

shores, personal space is our individual border beyond which no stranger can penetrate without making us uneasy.

3   Lately, I've found that my personal space is being violated more than ever before. In elevators, people are wedging themselves in just before the doors close; on the street, pedestrians are zigzagging through human traffic, jostling others, refusing to give way; on the subway, riders are no longer taking pains to carve out little zones of space between themselves and fellow-passengers; in lines at airports, people are pressing forward like fidgety taxis at red lights.

> **Malthusian:** the idea that population increases at a faster rate than the world can support

4   At first, I attributed this tendency to the "population explosion" and the relentless **Malthusian** logic that if twice as many people inhabit the planet now as did twenty years ago, each of us has half as much space. Recently, I've wondered if it's the season: T-shirt weather can make proximity more alluring (or much, much less). Or perhaps the **proliferation** of coffee bars in Manhattan—the number seems to double every three months—is infusing so much caffeine into the already jangling locals that people can no longer keep to themselves.

> **proliferation:** fast growing

5   Personal space is mostly a public matter; we allow all kinds of invasions of personal space in private. (Humanity wouldn't exist without them.) The **logistics** of it vary according to geography. People who live in Calcutta have less personal space than folks in Colorado. "Don't tread on me" could have been coined only by someone with a spread. I would wager that people in the Northern Hemisphere have roomier conceptions of personal space than those in the Southern. To an Englishman, a handshake can seem like trespassing, whereas to a Brazilian, anything less than a hug may come across as chilliness.

> **logistics:** science of

6   Like drivers who plow into your parked and empty car and don't leave a note, people no longer mutter "Excuse me" when they bump into you. The decline of manners has been widely lamented. Manners, it seems to me, are about giving people space, not stepping on toes, granting people their private domain. I've also noticed an increase in the ranks of what I think of as space invaders, mini-territorial expansionists who seize public space with a sense of manifest destiny. In movie theatres these days, people are staking a claim to both armrests, **annexing** all the elbow room, while at coffee shops and on the L.I.R.R. [Long Island Rail Road], individuals routinely **commandeer** booths and sets of facing seats meant for foursomes.

> **annexing:** claiming

> **commandeer:** seize

7   Ultimately, personal space is psychological, not physical: it has less to do with the space outside us than with our inner space. I suspect that the shrinking of personal space is directly proportional to the expansion of self-absorption: people whose attention is inward do not bother to look outward. Even the focus of science these days is micro, not macro. The Human Genome Project is mapping the universe of the genetic code, while neuroscientists are using souped-up M.R.I. machines to chart the flight of neurons in our brains, taking snapshots of a human thought.

> **breeze from a butterfly's wings:** the idea that small actions can cause large reactions in an unpredictable future

8   In the same way that a **breeze from a butterfly's wings** in Japan may eventually produce a tidal wave in California, I have decided to expand the contracting boundaries of personal space. In the line at my bank, I now refuse to move closer than three feet to the person in front of me, even if it means the fellow behind me starts breathing down my neck.

QUESTIONS FOR DISCUSSION

I nterest
1. What method does Stengel use in his introduction to generate reader interest? Does his method work in attracting your interest? Why or why not?
2. What might people who invade personal space have in common with beings from outer space who invade a planet?

D etails
3. How does Stengel support his point that personal space is not the same for everyone?
4. How does Stengel intend to address this problem of decreasing personal space in public places? Do you think his efforts will produce a "tidal wave" of change? Why or why not?
5. How does Stengel use the following strategies in this essay: narration, description, comparison/contrast, cause and effect, definition (see Chapter 4)?

E xplanation
6. How does Stengel make sure his readers understand what he means by "personal space"?
7. What evidence does Stengel give to show that his personal space is being violated? Is this evidence enough to convince you that the problem is widespread? Why or why not?
8. Ultimately, what does Stengel see as the principal reason people violate others' personal space? Explain why you agree or disagree with him on this point.

A udience
9. What suggests that Stengel is not being entirely serious when he presents the first set of possible causes for people's tendency to violate others' personal space?
10. This essay appeared in *The New Yorker*. What in the essay suggests Stengel is writing to an educated reader who is likely familiar with life in New York City?

Ⓢtyle

11. Notice some of the long sentences in this essay (such as the second sentence of the introduction). Find some others. What effect do you think Stengel is trying to create with these sentences?

Ⓘ Ⓓ Ⓔ Ⓐ Ⓢ for Your Own Writing   MyWritingLab

Respond to Stengel

Write a letter to Richard Stengel in response to his essay "Space Invaders." If you live in an area where you, too, have increasingly experienced a lack of respect for personal space, let Stengel know that you share his pain and then relate some of your own experiences. If, however, you have not experienced an invasion of your space, write to Stengel, suggesting that he leave New York and visit your area where personal space is respected. In either case, try to maintain a somewhat lighthearted tone.

Analyze a Public Behavior

Have you noticed a type of annoying public behavior occurring more frequently recently? Like Stengel, write an essay that analyzes this behavior using a variety of strategies—narration, description, cause and effect, comparison/contrast, and definition. Also like Stengel, you might try "framing" the essay by beginning with the impact of the behavior on yourself and ending with how you intend to deal with the behavior.

SELECTION 4

But What Do You Mean?

Deborah Tannen

This reading is by the language scholar Deborah Tannen, who has published many popular books on how we communicate with one another. The article was originally published in Redbook *magazine. In it she uses examples and explanation to analyze how men and women tend to communicate differently in the workplace.*

PRE-READING PROMPT

1. What differences have you noticed in the ways men and women speak?
2. What might account for the differences in the communication styles between men and women?

ritual: ceremonial practice

1   Conversation is a **ritual**. We say things that seem obviously the thing to say, without thinking of the literal meaning of our words, any more than we expect the question "How are you?" to call forth a detailed account of aches and pains.

2   Unfortunately, women and men often have different ideas about what's appropriate, different ways of speaking. Many of the conversational rituals common among women are designed to take the other person's feelings into account, while many of the conversational rituals common among men are designed to maintain the one-up position, or at least avoid appearing one-down. As a result, when men and women interact—especially at work—it's often women who are at the disadvantage. Because women are not trying to avoid the one-down position that is unfortunately where they may end up.

3   Here, the biggest areas of miscommunication.

1. Apologies

synonymous: the same as

4   Women are often told they apologize too much. The reason they're told to stop doing it is that, to many men, apologizing seems **synonymous** with putting oneself down. But there are many times when "I'm sorry" isn't self-deprecating, or even an apology; it's an automatic way of keeping both speakers on an equal footing. For example, a well-known columnist once interviewed me and gave me her phone number in case I needed to call her back. I misplaced the number and had to go through her newspaper's main switchboard. When our conversation was winding down and we'd both made ending-type remarks, I added, "Oh, I almost forgot—I lost your direct number, can I get it again?" "Oh, I'm sorry," she came back instantly, even though she had done nothing wrong and I was the one who'd lost the number. But I understood she wasn't really apologizing; she was just automatically reassuring me she had no intention of denying me her number.

5   Even when "I'm sorry" is an apology, women often assume it will be a first step in a two-step ritual: I say "I'm sorry" and take half of the blame, then you take the other half. At work, it might go something like this:

A: When you typed this letter, you missed this phrase I inserted.
B: Oh, I'm sorry. I'll fix it.
A: Well, I wrote it so small it was easy to miss.

6   When both parties share the blame, it's a mutual face-saving device. But if one person, usually the woman, utters frequent apologies and the other doesn't, she ends up looking as if she's taking the blame for mishaps that aren't her fault. When she's only partially to blame, she looks entirely in the wrong.

7   I recently sat in on a meeting at an insurance company where the sole woman, Helen, said "I'm sorry" or "I apologize" repeatedly. At one point she said, "I'm thinking out loud. I apologize." Yet the meeting was intended to be an informal brainstorming session, and everyone was thinking out loud.

8   The reason Helen's apologies stood out was that she was the only person in the room making so many. And the reason I was concerned was that Helen felt the annual bonus she had received was unfair. When I interviewed her colleagues, they said that Helen was one of the best and most productive workers—yet she got one of the smallest bonuses. Although the problem might have been outright sexism, I suspect her speech style, which differs from that of her male colleagues, masks her **competence**.

> **competence:** ability to do her job well

9   Unfortunately, not apologizing can have its price too. Since so many women use ritual apologies, those who don't may be seen as hard-edged. What's important is to be aware of how often you say you're sorry (and why), and to monitor your speech based on the reaction you get.

2. Criticism

10   A woman who co-wrote a report with a male colleague was hurt when she read a rough draft to him and he leapt into a critical response—"Oh, that's too dry! You have to make it snappier!" She herself would have been more likely to say, "That's a really good start. Of course, you'll want to make it a little snappier when you revise."

11   Whether criticism is given straight or softened is often a matter of convention. In general, women use more softeners. I noticed this difference when talking to an editor about an essay I'd written. While going over changes she wanted to make, she said, "There's one more thing. I know you may not agree with me. The reason I noticed the problem is that your other points are so **lucid** and elegant." She went on hedging for several more sentences until I put her out of her misery. "Do you want to cut that part?" I asked—and of course she did. But I appreciated her tentativeness. In contrast, another editor (a man) I once called summarily rejected an idea for an article by barking, "Call me when you have something new to say."

> **lucid:** clear

12   Those who are used to ways of talking that soften the impact of criticism may find it hard to deal with the right-between-the-eyes style. It has its own logic, however, and neither style is **intrinsically** better. People who prefer criticism given straight are operating on an assumption that feelings aren't involved: "Here's the dope. I know you're good; you can take it."

> **intrinsically:** fundamentally

3. Thank-You's

13   A woman manager I know starts meetings by thanking everyone for coming, even though it's clearly their job to do so. Her "thank-you" is simply a ritual.

14   A novelist received a fax from an assistant in her publisher's office; it contained suggested catalog copy for her book. She immediately faxed him her suggested changes and said, "Thanks for running this by me," even though her contract gave her the right to approve all copy. When she thanked the assistant, she fully expected him to **reciprocate**: "Thanks for giving me such a quick response." Instead, he said, "You're welcome." Suddenly, rather than an equal

> **reciprocate:** respond in a similar way

exchange of pleasantries, she found herself positioned as the recipient of a favor. This made her feel like responding, "Thanks for nothing!"

15   Many women use "thanks" as an automatic conversation starter and closer; there's nothing literally to say thank you for. Like many rituals typical of women's conversation, it depends on the goodwill of the other to restore the balance. When the other speaker doesn't reciprocate, a woman may feel like someone on a seesaw whose partner abandoned his end. Instead of balancing in the air, she has plopped to the ground, wondering how she got there.

4. Fighting

16   Many men expect the discussion of ideas to be a ritual fight—explored through verbal opposition. They state their ideas in the strongest possible terms, thinking that if there are weaknesses someone will point them out, and by trying to argue against those objections, they will see how well their ideas hold up.

17   Those who expect their own ideas to be challenged will respond to another's ideas by trying to poke holes and find weak links—as a way of helping. The logic is that when you are challenged you will rise to the occasion; Adrenaline makes your mind sharper; you get ideas and insights you would not have thought of without the spur of battle.

18   But many women take this approach as a personal attack.

19   Worse, they find it impossible to do their best work in such a **contentious** environment. If you're not used to ritual fighting, you begin to hear criticism of your ideas as soon as they are formed. Rather than making you think more clearly, it makes you doubt what you know. When you state your ideas, you hedge in order to fend off potential attacks. Ironically, this is more likely to invite attack because it makes you look weak.

contentious: argumentative

20   Although you may never enjoy verbal sparring, some women find it helpful to learn how to do it. An engineer who was the only woman among four men in a small company found that as soon as she learned to argue she was accepted and taken seriously. A doctor attending a hospital staff meeting made a similar discovery. She was becoming more and more angry with a male colleague who'd loudly disagreed with a point she'd made. Her better judgment told her to hold her tongue, to avoid making an enemy of this powerful senior colleague. But finally she couldn't hold it in any longer, and she rose to her feet and delivered an impassioned attack on his position. She sat down in a panic, certain she had permanently damaged her relationship with him. To her amazement he came up to her afterward and said, "That was a great **rebuttal**. I'm really impressed. Let's go out for a beer after work and hash out our approaches to this problem."

rebuttal: counterargument

5. Praise

21   A manager I'll call Lester had been on his new job six months when he heard that the women reporting to him were deeply dissatisfied. When he talked to them about it, their feelings erupted; two said they were on the verge of quitting

because he didn't appreciate the work, and they didn't want to wait to be fired. Lester was dumb-founded: He believed they were doing a fine job. Surely, he thought, he had said nothing to give them the impression he didn't like their work. And indeed he hadn't. That was the problem. He had said nothing—and the women assumed he was following the adage "If you can't say something nice, don't say anything." He thought he was showing confidence in them by leaving them alone.

22   Men and women have different habits in regard to giving praise. For example, Deirdre and her colleague William both gave presentations at a conference. Afterward, Deirdre told William, "That was a great talk!" He thanked her. Then she asked, "What did you think of mine?" and he gave her a lengthy and detailed critique. She found it uncomfortable to listen to his comments. But she assured herself that he meant well, and that his honesty was a signal that she, too, should be honest when he asked for a critique of his performance. As a matter of fact, she noticed quite a few ways in which he could have improved his presentation. But she never got a chance to tell him because he never asked—and she felt put down. The worst part was that it seemed she had only herself to blame, since she had asked what he thought of her talk.

23   But had she really asked for his critique? The truth is, when she asked for his opinion, she was expecting a compliment, which she felt was more or less required following anyone's talk. When he responded with criticism, she figured, "Oh, he's playing 'Let's critique each other'"—not a game she'd initiated, but one which she was willing to play. Had she realized he was going to criticize her and not ask her to reciprocate, she would never have asked in the first place.

24   It would be easy to assume that Deirdre was insecure, whether she was fishing for a compliment or **soliciting** a critique. But she was simply talking automatically. Performing one of the many conversational rituals that allow us to get through the day. William may have sincerely misunderstood Deirdre's intention—or may have been unable to pass up a chance to one-up her when given the opportunity.

soliciting: seeking out

6. Complaints

25   "Troubles talk" can be a way to establish **rapport** with a colleague. You complain about a problem (which shows that you are just folks) and the other person responds with a similar problem (which puts you on equal footings). But while such **commiserating** is common among women, men are likely to hear it as a request to solve the problem.

rapport: a bond

commiserating: sharing troubles

26   One woman told me she would frequently initiate what she thought would be pleasant complaint-airing sessions at work. She'd talk about situations that bothered her just to talk about them, maybe to understand them better. But her male office mate would quickly tell her how she could improve the situation. This left her feeling **condescended** to and frustrated. She was delighted to see this

condescended: talked down to

very impasse in a section in my book *You Just Don't Understand,* and showed it to him. "Oh," he said, "I see the problem. How can we solve it?" Then they both laughed, because it had happened again: He short-circuited the detailed discussion she'd hoped for and cut to the chase of finding a solution.

27   Sometimes the consequences of complaining are more serious: A man might take a woman's lighthearted griping literally, and she can get a reputation as a chronic malcontent. Furthermore, she may be seen as not up to solving the problems that arise on the job.

7. Jokes

28   I heard a man call in to a talk show and say, "I've worked for two women and neither one had a sense of humor. You know, when you work with men, there's a lot of joking and teasing." The show's host and the guest (both women) took his comment at face value and assumed the women this man worked for were humorless. The guest said, "Isn't it sad that women don't feel comfortable enough with authority to see the humor?" The host said, "Maybe when more women are in authority roles, they'll be more comfortable with power." But although the women this man worked for may have taken themselves too seriously, it's just as likely that they each had a terrific sense of humor, but maybe the humor wasn't the type he was used to. They may have been like the woman who wrote to me: "When I'm with men, my wit or cleverness seems inappropriate (or lost!), so I don't bother. When I'm with my women friends, however, there's no hold on puns or cracks and my humor is fully appreciated."

29   The types of humor women and men tend to prefer differ. Research has shown that the most common form of humor among men is razzing, teasing, and mock-hostile attacks while among women it's self-mocking. Women often mistake men's teasing as genuinely hostile. Men often mistake women's mock self-deprecation as truly putting themselves down.

30   Women have told me they were taken more seriously when they learned to joke the way the guys did. For example, a teacher who went to a national conference with seven other teachers (mostly women) and a group of administrators (mostly men) was annoyed that the administrators always found reasons to leave boring seminars, while the teachers felt they had to stay and take notes. One evening, when the group met at a bar in the hotel, the principal asked her how one such seminar had turned out. She retorted, "As soon as you left, it got much better." He laughed out loud at her response. The playful insult appealed to the men—but there was a trade-off. The women seemed to back off from her after this. (Perhaps they were put off by her using joking to align herself with the bosses.)

31   There is no "right" way to talk. When problems arise, the culprit may be style differences—and all styles will at times fail with others who don't share or understand them, just as English won't do you much good if you try to speak to

someone who knows only French. If you want to get your message across, it's not a question of being "right"; it's a question of using language that's shared—or at least understood.

QUESTIONS FOR DISCUSSION

Interest

1. Does Tannen's introduction spark your interest? If so, how? If not, what could she have done to make the topic more engaging for you?
2. Who is most likely to be interested in miscommunication in the workplace? How does Tannen try to appeal to these readers?

Details

3. Based on your experiences, do you think Tannen describes typical situations? Why or why not?
4. Which details about people's reactions work best to get across the impact of miscommunication in the workplace?

Explanation

5. Communication is an abstract concept, but Tannen uses several techniques to make her analysis clear and understandable. What does she do that helps you better follow her presentation of ideas?
6. Tannen frequently uses examples to show what she means. Which examples did you find the most helpful in understanding Tannen's analysis? Why?
7. As you read this essay, did you notice any of your own communication rituals? Give examples that you have noticed in yourself or in others at school or in the workplace.

Audience

8. Do you think Tannen shows sympathy for either gender? Why or why not?
9. Tannen ends her essay by stating, "There is no 'right' way to talk." Do you think most readers would believe this? Why or why not?

Style

10. Tannen breaks down the areas of communication into numbered sections. How effective is this strategy? Does it make the material easy for you to follow? Explain why or why not.
11. Even though the topic seems somewhat formal—rituals in conversation—Tannen has a number of very informal elements in her writing. What do you notice that Tannen does to keep her style down to earth and accessible for most readers?

I D E A S for Your Own Writing   MyWritingLab

Workplace Language Essay

Each workplace has its own methods of communication. Write an essay that analyzes the distinctive communication style of a place where you have worked. Consider spoken, written, and nonverbal communication such as certain glances, looks, and body language. The essay should have a thesis (controlling idea) that directs the action of the essay and provides an interesting take on the language patterns in your workplace.

Analyzing the Influence of an Idea

Your Writing Task: Analyze the importance of an idea and the influence it has had on your life and possibly on other people's lives. You can take either a serious or a humorous tone in analyzing how the idea has influenced people. You could also take a subject that on the surface seems to be not all that serious and then talk about it in a serious manner. For example, you could write about "double dipping" and the important reasons people should not do it. Or you could take a topic that some people might take quite seriously and try to show the humorous qualities of its influence. For example, you could write about how people think turkey should be the main course of Thanksgiving dinner, that idea's influence, and how you find it really funny (or dumb) and why. The important component of this assignment is to recount and analyze how this idea has an influence on our lives, for better or for worse.

Your Readers: These paragraphs are to be shared with your classmates, so you have to be sure to provide important details and think about how others would react to your examples, explanation, and depiction of the influence of a certain idea. But most importantly, the paragraphs have to stir readers' interest. They should make people want to read on.

A Successful Analyzing the Influence of an Idea Assignment . . .

- Is entertaining, easy to read, and thought provoking.
- Provides a strong background about a certain idea for readers.
- Offers strong details, examples, and explanation of how this idea has influenced and still influences people.
- Has focused and unified paragraphs.
- Uses a clear organization strategy with transitions and other coherence devices.
- Provides a medium level of tone and diction—not too formal but not too informal.
- Is free of distracting mechanical and proofreading errors.

Analyzing an Ad

Your Writing Task: Write an essay that analyzes a print advertisement from a magazine. The paper needs to describe the ad in detail so a reader can easily visualize it, but the main focus of the paper is analysis/critique. In addition to analyzing how the ad tries to persuade consumers, you need to discuss what the ad says about American culture.

You cannot assume that the reader can see the ad, so you have to write an essay that effectively introduces, provides a context for (what magazine it came from, whom the ad targets), and concisely describes the ad early on. Then offer a thesis that has a strong position on what the ad does and means. You need to support that position with detailed analysis. Here are questions you should consider:

- **How does the ad appeal to its target audience?** To what values does the ad appeal? And how is the ad constructed to appeal to those values (use of color, copy, document design, layout, graphics, and images)? What strategies does the advertiser use?

- **What does this ad say about American culture** (issues of gender, race/ethnicity, body image, beauty, health, self-esteem, sexuality, etc.)? Are the explicit and implicit messages positive, negative, wholesome, troubling, realistic, infuriating, noble, pathetic?

Your Readers: Address your paper to classmates who might be interested in your subject and could be interested in your analysis and/or findings. But also imagine that your audience is somewhat informed but undecided, and that they might take an opposing viewpoint from your own.

A Successful Analyzing an Ad Essay . . .

- Provides a concise, accurate, and descriptive summary of the ad early on to orient the reader.
- Offers an assertive thesis that makes an evaluative judgment about the effectiveness of the ad and how it reflects American culture.
- Offers strong support for its thesis by using specific details and detailed analysis of how the ad attempts to persuade.
- Contains focused and unified paragraphs that relate specific details about the ad.
- Provides strong explanation about the ad's effectiveness and what it says about American culture.
- Uses third person voice to analyze the article, not the first person (*I, we*) or second person (*you*).
- Uses a clear organization strategy with transitions and other coherence devices.
- Provides a medium level of tone and diction—not too formal but not too informal.

- Is free of distracting mechanical and proofreading errors.

See pages 260–264 for Janet Lopez's response to this assignment.

Case Study: PTA Memo

Your Role: You are the parent of a boy who is in the second grade at Whittier Elementary School. Ever since your child has been going to school, you have been an active member of the school district's parent–teacher association (PTA). This year you serve as President of the PTA Executive Board of Whittier Elementary. There are four other executive members on the PTA board.

The Situation: Because of the strong support of parents, last year the PTA raised enough money to replace the older playground equipment with three new pieces of playground equipment.

You and the rest of the board have agreed on replacing the old and somewhat dangerous main playground equipment with a larger and safer piece of equipment. Also, you all have agreed to replace an older swing set that had six swings with a new one that has ten swings. However, no one on the board can agree on what the third new piece of playground equipment should be.

The first option is a decades-old standard at playgrounds: the "monkey bars." The second option is a twelve-foot-long curvy tunnel that kids can crawl through. Two board members want the monkey bars, and the other two want the tunnel. The board even polled the kids who attend the school, and results were also divided roughly 50/50. You are the tie-breaking vote, so you have to make the decision for the PTA.

The Document and Your Reader: The superintendent of the school district, Rose Huffington, has asked you to send her a one-page memo that informs her of your decision to go with either the monkey bars or the tunnel. She has asked you to provide a "short analytical rationale why you chose what you did" in the memo.

Since you have done memos for your job and for Superintendent Huffington in the past, you know it is very important that your memo have a clear "bottom-line" in the first paragraph, meaning that you have to let the reader know your decision or point very early on. Then the following paragraphs simply explain the *why* of your bottom line. In this case, you will have to concisely state your decision and explain why in the first paragraph, and then in three or four paragraphs afterward you have to provide explanation and develop your ideas on why you have chosen either the monkey bars or the tunnel.

The Required Format: The memo needs to be formally addressed to the superintendent with her name and title, your name and title, the date, and a short but descriptive subject line at the top of the document. The paragraphs should be single-spaced with double-spacing between paragraphs.

A Successful PTA Memo . . .

- Asserts a strong bottom line in the first paragraph by offering a concise statement about your decision on the third piece of playground equipment.
- Provides a strong analysis and rationale why you chose one piece of playground equipment over the other.
- Explains and details your reasoning by analyzing what elementary school children want and need.
- Is persuasive and informative through detailed explanation of your reasoning.
- Has focused and unified paragraphs that are developed and connect to the bottom line in the first paragraph.
- Is free of irrelevant details.
- Follows the proper format of a memo.
- Uses a clear organization strategy with transitions and other coherence devices.
- Provides a medium level of tone and diction—not too formal but not too informal.
- Is free of distracting mechanical and proofreading errors.

CHAPTER AT A GLANCE

Learning Objectives	How they connect to writing at college . . .
❶ Analyze a subject by breaking it down and building it back up.	**Analysis** is separating something into its parts, so you can better understand how it works as a whole.
	The first step in analysis is to determine your purpose.
	Next, you need to figure out what parts of your subject you need to look at more closely to achieve that purpose.

Learning Objectives	How they connect to writing at college . . .

❷ Support your analysis (and your thesis) with details, examples, and explanation.

In analytical writing, you must use details, examples, and explanation to show readers how you reached your point, or your thesis.

❸ Be a critical thinker when analyzing.

Critical thinking requires looking at both the obvious and beyond the obvious, and then using that information either to make an informed decision or to offer a relevant insight.

Critical thinking requires questioning **assumptions**, **biases**, and **authorities**.

Critical thinking also requires that you present your points to readers who may not share your opinions and values.

❹ Put **I D E A S** to work in analytical writing.

Writers ask the following kinds of questions as they prepare to draft an analytical piece of writing:

- Which parts should I spend the most time analyzing?
- How do all these parts work together?
- Which details are important?
- How can I make this interesting to the reader?
- What's my point here?

MyWritingLab Visit **Chapter 9, "Analytical Writing,"** in MyWritingLab to test your understanding of the chapter objectives.

Evaluative Writing

10

Learning Objectives

In this chapter you will learn how to . . .

❶ Consider the criteria for success.

❷ Show how a subject is or is not a success.

❸ Put **I D E A S** to work in evaluative writing.

A sound evaluation depends on criteria, factors you consider when making a judgment. You use criteria to see whether something is excellent, good, average, or poor.

Every day we make evaluations, regardless of whether or not we are conscious of doing so. Consider these evaluations from people's personal, college, and professional lives:

- When Professor Baker's composition students turn in papers, he evaluates them according to the requirements of the assignment. In addition, each paper needs to be unified, well supported, and coherent—the qualities necessary for successful writing.
- When considering Jamie, a salesperson, for a promotion, her manager looks closely at Jamie's overall work ethic, her sales over the past year, and her leadership potential.
- Before accepting a job offer, Kei considers the salary, benefits, reputation, and working conditions at the law firm. He also thinks about the commuting distance to downtown.

We evaluate to make decisions based on the quality of something—such as a performance, an opportunity, or even a piece of furniture. As you can see from these examples, behind every evaluation is a set of standards or **criteria**. Carefully thought-out and thorough criteria are essential for evaluation.

❶ Consider the criteria for success.

Consider the Criteria for Success

Criteria are the principles or standards by which something is judged, or **evaluated**. Most judgments, or evaluations, take into account various criteria. So when evaluating something, you have to do this: *Consider the criteria for success.*

Identify Criteria

If you are choosing a restaurant, you are not going to decide based on quality of food alone. While the quality of the food is *very* important when you judge a restaurant, other factors that come into play could be the atmosphere, quality of service, speed of service, and type of food.

Depending on the circumstances, one criterion for a restaurant may be the most important. For example, if you have only thirty minutes to eat lunch, you are not likely to go to an eatery that serves at a slower pace. You will probably choose a drive-thru at a fast food joint.

For some, atmosphere would be the least important criterion when choosing a restaurant, whereas others might believe atmosphere affects the quality of the dining experience, which in turn affects how they feel about the food.

We also choose our criteria based on the object under evaluation. So, while most people consider that good acting, well-developed characters, and an engaging story line are all important to the success of a movie, you may have different criteria for diverse types of movies and place more emphasis on particular criteria for certain movies than others. Believability and realism might be important in a drama but not at all relevant in a horror flick, for example. Special effects may be important in an action film but not so important in a romantic comedy. Criteria depend on the subject matter.

Explain Criteria

When writing an evaluative piece, you also have to think about whether you want to be explicit or implicit about your criteria. When being explicit, a writer clearly mentions the criteria used for evaluation, such as acting ability, food quality, or cost. A writer evaluating with implicit criteria will simply explain the strengths and weaknesses of a product, a restaurant, a car, and so on without announcing to the reader which criterion is being evaluated.

In a number of cases, a piece of evaluative writing might do both—be explicit about some criteria and implicit about others.

EXERCISE 10.1   Identify Criteria   MyWritingLab

Directions: Working alone or with your peers, identify criteria for evaluating each of the following:

1. What should you consider when choosing a cell phone provider?

2. What should parents look for in choosing a babysitter?

3. What should college students consider when selecting an elective course?

4. How did you choose the best route to take to work or school?

5. What should one look for when choosing a credit card?

EXERCISE 10.2   Analyze Criteria   MyWritingLab

Directions: Identify criteria for each of the following sets of situations, noting the similarities and differences.

1. What are the characteristics of an ideal dog for a child under twelve? For a retired person?

2. What are the features of an ideal part-time job? A full-time job?

3. What should one look for in a restaurant for a special date? For a business lunch?

4. What are the traits of an ideal grade school teacher? A college professor?

5. What would be the features of an ideal fitness center for someone under 30? Over 50?

❷ Show how a subject is (or is not) a success.

Show How a Subject Is (or Is Not) a Success

Generating criteria is the first step in creating a strong evaluative paper. The second step is explaining *why* and *how* a subject is (or is not) a success based on those criteria.

"You're out here because you're supposed to receive a performance review? I'm out here because I'm supposed to give one!"

▲ Has your job performance ever been evaluated? What criteria were used for that evaluation?

For instance, if you had to evaluate whether it would be better to take public transportation or your car to travel to college each day, you would weigh a number of factors, of which cost is probably the most significant. If you add up the costs for a parking pass, gas, and additional car maintenance, coupled with the convenience of taking your own car, those factors will give you a picture of how successful using your own car will be. If you add up the costs for a bus/rail pass, the walking distance from bus/train stops to your home, and flexibility of the public transportation schedule, that would give you an idea of how successful taking public transportation to campus will be.

You figure out the best option by examining the details and reflecting about your transportation situation. You have to discover *why* one form of transportation is preferable to the other. In this instance, you use evaluation to determine what you will do.

You also use evaluation to determine the success of something you have already done. In a review of a restaurant, for example, you would use details, examples, and explanations to discuss your criteria—the food quality, service, cost, and atmosphere—and to support whether or not a certain restaurant warrants a return visit. Writers have to provide concrete details about taste, smells, visual imagery, sounds, and textures—connecting the five senses to show how a dining experience was or was not good. Sometimes the evaluation can be mixed since the atmosphere could be horrible, the food great, the service so-so, and prices decent.

EXERCISE 10.3   Applying Criteria   My**Writing**Lab

Directions: Choose one of the sets of criteria you developed for the previous exercise and apply it to a particular situation. For example, if you developed the criteria for an ideal part-time job, apply those criteria to a part-time job you have held. On the basis of this evaluation, was that job ideal?

❸ Put **I D E A S** to work in evaluative writing

Put **I D E A S** to Work in Evaluative Writing

Which criteria are important? How can I show my evaluation through strong details, examples, and explanation? How can the evaluation be interesting for the reader? How can I make my readers trust my evaluation?

MyWritingLab Visit Ch. 10 Evaluative Writing in MyWritingLab to access the IDEAS videos.

Writers ask themselves these questions as they prepare to draft evaluative writing. As you think through which examples and details are most important, keep in mind **I D E A S**, which stands for **I** nterest, **D** etails, **E** xplanation, **A** udience, and **S** tyle.

STUDENT WRITER AT WORK

In Karl Martinson's Introduction to College Writing class, his professor assigned the following Evaluation paper (see page 309 for the full assignment).

Business, Service, or Product Evaluation

As part of the "Everyday Critic" feature of a campus newspaper, you have been asked to write an article in which you judge a business or service situated on campus or within the local community. Another option is evaluating a new product on the market.

The "Everyday Critic" feature focuses on businesses, services, or products college students or locals might want to know about. Sometimes writers critique an established business or service, but often they evaluate new businesses or services that are offered at college or in the city in which you live. Whether you evaluate a dog-grooming business, the campus writing center, or a new hair-care product, your evaluation needs to clearly and explicitly establish criteria for evaluating the product or service, and then you must use specific and concrete details along with developed examples from your experience to support your evaluation.

Keep in mind that you need to use different sets of criteria for different products or services. For example, a critic would evaluate a hardware store differently than he or she would evaluate a college's math tutoring services. Therefore, it is important to think about the type of business, service, or product you are evaluating and clearly establish factors by which it should be judged.

Karl decided to write about his recent search for a kennel for his dog. He reviewed all his notes from the kennels he visited and then did some freewriting to generate more details from his memories of each place.

Using the **IDEAS** template as a way to brainstorm ideas for his paper, Karl asked these questions and had the following thoughts about his Evaluation paper:

Interest: What do I want to lead with to get the reader's attention?
I know a lot of students have dogs and may need to find a kennel. What details about my dog and my search will really interest them and tell them something new?

Details: Ben is old and spoiled, so I have to describe that, of course, and the reason I needed a kennel in the first place. I went to so many bad kennels. How will I narrow down my descriptions of the bad, so I can focus on the good features of the kennel I chose?

Explanation: I want my readers to know my criteria. Should I spell it out in the introduction or should I explain it in a separate paragraph? I could explain in separate paragraphs each important feature I looked for. The descriptions could keep the explanations from sounding too dull.

Audience: Some of my readers may have dogs, so they will be interested in knowing what to look for in a good kennel. But I want even non-dog owners to be interested in knowing whether or not I could find a good place for my dog to stay. What details about Ben can I include in the introduction to make the readers care about him?

Style: I have to balance the amount of details without going overboard since it's only a short review. The professor has also really talked about how this paper has to have a clear thesis. In my last paper I used "I think" and "I feel" too much, so I'll have to watch for those. I'll also try not to use so many linking verbs.

When Karl visited the Writing Center with a draft of his paper, the tutor there asked these questions and made these comments:

- I really like the details you provide about the various kennels—that's solid. But notice how in each paragraph you describe the good kennel first and then give details about the bad? Consider using a more emphatic organization. Describe the bad kennels first and then the good features you found in Happy Valley?

- Also, what about the price? Was the price fair and affordable? You mention affordability in the introduction, but you don't mention the cost again.

- You have strong details about Ben at the start of the essay. I like that a lot. But you don't have much about Ben in the body paragraphs. Can you explain how the kennel not only met your criteria but was particularly good for Ben?

- Right now, you have a thesis—it's a "great kennel"—but that's *really general*. Why is it a really good place to board your dog? Explain it to the reader. Be explicit. If you state why in the thesis, then the thesis sets up the details in the body paragraphs.

After his visit to the Writing Center, Karl revised his paper and turned in the following document for his writing class.

Karl's Review

Martinson 1

Karl Martinson
Professor Taylor
Introduction to College Writing
30 May 2014

A Kennel for Ben

I don't often get to go fishing with my buddies, so the chance to spend spring break at the lake was too good to pass up. The only problem was Ben, my nine-year-old Labrador. Years ago Ben would have come along and joined in on the fun, even diving off the dock for a swim in the lake. Now his grey muzzle, cloudy eyes, and hip problems did not make him the best camping companion. With all my close friends going on the trip and my family living out

> **Interest:** Here Karl includes details about his dog to evoke interest in his readers and curiosity about how he will solve this problem.

Martinson 2

of town, I didn't have anyone I trusted with the key to my apartment and the care of Ben. I decided to find a good kennel where I could board Ben for four days. I'm glad I started my search for a kennel early because finding one where I knew Ben would be safe, comfortable, and well-cared for was not easy. Luckily, I found Happy Valley Kennel, which met all my requirements at a price I could afford.

Explanation: Here are Karl's criteria for the kennel he wants for Ben.

First, I wanted a clean and safe kennel for Ben. The first kennel I visited was a private kennel in the owner's backyard. I was not impressed by the building's peeling paint and the scummy water in the water bowls. At another kennel I visited, the air inside the building was too warm, and the office area smelled of stale urine. The runs looked like they hadn't been cleaned in a couple days. Another kennel was fairly clean, but I didn't notice any smoke alarms, and the owners didn't ask if Ben's vaccinations were up-to-date. Happy Valley is a private kennel, but this owner keeps the building and grounds very clean. The building was well-ventilated and the only smell was from the disinfectant used to clean the floors. The building had smoke alarms, and the owners insisted on a letter from a veterinarian, showing all Ben's shots were current. They also wanted a number for Ben's vet in case of an emergency.

Details: Karl includes specific details to show how unsuitable these kennels are.

I also wanted a kennel where Ben could be comfortable. At home he sleeps in a huge, soft dog bed and can sit on the sofa to watch television. He has the run of my apartment, and I take him on daily walks to the park. He has arthritis, so I wanted him to have a soft place to sleep, and because he's big, I wanted him to have enough space to move around. Some of the kennels I visited had small cages and no bedding. The dogs had to lie down on concrete.

Details: Notice how Karl uses contrasting details to show how the preferred kennel does a better job of meeting his criteria.

Martinson 3

At Happy Valley, the cages were spacious, and each had an indoor-outdoor run. Ben would also be taken for a short walk four times a day. The kennel provides bedding for an extra fee, but the owners said I could bring Ben's bed, which I thought was a good idea because it would be something familiar for Ben in a strange place.

Most importantly, I wanted the people taking care of Ben to like dogs and treat him as though he was their own. One kennel I visited, part of a national chain, was safe and clean and offered lots of extras, but I felt the workers didn't really like the dogs. It was just a job to them. At Happy Valley, the owners genuinely love dogs. They have three of their own. They wanted to know all about Ben's favorite food and treats, whether he had a favorite toy, and when he was used to taking walks. They said I could bring him by, so he could walk around and get used to the place before I left him there. When I did that, the owners gave Ben so much attention that his tail didn't stop wagging. During Ben's stay, they spoiled him as much as I do.

Happy Valley is a clean, safe kennel where dogs can feel as comfortable as they do in their own homes. The owners are true dog lovers who treat their guests like their own pets. Since I brought Ben's food and bedding, his stay at Happy Valley cost me $30 per day, which I thought was a fair price. Ben was safe, comfortable, and spoiled while I enjoyed my fishing trip.

> **Explanation:** Here Karl uses specific examples to show the owners' love of dogs.

> Here Karl makes reference to the criteria and fishing trip he mentioned in the introduction.

MyWritingLab Visit Ch. 10 Evaluative Writing in MyWritingLab to access the IDEAS videos.

I D E A S in Action

In the first reading, commentary using the **I D E A S** template is provided to show how close, analytical, critical reading is important.

SELECTION 1   **MyWritingLab**

Reality Check: Your Social Media May Be Putting You in Danger

Adrienne Erin

The first reading of this chapter is a reporter's discussion and evaluation of the risks people take when they use social media. The article was published on Al.com, described as "a digitally-focused news organization" for the newspapers of Mobile, Birmingham, and Huntsville, Alabama.

PRE-READING PROMPT

1. Have you or someone you know had any negative experiences using social media? What do you think causes many of the problems that can arise from so many people using social media?
2. What are the positive outcomes of using social media sites?

1   Social media has undoubtedly become a highly integral part of life in the 21st Century. We constantly check our Facebook pages for notifications, live-tweet the latest happenings and Instagram our meals, using these mediums as a simple form of communication or entertainment. Let's face it, social media is just plain fun. But could you actually be putting yourself in danger from using it?

> **Interest & Details:** The author provides concrete examples and ends with a question to spark interest.

2   The internet itself is full of all sorts of threats, from identity theft to phishing scams, and more than 1 million people are at risk for being a victim of cyber crime every single day! Social media sites are no different, and what you may see as a harmless communication medium is just another way for criminals to target their prey.

Social Media Crime

3   There is a large portion of social media users who don't know the status of their privacy settings on these sites. When it comes down to it, this is seriously dangerous. Your profile can easily be hacked, giving someone access to quite a bit of information, and you can also fall victim to scams that could do quite a bit of damage to both your computer and your bank account. Ouch!

4   Furthermore, nearly 81 percent of internet crimes are somehow related to social media sites. With such a high population currently using these sites on a daily basis, just think about how frightening that statistic really is!

5   Keep in mind that your information isn't the only thing at risk when it comes to social media dangers. Your physical well-being could come into play, as well.

Style: Erin uses a strong transition to the next section.

Burglaries and Sex Crimes

6   Think of all of the information that you have on your social media profiles. You probably have your age, the city that you reside in, the school that you attend and even more. Not only that, but you probably post information about an upcoming trip or check-in at a restaurant. You may think that you are just keeping your friends up to date about your life, but in reality you are also paving the way for burglars to target your home.

Explanation: The author provides other effects of sharing information about yourself.

7   78 percent of burglars use social media platforms to locate properties that will be empty for the taking. Just by knowing your name and the town you live in, they can easily find your address. But that is only the first part. Once they have this information, they can track your posts to see if you are out of town or at a party somewhere. This gives the burglars an exact time to pull off the act.

8   What's even scarier is the fact that 33 percent of internet-initiated sex crimes happen through social media. In 50 percent of sex crime cases involving minors, the offender got their hands on information about the victim through their social profiles. Many people, teens especially, post so much information on sites that they are just setting themselves up for danger, and it shouldn't be that way.

Details: The writer provides specific statistics to support her points.

Keep Yourself Safe

9   Wouldn't it be amazing if there was some sort of electromagnetic shielding security technology that could just keep us all safe on the internet? With the ever increasing social media risks, it would be pretty great if it was that simple to block crime from happening to us.

10   The most obvious solution would be to just not use social media sites, right? Well, it really isn't that simple, especially when it is fully integrated into our lifestyles and is almost a necessity when procuring a new job. Regardless of the hazards, you will still want to be able to share photos and information with your friends, so instead of abstaining completely, you just need to be smart about it.

11   Knowing your security and privacy settings on your social media sites is extremely important and can really keep you safe from digitally-initiated harm. Be careful about what information you share and don't let the entire internet world know that you are going on vacation.

Audience: Instead of just evaluating how sites are dangerous, Erin provides realistic steps to protect people in her conclusion.

12   Lastly, if you are a parent, be sure to keep an eye on what your kids are posting and sharing on these sites, as well. It is important for users of all ages to protect themselves and be aware of potential dangers that could head their way.

QUESTIONS FOR DISCUSSION

1. Erin offers statistics to support her points. If you were to expand on her points, what examples or experiences would you use to provide more support for her evaluation of the dangers of these sites?
2. What are additional dangers or problems with social media that you see? What would you add to this article?
3. Do you think this is a fair evaluation of social networking sites? Do the risks outweigh the benefits?

I D E A S for Your Own Writing   MyWritingLab

Evaluate Your Productivity

Some claim social networking sites waste time. If you use a social networking site, do an experiment on yourself to see if those claims are true for you. Designate one typical weekday to record how often and how long you are on a specific site. Then designate one typical weekday during the same week to not use that site at all, ever. Finally, evaluate how productive you were on both days by using explicit criteria to evaluate productivity.

Evaluate Your Profile, Pictures, and Posts

Evaluate your profile, pictures, and posts on a social networking site from the past week or two. Could your privacy settings or posts lead to danger? Overall, evaluate the safety of your online activities. Also, some employers check people's social networking sites before they consider them for interviews. Evaluate your pictures and posts and consider how a potential employer would judge you. Would your online presence create a positive or negative impression?

SELECTION 2   MyWritingLab

Review of *Carrying Lightning*

Lee Zimmerman

This passage comes from Blurt Online *(http://blurt-online.com), a website that describes itself as "music news, reviews, videos, and more." Lee Zimmerman reviews an album by Amanda Shires, an artist whose music is usually classified as Americana. A native Texan, Shires started playing the fiddle when she was a young girl and has played with various bands and other recording artists.*

Now she is an accomplished solo artist who has three albums in her discography: Being Brave, West Cross Timbers, *and the album reviewed below.*

PRE-READING PROMPT

1. What do you think is probably the biggest challenge when writing about music?
2. Which criteria do you think a reviewer should include when evaluating an album?
3. Amanda Shires' music is often classified as Americana music. Look up the definition of Americana music on the Web to get a sense of that kind of music before reading the review.

[1]   Sounding like a confluence of Emmylou Harris and Lucinda Williams—packing their own mini orchestra to boot—Amanda Shires reemerges with her strongest-sounding effort to date, one that ought to boost her profile in Americana circles. She's come close before; both she and co-producing partner Rod Picott are formidable players and performers. But in a real sense, *Carrying Lightning* lives up to its branding, with an energy and emotion that's practically palpable.

[2]   Shires is a dynamic presence, and yet she's able to meld different personas; there's the sensitive strains of a singer songwriter—as delineated in the delicate touch of "Bees in the Shed" (which seems to draw on Joni Mitchell as an influence), "Detroit or Buffalo" (the album's sole cover) and "Sloe Gin"—as well as the feisty strains of a seductive siren, cast in the percolating, pent-up delivery of "Ghost Bird," the gypsy tango of "Shake the Walls" and the casual ukulele strum of "Lovesick I Remain." Violin is her primary instrument (she was prominently featured on Jason Isbell's latest album, *Here We Rest*), and she casts it well throughout, whether it's providing the searing strains that boost the brittle, emotionally-charged "She Let Go of Her Kite," or part of an entire string section on "Kudzu," a tender love song that earns its expansive treatment. Yet, she doesn't stop there; the whistling refrain of "Winner. . ." and the easy lope of "When You Need a Train, It Never Comes" define her to a fault and set her apart in the process.

[3]   A superb supporting cast also helps of course—Picott and noted guitarists Will Kimbrough and Neal Casal, among them—but there's no denying Shires herself as a tour-de-force, a singer, songwriter and musician who possesses the entire package and evidences it here. A revelatory offering in every sense, *Carrying Lightning* makes an indelible impression.

QUESTIONS FOR DISCUSSION

1. In the opening sentence of the review, Zimmerman compares Amanda Shires to Emmylou Harris and Lucinda Williams. If you do not know these artists, do a quick Web-based search about them and

their music. How does this comparison in the first sentence create a context for the reader? How does the comparison announce to the reader what kind of musician Shires is?

2. What is Zimmerman's overall evaluation of the album? What is his thesis? Where is it located? If you could summarize the evaluation in your own words, how would you state the thesis?

3. Zimmerman does not explicitly name his criteria for evaluating this album. List what you think his criteria are.

4. Pay attention to the important descriptive words that Zimmerman uses to describe Shires and her music. What do those words reveal about the way he feels about the album? How do those words detail his evaluation?

I D E A S for Your Own Writing   **MyWritingLab**

Evaluate a Product You Recently Purchased

Using two or three basic criteria, evaluate a product you have recently purchased. How good a product is it? Be sure to provide effective examples and strong details to support your overall evaluation (thesis), which comes at the end of the first paragraph.

Evaluating a Music Genre

Did you ever think about the challenges faced by a music critic? How does one explain what something should sound like? Try your hand at putting together criteria for evaluating a certain type of music—pop, heavy metal, hip-hop, bluegrass, or whatever genre you choose. As you explain your criteria for evaluating that type of music, use examples from various artists who perform in that genre to make your points clear.

SELECTION 3   **MyWritingLab**

4 Reasons Why the Library Should Affect Your College Choice

Jeff Greer

U.S. News & World Report, *a magazine that ranks colleges on an annual basis, features informative articles for students who are searching for and deciding on what colleges to apply to and attend. In this article, the author provides specific criteria for evaluating a library when considering colleges.*

1. What has been your experience with the services and staff of the library so far in college? Before you read the article, consider what services and characteristics are crucial for a good library. Why?
2. When you chose the college you attend now, what criteria did you use to evaluate the college? Do you wish you had considered other criteria? Why or why not?

1   If you talk to a college admissions officer or a high school guidance counselor about things to do when you visit a college campus, one of the first things they say is to visit the libraries on campus. Bring a book or some schoolwork, sit down, and soak up the environment.

2   Can you see yourself there for four years?

3   "The library is the backbone of a college or university's academic environment," says Kelly Alice Robinson, career information services manager at the Career Center Library at Boston College. Not only is the actual physical library one of the main spots where college students go to get work done (and socialize), it's also a useful resource of a wide range of information and services, she says. And that doesn't even scratch the surface of the digital capabilities that many library systems possess. *U.S. News* spoke to a handful of experienced librarians from colleges to find out what prospective students—and their parents—should look for when they check out a prospective school's library.

1. What is the staff like?

4   Chat with a reference desk staffer or two. How helpful are they? What kinds of information can they provide? Do they seem like they are prepared and willing to help students? These are important questions. "More and more college libraries have shifted to become service-oriented," says Cindy Fisher, a first-year experience librarian at the University of Texas–Austin who helps new students transition into college. "Think of some things you might need as a student and ask the librarian at the reference desk what kind of resources their school offers."

5   An important thing to note is that schools' libraries are different based on the school's size, Robinson says. Some bigger schools have subject librarians and libraries that specialize in certain topics, like history. Smaller schools may not have this specialization. But that doesn't mean the smaller schools and their libraries don't pack a punch: Many schools operate in consortia with other colleges and networks to give students a nice plate of resources.

2. How much does the library system and its librarians interact and work with faculty?

6   Find out what, if any, types of collaboration professors have with the libraries. Fisher says professors and librarians at many schools work together to create course content or inform each other's work and research. If you can get a sense

of the relationship and bond between these two major parts of campus life, you can get a nice picture of how smoothly you can research class topics and projects. "Try to get a sense of the fluidity of organization, the transparency of people and tools and access," says Sarah Bordac, the head of outreach and instructional design at Brown University Library.

3. What's the atmosphere like?

7   Walk into the library and go about your normal business. Some campuses have multiple libraries—one of which is likely to be more of a social environment than the other quieter, more serious locales. Test them all out. And within each library, there are places to chat and places to intently focus. Visit each spot. At Brown University, "we've made our library spaces more inviting, more personal," says Brown's University Librarian Harriette Hemmasi. "When you come in, you get the sense that someone cares about you as a student in that environment . . . That's really important. It becomes sort of a home away from home."

4. Check the library system website and digital resources. This is a big one.

8   It's a new digital age in information services, and academic libraries are on the cutting edge. From digital documents to ramped-up search engines, many library systems can help you find just about anything that can help you with your projects. And because a lot of libraries close at a certain hour—unless it's finals week—it's vitally important to see what they offer online when you're cranking out that term paper at 4 a.m. "Find out what happens after the physical library closes," Fisher, of UT–Austin, says. "Is the website easy to navigate? How easy is it to access all the great information that the school's library system has?"

9   A big part of Fisher's job is showing new students how to use the UT library system. She helps students get comfortable with their new academic atmosphere. When you talk to the librarians at your prospective schools, ask them if the school offers courses or seminars to new students. After all, libraries and their services are a major part of your college experience, and making sure that you can use them to your advantage should be among the top factors on your list for picking a school.

QUESTIONS FOR DISCUSSION

Interest

1. Authors often use quotations to get readers interested and keep their interest. What quotations does Greer use that stand out to you and why?
2. If you were to revise this article, what would you add, change, or delete in the first three paragraphs to make the article more interesting to a high school student thinking about college?

D etails

3. Which details about how to evaluate a library are likely to surprise some readers? Why?

4. The author provides four criteria to evaluate a library. What other criteria would you add and why?

5. Greer only uses statements from staff at libraries. If Greer had asked students' opinions about libraries, would those opinions and information points from students have strengthened his article? Why or why not?

E xplanation

6. The section about atmosphere is the least developed part of the article. What other reasons or supporting points would more fully explain why atmosphere is such an important aspect of a library?

7. The author compares how libraries at small and large colleges might differ. How important is that explanation to the article? The author notes "consortia" and "networks," but how could he have provided some examples to relate these concepts more clearly to the reader?

A udience

8. What is Greer's overall attitude or tone in this article? How does this tone affect your openness to his advice?

9. Quotations serve as support to explain why these criteria are important. How do they also establish the author's credibility with readers?

S tyle

10. The author uses a variety of types and lengths of sentences. Examine four paragraphs and analyze the types and lengths of sentences the author uses in this short article. How does the variety of sentences create strong cohesion, or flow, to the article?

I D E A S for Your Own Writing   MyWritingLab

Evaluate Your Library

Using Greer's criteria as your guide, visit your college's library and evaluate it. In a journal entry or short essay, judge the library by his criteria and offer a judgment about the library based on its staff, atmosphere, and online search engines. Be sure to provide specific details, examples, and explanation to support your judgment about the library.

Which Criteria Are Important?

Using your own expertise about a product, service, or profession, write an evaluative essay that explains the crucial traits of that product, service, or profession. For example, if you're a gardener and you know how to pick out the healthiest and best flowers and/or vegetables, provide characteristics of the plants and/or stores a new gardener needs to pay attention to. Like Greer does in his essay, be sure to explain why those criteria are important and quote fellow experts who agree with you. Unlike Greer, you can also use your personal experience for support.

SELECTION 4   My**Writing**Lab

The Flight from Conversation

Sherry Turkle

This essay was published in the New York Times. *In the article, which is based on her research and her book titled* Alone Together: Why We Expect More from Technology and Less from Each Other, *Sherry Turkle evaluates how the use of technology affects us and how that compares to her ideal/criteria of how good conversations work. Turkle is a Professor of Psychology at the Massachusetts Institute of Technology (MIT) and is the founder and Director of the MIT Initiative on Technology and Self.*

PRE-READING PROMPT

1. Professor Turkle studies how people use technology and how it affects our society and human behavior. From your own experience, have there been times where technology has been a negative influence in your life, especially in regard to relationships or working with people? Give some examples.
2. How would you define a "good conversation"? What has to be there? How often do you have good conversations each day, each week, or each month?

1   We live in a technological universe in which we are always communicating. And yet we have sacrificed conversation for mere connection.

2   At home, families sit together, texting and reading e-mail. At work executives text during board meetings. We text (and shop and go on Facebook) during classes and when we're on dates. My students tell me about an important new skill: it involves maintaining eye contact with someone while you text someone else; it's hard, but it can be done.

▲ Together, but not together.

3   Over the past 15 years, I've studied technologies of mobile connection and talked to hundreds of people of all ages and circumstances about their plugged-in lives. I've learned that the little devices most of us carry around are so powerful that they change not only what we do, but also who we are.

4   We've become accustomed to a new way of being "alone together." Technology-enabled, we are able to be with one another, and also elsewhere, connected to wherever we want to be. We want to customize our lives. We want to move in and out of where we are because the thing we value most is control over where we focus our attention. We have gotten used to the idea of being in a tribe of one, loyal to our own party.

5   Our colleagues want to go to that board meeting but pay attention only to what interests them. To some this seems like a good idea, but we can end up hiding from one another, even as we are constantly connected to one another.

6   A businessman laments that he no longer has colleagues at work. He doesn't stop by to talk; he doesn't call. He says that he doesn't want to interrupt them. He says they're "too busy on their e-mail." But then he pauses and corrects himself. "I'm not telling the truth. I'm the one who doesn't want to be interrupted. I think I should. But I'd rather just do things on my BlackBerry."

7   A 16-year-old boy who relies on texting for almost everything says almost wistfully, "Someday, someday, but certainly not now, I'd like to learn how to have a conversation."

8   In today's workplace, young people who have grown up fearing conversation show up on the job wearing earphones. Walking through a college library or the campus of a high-tech start-up, one sees the same thing: we are together, but each of us is in our own bubble, furiously connected to keyboards and tiny touch screens. A senior partner at a Boston law firm describes a scene in his office. Young associates lay out their suite of technologies: laptops, iPods and multiple phones. And then they put their earphones on. "Big ones. Like pilots. They turn their desks into cockpits." With the young lawyers in their cockpits, the office is quiet, a quiet that does not ask to be broken.

9   In the silence of connection, people are comforted by being in touch with a lot of people—carefully kept at bay. We can't get enough of one another if we can use technology to keep one another at distances we can control: not too close, not too far, just right. I think of it as a Goldilocks effect.

10   Texting and e-mail and posting let us present the self we want to be. This means we can edit. And if we wish to, we can delete. Or retouch: the voice, the flesh, the face, the body. Not too much, not too little—just right.

11   Human relationships are rich; they're messy and demanding. We have learned the habit of cleaning them up with technology. And the move from conversation to connection is part of this. But it's a process in which we shortchange

ourselves. Worse, it seems that over time we stop caring, we forget that there is a difference.

12   We are tempted to think that our little "sips" of online connection add up to a big gulp of real conversation. But they don't. E-mail, Twitter, Facebook, all of these have their places—in politics, commerce, romance and friendship. But no matter how valuable, they do not substitute for conversation.

13   Connecting in sips may work for gathering discrete bits of information or for saying, "I am thinking about you." Or even for saying, "I love you." But connecting in sips doesn't work as well when it comes to understanding and knowing one another. In conversation we tend to one another. (The word itself is kinetic; it's derived from words that mean to move, together.) We can attend to tone and nuance. In conversation, we are called upon to see things from another's point of view.

14   Face-to-face conversation unfolds slowly. It teaches patience. When we communicate on our digital devices, we learn different habits. As we ramp up the volume and velocity of online connections, we start to expect faster answers. To get these, we ask one another simpler questions; we dumb down our communications, even on the most important matters. It is as though we have all put ourselves on cable news. Shakespeare might have said, "We are consum'd with that which we were nourish'd by."

15   And we use conversation with others to learn to converse with ourselves. So our flight from conversation can mean diminished chances to learn skills of self-reflection. These days, social media continually asks us what's "on our mind," but we have little motivation to say something truly self-reflective. Self-reflection in conversation requires trust. It's hard to do anything with 3,000 Facebook friends except connect.

16   As we get used to being shortchanged on conversation and to getting by with less, we seem almost willing to dispense with people altogether. Serious people muse about the future of computer programs as psychiatrists. A high school sophomore confides to me that he wishes he could talk to an artificial intelligence program instead of his dad about dating; he says the A.I. would have so much more in its database. Indeed, many people tell me they hope that as Siri, the digital assistant on Apple's iPhone, becomes more advanced, "she" will be more and more like a best friend—one who will listen when others won't.

17   During the years I have spent researching people and their relationships with technology, I have often heard the sentiment "No one is listening to me." I believe this feeling helps explain why it is so appealing to have a Facebook page or a Twitter feed—each provides so many automatic listeners. And it helps explain why—against all reason—so many of us are willing to talk to machines that seem to care about us. Researchers around the world are busy inventing sociable robots, designed to be companions to the elderly, to children, to all of us.

18   One of the most haunting experiences during my research came when I brought one of these robots, designed in the shape of a baby seal, to an elder-care

facility, and an older woman began to talk to it about the loss of her child. The robot seemed to be looking into her eyes. It seemed to be following the conversation. The woman was comforted.

19   And so many people found this amazing. Like the sophomore who wants advice about dating from artificial intelligence and those who look forward to computer psychiatry, this enthusiasm speaks to how much we have confused conversation with connection and collectively seem to have embraced a new kind of delusion that accepts the simulation of compassion as sufficient unto the day. And why would we want to talk about love and loss with a machine that has no experience of the arc of human life? Have we so lost confidence that we will be there for one another?

20   We expect more from technology and less from one another and seem increasingly drawn to technologies that provide the illusion of companionship without the demands of relationship. Always-on/always-on-you devices provide three powerful fantasies: that we will always be heard; that we can put our attention wherever we want it to be; and that we never have to be alone. Indeed our new devices have turned being alone into a problem that can be solved.

21   When people are alone, even for a few moments, they fidget and reach for a device. Here connection works like a symptom, not a cure, and our constant, reflexive impulse to connect shapes a new way of being.

22   Think of it as "I share, therefore I am." We use technology to define ourselves by sharing our thoughts and feelings as we're having them. We used to think, "I have a feeling; I want to make a call." Now our impulse is, "I want to have a feeling; I need to send a text."

23   So, in order to feel more, and to feel more like ourselves, we connect. But in our rush to connect, we flee from solitude, our ability to be separate and gather ourselves. Lacking the capacity for solitude, we turn to other people but don't experience them as they are. It is as though we use them, need them as spare parts to support our increasingly fragile selves.

24   We think constant connection will make us feel less lonely. The opposite is true. If we are unable to be alone, we are far more likely to be lonely. If we don't teach our children to be alone, they will know only how to be lonely.

25   I am a partisan for conversation. To make room for it, I see some first, deliberate steps. At home, we can create sacred spaces: the kitchen, the dining room. We can make our cars "device-free zones." We can demonstrate the value of conversation to our children. And we can do the same thing at work. There we are so busy communicating that we often don't have time to talk to one another about what really matters. Employees asked for casual Fridays; perhaps managers should introduce conversational Thursdays. Most of all, we need to remember—in between texts and e-mails and Facebook posts—to listen to one another, even to the boring bits, because it is often in unedited moments, moments in which we hesitate and stutter and go silent, that we reveal ourselves to one another.

26   I spend the summers at a cottage on Cape Cod, and for decades I walked the same dunes that Thoreau once walked. Not too long ago, people walked with their heads up, looking at the water, the sky, the sand and at one another, talking. Now they often walk with their heads down, typing. Even when they are with friends, partners, children, everyone is on their own devices.

27   So I say, look up, look at one another, and let's start the conversation.

QUESTIONS FOR DISCUSSION

I nterest

1. At the start of her essay, specifically in the second paragraph, Turkle uses a number of examples in an attempt to hook the reader. Do these examples seem realistic to you, and do you think they will make a reader of the *New York Times* want to read on? Why?

D etails

2. Turkle generally moves from examples to specific assertions to make her main points later in the essay. Do you find that organization effective? Why or why not? Would the article have been stronger if it had been organized differently?

3. Turkle states, "When people are alone, even for a few moments, they fidget and reach for a device." Reflecting on your friends' and your own use of technologies, does this assertion seem true? Why or why not?

4. Turkle uses a few direct quotations in her article. What purpose do these serve, and how effective are they in making her points?

E xplanation

5. The author explains "the Goldilocks effect" in her essay. What is that effect, and do you find that she is accurately describing the way people act online? Why or why not?

6. What examples does Turkle use to support her idea that the technologies we use do not foster patience and self-reflection? Can you think of any examples to further support those points or go against them?

7. Face-to-face conversation is set as the benchmark, the ideal, of conversation. Do you agree with this implied criteria, or do you disagree with Turkle in that online conversations can be reflective, slow, and deep? Why or why not?

A udience

8. Writing an essay that critiques the use of technology in American culture can be risky because many people assume that technological advances are always good. How would you describe Turkle's tone in this article? Is her tone effective in going against the mainstream point of view about the goodness of technological advances?

9. In what ways does the author directly reach out to her audience? Are there places in the essay where she is in risk of losing her audience because of word choice or the tone used? Give examples.

S tyle

10. Pick one paragraph in this article and examine the sentence variety the author or the people she quotes from use. Try putting each sentence into its own bulleted list to make it easier to notice the different structures (compound, complex, etc.) and lengths of the sentences in the paragraph.

I D E A S for Your Own Writing   MyWritingLab

Evaluate Your Text Messages

In her article, Turkle makes this statement: "Now our impulse is, 'I want to have a feeling; I need to send a text.'" Select five text messages you have sent and evaluate whether they fit into the category of "texting just to share something." In one paragraph, examine the specific messages and analyze whether they connect with or go against Turkle's point. In a second paragraph, explain what you think these text messages say about how you communicate with others and whether you are engaging in true conversations.

Evaluate Your Face-to-Face Conversations

How many face-to-face conversations do you think you should have per day, and how long should they be on average? Over the next three days, track how many face-to-face conversations you have. In addition, track how long these conversations last and examine their depth/quality. In other words, do the conversations move beyond small talk (i.e., saying hello or discussing the weather)? After tracking and compiling the results of your conversations for the three-day period, write a short essay that has four sections:

- Introduce the criteria you thought your day should have (how many conversations, average length of them) and why you chose those numbers.
- Detail the three days in three separate paragraphs by relating the number and average length of conversations for each day.
- Reflect on the quality of these conversations and what you got out of them.
- Conclude by talking about what you learned by doing this writing project.

Evaluating the Credibility of an Online Source (.org)

Your Writing Task: Evaluate an online source by focusing on appropriate criteria to examine the source's authority and objectivity. The source needs to have an *.org* designation.

When evaluating a *source's authority*, use these questions to brainstorm your evaluation:

- Who is the author or organization? Is it clear who is behind the information?
- Does the author or organization have any important credentials that might instill trust or distrust in the reader?
- Why is the source providing this information? What is motivating the source to write this?

When evaluating a *source's objectivity*, use these questions to brainstorm your evaluation:

- What is the source trying to do to the reader: to inform, persuade, please/entertain? Is it clear what the source is trying to do?
- Does the source have any bias or prejudice toward or for certain viewpoints?

Your Readers: This document is written for your classmates and instructor. Your evaluation needs to make them aware of an online source and how it is or is not a credible source of information. You should support your evaluation with strong reasoning and developed answers to the above questions.

A Successful Evaluating the Credibility of an Online Source (.org) Assignment . . .

- Details and provides a concise introduction to the online source by offering one to three sentences that give background information about the source.
- Provides a thesis that clearly presents an evaluation of the source's credibility.
- Offers strong details and explanation of the source's authority and objectivity.
- Has focused and unified paragraphs.

- Utilizes a clear organization strategy with transitions and other coherence devices.
- Provides a medium level of tone and diction—not too formal but not too informal.
- Is free of distracting mechanical and proofreading errors.

Business, Service, or Product Evaluation

Your Writing Task: As part of the "Everyday Critic" feature of a campus newspaper, you have been asked to write an article in which you judge a business or service situated on campus or within the local community. Another option is evaluating a new product on the market.

The "Everyday Critic" feature focuses on businesses, services, or products college students or locals might want to know about. Sometimes writers critique an established business or service, but often they evaluate new businesses or services that are offered at college or in the city in which you live. Whether you evaluate a dog-grooming business, the campus writing center, or a new hair-care product, your evaluation needs to clearly and explicitly establish criteria for evaluating the product or service, and then you must use specific and concrete details along with developed examples from your experience to support your evaluation.

Keep in mind that you need to use distinct sets of criteria for different products or services. For example, a critic would evaluate a hardware store differently than he or she would evaluate a college's math tutoring services. Therefore, it is important to think about the type of business, service, or product you are evaluating and clearly establish factors by which it should be judged.

Your Readers: The audience you are writing for is the campus community of your college. The review is mostly aimed at students like yourself, but professors, administrators, and staff might also read your article.

A Successful Evaluation Paper . . .

- Provides a concise, accurate, and descriptive background for introducing the business, service, or product to orient the reader.
- Has a thesis that is assertive, one that clearly makes a judgment about the merit of the business, service, or product by the end of the first paragraph.
- Offers strong support for its thesis by using specific and concrete details along with detailed examples and explanation to support the evaluation.
- Has focused and unified paragraphs that relate specific details connected to criteria appropriate for evaluating this subject.

- Uses a clear organization strategy with transitions and other coherence devices.
- Provides a medium level of tone and diction—not too formal but not too informal.
- Is free of distracting mechanical and proofreading errors.

See pages 289–293 for Karl Martinson's response to this assignment.

Case Study: Letter about Whether Dexter Jones Should Be Paroled

Your Role: In this case, you will act as one of the few friends of Dexter Jones, an inmate in the Northman State Penitentiary in central Minnesota. Dexter, your friend from high school, is serving a fourteen-year sentence for second-degree assault and armed criminal action since he was certified to stand trial as an adult during the court case. Dexter was put in jail when he was fifteen.

Dexter's Background and the Situation: During Dexter's early life, his family often fell on hard times—renting houses, getting evicted, and living in cheap hotels. Occasionally, the family—mom, dad, Dexter, and his sister—would have to be homeless and sleep in tents by the river. While Dexter's mom had a steady job as a waitress at a local diner, Dexter's dad was fired from his factory job after he hit a supervisor when Dexter was around eight years old. For a significant portion of Dexter's life, his dad was either looking for a job or losing his job because of drinking and not showing up to work. When Dexter was in junior high school, his dad spent time in jail for producing and dealing crystal meth. Dexter's parents divorced when Dexter was in sixth grade.

After the divorce, Dexter was mostly left alone. He often got into fights in school with kids who were bigger than he was. He experimented with drinking, smoking marijuana, and dropping acid. He was often suspended for long periods of time from both junior high school and the early part of high school for fighting and acting up in class.

During the summer before his sophomore year, he was riding around drinking whiskey with his buddies. Dexter and his friends stopped at a parking lot where lots of teens were hanging out on a Friday night. Dexter and another young teen, Lee Fowler, began yelling at one another. The words eventually led to a fight. Fowler, much larger than Dexter, knocked him down and started pummeling him, and Dexter pulled out his large pocketknife.

Dexter stabbed Lee Fowler six times, puncturing Fowler's lung and creating multiple, deep lacerations. Dexter fled the scene with his friends and was picked up by police about two hours later and confessed to what he had done. Thinking Dexter would get leniency because he was a minor, his lawyer suggested he plead guilty to the charges. However, the judge certified Dexter as an adult and gave him fourteen years behind bars with hardened criminals.

It has been four years since Dexter went into Northman, and he is now nineteen. His first two years were difficult because he often got into fights with other inmates, but in the third year he settled down, got into lifting weights, began attending religious services, and earned his G.E.D.

While he only occasionally gets into fights or trouble at Northman, Dexter has told you that he thinks Fowler needed to be put on trial too since Dexter suffered a severe concussion and claims Fowler had a knife that the police never found. He told you one time, "If I hadn't have gotten caught, something like that would have probably happened sometime in high school or later on. I got anger issues."

You have known Dexter since grade school and share a love of cars with him. The two of you would often hang out at your cousin's gas station and garage, earning some money by helping with detailing automobiles. Dexter was a hard worker, but your cousin banned him from the shop after Dexter was caught stealing some money from the cash box. Dexter claimed it was to help his mother pay rent, but you don't know for sure that's where the money went.

The Document and Your Reader: Since you are one of the few people who have visited Dexter in Northman besides his mother and you have had close contact with him the past four years, the parole officer asked you to write a letter. Dexter does not and will not ever know that you are writing the letter. The parole officer has asked for a letter that evaluates whether you think Dexter is ready to go back into society. The letter will be read by the parole board and filed away for reference.

Based on Dexter's background, past behavior, and current behavior, your letter to the parole board should either encourage or discourage board members from granting Dexter Jones parole.

The Required Format: The letter needs to be formally addressed to the Parole Board of the State of Minnesota. The paragraphs must be single-spaced and have double-spacing between paragraphs.

A Successful Parole Board Letter . . .

- Presents in the first paragraph a clear and concise thesis about whether Dexter should earn parole and why.
- Evaluates Dexter's situation with strong explanation and sound reasoning based on important criteria.
- Is persuasive and informative through details and examples.
- Has focused and unified paragraphs that are developed and connect to the thesis.

- Is free of irrelevant details.
- Follows the proper format of a memorandum.
- Utilizes a clear organization strategy with transitions and other coherence devices.
- Provides a medium level of tone and diction—not too formal, but not too informal.
- Is free of mechanical and proofreading errors.

CHAPTER AT A GLANCE

Learning Objectives	How they connect to writing at college . . .
❶ Consider the criteria for success.	*Criteria* are the principles or standards by which something is judged or evaluated. Before evaluating, you must be able to identify the criteria you are using to determine success.
❷ Show how a subject is (or is not) a success.	The second step in evaluation is explaining *why* and *how* a subject is (or is not) a success based on those criteria.
❸ Put **I D E A S** to work in evaluative writing.	In drafting evaluative writing, writers ask the following kinds of questions: • Which criteria are important? • How can I show my evaluation through strong details, examples, and explanation? • How can the evaluation be interesting for the reader? • How can I make my readers trust my evaluation?

> **MyWritingLab** Visit **Chapter 10, "Evaluative Writing,"** in MyWritingLab to test your understanding of the chapter objectives.

Persuasive Writing

11

The courtroom is a place where persuasion and argumentation take place. Persuasion also is part of our everyday lives. How has a piece of writing persuaded you? What aspects of that writing influenced you to agree with the writer's point of view? How have you persuaded people in college, in the workplace, and in your personal life?

Most writing can be considered persuasive because as a writer you want to persuade your readers either to agree with your way of thinking about a subject or to clearly understand your message. This chapter, however, focuses exclusively on writing with a central aim to persuade readers to do, change, or rethink something. You probably attempt to persuade people every day, whether it is talking your friends into seeing a particular movie or convincing an employer you are the best person for a job. Of course, people try to persuade you every day, too. Advertising is the most visible form of persuasion we see on a consistent basis, whether it is a banner ad on the Web, a billboard, or a print ad in a magazine.

Some people may think of persuasion as manipulative or deceptive. Your persuasive writing, however, should be ethical. You should not make up information or exaggerate. You should speak the truth from your point of view and support your point or thesis effectively.

MyWritingLab Visit Ch. 11 Persuasive Writing in MyWritingLab to access the IDEAS videos.

In addition to the **I D E A S** explained in Chapters 2 and 3, persuasive writing includes a number of other important principles.

❶ Know your audience's expectations.

Know Your Audience's Expectations

Since the goal of persuasive writing is to move readers to action, to change their minds, or to challenge them to rethink something, **audience awareness**, or anticipating your readers' wants and expectations, is crucial. Knowing your audience's expectations involves using evidence they will find convincing, presenting your writing in a way they think is appropriate, and showing how what you are saying connects to them or to the common good.

▲ What evidence would you use to convince peers not to text while driving?

Use Convincing Evidence for Your Audience

Different kinds of evidence work better in convincing various groups of people. For example, a state senator who supports a bill proposing severe penalties for texting while driving will try to persuade her fellow legislators by using facts, statistics, and realistic examples of how texting while driving has harmed people.

However, that same state senator might have to use different types of evidence when convincing her seventeen-year-old daughter to stop texting while driving. Facts and statistics may not work as well because they could seem impersonal, so as a mother, she would use more emotional examples to get the point across.

Choose an Appropriate Format

How you present information to your readers is critical to its success in persuading them. For instance, if you were trying to convince a company manager to switch supply vendors, you would achieve your persuasive aim more effectively by presenting your evidence in charts, graphs, and bulleted lists rather than in an essay.

Connect with Your Readers

The best persuasive writing connects with readers. You want to show readers that the action you would like them to take or the point of view you hope they will accept is in *their* best interest. The state senator will emphasize how much she wants her daughter to be safe. You will show the manager how the change in vendors will increase the company's profits. Readers are more open to being convinced when they think a writer is genuinely concerned about them.

EXERCISE 11.1   Analyze Audience Expectations   MyWritingLab

Directions: For each of the following situations that call for persuasive writing, analyze the audience expectations by addressing these questions:

- What kinds of authoritative evidence could the writer include?
- What tone should the writing convey? Should the writing be formal? Conversational?
- How can the writer connect this issue to the reader(s)? How can the writer show concern and respect for the readers, especially if they may have an opposing view?
- Is using personal experience appropriate for this writing situation? Explain why or why not. If it is, explain what types of experiences would be appropriate.

1. A union representative, negotiating with management for improved wages and benefits, submits a written proposal.

2. A student missed an important test because of a family emergency and sends an email to the teacher requesting an opportunity to make up the test.

3. A homeowner, concerned that a proposed convenience store with a liquor license will disrupt the neighborhood, writes to the city council.

4. Because of a faulty repair at a local automotive repair company, you were involved in a car accident and missed several days of work. You write to the company asking to be compensated for the damages to your car and for the lost income.

5. A company is offering paid internship positions for the summer, and you send a letter of application.

❷ Use the rhetorical toolkit: *ethos, logos,* and *pathos.*

Use the Rhetorical Toolkit: *Ethos, Logos,* and *Pathos*

Particularly in persuasive writing, it is helpful to analyze or brainstorm about the subject by using what are commonly called the three **rhetorical appeals**, or what we call the rhetorical toolkit: *ethos, logos,* and *pathos.* If something *appeals* to you, it catches your attention. Using these appeals in the rhetorical toolkit is also a way to connect with your readers and capture their attention, so they consider your points carefully.

Ethos: Establishing Credibility

Ethos refers to the way writers show their credibility in a piece of writing. They want readers to trust them because readers are more likely to be convinced by writers whom they perceive as honest, fair, and knowledgeable.

The following strategies can help you show strong *ethos*—credibility or trustworthiness—in a paper:

- Using a strong style
- Showing a proper attitude or tone
- Citing reputable authorities
- Sharing relevant personal experience
- Showing respect for your audience and the views of others

Strong Style

Just as people are often judged—accurately or not—by the clothes they wear, your ideas will be judged in large part by the writing style you use to present them. A young man applying for a job as an engineer may have the education, experience, and work ethic to do the job well; however, if he shows up wearing a stained shirt, old jeans, and grungy flip flops, he is not likely to get the job. Similarly, you can build a convincing case, but if it is "dressed" in poor writing style, your readers are not as likely to be persuaded. In contrast, a cover letter and resume that are properly formatted, appropriate to the job being offered, and convincing through examples and details will establish a person's authority and perhaps earn that person an interview.

One of the easiest ways to show strong *ethos* or credibility is to submit work that is neatly typed, well written, and carefully proofread. For a reader to trust what you are presenting, proper word choice, appropriate tone, and respect for readers are key elements for establishing strong credibility.

Proper Attitude or Tone

Again, remember the importance of connecting with your audience. A paper with an angry tone seldom persuades anyone other than people who already think exactly like the writer. However, a writer whose tone is rational and reasonable can persuade a wider audience. Since an important component of tone is diction, or choice of words, you should avoid words that suggest unreasonable bias or prejudice.

Reputable Authorities

Just as you want to convey your own knowledge, fairness, and credibility, you want your sources to do so as well. Choose sources that are widely respected in their fields, accurate, and up to date. Presenting the ideas of others accurately and acknowledging them with proper documentation also establishes your *ethos* by showing you are an honest writer who gives credit to others when it is due.

Personal Experience

Using personal experience can strongly establish your *ethos* and personal investment in a topic by showing your connection to it. But, depending on the topic, the paper, and the class, using personal experience may or may not be a good idea. Always consider the kind of persuasive writing you are doing and your audience's expectations.

Respect for the Audience and Others' Views

Often, when your aim is to persuade, your audience may not initially agree with your position. An ethical approach to persuasion does not ignore these opposing views, nor does it ridicule or treat them with disrespect. As a knowledgeable and fair writer, you need to address opposing views respectfully. The part of a persuasive paper in which you show how the evidence for your position is stronger and more extensive than that of the opposition is called the **rebuttal**. While you should also admit when the opposition has a good point that cannot be disproved, you can emphasize that you still have the strongest evidence for your position.

▲ If you were hiring a new marketing representative for your company, how would you expect job candidates to dress for interviews? Why?

EXERCISE 11.2   Improve *Ethos* MyWritingLab

Directions: Your friend Sam, an employee of Baxter's Auto Body Shop, wrote the following letter to try to get some safety concerns addressed by the shop owner. He knows you are taking a college writing course and has asked for your advice before he gives the letter to his boss. What changes would you suggest so Sam can improve his *ethos*?

Dear Mr. Baxter,

I thought working at your auto body shop would be a good opportunity, but it sure hasn't been all it was cracked up to be. Here is the problems.

Your shop has some major hazards that any moron should see and defiantly do something about. For one thing we use some of the most toxic solvents and cleaners around. Did you ever hear of water-based or citrus-based cleaners? They do a good job and won't eat through my skin if I get splattered. Don't get me started on what these toxins are also doing to the environment. And have you ever tried mixing paint in an enclosed room with a screwed-up ventilation system? I have—every single day since I started working for you. After breathing in those vapors every day, I'm surprised I have any brain cells left to write this letter.

Do you not care about your employees, or are you just too cheap? I hope you fix the problems soon cause I'd hate to have to find another job.

Sam

Logos: Using Logic and Reason

From the Greek term *logos*, we get the word *logic*, which refers to the use of sound reasoning and judgment. You use *logos* when your supporting evidence appeals to your readers' intellect and their ability to think critically. Most readers expect this to be the strongest part of a persuasive paper.

But what do you have to do to show logic? Your first step should be to gather the following kinds of evidence to support your point or thesis:

- Real or realistic examples
- Testimony or research by experts

- Details that show and explain
- Relevant facts
- Relevant statistics
- Charts and graphs that show data

When working with *logos* in persuasive writing, you tend to work mostly in the **E** of **I D E A S** : Explanation. Most persuasive writing will require that you find this material in outside sources, so finding *experts* and *valid* and *reliable sources* of information is extremely important.

Before you begin working with the information you have gathered, ask yourself these important questions:

- Have I gathered enough evidence to make a strong case for my point?
- Is the evidence up to date and accurate?
- Have I used reliable sources and the opinions of respected experts?
- Is the evidence relevant, or clearly connected, to the point I want to make?

▲ What advice would you give a young person trying to convince skeptical parents that tattoos are acceptable forms of self expression?

Next, you have think about that information, see connections, and draw conclusions that you can present to your readers in a convincing way. Richard Fulkerson, a professor of writing and author of *Teaching the Argument in Writing*, recommends some basic logical strategies which you can use to connect your evidence to your thesis:

- Draw general conclusions from specific samples.
- Show connections between similar situations.
- Link causes and effects.
- Apply widely accepted principles to specific situations.
- Connect signs or clues to what they suggest.
- Use respected experts with relevant knowledge to reinforce points.

We will examine these strategies through the example of Marta, a high school senior, who is trying to convince her parents to allow her to get a tattoo. Her parents' position is that only criminals get tattoos. They also worry about physical risks like catching a serious disease such as hepatitis or AIDS from contaminated needles. If Marta hopes to persuade her parents, she must first do some research to gather enough accurate and relevant supporting evidence to back up her thesis or point: *Tattoos are a safe form of artistic expression shared by many people from all walks of life.*

Once she has her evidence, Marta can begin applying logical strategies to the way she presents it to her parents. As you read these points, think about how logical and effective they might be in persuading her parents. Read them critically.

Logical Strategy ⟶	Marta Applies the Strategy
Draw general conclusions from specific samples: The reasoning here is that what is true of a well-chosen sample will likely hold true for the larger group. It is important when using this kind of logical reasoning that you try to base your conclusions on a large enough representative sample of the group.	Marta finds that at least thirty of the girls and almost fifty of the boys in her senior class of three hundred have tattoos, and none of them are criminals. She also finds a survey by the Pew Research Center that says 36 percent of Americans in the 18–25 age bracket have tattoos. From these samples, Marta feels confident that a significant number of people in her age group who are not disreputable characters have tattoos.
Show connections between similar situations: Analogies are comparisons between two situations, things, or ideas that are somewhat similar. The thinking is that if they are similar in obvious ways, they are similar in other ways, too.	Marta knows that one of her parents' objections to tattoos is that they are "permanent." Marta plans to compare getting a tattoo to getting her ears pierced—something her parents allowed her to do when she was much younger.
Explore cause and effect relationships: If two situations nearly always occur together, a logical line of thinking perceives the two as causally related—that is, one causes the other. While often this is the case, sometimes other contributing causes might be at work.	One of Marta's cousins was recently turned down for a job, and Marta's parents say it was because he has a tattoo. Marta will have to be careful here because she will have to explain to her parents that they are not being completely logical. Her cousin applied for a job that he was not qualified for, so he was likely turned down for reasons other than a tattoo.
Apply widely accepted principles to specific situations: Another way to support a position is to take a well-accepted or popular principle and show how a particular situation applies to it. Marta knows her parents are proud of her creativity and believe in every person's right to self-expression.	Marta will explain to her parents that to her the tattoo is an artistic expression, personally designed to represent her strong stands on protecting the environment.

Logical Strategy ⟶	Marta Applies the Strategy
Connect signs or clues to what they suggest: Visible evidence or clues can be presented as evidence of something not visible.	In order to persuade her parents to accept the safety of tattoos, Marta might point out that the tattoo parlor in their town has a state license and accreditation from the Alliance of Professional Tattooing. These "clues" suggest that the tattoo parlor Marta would use is highly safe.
Logical Strategy ⟶	Marta Applies the Strategy
Use respected experts with relevant knowledge: An authority whose integrity and expertise is widely accepted can be strong support in persuasion.	Marta might cite the Centers for Disease Control and Prevention (CDC) to point out that there has not been a documented case of AIDS transmission from a tattoo and that current data does not indicate that people who get tattoos are at increased risk of hepatitis infection.

EXERCISE 11.3   Make Logical Connections   MyWritingLab

Directions: Return to Sam's letter from Exercise 11.2 on page 318. Using Fulkerson's strategies, briefly explain how you could connect the evidence listed below to Sam's point: working conditions at the auto body shop must be made safer for employees.

1. The EPA recently fined another auto body shop for improper disposal of hazardous wastes.

2. The ten employees at Baxter's Auto Body Shop each miss an average of three to five days of work each month because of headaches and nose bleeds.

3. Customers frequently ask if the shop uses environmentally friendly products.

4. A faulty ventilation system led to a fire at a similar auto body shop in a nearby town.

5. Shops using environmentally friendly and safer paints and solvents have seen no significant increase in costs or decrease in the quality of work.

Pathos: Working with Emotions, Values, or Beliefs

While appeals to reason and logic should be strong components of a persuasive paper, your readers are also inspired by their emotions or feelings, by what they value and believe. *Pathos* refers to ways you appeal to your readers' emotions, values, and beliefs. Writers express *pathos* through these means:

- Emotional stories, examples, and details
- Emotionally loaded language and emotional word choice
- Graphic images
- Assumptions and beliefs important to the audience

Emotional Stories, Examples, and Details

Emotional stories and examples *show* the readers what you mean and help them understand why you want them to think or act a certain way. By putting a "face" on a serious social problem, the writer is more likely to evoke sympathy from readers and inspire them to take action as the following examples show:

Emphasis on *Logos*	Emphasis on *Pathos*
Over one million school-age children in America are homeless. About one-fifth of these children do not attend school at all, often because they lack transportation from homeless shelters to schools. Homeless children who are able to attend school are more likely to do poorly in their classes and to be suspended for behavior problems. Only one in four graduates from high school. Fortunately, our community has a program to help provide a safe environment and a good education for homeless children, but your help is needed to keep this program alive.	Eight-year-old Michael lives out of a suitcase he must haul to school every day because he cannot risk leaving his few belongings at the homeless shelter where he lives with his mother and two-year-old sister. Michael struggles with math and reading but worries more about where his family will stay when their time is up at this shelter. After school, he returns to the corner of the church basement where a row of cots and a small locker make up his current home. Four families are currently staying at this shelter, so there is little privacy, little quiet time to study. There is a way to help Michael, to allow him to achieve the education that will lift him from this life of poverty. But rescuing Michael and children like him takes help from citizens like you.

EXERCISE 11.4   Use *Pathos* to Persuade   MyWritingLab

Directions: Provide examples or stories that could be used to persuade people in each of the following instances. Explain how the examples could appeal to the audience's emotions, values, or beliefs.

1. A young teen tries to convince his parents to get him his own cell phone.

2. During a job interview, a candidate tries to show that she has strong people skills.

3. A research paper for a biology class argues for restrictions on animal testing in medical research.

4. A student has missed an important test and asks for an exception to the professor's "no make-up" policy.

5. An advertiser targets the 40+ crowd in promoting a new energy drink.

Emotionally Loaded Language, Emotional Word Choice

Another way to observe the use of *pathos* is in the way writers use emotionally loaded language to create a built-in bias for the reader. To show you how word choice matters, think about the differences between the following sets of word choices:

Neutral Words	Emotional Words
situation	crisis, tragedy, disaster
correctional facility	prison
government assistance	welfare
reduction in force	lay-off
biosolids	sewage
associate	low-level employee
sub-standard housing	slums
casualty	person killed or maimed
person of interest	criminal suspect
replacement workers	scabs

Look at the following statements, written in relatively neutral language:

- The basketball player caught the ball and tossed it into the net.
- The singer walked on to the stage wearing a tight dress and sang one of her new songs.
- As a replacement worker for our company, you will remove biosolids from basements experiencing a temporary inundation of water.

Now look at the same statements charged up with more emotional words:

- The basketball legend made a spectacular rebound and slammed the ball into the net.
- Her sequined designer gown hugging her svelte figure, the diva strolled on to the stage and belted out her next smash hit.
- As a company scab, you will remove sewage from flooded basements.

Think carefully about your choice of words when trying to persuade an audience. Of course, you want to present your position in positive terms, but you also want to be clear and honest in your presentation.

EXERCISE 11.5   Notice Biased or Emotional   MyWritingLab
Word Choices

Directions: As you read an essay or article for this class or another class, use a piece of paper with two columns to record biased or emotional word choices in the left column. Once you are done reading the essay or article, write down more objective word choices in the right column. Then, write a one-paragraph analysis of how the biased word choices show the author was trying to persuade you to agree with his or her point of view.

Graphic Images

Through images, advertising frequently exploits emotions to persuade. Flood victims stranded on roof tops, oil-soaked pelicans on the Gulf Coast, a dog pitifully looking at the camera as it sits among squalor in a pen— these images all might arouse emotions in certain people, making them sympathetic to what is presented.

EXERCISE 11.6   Analyze Graphic Images   MyWritingLab
Directions: Examine the following sets of images used in persuasive messages. Think about the emotions evoked by the images and their appropriateness for the audience and purpose of each piece.

Image 1 This Thai Health Promotion Foundation ad is trying to persuade motorcyclists to wear helmets.

- Will the image of the hot air balloon working like a helmet surprise viewers of this ad?
- How does the use of dark colors and the man's body make a statement about what happens when helmets are not worn?
- Does the contrast of the smile and accident scene play effectively with the audience's emotions and assumptions?
- Do you think this ad would effectively reach its intended audience? Why or why not?

Image 2 This billboard in Australia warns people about the dangers of driving when tired.

- Does this billboard use *pathos* effectively or do you think it merely exploits the viewer's emotions? Explain.
- What words are the most powerful and persuasive in this ad? Why?
- How does the use of black and white colors with red send a message?
- Do you think this ad would effectively reach its intended audience? Why or why not?

Image 3 This ad by the California Department of Health warns parents about how second-hand smoke affects their children.

- How does the image of the cigarette sandwich next to a glass of milk stir up emotions?
- How does the copy (writing) of the ad prey on guilt to move viewers?
- Which emotionally laden word choices are most effective? Which ones are not as effective?
- Do you think this ad would effectively reach its intended audience? Why or why not?

Assumptions and Beliefs Important to the Audience

Sometimes people can have the same facts, statistics, examples, data, and studies in front of them, but they will disagree about an issue based on beliefs and assumptions they do not share. For example, two people could look at a country's economic situation—high unemployment, a large national debt, the loss of manufacturing jobs—and come to completely different conclusions about what needs to be done:

- One person, who believes in the "free market" and less governmental intervention into industry, could argue to cut funding of specific governmental programs and to offer tax breaks to wealthy business owners in order to expand those businesses and invest.
- Another person, who feels the country needs stronger governmental regulation of the financial industry and rails against "corporate welfare," may want to end tax breaks and establish a tax system that would bring in more revenue to support education and offer incentives to "green" companies.

You should consider how *pathos* relates to *beliefs and assumptions* because if you connect to readers' beliefs and assumptions, you have a better chance of persuading them. In addition, when you read persuasive writing, it is important to critically unpack a writer's assumptions. Often when you disagree with a point, it could be because your assumptions do not match those of a writer.

Put I D E A S to Work in Persuasive Writing

❸ Put **I D E A S** to work in persuasive writing.

How do I want to persuade my reader? What do I want them to think or do after they are done reading my paper? What examples and details are useful and important in persuading my reader? How can I make the reader care? How can I establish my credibility? How can I tap into emotions?

MyWritingLab Visit Ch. 11 Persuasive Writing in MyWritingLab to access the IDEAS videos.

Writers ask themselves these questions as they prepare to draft a persuasive piece of writing. As you think through what examples and details are most important, keep in mind **I D E A S**:

- **I** nterest
- **D** etails
- **E** xplanation
- **A** udience
- **S** tyle

STUDENT WRITER AT WORK

Navid Montazeri's professor gave him the following assignment, which ties together a variety of reading and writing skills Navid has been practicing this semester: close, careful reading as a believer and a doubter, summarizing and paraphrasing, and analysis. The full assignment is on pages 345–347 of this chapter, but here is the general topic:

Summary-Analysis-Response Essay

Your Task

Actively and critically read an article that has a primarily persuasive aim. Your goal is to demonstrate that you can objectively summarize the article with the author's position, analyze the author's use of the rhetorical toolkit (ethos, logos, pathos), and respond to the essay with an informed opinion of what you read.

Follow Navid as he works through this assignment, a paper that demands close reading and critical thinking. He has to summarize the article (summary), evaluate the article using the rhetorical toolkit (analysis), and provide a reasoned response to that reading material (response).

Active Reading

Navid chose the essay "Put the Brakes on Driving While Texting" by Leonard Pitts as the piece he would read, summarize, analyze, and respond to for this assignment. As he read the essay, Navid made notes about the author's strategies by using the **I D E A S** template.

Put the Brakes on Driving While Texting
Leonard Pitts

Leonard Pitts has been writing his syndicated column for The Miami Herald *since 1994, winning a Pulitzer Prize for his work in 2004. Pitts has won numerous other awards and recognition for his work, which appears in 150 newspapers across the United States. He offers insights on the American experience, particularly that of African Americans. In this column he weighs in on the issue of texting while driving.*

1. What are some of the obvious dangers of texting while driving?
2. Why do you think so many people continue to text while driving even when they know the dangers?
3. What do you think it would take to convince someone to stop texting while driving?

Interest: The author grabs the reader's interest with an up-front statement.	1 The amazing thing about the debate over the need for laws to ban texting while driving is that there is a debate over the need for laws to ban texting while driving.

2   In the first place, you'd think you wouldn't need a law, that simple common sense would be enough to tell us it's unsafe to divert attention to a tiny keyboard and screen while simultaneously piloting two tons of metal, rubber, glass and, let us not forget, flesh, at freeway speeds—or even street speeds. In the second place, if common sense were insufficient, you'd think lawmakers would have rushed to back it up with tough laws.

Style: Pitts uses a short sentence to make a point with attitude and a conversational style.

3   Think again.

4   The issue has been moved to the front burner recently by a confluence of events. In late July, a study by the Virginia Tech Transportation Institute quantified the blatantly obvious: texting while driving is dangerous. Researchers found that the person who does so is the functional equivalent of a drunk driver, a whopping 23 times more likely to be involved in an accident or near-collision. Actually, according to a study in *Car and Driver* magazine, the texter is a significantly greater threat than a mere drunk.

Explanation: Pitts explains why texting is dangerous through a research study and another source.

5   About the same time the VTTI study was released, four senators introduced legislation that would require states to pass laws banning drivers from texting or risk losing federal highway funds. According to the *Los Angeles Times*, only 16 states and Washington, D.C., already have such laws on the books.

6   And last week, Transportation Secretary Ray LaHood announced a September summit in which lawmakers, law enforcement, academics, safety experts, and other stakeholders will study texting and other driving distractions.

7   You want my response to this flurry of attention and activity? I can give it to you in a syllable:

8   Duh.

9   What else is there to study? What more is there to say? The danger is all too self-evident. And if it were not, it has been quite aptly illustrated in episodes like last year's commuter train crash in California in which the operator was texting and 25 people died.

Details: Pitts presents the laws as common sense.

10   Enough. Ban texting while driving. And cell phone use, too. Because what researchers tell us is that it's not the physical difficulty of juggling the devices that endangers us. It is the distraction: a driver so wrapped up in communicating

with a person who isn't there that he is drawn away from his primary duty: keep the car between the lines. The brain simply doesn't have sufficient bandwidth for both.

11   So yeah, there ought to be a law. And it ought to have some teeth in it. On the second offense, maybe a hefty fine, or brief loss of driving privileges. On the third, maybe you earn a free stay of a couple days and nights at the lovely graybar hotel.

12   If you sense here the zeal of the newly converted, congratulations on your perception.

13   I stopped using my cell behind the wheel (I was never dumb enough to text) two weeks ago. Had myself an epiphany, I did: was reviewing last night's game with my son really worth dying for? I decided it was not. So I no longer make or take calls while driving.

> **Details:** He uses a personal example to support his point.

14   If it's an emergency, I told my family, dial me again and I'll call you back. But the calls are hardly ever urgent, are they? That's not what this epidemic is about. Rather, it's about this idea—new within the last 15 years or so of our hyper-connected, hyper-productive culture—that it's never OK to be out of touch, unreachable, unreached.

15   Whither solitude? Whither the moment just spent communing with your own thoughts? Do you really have that much to say? I'll save you the trouble: you don't.

16   Phoning while driving, texting while driving . . . here's a novel idea. How about driving while driving? And for those truly urgent messages that just can't wait, I propose a simple solution:

17   Pull over.

Planning

Using the **I D E A S** template as a way to brainstorm ideas for his paper, Navid asked the following questions and had these thoughts about his paper:

Interest: So how do I spark interest? Most of my readers are probably like me and use cell phones when they drive, so I don't want to turn them off or sound preachy. Can I use some shocking statistics to show the problem? That way I can at least spark my readers' curiosity about what Pitts has to say. I think it's important to show my readers that I'm like them, and I don't automatically agree with everything Pitts writes.

Details: I want to be sure to cover all of Pitts's main points in my summary, so I can comment on them in more detail in the analysis section. I need to be specific in presenting the research Pitts uses to make his points about distracted drivers. His most emotional example is the commuter train crash, so I want to be sure to work that in. I have highlighted specific places in the article where Pitts uses emotional or biased language, so I can include specific references to that.

Explanation: The appeals to ethos and pathos were easier to find than logos. I want to be sure to connect what Pitts says to Fulkerson's techniques we talked about in class. The section where Pitts mentions almost having an accident might be unclear to readers because he only implies what happened. I have to make sure I explain that part accurately. In the conclusion, I should also mention that a lot has changed since Pitts wrote this article.

Audience: I have to create a thesis after my short introduction that grabs the reader's attention. The professor said it's ok to use "I" when stating my response to the essay. In the summary and analysis sections of the essay, I definitely want to come across as objective. No "I" in those sections. While I don't agree with all of what Pitts says, I want to come across as fair in the response section.

Style: My professor commented on my last paper that I need more sentence variety. I also need to choose quotes carefully and be sure to introduce them properly. In my last paper, I lost points for "dumping" quotes. I want to avoid using "I think" and "I feel" since those are wordy constructions.

Navid's Essay

The following essay is Navid's Summary-Analysis-Response to Leonard Pitts's essay "Put the Brakes on Driving While Texting." As you read, notice how he carefully follows the specific guidelines of the assignment.

Montazeri 1

Navid Montazeri

Prof. Copeland

Introduction to College Writing

7 November 2014

A Closer Look at

"Put the Brakes on Driving While Texting"

> Navid tries to capture his readers' interest with surprising statistics and facts.

Surveys taken in 2011 and 2012 by the U.S. Department of Transportation's National Highway Traffic Safety Administration found that during every minute of daylight, 660,000 drivers use cell phones or manipulate electronic devices while driving (United States, "NHTSA"). Other research shows that texting drivers take their eyes off the road for an average of 4.6 seconds. If the car is going fifty-five miles per hour, a driver will travel the length of a football field without looking at the road (United States, "No Texting"). I learned these facts after my curiosity about texting and driving was raised by Leonard Pitts's article "Let's Put the Brakes on Driving While Texting." Despite my initial negative reaction to the article, the more I thought about Pitts's message, the more sense it made to me. While I may not completely give up my cell phone while driving, Pitts has convinced me that texting while driving is dangerous.

> After giving the author's full name in the introduction, Navid will refer to the author by only his last name.

> Here Navid presents a tight summary of the article he is analyzing. Note how the summary contains only the main points of Pitts's article.

In "Put the Brakes on Driving While Texting," Pitts addresses the danger of using a cell phone while driving. He says that common sense alone should keep drivers from engaging in distracting activities while driving and is surprised that drivers continue this unsafe practice. He is astounded that lawmakers have not immediately passed laws banning texting while driving. Although recent studies have confirmed the dangers, few states currently have laws restricting the practice, and the federal government only calls for more study of the issue. Pitts argues that texting and even talking on cell phones while driving should be banned because both distract drivers whose brains cannot focus on both communicating

Montazeri 2

and driving. Pitts supports tough laws with punishments ranging from fines to prison times. To explain his strong position, Pitts admits nearly having a car accident while talking to his son on a cell phone. Since calls are seldom for emergencies and since being out of touch is not so bad, Pitts says drivers should focus on driving. If they must take an emergency call, they should pull over.

Pitts's *ethos* is inconsistent in this article. A Pulitzer Prize-winning author, Pitts brings a strong writing style to this piece; however, his attitude comes across as sarcastic, and he is clearly biased. Pitts begins by calling the debate on laws to ban texting while driving "amazing" since "common sense" should be enough to tell people it's dangerous (328). After basically saying those who disagree with him have no common sense, Pitts responds to the studies on texting and driving and the efforts to pass legislation banning this practice with "Duh"(328). Even though Pitts is clearly frustrated by all the time and studies it takes to realize an obvious danger, this response seems disrespectful towards efforts by those who are on his side. Pitts explains his strong feelings on this issue by relating his experience of nearly having an accident while driving and talking on a cell phone. His honesty in relating this experience helps his *ethos*, but even in this admission, he includes a disrespectful dig at those who disagree with him: "(I was never dumb enough to text)" (329). Calling those he is trying to persuade "dumb" isn't showing much respect for opposing viewpoints.

With emotion running so high in this article, I didn't expect to find much evidence of *logos*, but I did find some of the strategies Richard Fulkerson recommends. The example of a commuter train crash caused by the operator's texting is effective because even though this example involves a train, it suggests that texting while driving a car could also have deadly results. Pitts draws conclusions from another similar situation by

Here Navid points out a specific concern with *ethos*.

Navid makes another reference to a specific type of appeal to *ethos*: personal experience.

Navid gives a specific example to support his criticism of the author.

Navid points out how the author makes connections between similar situations.

Montazeri 3

Using research by respected experts is an appeal to *logos*.

pointing out the studies by Virginia Tech Transportation Institute and *Car and Driver* magazine that found a texting driver is as dangerous as a drunk driver. Most readers will agree that drunk drivers are dangerous, so this research by respected authorities is persuasive. Pitts also mentions research that found the brain can't effectively handle both using a cell phone and driving a car.

This shows Navid is approaching this article as a critical thinker.

However, Pitts gives no specifics about who conducted this research, which reduces its effectiveness as logical support. Still,

Linking causes and effects is another appeal to *logos*.

the research Pitts cites along with the examples of the commuter train crash and his own near-accident work together to show the reader a strong cause and effect relationship between distracted drivers and potentially deadly accidents.

Pathos is Pitts's strongest appeal. His own near accident was a wake-up call for him, and he clearly wants to get his message out to readers. Early in the article, Pitts presents the danger in descriptive and emotional language: "it's unsafe to divert attention to a tiny

Here Navid gives a specific example of emotional language used in the essay.

keyboard and screen while simultaneously piloting two tons of metal, rubber, glass and, let us not forget, flesh, at freeway speeds . . ." (328). That sentence drives home to readers how fragile the human body is when involved in a car crash. If our own safety is not enough to consider, Pitts's example of the deadly train crash makes clear that one person's inattention can cause the deaths of others. Most people would agree that our rights to do what we want end when our

Appealing to readers' beliefs or assumptions is another appeal to *pathos*.

actions put others in serious danger. Pitts's appeal to this belief is an effective use of *pathos*.

Notice how Navid's uses first person "I" when he discusses his personal response to the article.

I easily read Pitts's article as a doubter because I use my cell phone when I drive. I seldom text and drive, but I text while waiting at a stop light, and I have read texts while driving. When talking on my cell phone, I have always felt in control of my car and aware of my surroundings. I don't see it as being much different from talking to a passenger in my car. Yes, I am part of that "hyper-connected" culture Pitts finds a problem, but I don't

Montazeri 4

Here Navid uses his personal experiences to go against what the author writes.

see being connected to people as a problem. When I want to be alone, I can turn off my cell phone or ignore calls and messages. Using the cell phone when I drive is a convenient way to stay in touch or conduct business and save time. Obviously an older man, Pitts is not as comfortable with the technology I have grown up using. As a doubter, I was also not impressed with Pitts's sarcasm. In addition to "Duh," he writes "Think again," "congratulations on your perception" (329), and "Do you really have that much to say? I'll save you the trouble: you don't" (328). I felt he was talking down to me, and he has written off those who use cell phones while driving as "dumb."

Navid gives specific examples from the essay to suppor this negative reaction.

As a believing reader, I put aside my irritation with Pitts's sarcasm and tried to understand his position. His honesty in admitting his near-accident helped me see why Pitts is determined to wake up his readers to the dangers of texting and driving. I have a friend who was in an accident because he was texting and driving. He hit the car in front of him when it slowed to make a turn, and though there were no serious injuries, this accident made my friend swear off texting and driving. That incident and Pitts's article have led me to reduce using my cell phone while driving. The research about how texting impairs drivers is persuasive, so I probably won't wait for an accident as my wake-up call.

As a believing reader, Navid draws upon personal experiences to support what he read in the article.

When Pitts wrote this article in 2009, only sixteen states had banned texting while driving. Today, that number is up to thirty-nine states and ten states prohibit all drivers from using handheld cell phones while driving (United States, "NHTSA"). These laws have come about because of the dramatic increase in accidents caused by distracted drivers. While Leonard Pitts has not totally convinced me to put down my phone when I drive, I'll definitely not be texting any more.

Here Navid shows he was interested enough in the subject to go to outside sources to find updated information. It's an impressive way to wrap up a paper.

Navid has a mixed reaction to the article, which he re-emphasizes in his conclusion.

Montazeri 5

Works Cited

National Highway Traffic Safety Administration. "NHTSA Survey Finds 660,000 Drivers Using Cell Phones or Manipulating Electronic Devices at Any Given Daylight Moment." United States Department of Transportation, 5 Apr. 2013, www.transportation.gov/briefing-room/nhtsa-survey-finds-660000-drivers-using-cell-phones-or-manipulating-electronic-devices.

Pitts, Leonard. "Put the Brakes on Driving While Texting." *IDEAS & Aims for College Writing*, by Tim Taylor and Linda Copeland, Pearson, 2016, pp. 327-29.

United States Department of Transportation. "No Texting Rule Fact Sheet." Federal Motor Carrier Safety Administration, May 2012, www.fmcsa.dot.gov/driver-safety/distracted-driving/no-texting-rule-fact-sheet.

MyWritingLab Visit
Ch. 11 Persuasive Writing
in MyWritingLab to access
the IDEAS videos.

I D E A S in Action

SELECTION 1   MyWritingLab

The Attendance Policy

Mrs Chili

The next essay comes from a blog called "A Teacher's Education." The author describes herself as an "English Teacher, reader, writer, all-around lover of language." Mrs. Chili works as an instructor at a two-year college.

PRE-READING PROMPT

1. If you were a college instructor, would you have an attendance policy? Why or why not?
2. What are the similarities between going to college and working at a job? How are they similar? How are they different?

1   Several years ago, the Local University English Department established a strict attendance policy for its Freshman Writing courses. The policy states that students are allowed three absences without penalty, and that every absence after the third will cost the student one letter grade from his or her final score. For example, a student who earned an A in the course but was absent five times will leave the class with a C. The rule makes no distinction between excused and unexcused absences, and it is up to the individual instructors to monitor student attendance and implement the policy. Although the rule is met with nearly universal disapproval by students in English 101, I contend that the policy is not only fair, but that it is necessary.

2   Freshman year is, under the best of conditions, a profoundly difficult time for students. Most freshmen come to college straight from high school and have little, if any, experience in being responsible for themselves. Most students are living away from home for the first time in their lives and are expected to attend to all of their own needs; to make sure they are out of bed in time to get to morning classes, to see to their own personal care and laundry, and to budget their time so that they can balance the responsibilities of their studies with their desires to experiment with their newly obtained freedom. Students are often ill-prepared to deal simultaneously with that freedom and the responsibilities of functioning in an environment which demands their mature and attentive participation. One of the objectives of those who teach freshmen in particular is

to create an environment where students can learn to balance what they have to do with what they want to do.

3   Because the successful completion of freshman year is a prerequisite to the successful completion of college, it is important that students be given an opportunity to learn to function as responsible adults as soon as classes begin in September. The point of freshman classes goes far beyond the material listed on the syllabus; most responsible freshman instructors understand that they are educating their students not only in the discipline of the course, but that they are also teaching their students what is required to successfully navigate college life and, eventually, the professional world which the students will enter after graduation. Freshman instructors impose deadlines and require that the student demonstrate a great deal of initiative and comprehension of the material because that is what professors expect of their students and employers expect of their employees. The three-absence attendance policy is a good one in that it reinforces the expectations of the professional world, and is, in fact, more generous than the expectations for attendance at most businesses. The policy reflects the conditions which the students will encounter in their professional lives.

4   Opponents of the rule claim that it is unfair because it assumes that attendance in the course is necessary for a student to do well. While it is true that one or two students come to freshman writing classes with a strong set of foundational skills and perhaps could do well in the course without attending every class, those students are exceptions rather than the norm. While they may have been good writers in a high school setting, the expectations for college-level thinking and writing are quite a bit more rigorous than A-level work in high school. Because clear, thoughtful, and expressive writing is vital for success in college, it is critical that students begin their college experiences with a strong and comprehensive understanding of the writing process and of how to compose professional, ethical, and well-researched pieces. Learning how to be analytical and critical of one's own writing is a process of trial and error that is best understood in the context of group work and guided examples. Consider a player on a sports team; a player who fails to report to practice sessions won't be allowed to remain on the team for very long because his or her skills won't be as polished and consistent as the players who do practice. Skillful writing is similar in that it is less a knowledge than a practice.

5   Freshman writing classes at LU are about far more than the reading and writing assignments. The class meetings are often filled with lively discussions about current events, dissection and analysis of readings, and the implications of the use of language. It is this collaborative effort, where teacher and students interact and learn from one another, that is at the heart of the attendance policy. My own professional experience has shown me that students benefit

greatly from guided class discussions about the material that is assigned. More often than not, students report to me that they didn't really "get" the reading assignments until they were discussed in class, and they will write that they see things differently at the end of the course than they did at the beginning. The instructor encourages students to ask their own questions and to wander out beyond their comfort zones of "right and wrong" answers to test the limits of their own thinking.

6   Finally, students who disagree with the attendance policy claim that because they are assigned 101 classes and have no choice in which classes they attend, there should be more leniency in the rule. While there may be some merit in this point—it is true that I, as a mother of two small children, would not choose to take a class that would conflict with my ability to be home after my daughters return from school—it is, at its heart, an insufficient argument. Students can make use of the University's add/drop policy to switch sections if they find they have a critical conflict with the course that has been assigned to them. It is true that the employee does not often get to dictate the terms of his or her working day, and finding a way to balance outside responsibilities with school or work is an important skill that mature adults should possess. The fact that the policy applies to all 101 courses, regardless of the time of day they're offered, evens the proverbial playing field for students. A student in one section doesn't get to benefit from a more lenient attendance policy than a student in another section whose instructor is insistent that students be in class. Though many may look upon the policy as being strict and unforgiving, the consistency across the program is fair in that each student is held to the very same standard.

7   Freshman year is, in my mind, less about academics and more about maturity. Students come to their first college classes with apprehension and excitement, and it is up to the professors who teach freshman classes to give their students the skills they'll need to succeed beyond their first year. The 101 attendance policy is an important part of a student's development into a responsible, mature professional. It should continue to be a component of the freshman writing curriculum specifically because it fosters in students a recognition that rules—even the ones that are unpleasant and difficult to follow—are put in place for valid reasons, and often have serious consequences when they're broken.

QUESTIONS FOR DISCUSSION

Interest

1. The author of the essay provides a calm, dispassionate defense of the attendance policy. Did this help you as a reader or make you less interested in her argument? Why?

2. If Mrs. Chili asked for advice on how to make this more interesting and persuasive for readers, what would you tell her to do?

D etails

3. One of her main points of support is the attendance policy reflects a workplace environment and the "professional world." What details does she use to back up that claim? Should she have developed that point more through stronger details? How?

4. In the author's essay, she makes a concession that one or two people might not need to take the composition course. However, what details are effective in arguing that they should take the course?

5. Another comparison the instructor makes is that writers need practice just like athletes do. Do you find that comparison valid? Why or why not?

E xplanation

6. Mrs. Chili does not provide many concrete and descriptive examples to show how the attendance policy is good rule. What are some examples or experiences that might help her argument? What are some examples or experiences that might hurt her points?

7. Chili claims that instructors try to teach freshmen how "to successfully navigate college life." Does she sufficiently explain what this means? Why or why not?

A udience

8. Has Mrs. Chili persuaded you that the attendance policy is fair and necessary? Why or why not?

9. How persuasive do you think her argument will be to students who are older, who have jobs, who have kids, and/or who commute to school?

S tyle

10. Take one paragraph of the essay and analyze the types and lengths of sentences that Mrs. Chili uses. How much sentence variety does the paragraph have?

I D E A S for Your Own Writing

Design a survey to determine students' attitudes toward attendance policies in their classes. Then survey a number of students from several of your classes. Use the data to write up a report on student attitudes toward attendance policies for your campus newspaper. Include examples and short quotes as well as statistical data to make your report lively reading. See Chapter 12, pages 358–360, for information and advice about creating surveys.

SELECTION 2
Don't Let Stereotypes Warp Your Judgment

MyWritingLab

Robert L. Heilbroner

The following essay is from the Harvard-educated economist Robert Heilbroner and first appeared in Reader's Digest in 1962. In this essay Heilbroner explains the pervasiveness of stereotyping and urges readers to take steps to avoid it.

PRE-READING PROMPT

1. Heilbroner wrote this article in 1962. What stereotypes are still pervasive today? What are some stereotypes you have encountered?
2. Why do you think people stereotype others? Is the intent behind stereotyping always malicious?
3. We often think of stereotypes as being harmful to the people who are stereotyped. How can stereotypes hurt the people who believe them?

1   Is a girl called Gloria apt to be better looking than one called Bertha? Are criminals more likely to be dark than blond? Can you tell a good deal about someone's personality from hearing his voice briefly over the phone? Can a person's nationality be pretty accurately guessed from his photograph? Does the fact that someone wears glasses imply that he is intelligent?

2   The answer to all these questions is obviously, "No."

3   Yet, from all the evidence at hand, most of us believe these things. Ask any college boy if he'd rather take his chances with a Gloria or a Bertha, or ask a college girl if she'd rather blind date a Richard or a Cuthbert. In fact, you don't have to ask: college students in questionnaires have revealed that names conjure up the same images in their minds as they do in yours—and for as little reason.

4   Look into the favorite suspects of persons who report "suspicious characters" and you will find a large percentage of them to be "swarthy" or "dark and foreign-looking"—despite the testimony of criminologists that criminals do *not* tend to be dark, foreign or "wild-eyed." Delve into the main asset of a telephone stock swindler and you will find it to be a marvelously confidence-inspiring telephone "personality." And whereas we all think we know what an Italian or a Swede looks like, it is the sad fact that when a group of Nebraska students sought to match faces and nationalities of 15 European countries, they were scored wrong in 93 percent of their identifications. Finally, for all the fact that horn-rimmed glasses have now become the standard television sign of an

"intellectual," optometrists know that the main thing that distinguishes people with glasses is just bad eyes.

5   Stereotypes are a kind of gossip about the world, a gossip that makes us prejudge people before we ever lay eyes on them. Hence it is not surprising that stereotypes have something to do with the dark world of prejudice. Explore most prejudices (note that the word means prejudgment) and you will find a cruel stereotype at the core of each one.

6   For it is the extraordinary fact that once we have typecast the world, we tend to see people in terms of our standardized pictures. In another demonstration of the power of stereotypes to affect our vision, a number of Columbia and Barnard students were shown 30 photographs of pretty but unidentified girls, and asked to rate each in terms of "general liking," "intelligence," "beauty" and so on. Two months later, the same group were shown the same photographs, this time with fictitious Irish, Italian, Jewish and "American" names attached to the pictures. Right away the ratings changed. Faces which were now seen as representing a national group went down in looks and still farther down in likability, while the "American" girls suddenly looked decidedly prettier and nicer.

7   Why is it that we stereotype the world in such irrational and harmful fashion? In part, we begin to typecast people in our childhood years. Early in life, as every parent whose child has watched a TV Western knows, we learn to spot the Good Guys from the Bad Guys. Some years ago, a social psychologist showed very clearly how powerful these stereotypes of childhood vision are. He secretly asked the most popular youngsters in an elementary school to make errors in their morning gym exercises. Afterwards, he asked the class if anyone had noticed any mistakes during gym period. Oh, yes, said the children. But it was the *unpopular* members of the class—the "bad guys"—they remembered as being out of step.

8   We not only grow up with standardized pictures forming inside of us, but as grown-ups we are constantly having them thrust upon us. Some of them, like the half-joking, half-serious stereotypes of mothers-in-law, or country yokels, or psychiatrists, are dinned into us by the stock jokes we hear and repeat. In fact, without such stereotypes, there would be a lot fewer jokes. Still other stereotypes are perpetuated by the advertisements we read, the movies we see, the books we read.

9   And finally, we tend to stereotype because it helps us make sense out of a highly confusing world, a world which William James once described as "one great, blooming, buzzing confusion." It is a curious fact that if we don't *know* what we're looking at, we are often quite literally unable to *see* what we're looking at. People who recover their sight after a lifetime of blindness actually cannot at first tell a triangle from a square. A visitor to a factory sees only noisy chaos where the superintendent sees a perfectly synchronized flow of work. As Walter Lippmann has said, "For the most part we do not first see, and then define; we define first, and then we see."

10   Stereotypes are one way in which we "define" the world in order to see it. They classify the infinite variety of human beings into a convenient handful of "types" towards whom we learn to act in stereotyped fashion. Life would be a wearing process if we had to start from scratch with each and every human contact. Stereotypes economize on our mental effort by covering up the blooming, buzzing confusion with big recognizable cut-outs. They save us the "trouble" of finding out what the world is like—they give it its accustomed look.

11   Thus the trouble is that stereotypes make us mentally lazy. As S. I. Hayakawa, the authority on **semantics**, has written: "The danger of stereotypes lies not in their existence, but in the fact that they become for all people some of the time, and for some people all the time, *substitutes for observation.*" Worse yet, stereotypes get in the way of our judgment, even when we do observe the world. Someone who has formed rigid preconceptions of all Latins as "excitable," or all teenagers as "wild" doesn't alter his point of view when he meets a calm and deliberate Genoese, or a serious-minded high school student. He brushes them aside as "exceptions that prove the rule." And, of course, if he meets someone true to type, he stands triumphantly vindicated. "They're all like that," he proclaims, having encountered an excited Latin, an ill-behaved adolescent.

> **semantics:** the study of meaning

12   Hence, quite aside from the injustice which stereotypes do to others, they impoverish ourselves. A person who lumps the world into simple categories, who type-casts all labor leaders as "racketeers," all businessmen as "reactionaries," all Harvard men as "snobs," and all Frenchmen as "sexy," is in danger of becoming a stereotype himself. He loses his capacity to be himself, which is to say, to see the world in his own absolutely unique, inimitable and independent fashion.

13   Instead, he votes for the man who fits his standardized picture of what a candidate "should" look like or sound like, buys the goods that someone in his "situation" in life "should" own, lives the life that others define for him. The mark of the stereotype person is that he never surprises us, that we do indeed have him "typed." And no one fits this straitjacket so perfectly as someone whose opinions about *other people* are fixed and inflexible.

14   Impoverishing as they are, stereotypes are not easy to get rid of. The world we typecast may be no better than a Grade B movie, but at least we know what to expect of our stock characters. When we let them act for themselves in the strangely unpredictable way that people do act, who knows but that many of our fondest convictions will be proved wrong?

15   Nor do we suddenly drop our standardized pictures for a blinding vision of the Truth. Sharp swings of ideas about people often just substitute one stereotype for another. The true process of change is a slow one that adds bits and pieces of reality to the pictures in our heads, until gradually they take on some of the blurriness of life itself. Little by little, we learn not that Jews and Negroes and Catholics and Puerto Ricans are "just like everybody else"—for that, too, is a

stereotype—but that each and every one of them is unique, special, different and individual. Often we do not even know that we have let a stereotype lapse until we hear someone saying, "all so-and-so's are like such-and-such," and we hear ourselves saying, "Well—maybe."

16   Can we speed the process along? Of course we can.

17   First, we can become aware of the standardized pictures in our heads, in other people's heads, in the world around us.

18   Second, we can become suspicious of all judgments that we allow exceptions to "prove." There is no more chastening thought than that in the vast intellectual adventure of science, it takes but one tiny exception to topple a whole edifice of ideas.

19   Third, we can learn to be chary of generalizations about people. As F. Scott Fitzgerald once wrote: "Begin with an individual, and before you know it you have created a type; begin with a type, and you find you have created—nothing."

20   Most of the time, when we typecast the world, we are not in fact generalizing about people at all. We are only revealing the embarrassing facts about the pictures that hang in the gallery of stereotypes in our own heads.

QUESTIONS FOR DISCUSSION

I nterest

1. Heilbroner sets up or introduces his topic with three short paragraphs. How do these paragraphs work together, and how effective are they in capturing your interest?

2. Does Heilbroner touch upon any stereotypes you have experienced—either as the one stereotyped or as the one stereotyping another? How does this contribute to your interest in what he has to share?

D etails

3. What information about stereotyping does Heilbroner present before he explains how to avoid it?

4. At the end of the essay, Heilbroner offers steps for avoiding stereotypical thinking. Has he convinced you to take those steps? Why or why not?

E xplanation

5. Are Heilbroner's examples of faulty assumptions typical? Are his examples enough to convince you that many of people's preconceptions based on appearance are false? Explain why or why not.

6. What does Heilbroner offer as the causes of stereotyping? What other causes could he have included?

7. What effects do stereotypes have on the people who rely on them for judgments?

8. Why do you think Heilbroner does not discuss the effects of stereo-typing on the people who are stereotyped? Does that omission make his essay less persuasive? Why or why not?

Audience

9. While Heilbroner obviously wants his readers to avoid stereotyping, he avoids coming across as didactic or "preachy." How does he avoid sounding like he is preaching proper behavior?

Style

10. Notice Heilbroner's use of quotes. Does he use them effectively? While he has identified S. I. Hayakawa, he does not provide background for William James, Walter Lippmann, or F. Scott Fitzgerald. Does that detract from the effectiveness of the quote? Why or why not?

11. In one paragraph near the beginning of the essay, Heilbroner uses the words *gossip*, *prejudice*, and *cruel* to describe stereotyping. Considering that Heilbroner has said that all of us stereotype, is this negative tone appropriate? At this point in the essay do you think readers are ready to see stereotyping as such a negative behavior? Explain why or why not.

I D E A S for Your Own Writing   MyWritingLab

Paraphrase Challenge

Practice paraphrasing by putting Heilbroner's three suggestions for avoiding stereotypical thinking into your own words and style. Remember, unlike summaries, paraphrases include all the points in the original piece and may even be a bit longer than the original.

Debunking a Stereotype

Tackle one stereotype that you have frequently encountered and write a short piece that debunks the stereotype—that examines all the supposed traits of the stereotyped individual and shows how they are simply not applicable. Your purpose is to persuade your readers to see an *individual* where previously they might have seen only a preconceived "type."

Consequences of a Problem Paper

Your Task: What problem in your state or local community particularly concerns you? Write a paper in which you show readers that the problem is a serious issue and move them toward thinking that something needs to be done about this issue. To do this, you should describe the problem you are concerned with, demonstrate its existence, explain its consequences, and show why it is a pressing problem that citizens need to address.

Your Audience: Address your paper to peer-scholars who might be interested in your subject and could be interested in your analysis and/or findings. But also imagine your audience as somewhat informed but undecided people who might take a viewpoint that opposes yours. Consider what they might already know about the subject and how your essay might add to what they know. Consider, too, why this problem or issue is important to you and why others should care about it.

A Successful Consequences of a Problem Paper . . .

- Offers a clear and assertive thesis that presents your position on the problem.
- Provides context and background on the problem for the readers.
- Uses appropriate, accurate, and logically sound opinions, examples, details, and explanation to show the severity and consequences of this problem while avoiding irrelevant details.
- Employs all three rhetorical appeals—*ethos*, *logos*, and *pathos*—to persuade the reader.
- Has unified, coherent, and sufficiently developed paragraphs.
- Utilizes a clear organization strategy with transitions and other coherence devices.
- Provides a medium level of tone and diction—not too formal but not too informal—with appropriate word choice and varied sentence types.
- Is free of distracting mechanical and proofreading errors.

Summary-Analysis-Response (SAR) Essay

Topic: Actively and critically read an article that has a primarily persuasive aim. Then demonstrate that you can objectively summarize the article with the author's position, analyze the author's use of rhetorical appeals (*ethos, logos, pathos*) and respond to the essay with an informed opinion of what you read. Use the following organization:

Introduction: Introduce the topic with a "hook" to grab your readers' attention and interest. Let the readers know the title and author of the article you are analyzing. Your thesis should present your overall assessment of the author's ability to present an effective persuasive piece.

Body (3 parts):

- **Summary**—Begin the body of your essay with a concise summary (no personal views) of the article. Present in *your words* the main ideas of the piece; however, you may occasionally quote the author's words to tie both you and your reader to the original text. Your goal in this part of the paper is to provide your reader with *your* understanding of what the text actually says or means.

- **Analysis section**   Next, analyze (break down) the persuasive elements of the article. Consider the following points as you analyze the article:

  - What is the author's thesis or main point?
  - Does the author establish *ethos*?
  - Does the author make good use of *logos*?
  - Does the author use *pathos* effectively?

- **Response section**—The final section of the body should be your personal response to what you have read. Here, your goal is to explain to your readers where you do and/or do not feel comfortable accepting the author's position. The response portion of the paper should focus on what the text means to you. (In preparation for writing this essay, it would be a good idea to review the reading as a believer and reading as a doubter strategies presented in Chapter 2.)

Conclusion: Re-emphasize, without simply being repetitive, whether you agree or disagree with the article's point and how persuasive you think the author is. Emphasize your assessment's credibility.

Works Cited Page: You must have a Works Cited page on which you list the article and any other material you consult. (See Chapter 12 for documentation guidelines.)

A Successful SAR Essay . . .

- Demonstrates your ability to read carefully and summarize the main ideas of a writer.
- Applies a clear understanding of the three persuasive appeals—*ethos, logos,* and *pathos*—to show what makes a piece of persuasive writing successful.
- Presents your well-supported opinion in a clear, direct manner.
- Incorporates and documents short, effective direct quotes from another writer's work.
- Has unified, coherent, and sufficiently developed paragraphs.
- Utilizes a clear organization strategy with transitions and other coherence devices.
- Provides a medium level of tone and diction—not too formal but not too informal—with appropriate word choice and varied sentence types.
- Is free of distracting mechanical and proofreading errors.

Job or Internship Application Letter

Your Research and Writing Task: Find a job you are interested in or an internship you might want to get for next semester to make you a better job candidate once you graduate. Then write a cover letter that will go along with a résumé once you apply for this opening. If you are not ready to apply for a job or an internship, then find one that appeals to you, so you can get practice writing a strong and persuasive cover letter. When you turn in the letter, also submit the job/internship ad you are applying for.

Recommended Structure and Formatting: Your one-page cover letter needs to have specific details, clear reasons, and strong explanations. The first paragraph should contain a confident and persuasive bottom line—a thesis-like statement that explains why you would be a good candidate for the position. The body paragraphs afterward need to support that thesis.

In general, a strong cover letter has at least four paragraphs with single-spacing and double-spacing between paragraphs. Following are recommendations and details about the structure of the letter:

- **Beginning Information:** Insert (1) your address at the top, (2) a space and then the date you will send the letter, (3) a space and then the person and/or organization you are sending the letter to, and (4) a formal address followed by a colon, such as "Dear Ms. Tyler:".

- **Paragraph 1:** Inform the reader about what you are applying for and then provide a concise statement (thesis) stating why you would be a good candidate for the position that connects to the information in paragraphs 2 and 3.

- **Paragraph 2:** Provide details and explanation about either your educational background (major, minor, coursework related to the opening) connected to the opening or work experience that links to the opening. If you have a lot of work experience, it is smart to lead with that. If you do not, lead with your education, knowledge, and personal characteristics (work ethic, self-discipline, ability to work with others, etc.) that connect to the opening.

- **Paragraph 3:** Provide details and explanation about either your work experience or your education (opposite of paragraph 2).

- **Paragraph 4:** Thank the person or organization for reviewing your application and then reinforce your thesis by reminding the reader why you would be a good candidate for the job.

- **Closing:** Go down two spaces and then type "Sincerely" followed by a comma. Type four spaces and then type your name. Sign your name in the space provided between "Sincerely" and your name.

A Successful Application Letter . . .

- Asserts a strong bottom line in the first paragraph by offering concise but specific reasons about how your background and attributes strongly connect to the opening.

- Is persuasive through substantial support about your experience and background that connects to the opening available.

- Has focused and unified paragraphs that are highly developed and connect to the bottom line in the first paragraph.

- Follows the formatting guidelines for cover letters.

- Exhibits strong concision, cohesion, transitions, and sentence variety in length and type.

- Provides a medium level of tone and diction—not too formal but not too informal.

- Is free of mechanical and proofreading errors.

Learning Objectives	How they connect to reading, writing, and critical thinking at college . . .
❶ Know your audience's expectations.	When trying to persuade an audience, you need to think about how to provide convincing evidence, use the appropriate format, and connect with readers.
❷ Use the rhetorical toolkit: *ethos, logos,* and *pathos*.	You can use these concepts to analyze and create persuasive writing: • *Ethos*—Writers can establish their credibility by using a strong style, providing the proper tone, using respected authorities/sources, employing personal experience, and showing respect for other viewpoints. • *Logos*—Writers can appeal to logic and reason by using valid generalizations, making connections between ideas and issues, showing cause and effect relationships, arguing from strong principles, showing signs or clues that relate to the issue, and citing respected experts. • *Pathos*—Writers can work with emotions, values, and beliefs by providing examples and details that convey emotions, using emotional word choices, presenting graphic images, and working with readers' assumptions, beliefs, and values.
❸ Put **I D E A S** to work in persuasive writing.	You can use the **I D E A S** tool (**I** nterest, **D** etails, **E** xplanation, **A** udience, and **S** tyle) to generate content for your papers and to analyze other people's writing.

> **MyWritingLab** Visit **Chapter 11, "Persuasive Writing"** in MyWritingLab to test your understanding of the chapter objectives.

12

Working with Sources

Learning Objectives

In this chapter, you will learn how to…

1. Find sources.
2. Evaluate sources.
3. Summarize, paraphrase, and quote effectively and ethically.
4. See research as discovery.
5. Write an I-Search paper.

The library is one of your most important campus resources. How well do you know your library? Knowing how to use your library's many resources will make your research process more efficient and enjoyable.

As one of our students once said, college is about "reading, reading, and more reading." If your professors have assigned reading, then they also expect you to think critically and write about the materials you are reading or sources they expect you to find on your own.

Chris Thais and Terry Myers Zawacki, two scholars who researched how writing is used across college courses at their university, discovered that professors want "Clear evidence in writing that the writer(s) have been persistent, open-minded, and disciplined in study" (5). Research-based writing offers perhaps the best opportunity to demonstrate what professors want.

Through research, you will learn more about a subject, and you will demonstrate critical thinking as you read, analyze, and write about the material you have found. Finding appropriate sources requires reading, evaluating, and analyzing a variety of materials. Then writing involves bringing sources together in a way that shows your point of view or your voice responding to those sources. You can use sources to answer questions you have, support your points, or present alternate points of view.

To make your transition to working with sources in college papers easier, this chapter offers advice about finding, using, and connecting with source material effectively, ethically, and stylistically.

❶ Find sources.

Find Sources

Research involves searching for information that contributes to your understanding of your subject. The best research comes from a variety of sources—interviews, journals, books, blogs, online encyclopedias, pamphlets, historical documents, lectures, and so on.

Being "disciplined in study" begins at the research level because you do not want to gather material indiscriminately. You want to view all of your resources with a critical eye, asking questions such as:

- Is the source authoritative?
- Is the source reliable?
- Is the accuracy of the information verifiable?
- Is the material up to date?

▲ The root of the word "research" is "search." One of the first steps of doing research is searching for varied, reputable sources.

Research is not simply finding information; it is finding, critiquing, and responding to information. To conduct effective research, you also need to interact with and interpret the materials you have gathered.

Library Resources

Very often college students begin their research assignment by using Web-based search engines like Google, Yahoo!, or Bing. While such searches may yield some valuable and useful information, you need to keep in mind that anyone can put anything on the Web. Also, many websites pay search engines to place them on the first page of search results. For these reasons, the Web does not always provide the most relevant and accurate information.

All too often college students rely heavily on these search engines and fail to make use of the *more efficient* resource at their disposal: *the library*.

Getting to Know Your Library

One of the best ways to understand what your library offers is by attending a library orientation session; these are usually offered throughout the semester. However, if you get stuck or frustrated, do not forget to use another widely available resource: *librarians*. Librarians can troubleshoot where you might be going wrong in your research process and point you toward the resources, books, and databases that you should be using—making your whole research process much more efficient and pleasant. Often librarians can help you refine your searches and understand the best way to find what you need.

Use the Library's Catalog

Libraries have their own search engines, which are usually called "catalogs," where you can look for books, videos, audio recordings, and other materials housed in the library. You can search by "Subject," "Key Word," "Author," or "Title" to see if there are any resources there in the library that you might be able to use in your research (see Figure 12–1).

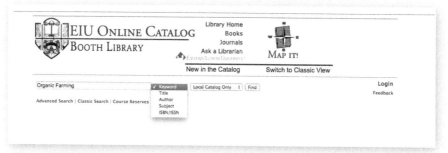

Figure 12–1   **Search Page**

The basic search page of the library catalog at Eastern Illinois University. Your library catalog mostly likely has similar search options.

For example, if you were looking for books on the general subject of "Organic Farming," a university's library might provide pages of titles you would have to wade through when researching. However, most catalogs will provide options to narrow the search; for example, the EIU Online Catalog offers related topics such as "Organic Farming—History" and "Organic Farming—Environmental Aspects" (see Figure 12–2).

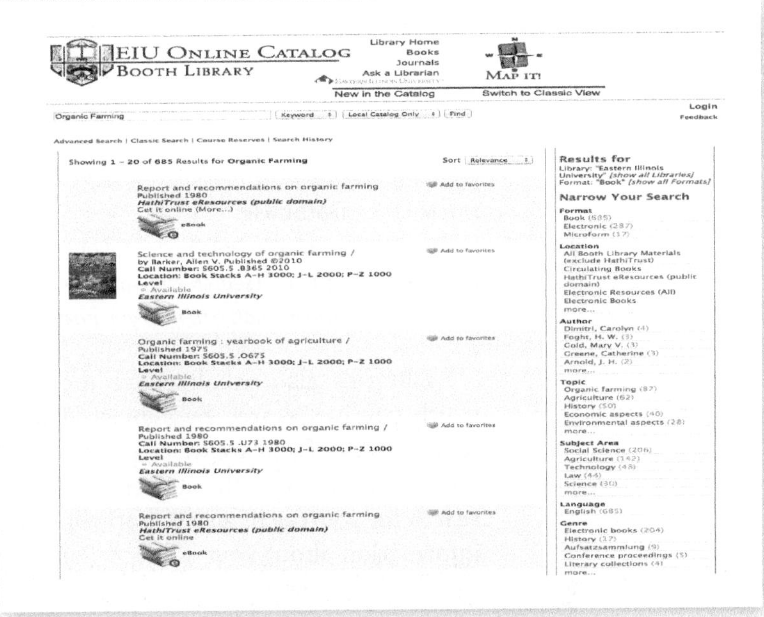

Figure 12–2   Search Results

Search results for "Organic Farming" from the EIU Online Catalog. While your library catalog may look different, it probably offers similar tools for narrowing your search.

Many libraries also participate in interlibrary loan programs, allowing you to search for books in every library that has joined the program. You can request books from other libraries and have them delivered to your college's library for your use.

Use the Library's Databases—Articles and Reports

Academic libraries also have "academic search engines" or "proprietary databases," which we will just call databases. In a database, you can search for articles and retrieve them through your college library's website.

Find and Select a Database. Often, college libraries have a link explicitly for searching either "Databases" or "Magazine and Journal Articles." Once on the databases page, you select which database you want to search. In most cases, students in a writing class will use standard databases like EBSCOhost Academic Search Elite, Gale Academic on File, or LexisNexis Academic. The first two databases search mainly for articles in magazines and journals, whereas LexisNexis also looks for newspaper articles, TV transcripts, and more. Databases should be *your go-to resources* when you do research during college (see Figure 12–3).

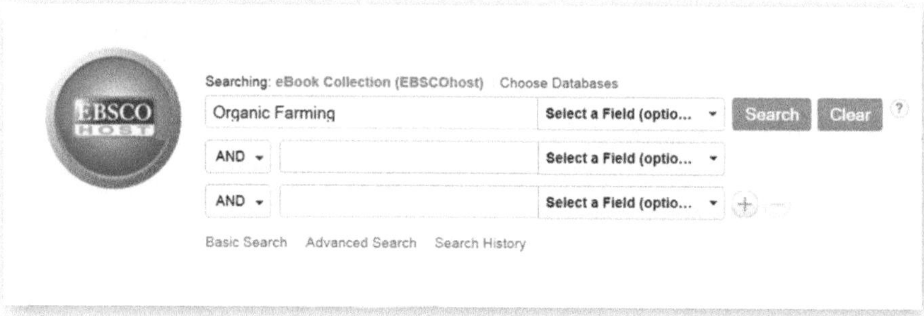

Figure 12–3   **Database**
In many ways, the basic search page for online databases is similar to that of your library catalog or your favorite search engine. To begin, simply type in your search term. Advanced search options are available to help you narrow your results.

Libraries also usually have more specialized databases available, in which you can search by subject. These specialized online databases are really helpful if you are writing for a specific discipline like biology, political science, and so on. No matter what database you use, it is important to search for sources in a way that will *save you time* and also provide relevant information about your subject. For example, if you were looking for articles on the general subject of "Organic Farming" in EBSCOhost, you would take these steps:

1. Type "organic farming" into the search field.

2. Limit the range of your search to the last ten years.

3. Hit the "Search" button.
   - Result: The database provides 3,253 results over the last ten years—far too many articles to look through.

   To limit the search more effectively, you would take the same steps, but you could also do this:

4. Click the "full text" box.
   - Result: The database provides 1,999 full text articles, which is still far too many.

Use a Boolean Search. Because it is better to narrow a research topic, you could then do what is called a **Boolean search**, which makes the research process more efficient by cutting the number of sources you have to skim and scan, and thus saving you time.

For example, here is a search strategy you could use if you want to find out if there are any health benefits associated with organic farming:

5. Type "organic farming" into the first field.

6. Type "health" into the second field.

7. Make sure the connecting word between the two fields is *and*.

   - Result: The database provides 212 articles over the past ten years, which is a much more manageable number.

If you were to limit the same Boolean search to the past five years, the search would provide 112 full text articles.

However, if you are specifically interested in research about organic farming and its possible health benefits for humans, you could add a third search term in the Boolean search:

8. Type "humans" into the third field.

   - Result: The database provides 26 full text articles, a very manageable amount of articles.

Use Peer-Reviewed Articles. Actively search for peer-reviewed articles because they usually relate very detailed information or arguments by specialists and experts in the field. They are particularly strong sources of information because experts in the field review them initially to see if the research is sound and appropriate to the discipline in which they work.

For example, here is a simple search for peer-reviewed articles about organic farming and health in EBSCOhost:

1. Type "organic farming" into the first field for the search.

2. Type "health" into the second field for the search.

3. Make sure the connecting word between the two fields is *and*.

4. Limit the articles to the past five years.

5. Click the check box labeled "scholarly/peer reviewed journals."

   - Result: The database provides 63 articles.

Work the Search Process. We have shown a methodical step-by-step walkthrough of the research process. However, you need to keep in mind while researching that it is not always going to go smoothly. Sometimes you might use the wrong search terms or phrases, and you will have to tinker with and revise them while doing research.

For example, in these searches, "health" is a broad term that could cover a number of areas. Using the word "nutrition" instead of "health" would refine a Boolean search and make it more specific. Doing a Boolean search using "organic farming," "humans," and "nutrition" for text articles over the last ten years turns up 11 articles compared to the 26 found using "organic farming," "humans," and "health."

EXERCISE 12.1   Evaluate a Google Search Versus a Database Search

Directions: Think of a serious topic you want to find more information about. With that topic in mind, search for information using a Web-based search engine. Take notes on the quality of information you get on the first ten links the search provides. Print out a page that offers the search results. Next, go to the library and search for information about your topic using a Web-based database such as Infotrac or EBSCOhost. Print out the page that offers the first ten results of your search and take notes about the quality of information you get from that search. For discussion during class, compare the information available from the two searches and discuss the positives and negatives of both search methods.

"Do-It-Yourself" Research—Primary Sources

Primary sources are original documents or first-hand information. Primary sources include eyewitness accounts; interviews; dissertations; the results of an experiment, study, or survey; historical and legal documents; clinical studies; government statistics; diaries and autobiographies; and original works of art such as novels, plays, short stories, poems, songs, and paintings.

In this section we focus on two types of primary research that you can do on your own: interviews and surveys. While the title of this section includes the phrase "Do It Yourself," you should not think this type of research is going to be simple or easy. You will have to prepare appropriately if you are going to interview someone or administer a survey in your community. This section offers a number of tips and ideas to think about as you prepare to conduct an interview or survey.

Interviews

When doing an interview, there are three distinct phases, which you can probably guess already: Before, During, and After.

Guidelines for Interviews

1. **Before:** Identify whom you are going to interview. Usually when you conduct an interview, it is because the interviewee has some type of expertise or interesting perspective on the topic you are researching. So once you have selected an expert to interview, here are some further steps you should take:

   - Research the person's background and expertise—be familiar with his or her work and ideas.
   - Ask for a résumé from the person if it would be helpful.
   - If it is a face-to-face interview, dress professionally.
   - Create questions ahead of time that offer the interviewee an opportunity to provide an opinion or interesting response with reasons why he or she feels that way.
     - Avoid asking questions that can be answered with a "yes" or a "no."
     - Do not ask leading questions that show a preference for an answer—let the person provide the opinion in the interview.
     - Prepare different, varied, and open-ended questions.
     - Have more questions than you need.
   - Consider sending some of your questions to the interviewee ahead of time.

2. **During:** Regardless of the type of interview you might conduct (face-to-face email, or phone), it is important to build a strong rapport with the person you interview; you do not want to alienate him or her. Once you have established a connection, it is time to start asking questions. As an interviewer, you need to take notes, but it is also a good idea to record the interview, so you can review the conversation and ensure you quote the person accurately. Here are some pointers on how to conduct the interview:

   - Think of your encounter with this person as a friendly conversation.
   - Begin with simple questions that will put your interviewee at ease. Then, prioritize your questions to make sure you cover the most important points.
   - Look the interviewee in the eye and use body language (head nodding, smiling, laughing, etc.) that shows you are interested in what he or she has to say.
   - Focus on what the person is saying (instead of being concerned with what question you are going to ask next).
   - Use silence appropriately since people need time to think and will speak more if you do not jump in to fill awkward pauses.

- Use follow-up questions to encourage specific details by asking for examples or further explanation of what the person means.
- Be flexible and unafraid to stray from your list of questions based on how the conversation progresses. Keep in mind that a good interview feels like a productive conversation.
- Make sure to thank the interviewee for his or her time at the end of the interview.

3. **After:** After you have thanked the interviewee, look for the most important information contained in your notes and/or recording:

- Summarize the main points from the interview in your own words to get the big picture.
- Select the strongest statements and quotations from the interview that provide vividness and color to your research.
- Examine statements, ideas, and points that support or connect to your ideas and points.
- Find statements, ideas, and points that contrast with your ideas or other sources.
- Contact the person if you need to follow up on a question or check his or her statements for accuracy.

EXERCISE 12.2   Conduct an Interview

Directions: Choose a professor on your campus—not your writing teacher—who regularly assigns research-based writing assignments. Interview that professor to learn more about the kinds of assignments given, his or her goals for assigning them, and typical results. Write up the results of your interview to report back to your class.

Surveys

A survey, if done appropriately, can be a very powerful piece of research because it provides data for analysis. You can take the traditional approach by making up a paper survey, or you can create an online survey through survey-generator databases, such as Survey-Monkey, or even through social networking sites, like Facebook. Whichever approach you take, a successful survey requires strong preparation.

Before beginning to compose the questions for your survey, you should take these steps:

- Decide on the goals or objectives of your research.
- Consider what you want to learn from this survey.
- Think about whom you should survey to find out what you want to know.
- Make a list of these goals and check each question you develop against them.
- Identify and eliminate questions that are not clearly relevant to your goals or do not ask respondents to provide necessary information.

Since people will likely want to know why you are collecting information and may want their privacy respected before answering survey questions, you should include a short statement of the survey's purpose at the top of the questionnaire and reassurance that each response will be kept anonymous.

Next, you should include instructions on how to answer the questions. These may be as simple as "Place an X in the box that indicates your answer." Explain whatever the method is for marking answers and try to keep that method consistent throughout the survey. Include additional instructions for specific questions if needed.

Keep your survey questions clear and concise, asking only one question at a time. Avoid questions that are biased or that direct your respondents to a particular answer. Also, make sure you ask questions that your respondents can actually answer. Be especially careful about asking for information they cannot reasonably be expected to remember.

Ways to Write Survey Questions

Imagine that you are conducting a survey about midterm exams in college courses. Here are some ways you can write the survey questions:

1. Structured Question

- How many hours do you spend studying for a typical midterm exam?
  - 0–2 hours
  - 2–4 hours
  - 4–6 hours
  - more than 6 hours

Be sure the list of answers includes all possible responses and confirm that none overlap. Sometimes you may want to include choices such as "other," or "none of the above."

2. Rating Question

- How important is the midterm exam to your understanding of the course material?

Not Important at All   Somewhat Important   Important   Very Important

(1)   (2)   (3)   (4)

3. Ranking Question

- Please rank the following kinds of exam questions in order of preference with 1 for your most preferred type of exam question.

      ___ Multiple Choice

      ___ Short Answer

      ___ Essay

      ___ Matching

      ___ Other (specify) _____

Rating and ranking questions are best suited for determining your respondents' emotions about a subject.

4. Open-Ended Question

- What do you see as the biggest advantage of having required midterm exams in all courses?

_____

_____

While open-ended questions can give insight into your respondents' thoughts, they are sometimes difficult to analyze and quantify when you are gathering data. Use them sparingly.

Once you have composed your survey questions, make sure the overall layout of your survey is clear and easy for respondents to follow. You may find it helpful to test the survey on a few people to make sure respondents understand the questions and the questions are eliciting the information you need.

EXERCISE 12.3   Devise a Survey

Directions: Devise a survey to determine first-year college students' familiarity with and attitudes toward research papers. You may want to look at such elements as experience with writing research papers, familiarity with documentation, and courses requiring research papers. Administer your survey to 15 to 20 students who are not in your writing class. Share the results of your survey with your writing professor and fellow writing students.

Secondary Sources

Secondary sources include all materials that comment on, discuss, or interpret primary sources. Here are some examples to help you understand the difference between primary and secondary sources:

Primary Source	Secondary Source
• The movie *Twilight Saga: New Moon*	• Roger Ebert's review of *Twilight Saga: New Moon*
• Autobiography of Mark Twain	• Biography of Mark Twain
• U.S. government statistics on white collar crime	• Magazine article about white collar crime
• Results of a clinical study on the use of omega-3 oils to reduce heart disease	• Journal article on diet modifications that can improve health
• Photographs by Ansel Adams	• Book about the work of nature photographers
• The novel *Of Mice and Men*	• A collection (book) of articles about *Of Mice and Men*

❷ Evaluate sources.

Evaluate Sources

When using secondary sources, there are a number of factors to consider because you want to make sure you are using objective, reputable, and recent sources.

Look for Objective and Non-Biased Sources

It is important to always check the credentials of authors or publishers to make sure they are authoritative and reliable. For example, Seth is doing a paper on Martin Luther King, Jr. Instead of using the online databases on his college library's website, he decides to "google" information about King. In the first page of hits on his search, he finds what looks to be a reputable website with the Web address of martinlutherking.org.

When he investigates further though, he discovers that the website is written and published by a white supremacist group. He probably would not want to use information from such a biased organization unless he was writing a paper about white supremacist groups.

Especially when searching on the Web, you cannot simply assume the information you find is reliable. As one librarian we know says repeatedly in library orientations for college students, "Any fool can have a website, and many do." Just because information is on the Web does not mean it is reliable or accurate. Solid research entails checking credentials and thinking about the possible biases of sources. Even if you are using reliable and strong sources, remember that writers have certain points of view and sets of beliefs and assumptions that frame how they present material and make arguments.

Consult Peer-Reviewed or Refereed Journals and Academic Books When Possible

Scholarly/peer-reviewed articles are written by experts in a field, and then reviewed by other experts in that field to verify that the research is sound and appropriate to the discipline in which they work. This careful quality control makes these articles strong sources of information. If you use an online database through your college's library, look for a simple check box for "scholarly" or "peer-reviewed" articles that you can use to focus your search on these sources.

Look at Publication Dates of the Work and Works Cited in the Text

For many topics, you are going to want the most up-to-date material. Also, checking the list of Works Cited or References page in an article can reveal incomplete or biased research as well as outdated material. Once you have found sources that you plan to use in a paper, the next step is using those sources effectively and ethically as "back-up singers."

❸ Summarize, paraphrase, and quote effectively and ethically.

Summarize, Paraphrase, and Quote Effectively and Ethically

One trap inexperienced writers sometimes fall into is relying too heavily on sources to do the talking for them. Instead of using sources as support or as launching points to argue against others' ideas, they just stitch together a variety of quotes. Unfortunately, their voices get lost in all of the source work.

Your Voice Is the Star and Sources Are the Back-Up Singers

The scholar Ben Rafoth has an excellent recommendation to keep in mind when you use sources in your papers: "Use outside sources as *back-up singers* for the author's voice" (111). It is easy to get bogged down when working with sources, but when you write, your voice has to be the dominant one.

In other words, *you are the lead singer of your paper*, and the sources are there to help you along and act as a complement to what *you are writing*. Since you are the leader of the document, you provide how *your ideas* connect or contrast to the ideas of sources.

"So What?" with Sources

Another trap inexperienced writers might fall into is providing material from various sources but not explaining or connecting why that source material is important or relevant to their purposes. Your lead singing needs to show what you think about those ideas or quotations and connect how they are relevant to what you might be uncovering in a specific paragraph or point in your paper. You must connect your voice to the voices you present. And your voice needs to be the strongest, the lead singer.

Use sources as a springboard to get into your own ideas on the subject, to *support your agenda* in the paper. Use source materials to support your thesis and the controlling ideas of your paragraphs. In the end, you do not want your readers thinking "So what?" after you have provided a summary, paraphrase, or quotation from a source. *You want readers thinking, "I see why you used that source."*

Summarizing, Paraphrasing, and Quoting

You can incorporate outside sources into your writing in three ways:

- **Condense** in Your Own Words: You *summarize* what the author says.
- **Translate** in Your Own Words: You *paraphrase* a specific point or set of points the author makes.
- **Present** the Author's Words: You directly *quote* the author to show what he or she says.

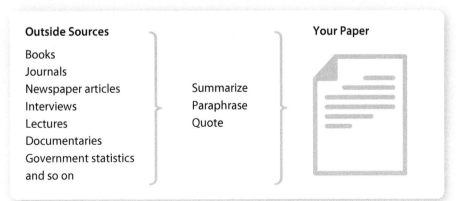

Outside Sources		Your Paper
Books		
Journals		
Newspaper articles	Summarize	
Interviews	Paraphrase	
Lectures	Quote	
Documentaries		
Government statistics		
and so on		

Summarizing, paraphrasing and quoting were introduced in Chapter 2 (43–53). Here, again, are the essentials of these ways of incorporating your sources into your writing:

Summarizing	Paraphrasing	Quoting
• **Introduce the summary.** Provide the author's name and possibly the source in order to show whom you are summarizing. Present the author's main idea or thesis. An *Introductory Phrase (IP)* needs to orient the reader about where you got the information.	• **Introduce the paraphrase.** Provide the author's name and possibly reference the title of the book, article, or other source. An *Introductory Phrase (IP)* needs to orient the reader about where you got the Information.	• **Provide an Introductory Phrase (IP)** to give a context for the quotation.
		• **Do not "dump" direct quotes into your paper.** Instead incorporate them smoothly with verbs like *explains, presents, argues, and notes.*
• **Condense.** Shorten what the author says to only the main points that support the thesis.	• **Write the paraphrase so that it is the approximate length of the original.** It may even be a little longer.	• **Use direct quotes sparingly.** Generally, the following are the situations that require direct quotes rather than summaries or paraphrases:
• **Write the summary *in your own words and style.***	• **Do not use the same words or phrases that are in the original piece of writing.** *Use your own words and style.* Remember that a paraphrase is similar to a translation.	• The author's words are particularly striking or memorable.
• **Use quotation marks.** Place important phrases or terms from the author that you want to keep in quotations marks.		• You plan to refute, agree with, or develop what the author is saying, so it's important that you present his or her position accurately.
• **Maintain the author's attitude and tone.** Keep your summary's overall attitude and tone consistent with that of the original author.	• **Maintain the author's attitude and tone.** Keep the paraphrase's overall attitude and tone consistent with that of the original author.	• The author is a notable, recognized authority on the topic.
• **Keep your own comments and opinions separate.**	• **Keep your own comments and opinions separate.**	• **Make sure direct quotes are accurate.** Do not change words within the quotation marks.
• **Properly use an in-text citation** to show the page number(s) of the summarized material.	• **Properly use an in-text citation.** Include the page number of the paraphrased material where the paraphrase ends.	• **Properly use an in-text citation** to show the page number of the quoted material.

The Purposes of Summarizing, Paraphrasing, and Quoting

To help you determine when and how to use sources, consider the following reasons why and when writers often choose to summarize, paraphrase, and quote.

1. **Writers summarize to . . .**
   - Show they have read and understood the material.
   - Provide a general overview of what a source relates before getting into specifics.
   - Show a comparison or contrast between different authors.

2. **Writers paraphrase to . . .**
   - Provide specific details that are important when they feel quoting is not necessary because the author's language is not very appealing or bold.
   - Offer specific statistics, facts, or figures that they found through doing research.
   - Lead in to their own thoughts about the information—whether they agree, disagree, question, or have mixed feelings.

3. **Writers quote sources to present the author's writing because the . . .**
   - Language is unusually vivid, bold, or inventive, and the statement cannot be paraphrased without distortion or loss of meaning.
   - Quotation represents and emphasizes a body of opinion or the view of an important expert.
   - Quotation emphatically reinforces their ideas and presents material relevant to their points.
   - Quotation emphatically goes against their ideas and presents material counter to their points.
   - Word choices, evidence, and/or assumptions in the quotation need to be analyzed and discussed.

❹ See research as
discovery.

See Research as Discovery

All too often college students think of research as a pain. But it is not. At least it shouldn't be. Another perspective, one that you should seriously consider, is this: *research is an act of discovery.*

That simple statement sums up how many people feel about research. In their view, through doing research they learn new ideas, they see how others think about a topic, they consider different arguments, they reflect on what new information means to them, and they get new outlooks on the world.

This happens all the time in our lives. For example, say you are in a conversation with your friend about different restaurants you like in your metro area. She tells you about a Nepalese restaurant that recently opened downtown that she has not been to yet. Because you are interested in what kind of food the new restaurant might serve, you type "Nepalese food" into your search engine to discover and learn about the traditional cuisine of Nepal: *chatamari, moma, masu, aloo tama*, and *tarkari*. By that simple act of looking up information about traditional Nepalese cuisine, you have done some research *because you wanted to learn*.

That love of learning is what drives many people who do research in their careers. Ecologists study watersheds because of their love for and interest in how ecosystems work. Oncologists do experiments because they are dedicated to curing cancer. Psychologists study facets of human behavior in an attempt to better understand human beings.

The writing assignment that follows is based on the work of Ken Macrorie, a writing teacher and scholar who wrote the book *The I-Search Paper*. This paper strongly reinforces the idea that research is a process of discovery.

⑤ Write an I-Search paper.

Write an I-Search Paper

MyWritingLab

The Assignment

The I-Search paper allows you to learn about a topic, and then reflect and comment on both the topic and the experience of searching for and discovering information about the topic.

Format

The paper should be written in three sections: Part I, What I Know, Assume, or Imagine; Part II, The Search; and Part III, What I Discovered.

Part I: What I Know, Assume, or Imagine You should write this section of the paper *before you begin your research*. As the heading says, this section should reflect what you know or think you know about your subject before doing any formal research.

Part II: The Search In this part of the paper you will write the "story" of your search—a narrative of your experiences searching the library, investigating and reading sources, interviewing people if needed. While you do not need to describe every resource you consulted, you should include all the *highlights of your research process*—successes, problems, and ways you approached the research task. In formal research, a dead end is a problem. In an "I-Search" paper, it is part of the story.

Part III: What I Discovered In this part of the paper, you should compare what you thought you knew with what your research has taught you. What important information did you find? What are the answers? Where do you stand after learning all this information? What did you learn? Emphasize the highlights of what you learned about your subject. In this part of the paper you will also use parenthetical citations to indicate the information you learned from your sources. You must use introductory phrases when summarizing, paraphrasing, and quoting sources, and you must use in-text citations when paraphrasing and quoting sources.

A Successful I-Search Essay . . .

- Is written in three sections: Part I, What I Know, Assume, or Imagine (written prior to search); Part II, The Search (highlights of the research process); and Part III, What I Discovered (comparing what the writer thought he or she knew with what was learned, and offering commentary and conclusions).
- Conveys a clear sense of the writer's attitude and style.
- Showcases that the writer has taken an active rather than a passive role in the search and that the assignment has been a genuine learning experience for the writer.
- Engages the reader through specific details, developed ideas, and sustained reflection.
- Displays evidence of critical thinking and offers insights about this topic in an interesting way.
- Offers a "What I Discovered" portion of the paper that is properly documented with citations in the correct format.
- Presents research as a supplement to, but not a substitute for, the writer's own ideas.
- Uses a minimum of four different sources by quotation, paraphrase, or summary with all outside information documented in MLA Style.
- Does not use long (block) quotations (more than four lines).
- Uses sources from databases (EBSCOhost, Infotrac, LexisNexis, etc.).
- Provides a properly formatted MLA Works Cited page.
- Employs ample transitions between ideas, paragraphs, and sections.
- Has focused and unified paragraphs that relate specific, concrete, and vivid details about the topic or question that the writer researched.
- Exhibits strong concision, cohesion, transitions, and sentence variety in length and type.

- Provides a medium level of tone and diction—not too formal but not too informal.
- Does not have editing errors that distract the reader or disrupt the meaning of sentences.
- Is relatively free of mechanical and proofreading errors.

Student Writer at Work

For his I-Search paper, Darrius Johnson chose to explore a sport he became intrigued with when he watched the Winter Olympics on TV. Before doing any research, he was required to write an abstract explaining what he was going to write about.

Johnson 1

Darrius Johnson

Professor Taylor

Introduction to College Writing

April 2, 2013

I-Search Abstract

    I've been watching curling during the Winter Olympics, and I'm just wondering how this curling even started. Or should even be considered a sport? This Olympics I have become more interested in the sport of curling. Curling is not one of the more popular sports of the Olympics, and it is usually seen on CNBC instead of NBC. While I watched highlights, many questions came to mind about curling. What exactly is curling? Where did it come from? And how did it become an Olympic sport before golf? Is it really that much more popular than golf, which isn't an Olympic sport? From what I've seen already, curling seems very simple, and I've picked up a lot about the sport. A curling competition is between two teams that push an object towards a target down a lane of what looks to be artificial ice. The object that is being pushed looks likes a sphere shaped stone with a handle on top to push it down the lane. There are usually two three-member teams competing against each other.

MyWritingLab Visit
Ch. 12 Working with
Sources in MyWritingLab
to access the IDEAS
videos.

Johnson eventually produced the following I-Search Paper on the sport of curling. He first thought about what he knew and observed about the sport in Section I; he related his research process in chronological order while reflecting on what he learned during the process in Section II; and then he finished with the information he uncovered in research in Section III. Commentary using the I D E A S template is provided to show how close, analytical, and critical reading is important.

Johnson 1

Darrius Johnson
Professor Taylor
Introduction to College Writing
10 April 2013

Curling

Section I

For the last couple of years, I have watched the winter Olympics. I usually catch a glimpse or some highlights of every event at least once in the six-week period the Olympics are shown. Ice skating, snowboarding, skiing, and hockey are all some of the more popular events. But this Olympics I have become more interested in the sport of Curling. Curling is not one of the more popular sports of the Olympics, and it is usually seen on CNBC instead of NBC. While I watched highlights, many questions came to mind about curling: What exactly is curling? Where did it come from? And how did it become an Olympic sport before golf? Is it really that much more popular than golf?

Curling is a very different type of Olympic sport. I haven't really watched a full curling competition, but from the highlights I have seen, curling seems very interesting and simple. From the curling competitions I have seen, I have picked up a lot about the sport. A curling competition is between two teams that push an object towards a target down a lane of what looks to be artificial ice. The object that is being pushed looks likes a sphere shaped stone with a handle on top to push it down the lane. There are usually two three-member teams competing against each other.

Before getting into fierce competition, the teams huddle up and discuss a strategy that will best help their chances of winning. The captain or leader of the team is usually the one who comes up with

Explanation: Here Johnson provides a context for the paper.

Interest: The author establishes questions he might answer.

Johnson provides his observations to orient the reader.

Details: The author further details the intricacies of the sport.

Johnson 2

the strategy and pushes the stone down the ice. The captain gets on his hands and knees and slides the stone down the lane. After the captain releases the stone, the other two members are equipped with what looks like regular brooms and sweep in front of the stone. Watching this game, I assumed that the sweeping of the ice helps dictate the direction of the stone. The sweeping of the ice helps the team put the stone in an offensive position to score or a defensive position to stop the other team from scoring. After observing several events this winter, I can only assume that the object of the game is to get more spherical stones in the target area.

Section II

Searching for information about curling wasn't hard, but at times I had difficulties. Starting the search, I first used the Internet and the search engines as my primary choice to find information. Using Internet search engines like Google, Yahoo, and Ask Jeeves were helpful in getting me started on my search and giving me some results that mentioned curling, but they didn't give me the best information.

I first started by just typing *curling* into the three search engines. Tons of information from multiple Internet sites came back as a result in my search. This was a problem because so many results from the search engines put me at a halt in my research. The results that were given were very broad and not very accurate to my topic. The results that the search engines provided were mainly sites and pages that had the word *curling*, but not the curling associated with the Olympic sport. Out of all the results, there were only a few sites that scratched the surface of what I was really looking for. Most results were just information about countries and individual success stories in curling. One result really stuck out to me and was at the top of the searches. The headline reads, "Curling Irons caused third degree burns on a child." This headline was all the way off topic and had nothing in common with what I was looking for. Using the Internet search engines was a waste of time and really steered me in the wrong direction.

My next option was a closer approach to the more traditional way to research for a topic. Use of the Internet was present again but in a more helpful way. On the Eastern Illinois University website, I

Details: Johnson provides general details to set up the concrete details in Section II.

Explanation: He describes the search process in chronological order.

Explanation: Johnson provides a headline of a source that wouldn't have helped him.

Style: Johnson transitions the reader toward the next stage of the research process.

Johnson 3

used the online databases to find newspaper and magazines articles that were relevant to my topic. EBSCOHost and LexisNexis were very helpful in refining my search and finding the most credible articles. *Curling* was my main search term, but using the refining method on the databases I found specifics about its history and importance as an Olympic sport. These search engines provided me with several articles about the origin, strategy, and other factors associated with the sport of curling.

Then I tried to find even more information about curling. I tried the traditional and old fashioned way and looked for books on curling in the EIU library. This turned out to be a complete dead end. Searching the whole library, I only found two books with little relevance to my topic. The two books that I found were over twenty-five years old. One was published in 1977 and the other in 1973. One was a handbook about curling techniques and strategies for coaches by Roy D. Thiessen. And the other was an article in the 1973 issue of *Sports Illustrated*. For this topic, going completely traditional was not the best way.

> **Audience:** The author shows the disappointment through the analogy of a "dead end."

> **Details and Explanation:** Johnson gives examples to develop his points.

Section III

Doing this research, I have learned through experience that Internet search engines are a faster way to research information, but results are not always accurate. The best way to research for a topic is still the old traditional way using books, magazine, and newspaper articles. A year ago in my high school English class, I had to do a paper with similar criteria. The paper had to be about a topic that we knew little or nothing about, so a lot of research was involved. My topic was the infamous Jack the Ripper. At this time I was even more dependent on Internet search engines. Because the Ripper murders happened centuries ago, loads of information piled up, which led to thousands of results. The results all displayed the same information, so instead of looking through thousands of sites, I relied on my high school library. Searching the library, right away I found three books and a newspaper article. The information provided by the books and articles was all the information from the search engines only more organized. Even from experience, books and articles were the better choice and displayed more accurate facts. Internet search engines give the least accurate information and can steer you away from your topic, and books and articles can usually give you the best information and quality for a paper.

> **Detail and Audience:** Here Johnson uses a comparison to provide proof for his assertion about "Internet search engines."

Johnson 4

Before starting my research on curling, I had many assumptions and asked many questions. Although I am a big fan of all sports, curling was one sport that had yet to gain my support. My first opinion about curling was that it is very boring and stupid. Jon Saraceno in his column for *USA Today* in 2002 agrees by saying, "I'd get more enjoyment strolling into my local supermarket late at night and watching sneaky stock boys whip frozen fowl down the cereal aisle" (10). One important question I needed answered was "Where was this sport created and why?" The World Curling Federation acknowledges curling as being "one of the world's oldest team sports" (WCF "History"). It was first established in Scotland in the mid 1500s, and it was known centuries ago as a "past time sport" (WCF "History"). In addition, American Fitness insists that the first competition took place around 1546 between two monks in the streets of Scotland (Winter Olympics Fun Facts). For the next few hundred years, curling was still only popular in Scotland. It wasn't till the late 1800s when the sport of curling began to gain popularity outside of Scotland. In the 1900s international curling clubs started to form and curling competitions were held in Canada, the USA, Sweden, Switzerland, Norway, and New Zealand (WCF "History").

Curling battles centuries ago were very different from modern day competitions. In the 1500s, 1600s, and 1700s, some competitions weren't even held on ice; they were mainly held in the middle of the street or on frozen lochs and ponds (WCF "History"). Also back then it was one on one competition and not between teams (WCF "History"). Unlike curling hundreds of years ago, a curling competition today is between two teams consisting of four members each (Saraceno 10). The game takes place at indoor rinks on frozen ice, and the official object is to get more of your team's stones closer to the circle target down the lane several feet away (Saraceno 10). Three objects are used for this sport, a stone and two brooms. What exactly is "the stone"? "The stone is actually granite and is a smooth sphere that weighs 38-44 pounds," ACF reports. Now the brooms are used to sweep in front of the stone to help with the direction and speed (Saraceno 10). The four members all have different roles for their team. There is usually one member of the

---

Style: The writer uses an introductory phrase (IP) to provide a context for the quotation.

Style: The author provides the page number in the in-text citation.

Style: Because this is a website, he cites the agency and title.

This is paraphrased material, so the author provides an in-text citation.

Johnson 5

team who is a designated pusher or slider while the other three members rotate the sweeping positions (Mulvoy).

The sweeping positions are arguably the most important positions in the game. In an interview with *USA Today*'s Jon Saraceno, Steve Rankin, a fan and curler, explains why. "Curling's all about basic friction." Rankin explains, "When you sweep, the friction melts the ice. That slight film of water lubricates between stone and ice, reducing friction, meaning the stone will travel further" (10). Both teams are given eight chances to get more stones in the target area than their opponent (Mulvoy). Curling is a very intense and competitive sport without any physical contact with the other team. You don't have to be a world-class athlete to curl. Much like chess, curling is a game of strategy, and you have to be mentally strong (Saraceno). Being mentally strong is very important. If you're strong mentally, then you will be a stronger competitor and curler (Saraceno). Not cracking under pressure, thinking ahead for future moves, keeping your composure, and outthinking your opponent are all characteristics of being mentally strong.

Another question I had about curling, I think was the most important for me to find out. How and why did curling become an Olympic sport? WCF explains that since the early 1900s curling has been a part of the Winter Olympics, but only as a "demonstration sport." This means that teams representing different countries would compete every four years in the Olympics, but no medal would be given. The first demonstration was in 1924 between Great Britain and France, Great Britain won (WCF "History"). Two more demonstrations were displayed in the winter games of 1988 and 1992 for men and women. After the 1992 demonstration on July 21, 1992 the International Olympic Committee presented medals to teams in Barcelona, Spain (WCF "History"). After multiple years of demonstrations in front of the International Olympic Committee, more countries started to gain interest and the popularity largely increased (WCF "History"). So in 1998 curling officially became an Olympic sport. Curling has become so popular that it is now a favorite video game for the Nintendo Wii System (AF2).

Style: Here Johnson uses an IP in the middle of a quotation to vary the way he uses IPs when introducing information.

Interest and Explanation: The author once again refers to a question he provides in section I.

Johnson 6

After researching the importance and competiveness of curling,
I am still not sold on why it is an Olympic sport. Jon Saraceno agrees
saying "I find it fascinating that anyone finds curling, well,
fascinating." He follows by saying, "I just can't seem to get swept up
in all the madness at the Ice Sheet venue, where the only thing
curling for sure are my nearly frostbitten toes."

Johnson 7

Works Cited

A print book.

Mulvoy, Mark. *Curling*. Lippincott, 1973.

A Web-based article found through a database.

Saraceno, Jon. "Curling More Than Stone's Throw from Being a
Sport." *USA Today*, 14 Feb. 2002. *Academic Search
Complete*, doi:JOE009673793202.

"Winter Olympics Fun Facts." *American Fitness*, Jan./Feb. 2010,
p. 51. *Academic Search Complete*, doi:47759113.

An article on a website.

World Curling Federation. "History of Curling." World Curling
Federation, www.worldcurling.org/history-of-curling.

Mulvoy, Mark. *Curling*. Lippincott, 1973.

Saraceno, Jon. "Curling More Than Stone's Throw from Being a Sport." *USA Today*, 14 Feb. 2002. *Academic Search Complete*, doi:JOE009673793202.

"Winter Olympics Fun Facts." *American Fitness*, Jan./Feb. 2010, p. 51. *Academic Search Complete*, doi:47759113.

World Curling Federation. "History of Curling." World Curling Federation, www.worldcurling.org/history-of-curling.

QUESTIONS FOR DISCUSSION

1. After reading the sample I-Search paper by Darrius Johnson, where do you feel he captured and kept your interest as a reader? What parts of the paper were the most interesting to you and why?
2. Some college writing instructors advise students not to use rhetorical questions in their papers because such questions can annoy readers. How do the questions in Johnson's paper serve a good purpose?
3. Johnson asserts that just using basic search engines like Google or Yahoo! didn't give him "good information," "were a waste of time," and "steered

[him] in the wrong direction." He is more positive about the effectiveness and efficiency of the online databases at his college's library. From your experience, do you agree with his points? Are the databases available though a college's library more effective, and do they save time? Why or why not? Explain your reasons based on your experiences.

4. One could argue that one of the weaknesses of Johnson's paper is that Section III does not have enough of his voice and his thoughts in it. The section provides a great deal of information he found through his research, but what about his thoughts? With that criticism in mind, go back through Section III and find places where Johnson could have presented his viewpoint more clearly.

CHAPTER AT A GLANCE

Learning Objectives	How they connect to reading, writing, and critical thinking at college ...
❶ Find sources.	Finding primary and secondary sources entails getting to know your library, using its catalog, and searching its databases to find articles and reports. In addition, you can perform "do-it-yourself" research by doing interviews and conducting surveys.
❷ Evaluate sources.	When considering which sources to use, you should seek objective and non-biased sources, use peer-reviewed articles, and consider the publication dates of sources.
❸ Summarize, paraphrase, and quote effectively and ethically.	When writing papers, keep in mind that your voice should be the star. You should use sources only as "back-up singers." When *summarizing*, you condense a source, use an introductory phrase, and put the information into your own words. When *paraphrasing*, you provide detailed information about a section of a source in your own words, use an introductory phrase, and provide an in-text citation. You cannot use the exact words of the source.

Learning Objectives	How they connect to reading, writing, and critical thinking at college . . .
	Both summary and paraphrase should offer an objective presentation of the source.

When *quoting*, you need to use an introductory phrase, provide an in-text citation, accurately quote the source, and use quotation marks. You should use a quotation only when the material is especially memorable or important; when you want to refute, agree, or develop what an author is saying; or when you want to use an expert for support. |
| ❹ See research as discovery. | Consider research an act of discovery—you are doing research to find out new and important information. |
| ❺ Write an I-Search Paper. | Follow a three-section format:

    I. What I know, assume, or imagine

    II. The search

    III. What I discovered |

MyWritingLab Visit **Chapter 12, "Working with Sources,"** in MyWritingLab to test your understanding of the chapter objectives.

Documenting Sources

13

Learning Objectives

In this chapter, you will learn how to…

❶ Document sources.

❷ Avoid plagiarism.

❸ Correctly use the MLA documentation style.

❹ Correctly use the APA documentation style.

❺ Write a research-based position paper.

Part of the challenge of working with sources is making sure you keep track of your sources and document them properly. What are some methods that work well to make sure you are working with sources correctly and keeping track of them? What don't you want to do?

This chapter provides guidance about using and documenting sources effectively and ethically, while using the appropriate style for the discipline in which you are writing.

❶ Document sources.

Document Sources

Whether you summarize, paraphrase, or quote material, the outside sources you use in your papers *must be documented.* There are three primary reasons you have to document your sources:

- Documentation gives proper credit to words and ideas that are not your own.

- Documentation gives interested readers a way to learn more about your topic by consulting your sources.

- Documentation shows your honesty as a writer (*ethos*) and lends credibility to your ideas.

All outside source information that you did not already know before you began your research and that is not common knowledge must be documented in two ways: in-text citations and Works Cited or References page entries.

In-text citations, sometimes called "parenthetical citations," indicate exactly where in your paper outside source material is used. The information within the citation allows readers to locate the source on the Works Cited or References page and the place in the original source where the material was found.

For example, say a student is writing about the adaptation of *Harry Potter and the Deathly Hallows* to the movie screen and uses some material found in a *Time* magazine review. The material is quoted and followed by an in-text citation in MLA style:

> Perhaps dividing the final book into two feature films was a good business strategy, but it did nothing for the pace of the plot in *Harry Potter and the Deathly Hallows Part I.* One reviewer calls the film's full hour of the main characters sitting in the woods waiting for Voldemort to unleash his evil "a minimalist indie horror film" (Corliss 68).

Readers of this paper can then turn to the Works Cited page and find the author of the review listed alphabetically by his last name:

> Corliss, Richard. "A Hollow Hallows: The First Film in the Harry Potter Finale Gets Lost in the Woods." *Time,* 29 Nov. 2010, pp. 67-68.

Now interested readers know exactly where to go to find the whole review and read it if they wish.

❷ Avoid plagiarism.

Avoid Plagiarism

The word *plagiarism* originates from the Latin verb *plagiare*, which means "to kidnap." It makes sense that plagiarism is like kidnapping since people who plagiarize attempt to benefit from using information or words that are not their own. The plagiarist takes credit for or profits from someone else's work, which is unethical.

Plagiarism can be intentional, such as when a student takes something from the Web or has a friend write a paper and tries to pass it off as his or her own. Or plagiarism can be unintentional, such as when a student tries to paraphrase someone else's writing but carelessly uses some of the same words and phrases as the original author. A writer might also mistakenly omit a citation or other acknowledgment of source material. Writing instructors are very capable of noticing writing style and content that is not typical of a student's work. Some professors even use online systems, such as Turnitin, to ensure students are doing their own writing and not plagiarizing or being sloppy when they summarize or paraphrase.

Whether it is the result of dishonesty or the outcome of not doing the fine detail work, plagiarism is a serious mistake that may have severe consequences. Plagiarizing in a paper could result in a student's receiving a zero on the assignment or an F in a course along with having to go before a college's judicial board. Students who plagiarize are sometimes even expelled.

In fact, the only material in a research-based paper that does not have to be documented is what you already knew before doing any reading or other research and what is referred to as *common knowledge*.

According to the Purdue Online Writing Lab, "you can regard something as common knowledge if you find the same information undocumented in at least five credible sources. Additionally, it might be common knowledge if you think the information you're presenting is something your readers will already know, or something that a person could easily find in general reference sources" ("Is It Plagiarism Yet?").

For example, if you were writing about the first time human beings walked on the moon, you could include the date (July 20, 1969), but you would not have to cite it. Another example would be that most people know the process by which plants make food is called *photosynthesis*, so you would not have to cite that information. When you are not sure whether information is considered common knowledge, *always play it safe and document*.

Simply put, students need to do their own writing and to cite properly the sources they have used. The following are strategies you can use to avoid unintentional plagiarism.

Strategies for Avoiding Unintentional Plagiarism

1. **Double-check your work for accuracy.** The easiest way to plagiarize unintentionally is to fail to check your writing against your sources. If you paraphrase two sentences from a source but use the exact phrasing of the author, then you have plagiarized. In this case, it would be better to just quote the source and provide an in-text citation.

2. **Make sure to use introductory phrases and in-text citations.** The easiest way to signal to your reader that you are using someone else's writing is to provide an introductory phrase that includes the author or title of the work you are presenting, which makes it absolutely clear to your reader that you are presenting someone else's ideas or writing. The in-text citation at the end of the summary, paraphrase, or quotation is a sign to readers that your use of the source is over and acts as a cue that you are now going to develop your own ideas in light of the material you have just presented.

3. **Use your own words when summarizing and paraphrasing.** When you put writing into "your own words," which is crucial for both summarizing and paraphrasing, you do not want to accidently kidnap the author's words and present them as your own. If you need to present an author's ideas in your own words, then a good trick to use is to put away the source you are writing from or simply turn the source face down, so you do not veer toward reading the exact words of the source.

As this section of the chapter relates, while you do research, it is best to take good notes and make sure you use sources correctly. When writers do research, they often make notes on different pieces of paper or in files, so they can keep their sources organized. For each source you use, make sure you have all the necessary information to create an entry for your Works Cited (MLA) or References (APA) page. Keeping a running list of these sources along with information and quotations you retrieved is crucial for efficient, ethical, and effective research. If you found a fact (paraphrase), have important information that you want to relate in your own words (paraphrase), or plan to use an exact quotation (word for word) from a source, you need to be sure to note the page numbers of those bits of information and make sure you are paraphrasing and quoting accurately.

❸ Correctly use the MLA documentation style.

Use the MLA Documentation Style

When working with sources for papers, one system that many classes in the humanities use is the Modern Language Association (MLA) style. If you are using American Psychological Association (APA) style, turn to pages 390–402. The sections that follow provide guidance about how to provide in-text citations, how to introduce sources by using introductory phrases (IPs), and how to create a Works Cited page in MLA style.

The Basics of MLA In-Text Citations

In-text citations typically come at the end of the sentence containing the information from an outside source. Note how sentences ending in citations should be punctuated:

> Paraphrase or summary sentence (in-text citation).
>
> "Direct Quote Statement" (in-text citation).
>
> "Direct Quote Question?" (in-text citation).
>
> "Direct Quote Exclamation!" (in-text citation).

Here are some examples of the more common kinds of in-text citations:

1. **A work by one author not named in text**

   Research has shown that preschoolers as young as two have an intuitive understanding of what makes a story (Tompkins 217).

2. **A work by one author named in text**

   As Tompkins points out, research shows that preschoolers as young as two have an intuitive understanding of what makes a story (217).

3. **A work by two authors not named in text**

   A striking feature of Shel Silverstein's poetry is the way he directly addresses the audience, pulling the readers into an intimate involvement with the poetry (Winter and Schmidt 92).

4. **A work by three or more authors not named in text**

   Remote-sit students most often criticize the lack of opportunity for one-on-one interaction with their instructors (Simonson et al. 80).

   Note: The abbreviation et al. *comes from the Latin* et alii *and means "and others."*

5. Indirect source

When an author you are reading quotes someone else and you want to use that quote, first try to find the original work and quote directly from it. If this not possible, your citation must indicate the quote is indirect.

> Psychological research confirms this statement by Michael Jordan: "The mental toughness and the heart are a lot stronger than some of the physical advantages you might have. I've always said that and I've always believed that" (qtd. in Dweck 86).

6. An online newspaper article with an unnamed author

The full title of this article is "A Stinky Ambassador." The citation needs only the first key word of the title since that is how an article with no author will be listed on the Works Cited page. Since this is material from the Web, there are no page numbers. However, some professors might ask for paragraph numbers for direct quotations and paraphrased material.

> With the gender gap in reading skills growing, Jon Scieszka believes teachers should "exploit" young boys' interest in weird and gross topics ("Stinky").

7. Non-print source author named in text

This material is from a web page, so there are no page numbers.

> Educator Jeff Lowe suggests that the best classroom library encourages the students' involvement in its management.

8. Non-print source author not named in text

> The best classroom library encourages the students' involvement in its management (Lowe).

Introducing Source Material in MLA Style

You should always make it clear within the text of your paper where material from your sources begins and ends. One way to do this is to use an introductory phrase (IP) in addition to an in-text citation. An **introductory phrase** provides an introduction and a context for source material, making it clear to the readers that you are working with someone else's ideas or written material. Note, for example, how a writer can use an introductory phrase to introduce a paraphrase:

Rhoda J. Maxwell believes it is important for teachers to convey expectations regarding the formality and technical correctness expected in assigned writing. Class notes, read only by the student who takes them, for example, may be messy with little regard for punctuation and spelling. However, essay assignments must be unified, coherent, and technically correct to meet the needs of a wider audience (34).

The introductory phrase at the beginning and the page number at the end make it clear where the borrowed material begins and ends. (Remember, if the author is mentioned in the text of the paper, there is no need to include the author's name in the citation.)

It is particularly important to use introductory phrases when presenting quoted material or paraphrasing a source. You do not want your reader to suddenly encounter quoted or paraphrased material and have no idea where it came from. Such quotes are sometimes called "dumped quotes" because the writer has simply dumped another's words into the paper without a context.

Five Introductory Phrase (IP) Patterns in MLA

Here are five introductory phrase patterns that you can use when presenting quoted material. In **MLA style** the introductory phrases use the *present tense*, and the period comes after the in-text citation in parentheses.

1. **IP = Author + Verb followed by a Comma (,) "_____" ( ).**

   Taylor and Copeland relate, "An introductory phrase provides an introduction and a context for source material, making it clear to the readers that you are working with someone else's ideas or written material" (382).

2. **IP = Author + Verb + *that* "_____" ( ).**

   In *IDEAS & Aims*, Taylor and Copeland inform us that "An introductory phrase provides an introduction and a context for source material, making it clear to the readers that you are working with someone else's ideas or written material" (382).

3. **IP = Complete Sentence that has the Author and Verb followed by a Colon (:) "_____" ( ).**

   Taylor and Copeland stress the importance of introducing source material: "An introductory phrase provides an introduction and a context for source material, making it clear to the readers that you are working with someone else's ideas or written material" (382).

4. "_____," IP = Verb + Author, "_____" ( ).

"An introductory phrase provides an introduction and a context for source material," explain Taylor and Copeland, "making it clear to the readers that you are working with someone else's ideas or written material" (382).

5. "_____," IP = Verb + Author ( ).

"An introductory phrase provides an introduction and a context for source material, making it clear to the readers that you are working with someone else's ideas or written material, " assert Taylor and Copeland (382).

As you can see, the sentences have complete introductory phrases because they have clear subjects (who is saying what) and verbs to indicate the owners of the quoted material to readers. Keep variety in mind when you work with quotations because if you use the same type of introductory phrase every time you present a quotation, the paper is going to become very repetitive and potentially boring to the readers.

In your introductory phrases, use specific verbs that clearly reflect what the author is saying. Using the verbs "says" or "states" or "relates" too often can lead to a lack of variety with the verbs used to introduce quotations. The following chart provides a listing of verbs you can use to introduce a source through summary, paraphrase, or quotations. However, you must choose verbs that connect to and make sense with the information or quotations you present because these words do not have the same meanings.

Verbs for Introductory Phrases

accepts	cautions	denies	lists	reveals
acknowledges	comments	describes	maintains	says
adds	compares	disagrees	observes	shares
admits	complains	discusses	outlines	shows
affirms	concludes	emphasizes	points out	speculates
agrees	condemns	explains	praises	states
analyzes	confirms	highlights	predicts	stresses
argues	considers	hypothesizes	proposes	suggests
asks	contradicts	identifies	proves	summarizes
asserts	contrasts	illustrates	rejects	urges
assesses	criticizes	insists	reports	warns
believes	defends	interprets	responds	writes

EXERCISE 13.1   Practice Integrating Quotations   MyWritingLab

Directions: Integrate the following quotation using each of the five IP patterns discussed above. Here is the essential information you need to have:

- The quote is "Of all the things we need to know about grammar, the verb is first."
- Don Watson makes this statement in his book *Death Sentences*.
- The quotation is on page 20.

Providing a Correctly Formatted Works Cited Page

In addition to documenting sources within the text of your paper, you will also document your outside sources on a separate **Works Cited** page at the end of your paper that details the sources you have used.

Based on the specifications from the *MLA Handbook,* eighth edition, when formatting a Works Cited page, here are the essentials:

- Make sure the whole page is double-spaced.
- Center the words "Works Cited" at the top of the page.
- Provide the entries of your sources in alphabetical order.
- Begin each entry with the last name of the author, or if the source does not have an author, begin with the title of the article or book or Web page—alphabetizing by the first principal word of the title (not *A, An,* or *The*).
- Begin each entry at the left margin of the page.
- Indent the lines after the first line of each entry 5 spaces, so it creates a "hanging indentation."

As a general rule, when compiling information about a source, make sure you have these basics:

- Author's or authors' names
- Title of the article or Web page or book
- Date of publication
- Where you found the source, what MLA calls the "container"
- Page numbers, web address (URL), or the digital object indentifier (doi)

Following are guidelines for five common print sources and five common Web-based sources college students might typically use. While this list does not cover all of the different types of sources you could use for a paper, you can use these citations for guidance and as examples when you format a Works Cited page.

If none of the examples relate to a source you are using, you have three options to help you format source information correctly:

- Go to the **Writing Center** or the Academic Support Center on your campus. These wonderful facilities will have writing handbooks and style manuals for you to refer to. In addition, the tutors there can work with you in formatting your Works Cited page.

- Use an **Online Writing Lab (OWL)** to see how you should format the sources. The most famous and probably the most comprehensive OWL on the Web is the Purdue OWL: http://owl.english.purdue.edu/. On that site there are various links that will take you to pages that will help you properly format the sources you use in your papers.

- Use the *MLA Handbook*, **eighth edition,** which is probably available in your college's library, or you can look for examples on the **MLA website** (style.MLA.org).

- Use an online documentation software program. However, be sure to enter the information correctly and check the citations to make sure they are in MLA style.

▶ This annotated example shows where to look on a title page for the source information required for MLA documentation.

I D E A S
& Aims
for College Writing

Title

Tim N. Taylor
Eastern Illinois University

Linda Copeland
St. Louis Community College

Authors' names

PEARSON

Publisher

Boston   Columbus   Indianapolis   New York   San Francisco   Upper Saddle River
Amsterdam   Cape Town   Dubai   London   Madrid   ilan   Munich   Paris   Montreal   Toronto
Delhi   Mexico City   Sao Paulo   Sydney   Hong Kong   Seoul   Singapore   Taipei   Tokyo

Five Common Print Sources

1. Book

Author's Last Name, First Name. *Title of Book*. Publisher, Year of Publication.

Rose, Mike. *The Mind at Work: Valuing the Intelligence of the American Worker*. Penguin, 2004.

Thaiss, Chris, and Terry Myers Zawacki. *Engaged Writers, Dynamic Disciplines: Research on the Academic Writing Life*. Boynton/Cook, 2006.

2. Work in an Edited Collection or Anthology

Author's Last Name, First Name. "Title." *Title of Anthology/Collection*, edited by Editor's First Name and Last Name, Publisher's Name, Year of Publication, pp. Page Numbers

Effinger Wilson, Nancy. "Bias in the Writing Center: Tutor Perceptions of African American Language." *Writing Centers and the New Racism: A Call for Sustainable Dialogue and Change*, edited by Laura Greenfield and Karen Rowan, Utah State UP, 2011, pp. 177-91.

Thoreau, Henry David. "Walking." *The Norton Book of Nature Writing*, edited by Robert Finch and John Elder, Norton, 2002, pp. 180-205.

3. Newspaper Article

Author's Last Name, First Name. "Title." *Name of Newspaper*, Day Month Year, pp. Page Number/s.

Fopay, David. "Utility Bill Relief the Goal of Effort." *Journal-Gazette & Times Courier*, 7 Aug. 2012, pp. A1+.

Green, Logan. "Haiti Connection Transforms Newman Center." *Daily Eastern News*, 18 Nov. 2010, pp. 1+.

4. Article in a Magazine

Author's Last Name, First Name. "Title." *Name of Magazine*, Month Year, pp. Page Number/s.

Anderson, John Lee. "After the Warlords." *The New Yorker,* 27 Mar. 2006, pp. 58-65.

Bergsma, Ad. "No Silver Linings, Please." *Ode,* Sept. 2010, pp. 63-67.

5. Article in a Scholarly Journal

Author's Last Name, First Name. "Title." *Name of Journal,* Volume Number, Issue Number, Year of Publication, pp. Page Numbers.

Courtney, Jennifer. "Real Men Do Housework: Ethos and Masculinity in Contemporary Domestic Advice." *Rhetoric Review,* vol. 28, no. 1, 2009, pp. 66-81.

Kellogg, Ronald T. "Training Writing Skills: A Cognitive Developmental Perspective." *Journal of Writing Research,* vol. 1, no. 1, 2008, pp. 1-26.

Five Common Web Sources—MLA

1. Page or Article on a Website

Author's Last Name, First Name, or Name of Organization. Name of Article or Posting. *Name of Website*, Date, Web Address.

Henig, Jess, et al. "Whoppers of Campaign 2010." *FactCheck.org,* 26 Oct. 2010, www.factcheck.org/2010/10/whoppers-of-campaign-2010/.

"Renewable Energy Standards—Mitigating Global Warming." *The Union of Concerned Scientists,* 12 Feb. 2009, www.ucsusa.org/clean_energy/ smart-energy-solutions/increase-renewables/renewable-energy.html#. Vw7apHq8qSo.

2. Article in an Online Newspaper

Author's Last Name, First Name (if known). "Title of Article." *Title of Newspaper*, Date of Publication, Web Address.

Harvery, Chelsea. "Why Living Around Nature Could Make You Live Longer." *The Washington Post,* 19 Apr. 2016, www.washingtonpost.com/news/ energy-environment/wp/2016/04/19/why-living-around-nature- could-make-you-live-longer/.

Overbye, Dennis. "A Costly Quest for the Dark Heart of the Cosmos." *The New York Times,* 16 Nov. 2010, www.nytimes.com/2010/11/17/science/space/17dark.html?_r=0science/space/17dark.html?_r=0.

3. Article in a Web-Based Magazine

Author's Last Name, First Name. "Title of Article." *Name of Magazine,* Date of Publication, Web Address.

Wlizlo, Will. "Jonathan Safran Foer's Experimental Literature." *Utne Reader,* 15 Nov. 2010, www.utne.com/arts/jonathan-safran-foer-experimental-literature.aspx.

Giaimo, Cara. "Why Only Apple Users Can Trash Their Files." *Slate*, 19 Apr. 2016, www.slate.com/blogs/atlas_obscura/2016/04/19/the_history_of_the_apple_trash_icon_in_graphic_design_and_lawsuits.html.

4. Newspaper, Magazine, or Journal Article Accessed through an Online Database

Author's Last Name, First Name. "Title." *Name of Journal or Magazine,* Volume Number, Issue Number, and/or Day Month Year, pp. Page Numbers. *Title of Database*, Web Address.

Karwin, Tom. "Organic Gardening Demystified." *Monterey County Herald,* 11 Feb. 2008. *LexisNexis.*

Davidson, Steve. "Going Organic." *Ecos,* Oct./Nov. 2005, pp. 8-12. *Academic Search Complete*, doi:19214128.

Sommers, Nancy. "Responding to Student Writing." *College Composition and Communication*, vol. 33, no. 2, May 1982, pp. 148-56. *JSTOR*, www.jstor.org.proxy1.library.eiu.edu/stable/357622.

5. Video or Podcast

Author's Last Name, First Name (if known). "Title of Video." *Name of Site*. Name of Sponsoring Institution/Organization (if one is listed), Date of Creation (if available), Web Address. [Date of Access].

Note: If you cannot find a date of creation, or if you think the site is unstable, then include the date that you accessed the site at the end of the entry.

> Eastern Illinois University. "Integrative Learning: The Faculty Perspective." *YouTube*, uploaded by IAMEIU, 27 Feb. 2012, www.youtube.com/watch?v=iv-lhAS-4v8&list=PL3F2A6CC4B57B69.

> University of Virginia. "2013 Ridley Lecture: Carol Dweck on Student Mindsets." *YouTube*, uploaded by University of Virginia, 21 Mar. 2013, www.youtube.com/watch?v=eGnqgXmlTk4.

❹ Correctly use the APA documentation style.

Use the APA Documentation Style

When working with sources for papers, many classes in the sciences and social sciences use the American Psychological Association (APA) style. The sections that follow provide guidance about how to provide in-text citations, how to introduce sources by using introductory phrases (IPs), and how to create a References page in APA style.

The Basics of APA In-Text Citations

In APA style, in-text citations typically are presented in one of two ways: (1) the author's last name, date of publication, and page number are placed at the end of the sentence, or (2) the author's name and date of publication come earlier in the sentence in the introductory phrase, and the page number is cited at the end. Note the patterns of the sentences using APA style:

> Paraphrase or summary sentence (in-text citation).

> Author (date) Paraphrase or summary sentence (page number).

> "Direct Quote Statement" (in-text citation).

> Author (date) "Direct Quote Statement" (page number).

> "Direct Quote Question?" (in-text citation).

> "Direct Quote Exclamation!" (in-text citation).

Here are some examples of the more common kinds of in-text citations:

1. A work by one author (or several) named in the introductory phrase

As Dweck (2006) explained, "The passion for stretching yourself and sticking to it, even (or especially) when it is not going well, is the hallmark of the growth mindset" (p. 7).

Knowles, Holton, and Swanson (2005) argued that by involving the students in the evaluation process, an instructor can give them a better sense of their goals and progress (p. 6).

2. A work by one author not named in the introductory phrase

Research has shown that people who have a "growth mindset" work hard toward getting better and are persistent even when they suffer setbacks (Dweck, 2006, p. 7).

3. A work by two or three authors not named in the introductory phrase

As they have shown, intrinsic motivation is connected to stronger analytical abilities and enhanced critical thinking skills (Deci & Flaste, 1995, p. 51).

By involving students in the evaluation process, an instructor can give them a better sense of their goals and progress (Knowles, Holton, & Swanson, 2005, p. 6).

Remote-sit students most often criticize the lack of opportunity for one-on-one interaction with their instructors (Simonson et al., 2011, p. 80).

Note: The abbreviation et al. *comes from Latin* et alii, *and means "and others."*

4. Indirect source

When an author you are reading quotes someone else, and you want to use that quote, first try to find the original work and quote directly from it. If this not possible, your citation must indicate the quote is indirect.

Psychological research about motivation has confirmed this statement from Michael Jordan: "The mental toughness and the heart are a lot stronger than some of the physical advantages you might have. I've always said that and I've always believed that" (as cited in Dweck, 2005, p. 86).

5. A Web-based article without paragraph numbers

Since Web-based articles often do not have page numbers or paragraph numbers, you have to provide only the name of the author and the date of publication. If an online article does have paragraph numbers, you must cite the paragraph number where the paraphrased or quoted material came from in the article by using the abbreviation "para." followed by the number of the paragraph.

> As Harlan (2013) described in a recent article about the Japanese company Rakuten, "The company initially said workers had to study on their own time, and it offered almost no guidance on how they should learn. It also provided no money for classes or books. Employees say they watched English movies and emptied shelves in the foreign-language sections of bookstores. They downloaded iPhone apps. They made flashcards."

> As described in a recent article about the Japanese company Rakuten, the company gives its employees autonomy on how they want to learn the language and does not compensate for their work toward learning English (Harlan, 2013).

> Burton (2010) noted that psychological priming made people believe what they wanted to believe regardless of the facts, logical support, and experts cited (para. 2).

> The experiment showed that psychological priming made people believe what they wanted to believe even though facts, evidence, and experts contradicted their beliefs (Burton, 2010, para. 2).

6. A Web-based article with sections

If a Web-based article has specific headings or sections like "Introduction," "Discussion," etc., you need to *cite the heading and the number of the paragraph* to help the reader find the quoted or paraphrased material easily. For indicating the paragraph number, use the abbreviation "para."

> As Johnson (2012) noted, one easy solution for office workers who sit for long periods is "to set an alarm as a reminder to take a lap or two around your work area. It's a practice that might not seem like much, but Levine said short, sporadic movement really adds up" ("Off Your Duff" section, para. 5).

Wing Sue defined "racial microagression" in this way: "Racial microaggressions are the brief and everyday slights, insults, indignities and denigrating messages sent to people of color by well-intentioned White people who are unaware of the hidden messages being communicated" (2010, "What Are Racial Microaggressions?" section, para. 2).

7. Website sources

Because APA requires the date of publication, if there is no date indicated on a Web page, you should provide the abbreviation "n.d," which stands for "no date." For websites and electronic sources, you use the same format as you would for print documents: author (if provided), date (if provided), page number (if provided), and paragraph number (if the source has headings). If a source does not have an author, you can indicate its title in the introductory phrase.

As detailed by the Purdue Online Writing Lab in "In-Text Citations: Author/ Authors," "When an electronic source lacks page numbers, you should try to include information that will help readers find the passage being cited" ("Sources Without Page Numbers," n.d., para. 1).

On its "Mission & Philosophy" page (n.d.), the EIU Writing Center is described in this way: "a place where students can develop as writers and thinkers. We recognize that student writers come to the center with individual needs and individual writing processes, and we are committed to working with students from all disciplines, majors, and academic backgrounds at any stage of the writing process."

The research indicated that "more than 1,100 counties—one-third of all counties in the lower 48—will face higher risks of water shortages by mid-century as the result of global warming. More than 400 of these counties will face extremely high risks of water shortages" (Sierra Club, n.d.).

Debates about whether air conditioning is harmful have been around since the technology was created because some people think "stale, recycled air might be sickening or dangerous" (Engber, 2012).

Introducing Source Material in APA Style

You should always make it clear within the text of your paper where material from your sources begins and ends. One way to do this is to use an introductory phrase (IP). An *introductory phrase* provides an introduction and a context for source material, making it clear to readers that you are working with someone else's ideas or written material.

Note, for example, how a writer can use an introductory phrase to introduce a paraphrase:

> Rhoda J. Maxwell (2004) believed it is important for teachers to convey expectations regarding the formality and technical correctness expected in assigned writing. Class notes, read only by the student who takes them, for example, may be messy with little regard for punctuation and spelling. However, essay assignments must be unified, coherent, and technically correct to meet the needs of a wider audience (p. 34).

The introductory phrase at the beginning and the page number at the end make it clear where the borrowed material begins and ends. (Remember, if the author is mentioned in the text of the paper, there is no need to include his or her name in the citation.)

It is particularly important to use introductory phrases when presenting quoted material or paraphrasing a source. You do not want your reader to suddenly encounter quoted or paraphrased material and have no idea where it comes from. Such quotes are sometimes called "dumped quotations" because the writer has simply dumped another's words into the paper without a context.

Five Introductory Phrase (IP) Patterns in APA

There are five introductory phrase patterns that you can use when presenting quoted material. In APA style, introductory phrases use the *past tense*, provide the year of publication, offer the page (print) or paragraph number (Web), and the period comes after the in-text citation in parentheses.

1. **IP = Author + Date + Verb followed by a Comma (,) "_____" (p.).**

> Taylor and Copeland (2015) related, "An introductory phrase provides an introduction and a context for source material, making it clear to the readers that you are working with someone else's ideas or written material" (p. 394).

2. IP = Author + Date + Verb + *that* "_____" (p.).

   In *IDEAS & Aims*, Taylor and Copeland (2015) informed us that "An introductory phrase provides an introduction and a context for source material, making it clear to the readers that you are working with someone else's ideas or written material" (p. 394).

3. **IP = Complete Sentence that has the Author, Date, and Verb followed by a Colon (:) "_____" (p.).**

   Taylor and Copeland (2015) stressed the importance of introducing source material: "An introductory phrase provides an introduction and a context for source material, making it clear to the readers that you are working with someone else's ideas or written material" (p. 394).

4. "_____," IP = Verb + Author (Date), "_____" (p.).

   "An introductory phrase provides an introduction and a context for source material," explained Taylor and Copeland (2015), "making it clear to the readers that you are working with someone else's ideas or written material" (p. 394).

5. "_____," IP = Verb + Author (Date, p.).

   "An introductory phrase provides an introduction and a context for source material, making it clear to the readers that you are working with someone else's ideas or written material," asserted Taylor and Copeland (2015, p. 394).

As you can see, the sentences have complete introductory phrases because they have clear subjects (who is saying what) and verbs to indicate the owners of the quoted material to readers. Keep variety in mind when you work with quotations, too, because if you use the same type of introductory phrase every time you present a quotation, the paper is going to become very repetitive and potentially boring to the readers.

In your introductory phrases, use specific verbs that clearly reflect what the author is saying. Using the verbs "said" or "stated" or "related" too often can lead to a lack of variety with the verbs used to introduce quotations. The chart below provides a listing of verbs you can use to introduce a source through summary, paraphrase, or quotations. However, you have to choose verbs that connect to and make sense with the information or quotations you present because these words do not have the same meanings.

Verbs for Introductory Phrases

accepted	cautioned	denied	listed	revealed
acknowledged	commented	described	maintained	said
added	compared	disagreed	observed	shared
admitted	complained	discussed	outlined	showed
affirmed	concluded	emphasized	pointed out	speculated
agreed	condemned	explained	praised	stated
analyzed	confirmed	highlighted	predicted	stressed
argued	considered	hypothesized	proposed	suggested
asked	contradicted	identified	proved	summarized
asserted	contrasted	illustrated	rejected	urged
assessed	criticized	insisted	reported	warned
believed	defended	interpreted	responded	wrote

EXERCISE 13.2   **Practice Integrating Quotations**   MyWritingLab

Directions: Integrate the following quotation using each of the five introductory phrase patterns discussed above. Here is the essential information you need to have:

- The quote is "Of all the things we need to know about grammar, the verb is first."
- Don Watson makes this statement in his book *Death Sentences*.
- The quotation is on page 20.
- The book was published in 2005.

Providing a Correctly Formatted References Page in APA Style

In addition to documenting sources within the text of your paper, you will also document your outside sources on a separate References page at the end of your paper that details the sources you have used.

Based on the specifications from the *Publication Manual for the American Psychological Association*, sixth edition (2010), when formatting a References page, here are the essentials:

- Make sure the whole page is double-spaced.
- Center the word "References" at the top of the page.
- Provide the entries of your sources in alphabetical order.
- Begin each entry with the last name of the author, or if the source does not have an author, begin with the title of the article or book or Web page—alphabetizing by the first principal word of the title (not *A, An,* or *The*).
- Begin each entry at the left margin of the page.
- Indent the lines after the first line of each entry five spaces, creating a "hanging indentation."
- When providing the title of books, articles, Web pages, or chapters, capitalize only the first letter of the title, proper nouns, and the first word after a dash in a title. If there is a subtitle after a colon or a semicolon, capitalize the first letter of the subtitle.
- Capitalize all the major words in the title of a scholarly journal.

As a general rule, when compiling information about a source, make sure you have these basics:

- Author's or authors' names
- Title of the article or Web page or book
- When it was published
- Where it was published
- Page numbers
- Digital object identifier (DOI) if one is assigned

or

- Home page URL for the journal, magazine, or newsletter, using this format: "Retrieved from http://www._____"

In this section, we provide guidelines for five common print sources and six common Web-based sources you might typically use. While this list does not cover all of the different types of sources you could use for a paper, you can use these citations for guidance and as examples when you're formatting a References page.

If none of the examples relate to a source you are using, you have three options to help you format source information correctly on your References page:

- Go to the **Writing Center** or the Academic Support Center on your campus, which will have writing handbooks and style manuals for you to refer to. In addition, the tutors there can work with you in formatting your References page.

- Use an **Online Writing Lab (OWL)** to see how you should format the sources. The most famous and probably the most comprehensive OWL on the Web is the Purdue OWL: http://owl.english.purdue.edu/. On that site there are various links that will take you to pages that will help you properly format the sources in your papers.

- Use the *Publication Manual of the American Psychological Association*, sixth edition, which should be available in your college's library, or you can look for examples on the **APA website**.

- Use an online documentation software program. However, be sure to enter the information correctly and check the citations to make sure they are in APA style.

Date of publication	Copyright © 2016 by Pearson Education, Inc.
	Library of Congress Cataloging-in-Publication Data
Author name(s)	Taylor, Tim N., author.
Title of text	IDEAS & aims for college writing / Tim N. Taylor, Eastern Illinois University ; Linda Copeland, St. Louis Community College.
	pages cm
	Includes index.
Edition number appears here after first edition	ISBN 978-0-205-83060-2 (Student Edition) -- ISBN 0-205-83060-9 (Student Edition) -- ISBN 978-0-321-95603-3 (A la Carte) -- ISBN 0-321-95603-6 (A la Carte)
	1. English language--Rhetoric. 2. Report writing. 3. College readers. I. Copeland, Linda, author. II. Title. III. Title: IDEAS and aims for college writing.
	PE1408.T366 2015
	808'.042--dc23
	2014041653

▲ This annotated example shows where to look on a copyright page for the source information required for APA documentation.

Five Common Print Sources

1. Book

Author's Last Name, Initial(s). (Year of Publication). *Title of book*. City and State of Publication: Publisher's Name.

Rose, M. (2004). *The mind at work: Valuing the intelligence of the American worker*. New York, NY: Penguin.

Thaiss, C., & Myers Zawacki, T. (2006). *Engaged writers, dynamic disciplines: Research on the academic writing life*. Portsmouth, NH: Boynton/Cook.

2. Work in an Edited Collection or Anthology

Author's Last Name, Initial(s). (Year of Publication). Title of article or chapter. In A. Editor & B. Editor (Eds.), *Title of anthology or collection* (pages of chapter or article). City and State of Publication: Publisher's Name.

Author's Last Name, Initial(s). (Year of Publication). Title of article or chapter. In A. Editor (Ed.), *Title of anthology or collection* (pages of chapter or article). City and State of Publication: Publisher's Name. Reprinted from [ ], pp. [page numbers], by Initial(s) Last Name, Year of Publication, City of Publication: Publisher.

Effinger Wilson, N. (2011). Bias in the writing center: Tutor perceptions of African American language. In L. Greenfield & K. Rowan (Eds.), *Writing centers and the new racism: A call for sustainable dialogue and change* (pp. 177-191). Logan, UT: Utah State University Press.

Berry, W. (2002). Conservation and the local economy. In N. Wirzba (Ed.), *The art of the commonplace: The agrarian essays of Wendell Berry* (pp. 195-204). Washington, DC: Shoemaker & Hoard. Reprinted from *Sex, economy, freedom & community*, pp. 3-18, by W. Berry, 1992. New York, NY: Pantheon.

3. Newspaper Article

Author's Last Name, Initial(s). (Year, Month Day). Title of article. *Name of newspaper*, Page number/s.

Fopay, D. (2012, August 7). Utility bill relief the goal of effort. *Journal-Gazette & Times Courier*, pp. A1, A2.

Green, L. (2010, November 18). Haiti connection transforms Newman Center. *The Daily Eastern News*, p. 1.

4. Article in a Magazine

Author's Last Name, Initial(s). (Year, Month Day).Title of article. *Name of Magazine*, page number/s.

Bergsma, A. (2010, September). No silver linings, please. *Ode Magazine*, 63-67.
Anderson, J. L. (2006, March 27). After the warlords. *The New Yorker*, 58-65.

5. Article in a Scholarly Journal

Author's Last Name, Initial(s). (Year of Publication). Title of article. *Name of Journal, Volume Number*(Issue Number), page numbers.

Courtney, J. (2009). Real men do housework: Ethos and masculinity in contemporary domestic advice. *Rhetoric Review, 28*(1), 66-81.

Kellogg, R. T. (2008). Training writing skills: A cognitive developmental perspective. *Journal of Writing Research, 1*(1), 1-26.

Six Common Web Sources

1. Page or Article on a Website

Author's Last Name, Initial(s). (Year, Month Day—if known). Title of article or page. Retrieved from http://Web address

Note: If there is no year or date of publication available, simply place "n.d." in the parentheses.

Henig, J., Novak, V., & Jackson, B. (2010, October 26). Whoppers of campaign 2010. Retrieved from http://www.factcheck.org/2010/10/whoppers-of-campaign-2010/

2. Page or Article on a Website if no author named

Title of article or page (if no author provided). (Year, Month Day—if known). Retrieved from http://Web address

In-text citations: The basics. (2012, March 14). *APA formatting and style guide.* Retrieved from http://owl.english.purdue.edu/owl/resource/560/02/

3. Article in an Online Newspaper

Author's Last Name, Initial(s). (Year, Month, Day). Title of article. *Title of Newspaper.* Retrieved from http://Web address

Overbye, D. (2010, November 16). A costly quest for the dark heart of the cosmos. *The New York Times*. Retrieved from http://www.nytimes.com

Darrow, B. (2012, August 7). Steve Wozniak expresses concerns about cloud computing. *The Washington Post*. Retrieved from http://www.washingtonpost.com

4. Article in a Web-Based Magazine

Author's Last Name, Initial(s). (Year, Month Day). Title of article. *Name of Magazine*. Retrieved from http://Web address

Agger, M. (2010, November 17). Data for a better planet. *Slate*. Retrieved from http://www.slate.com

Wlizlo, W. (2010, November 15). Jonathan Safran Foer's experimental literature. *Utne*. Retrieved from http://www.utne.com

5. Journal Article Accessed through a Database

Author's Last Name, Initial(s). (Date of Publication). Title of journal article. *Name of Journal, volume number*(issue number), pages. DOI or Retrieved from http://Web address

Note: APA requires that you provide the digital object identifier (DOI) if one is available. If the DOI is not available, provide the database's URL.

Fehr, J., & Sassenbery, K. (2009). Intended and unintended consequences of internal motivation to behave non prejudiced: The case of benevolent discrimination. *European Journal of Social Psychology, 39*(6), 1093-1108. doi:10.1002/ejsp.620

Hall, A., & Mogyorody, V. (2007). Organic farming, gender, and the labor process. *Rural Sociology, 72*(2), 289-316. Retrieved from http://web.ebscohost.com

6. Visual Sources

Author's Last Name, Initial(s) or Primary Contributor/s or Agency/Organization. (Date of Publication). *Title of Video* [Type of media]. Retrieved or Available from http://Web address

- DVD

  Robertson, W. (2005). *Writing across Borders*. [DVD]. Available from
  http://cwl.oregonstate.edu/writing-across-borders/

- PowerPoint Presentation

  Office of Academic Affairs, Eastern Illinois University. (n.d.). *Integrative learning:*
  The faculty perspective. Integrative Learning at EIU [PowerPoint slides].
  Retrieved from http://www.eiu.edu

- Video

  University of Virginia. (2013, March 21). *Ridley Lecture: Carol Dweck on student*
  mindsets [Video]. Retrieved from http://www.youtube.com

- TV Episode

  Pizzolatto, N. (Writer), & Fukunaga, C. (Director). (2014). The long bright dark
  [Television series episode]. In N. Pizzolatto & C. Fukunaga (Producers),
  True detective. Los Angeles, CA: HBO Studios.

- Movie

  Allen, W. (Writer & Director). (1975). *Love and death* [Motion picture]. United
  States: MGM Studios.

❺ Write a research-based position paper.

Write a Research-Based Essay

A research-based essay is a position paper that requires a writer to take a stand and use documented sources to support it.

Researched-Based Position Paper

To write a position paper, follow these criteria.

Your Writing Task

Write an essay that takes a stand on an arguable issue and supports its position through the use of strong description and evidence, real and/or likely examples, clear terms, acknowledgment and analysis of counterarguments, and careful reasoning.

When selecting a topic, you are limited to a "local" problem such as one of the following:

- An issue at your college
- An issue in your college's town or city
- An issue in your neighborhood, city, or suburb
- An issue in your state

Required Organization

The essay should have this organization:

- **Introduction**: background, context, review of conversation, why the reader should care
- **Thesis**: statement of claim and reasons
- **Support** of reasons and assumptions
- **Answers to possible objections** (counterarguments)
- **Conclusion**: review of major points, the contribution of this argument, a call to action, possible solutions

Your paper should use *a minimum of four different sources*, either by quotation, paraphrase, summary, or display of information. One of the four sources must come from a peer-reviewed journal. The essay must follow APA style and provide a separate References page.

Your Role and Audience

You should write the essay from a position of power to readers who might take an opposing viewpoint from your own. You need to show that there is a problem or issue and point out its effects. Then present a logical and supportable position about the problem/issue.

A Successful Position Paper . . .

- Offers an introduction that provides context and background for the reader while briefly introducing your position and reasons for that position.
- Explains the problem by using appropriate, accurate, and logically sound assertions, examples, and details.
- Presents a position that persuades readers by making logical and ethical claims.
- Provides a concise conclusion section that connects to the bottom line (your solution).

- Addresses and works with counterarguments, meaning the writer contends with how skeptics might disagree with his or her position on an issue.
- Follows the required organization of the assignment.
- Offers strong support for its solution by using solid examples, strong explanation, valid and credible research, specific and concrete details, and professional tone.
- Uses at least four sources to support its argument, not to carry the argument.
- Has focused and unified paragraphs that are appropriately developed.
- Paraphrases and integrates quotations from sources effectively, smoothly, and ethically through appropriate introductory phrases and in-text citations in APA style.
- Exhibits strong concision, cohesion, transitions, and sentence variety in length and type.
- Avoids using "I" and "You."
- Does not have editing errors that distract the reader or disrupt the meaning of sentences.

MyWritingLab   STUDENT WRITER AT WORK

MyWritingLab Visit Ch. 13 Documenting Sources in MyWritingLab to access the IDEAS videos.

This student paper is an example of the type of research-based paper typically assigned in college writing classes, and it illustrates how a writer can effectively integrate sources. It is a position paper that requires the writer to make a stand and use sources in APA style. (Chapter 12 has a research-based I-Search Paper by Darrius Johnson that uses MLA style. See page 366.)

After visiting with her professor during her office hours to talk about her ideas, Marissa Torres decided to write about public profanity. It is an issue she recently read about in an online article about a Massachusetts town imposing fines for public swearing. Also, she has noticed the prevalence of public cursing on the campus at her community college. Commentary using the I D E A S template is provided to show how close, analytical, and critical reading is important.

Marissa's Position Paper

In APA style, an abbreviated title of the paper appears at the top of each page, flush left, and the page number top right. On the title page only, the abbreviated title is preceded by "Running head:"

No %#@$&*: Profanity on Campus
Should Be Banned
Marissa Torres
Professor Copeland
Introduction to College Writing
29 September 2013

No %#@$&*: Profanity on Campus
Should Be Banned

Washington Post columnist Kathleen Parker (2011) described an incident in which she and others in a crowded elevator were forced to listen to a woman curse non-stop at her male companion. Parker called this woman a "vile invader" and said the woman "made coarse and unlovely a period of time that was not her own." More recently, the residents of Middleborough, Massachusetts, voted to impose a $20 fine on those who curse in public. Many of the townspeople believed the excessive public profanity was hurting local businesses ("Town," 2012).

Unfortunately, our campus has many of these "vile invaders" who pollute the public airspace with profanity. It is not possible to walk down a hallway without hearing conversations that include most, if not all, of the "seven dirty words" that made comedian George Carlin the subject of a Supreme Court case ("Broadcast," 2004). Four letter words are literally shouted between groups on campus grounds, especially at sports events. Vulgarity even shows up in the classroom. A student in my history class called the professor an "ass****" for not accepting late work. A female psychology teacher was called a more gender-specific vulgarity when she tried to quiet a side conversation that was interrupting her lecture.

The old childhood chant "Sticks and stones may break my bones, but words will never hurt me" is simply not true. Public profanity invades the space of others in an ugly and disrespectful way. It degrades the English language, encourages a lack of civility in our academic community, and reflects poorly on the character of those who use it with total disregard of its inappropriateness. Our campus needs to follow the lead of Middleborough, Massachusetts. Students who use profanity in public areas on campus should be subject to a $10 fine.

The Federal Communications Commission (FCC) defines profanity as "Language so grossly offensive to members of the public who actually hear it as to amount to a nuisance" (2012). A survey of students across campus shows that most agree on what words are

---

In APA style, the date is indicated and past tense is used in the introductory phrase.

Interest and Explanation: She begins with a clear example.

Because there is no author, the title is used.

Interest and Audience: The author takes a clear stand in her thesis.

NO %#@$&*: PROFANITY ON CAMPUS   3

most inappropriate. Many of these are "obscenities" or the so-called "four-letter words" that refer to body parts and functions (Wajnryb, 2005, pp. 20-21). Taboo words that make derogatory reference to a person's race or religion (p. 22) also have no place in public conversation on campus. Working together, administration, faculty, and students should determine which words are not acceptable and make using them in public on campus a violation of the student conduct code with violators receiving a $10 fine.

> Because the author uses the same source, she provides only the page number.

One good reason to try to stop public profanity on campus is that profanity is often a "lazy language" because it more often creates discomfort or even anger rather than communicates ideas effectively (O'Connor, n.d.). One of the goals of a college education is to learn to be an effective communicator in both written and spoken English. In composition classes, for example, students learn the importance of audience and how to reach that audience by using the appropriate language. It is not appropriate to use profanity in papers intended for a general audience, so why should it be acceptable to use profanity in public speech? Edwin L. Battistella (2005), a professor of English and an author of books on language, said, "Avoiding coarse language in public signals an understanding of the boundary between public and private discourse and a tacit acceptance of that boundary" (p. 83). Careful consideration of audience and the best way to convey ideas should not be left behind in the writing and speaking classrooms. Careful and polite language should be practiced in public.

> n.d. = no date found.

> **Details & Explanation:** Torres provides her second supporting point.

Another reason to stop public profanity on campus is that it creates a general atmosphere of disrespect, which can lead to more serious consequences than making some people uncomfortable. As Parker (2011) related, "Lack of civility in words bleeds into lack of decency in behavior." Discussions full of profanity can turn into arguments, which can lead to emotional or physical violence. Restricting the use of profanity on campus will help to set a more positive and civil tone. This is the same reasoning behind the FCC's responsibility to restrict profanity in the media. Susan Ness, an FCC commissioner, stated, "As stewards of the airwaves, broadcasters play a vital leadership role in setting the cultural tone for our society.

NO %#@$&*: PROFANITY ON CAMPUS   4

They can choose to raise the standard or to lower it" ("Broadcast," 2004). Let us choose to raise the "cultural tone" of our campus.

> **Details & Explanation:** The author makes readers think about the effects.

Finally, a prohibition of public profanity will help individuals break a bad habit that could jeopardize their later success in the workplace. Those who do not learn to curb their use of profanity may use it without thinking in places where it is most inappropriate, such as at work or even during a job interview (Prontes, n.d.). People who use profanity are judged and labeled by those who hear them. Jim O'Connor, founder of the Cuss Control Academy and author of *Cuss Control: The Complete Book on How to Curb Your Cursing*, speculated that we no longer view people who swear as "low-class or unintelligent"; however, he says swearing does suggest people are "insufficiently in

> **She cites a quote that was quoted by someone else.**

command of their emotions or their vocabulary" (as cited in Stafford, 2009, p. D8). Those who lose self-control and curse around teachers are just as likely to do so around employers. Timothy Jay (1992), a professor of psychology who has studied profanity, reasoned, "The loss of control over one's anger . . . results in a lowering of one's esteem" (p. 102). Also, because so much vulgar language has sexual content, those who use it may open themselves up to charges of sexual harassment. Because employers are liable in such cases, many have rules forbidding offensive language in the workplace (Battistella, 2005, p. 74). Therefore, making students more aware of the importance of always being conscientious about language is another way to prepare them for success in the workplace.

> **Style & Interest:** The author moves to counterargument with a transitional sentence.

Despite these obvious reasons for curbing profanity on campus, there are those who will object. Some may argue that imposing fines for profanity will create resentment and cause people to rebel (McWhorter, 2012). Ashley Montague, an early researcher of swearing, found that "no people has ever abandoned its habit of swearing merely because the State . . . forbade it" (as cited in Wajnryb, 2005, p. 9). Yes, there will always be rebels who ignore any restrictions. But a major goal of this rule and a fine will be to heighten awareness and to curb a growing trend. Many believe that federal oversight of the media is needed or the lines of decency will "constantly be pushed outward"

NO %#@$&*: PROFANITY ON CAMPUS   5

Details & Explanation: She attempts to go against the ideas of her opponents.

("Broadcast," 2004). The same can be said of the use of profanity on our campus. If something is not done to restrict its use, profanity will increase without regard to its impact on the reputation of the speakers and our campus as a whole.

Details & Explanation: Torres grapples with a second counterargument.

Some will certainly claim that this restriction on profanity would violate their freedom of speech. No one wants to inhibit the free exchange of ideas on campus, even unpopular ideas. What this restriction will do is require that ideas be presented clearly without demeaning profanity. While the First Amendment protects free speech, it does not always protect profanity. David L. Hudson Jr., a First Amendment scholar, argued, "[D]on't assume you have a right to curse at your public employer or at your public school. Context—as well as content—is important in First Amendment law. The government has greater power to regulate speech when it acts as employer or educator than it does when it acts as sovereign" (2011). The college is within its rights to add restrictions on the use of profanity to its code of conduct.

Keep in mind, the goal of this restriction and fine is not to punish. The majority of people who use profanity are not "bad." Typically, they are those who have picked up bad speech habits because today's society is so tolerant of profanity. But even with this tolerance, those who use profanity still contribute to an uncivil environment and lower their own esteem. By raising their awareness about the negative consequences of profanity, perhaps the college can help them break the profanity habit. Mike Holder, an athletic director at Oklahoma State University, broke his own profanity habit with self discipline: "Profanity was a part of my normal conversation. I did it so often that I didn't even notice it. When I became the (golf) coach, I made the decision to cut out profanity. If I was going to be a coach, I realized that there was a higher standard. It was difficult for me to stop (cursing), but I just disciplined myself and stopped it, and I wouldn't tolerate it from my players" (as cited in Haisten, 2009).

Interest & Audience: Torres ends on a positive note and reasserts the thesis to state her case for the reader.

Let us all hold our campus to a higher standard and show some self-discipline like Holder did.

NO %#@$&*: PROFANITY ON CAMPUS   6

References

A print book.

Battistella, E. L. (2005). *Bad language: Are some words better than others?* New York, NY: Oxford University Press.

Broadcast Decency Rules. (2004, April 30). *Issues & controversies on file*. Retrieved from http://www.2facts.com /icof_home_feature.aspx

A guide provided by a US government agency.

Federal Communications Commission. (2012). *Guide: Obscenity, indecency and profanity*. Retrieved from http://www.fcc.gov /guides/obscenity-indecency-and-profanity

A newspaper article found through the library's database.

Haisten, B. (2009, February 15). Profanity remains a sports curse: Rough language must have its limits, former and present coaches say. *Tulsa World*. Retrieved from http://web .ebscohost.com

Hudson, D. L., Jr. (2011, October 6). Remember, profanity isn't always protected speech. *First Amendment Center*. Retrieved from http://www.firstamendmentcenter.org/

Jay, T. (1992). *Cursing in America: A psycholinguistic study of dirty language in the courts, in the movies, in the schoolyards and on the streets*. Philadelphia, PA: John Benjamins.

McWhorter, J. (2012, June 14). Ban swearing? No way. CNN.com. Retrieved from http://www.cnn.com/2012/06/13/opinion /mcwhorter-swearing-ban/index.html

A page on an organization's website.

O'Connor, J. V. (n.d.). So what's wrong with swearing? *Cuss Control Academy*. Retrieved from http://www.cusscontrol .com/

An online newspaper article.

Parker, K. (2011, August 23). Profanity erodes civility. *stltoday*.com. Retrieved from stltoday.com

Prontes, I. (n.d.). The effects of profanity. *eHow*. Retrieved from ehow.com

NO %#@$&*: PROFANITY ON CAMPUS SHOULD BE BANNED   7

A newspaper article.

Stafford, D. (2009, May 31). Companies try to rein in employees' blue streaks. *Waterloo-Cedar Falls Courier*, p.D8.

An online magazine article.

Town swears off swearing, passes $20 profanity fine. (2012, June 13). *The Christian Science Monitor*. Retrieved from http://www.csmonitor.com/

Wajnryb, R. (2005). *Expletive deleted $&#@*!: A good look at bad language.* New York, NY: Free Press.

QUESTIONS FOR DISCUSSION

1. In the sample position paper by Marissa Torres, which parts do you feel captured and kept your interest as a reader?
2. Some readers might strongly disagree with Torres' thesis and her supporting reasons. Examine the three reasons she thinks a fine for public profanity should be imposed, and then rank them. Which one is the strongest point, the second strongest, and the weakest? Explain why you think so.
3. Torres addresses two counterarguments that might be presented by people who oppose her idea. How effective is she in addressing those counterarguments?
4. What are other reasons she could have used to support her thesis? And what are other counterarguments that people might bring up?
5. Torres uses many different sources. Which ones are her strongest sources, and why do you think so?

CHAPTER AT A GLANCE

Learning Objectives	How they connect to writing at college ...
❶ Document sources.	When doing research, document your sources to give credit for material that is not your own, help readers know what sources you are using, and provide credibility to your ideas.

Learning Objectives	How they connect to writing at college . . .
❷ Avoid plagiarism.	You can avoid plagiarism by double-checking your work, using introductory phrases and in-text citations, and making sure you are using your own words when summarizing and paraphrasing sources.
❸ Correctly use the MLA documentation style.	To properly work with sources in MLA style, use in-text citations, use different types of introductory phrases (IPs), and provide a Works Cited page.
	MLA requires the use of present tense verbs when summarizing, paraphrasing, or quoting.
❹ Correctly use the APA documentation style.	To properly work with sources in APA style, use in-text citations, use different types of introductory phrases (IPs), and provide a References page.
	APA requires the use of past tense verbs and the date of publication when summarizing, paraphrasing, or quoting.

MyWritingLab Visit **Chapter 13, "Documenting Sources"** in MyWritingLab to test your understanding of the chapter objectives.

PART 5

Sentence Skills

IMPROVING STYLE AND CORRECTING ERRORS

14 | Style Matters

MyWritingLab All of the exercises and activities in this chapter can be completed in MyWritingLab.

Learning Objectives

In this chapter, you will learn and practice how to . . .

❶ Identify and create independent clauses, dependent clauses, and phrases.

❷ Understand and create simple sentences.

❸ Understand and write compound sentences.

❹ Understand and write complex sentences.

❺ Understand and write compound-complex sentences.

❻ Write sentences that contain well-placed modifiers.

❼ Write sentences containing appropriate appositives and parallel constructions.

❽ Eliminate wordy constructions to make sentences concise.

When people say that a writer has **style**, that usually means the writer has created **sentence variety**. In other words, the author has crafted different types of sentences and varied the lengths of those sentences. To have style as a writer, you need to know how to construct different types of sentences.

As a writer, you have all kinds of good ideas, but you need to make sure your sentences are properly constructed and punctuated. If there are mistakes in the sentences or your meaning is not clear, those distractions will damage your message and hurt your credibility.

This chapter provides information about the types of sentences you have available to you and offers helpful tips for editing and proofreading your sentences.

❶ Identify and create independent clauses, dependent clauses, and phrases.

The Building Blocks of Sentences: Clauses and Phrases

In order to construct a variety of sentence patterns, it is important to understand some basic terms and concepts fundamental to all sentences. Although you can probably write sentences without thinking about any of these terms and concepts, understanding the basic constructions behind sentences is essential if you are to recognize how to avoid many common grammar and punctuation errors. In addition, being able to craft a variety of well-written sentences is more likely when you have a clear understanding of the building blocks of sentences.

Independent Clauses

An **independent clause** can stand alone as a complete sentence. All sentences must have at least one independent clause.

An independent clause—or a complete sentence—has three parts:

- Subject
- Verb
- Complete Thought

Subjects

The **subject** of a sentence answers the question "Who or what is the sentence about?" The subject of a sentence is usually a noun or a pronoun.

A **noun** is a word that names a person, place, thing, or idea. Most nouns are **common nouns**. They are not capitalized. **Proper nouns**, which name particular persons, places, or things, are always capitalized. The following examples show the difference between common and proper nouns:

Common Nouns	Proper Nouns
country	France
language	English
boy	Andrew
gum	Trident
day	Wednesday
month	January

A **pronoun** is a word that takes the place of a noun. Examples of pronouns that can be used as subjects include the following:

Personal Pronouns

I	we	everybody	these
you	it	everything	those
he	they	someone	that
she		somebody	this
		everyone	which

Here are examples of independent clauses—complete sentences—with the subjects in bold:

- **Kara** hopes to complete her degree in occupational therapy in two years.
- The art **museum** will open an exhibit on impressionism next month.
- **I** plan to join the campus Horticulture Club.
- **Smoking** is not allowed in my community's businesses.
- **English** and **algebra** are my hardest subjects.

EXERCISE 14.1 Identify Subjects

Directions: Circle the word or words indicating the subject of each of the following sentences.

1. Roya plans to major in computer science.

2. She would like a career as a web designer.

3. Who will be able to drive car pool next week?

4. Regular dieting and exercising will control most people's weight.

5. Studying takes up most of my time on weekends.

Verbs

An independent clause must also have a **verb**. Most verbs are **action verbs**, which tell us what the subject is doing and when the action occurs, such as in the following examples:

eat	learned	fly
hope	made	sleep
sang	waited	catch
allowed	spoke	watch
taught	forget	run

Linking verbs connect the subject of a sentence to one or more words that describe or identify the subject. These are the linking verbs:

was	become	act	feel
were	has	turn	grow
am	have	sound	taste
is	seem	get	look
are	appear	remain	smell

Helping verbs can be used to help the main verbs express a special meaning or a particular time. These are some common helping verbs:

can	might	should	being	is	were
had	did	could	must	will	been
are	have	does	may	shall	
am	was	has	do	would	

Here are examples of independent clauses—complete sentences—with the subjects in bold and verbs underlined:

1. The **band** <u>played</u> for over two hours.
2. **Everybody** <u>was standing</u> and <u>swaying</u> to the music.
3. **This** <u>is</u> the best concert of the year.
4. The **dog** <u>leaped</u> into the air and <u>caught</u> the Frisbee.
5. **Alan** <u>should have been paying</u> more attention.

EXERCISE 14.2 Identify Subjects and Verbs

Directions: Circle the subject and underline the verb in each of the following sentences.

1. Your success will depend upon your effort.
2. Amy entertained us with her jokes.
3. The trip to Mexico sounded like an inexpensive vacation.
4. We had been planning this vacation for two years.
5. Who would have expected a hurricane?

Avoid Three Common Problems in Identifying Subjects and Verbs

While finding subjects and verbs in sentences can be relatively easy, there are constructions that can confuse writers and lead to errors in subject-verb agreement (see pages 479–482) and even fragments. The most common problems in identifying subjects and verbs are the following:

- Confusing words in prepositional phrases for subjects and verbs.
- Finding subjects after verbs.
- Confusing participles with verbs.

1. Confusing words in prepositional phrases for subjects and verbs. The subjects and verbs of independent clauses are never found in a *prepositional phrase*—a group of words following a preposition. Remembering this rule will help you avoid subject-verb agreement errors in your writing. Common prepositions are listed in the following box:

Common Prepositions								
about	among	beneath	concerning	from	of	over	to	within
above	around	beside	despite	in	off	past	toward	without
across	at	besides	down	inside	on	regarding	under	
after	before	between	during	into	onto	since	up	
against	behind	beyond	except	like	out	through	upon	
along	below	by	for	near	outside	till	with	

In the following sentences, the prepositional phrases have been crossed out, making it easier to clearly identify the subject and verb of each sentence.

- A **box** ~~of matches~~ sits ~~on the fireplace mantel.~~
- The **houses** ~~near the river~~ run the risk ~~of being flooded.~~
- The **villagers** tried ~~to flee~~ the approaching tsunami.
- **Letters** ~~in an old suitcase~~ were the basis ~~of a best-selling novel.~~
- **Jon** used several techniques ~~to try to relax before tests.~~

EXERCISE 14.3 Identify Prepositional Phrases, Subjects, and Verbs

Directions: Cross out the prepositional phrases in the following sentences. Then circle the subject and underline the verb in each one.

1. A can of month-old baked beans sits in my brother's refrigerator.

2. Amber wanted to impress her boss by taking on extra responsibilities without extra pay.

3. The screams of the unhappy baby echoed through the quiet church.

4. The origins of that word can be found in the *Oxford English Dictionary*.

5. The jockey urged his horse to reach the finish line first.

2. Finding subjects after verbs. Remember, too, that subjects can come after verbs—the words that describe the action or state of being of the subject. To determine the subject in these kinds of sentences, ask "Who or what is the sentence about?" or "Who or what is performing the action in the sentence?"

The following sentences have subjects that come after the verbs. Again, you do not want to be confused by prepositional phrases, so crossing them out will help you correctly identify subjects and verbs.

- Here are the **invoices** ~~from last month~~.
- There have been several **complaints** ~~about cars speeding in school zones~~.
- Running ~~through the city park~~ was a **pack** ~~of stray dogs~~.
- There goes the **man** ~~in charge of the recycling center in my city~~.
- ~~In my refrigerator~~ were expired **milk**, moldy **cheese** and a **box** ~~of baking soda~~.

EXERCISE 14.4 Identify Prepositional Phrases, Subjects, and Verbs

Directions: Cross out the prepositional phrases in the following sentences. Circle the subject and underline the verb in each one. *Note:* In each sentence the subject will come after the verb.

1. Scrambling across the field to kick the ball were three aspiring soccer stars.

2. Here are the tickets to get into the concert.

3. Rising over the mountains was a golden morning sun.

4. There have been three principals in three years at my son's school.

5. Huddled at the school bus stop were three small children in winter snowsuits.

3. Confusing participles with verbs. Do not confuse a participle phrase with the verb of a sentence. A **participle** is a verb form that functions as an adjective in a sentence. Participles ending in *-ing* often introduce phrases or groups of words that describe a noun or pronoun in a sentence—**participle phrases**. Writers sometimes mistake these participles as verbs and end up writing fragments.

Fragments with Bolded Participles	Fragments Corrected by Adding a Helping Verb	Fragments Corrected by Adding a <u>Verb</u> and Finishing the Thought
Jay **daydreaming** at his desk	Jay **had been daydreaming** at his desk.	Jay, daydreaming at his desk, <u>did</u> not <u>notice</u> his angry boss standing behind him.
Job applicants **hoping** for an interview	Job applicants **were hoping** for an interview.	Job applicants, hoping for an interview, <u>formed</u> a line stretching down the street.
Albert **being** an honest man	Albert **has been** an honest man.	Albert, being an honest man, <u>returned</u> the wallet he found to the owner.

EXERCISE 14.5 Correct Fragments

Directions: Correct each of the following fragments in two ways. First, add a helping verb to the participle to create a complete sentence. Then correct the fragment by adding a verb and completing the thought after the participle phrase.

1. Ansai hoping to impress his supervisor

2. Bags sitting unclaimed at the airport

3. The coach watching the young rookie in the bullpen

4. My car sputtering and smoking

5. Cody singing the national anthem

Dependent Clauses

A **dependent clause** has two parts:

- Subject
- Verb

A dependent clause cannot stand alone as a complete sentence because it does not express a complete thought. A dependent clause by itself is a *fragment*.

Because dependent clauses have both a subject and a verb, which is what many writers think is sufficient for a complete sentence, dependent clause fragments are among the most common. You can correct a dependent clause fragment by adding an *independent clause*.

Dependent Clause Fragment	Correction
Because my **alarm** <u>was</u> broken	Because my alarm was broken, *I overslept and missed class.*
Which <u>is</u> my favorite show	*A power outage interrupted Law and Order,* which is my favorite show.
So that I <u>will get</u> the classes I need	*I always register early* so that I will get the classes I need.
Although my **car** <u>is</u> old	Although my car is old, *it is still reliable.*

EXERCISE 14.6 **Correct Dependent Clause Fragments**

Directions: Add an independent clause to each of the following dependent clauses to create a complete sentence.

1. Before I begin drafting a paper

2. Even though my car is old and has a lot of miles on it

3. Which is why I attend college

4. When I have free time

5. Until I finish my education

Phrases

A **phrase** is a group of words that add detail to a sentence. Unlike a clause, a **phrase** may be missing a subject or a verb, or it may be missing both. As you can see from the following examples, a phrase may not stand alone as a sentence.

my role model and friend	someone to count on	the sun rising in the east
now and forever	finding the time	quickly yet efficiently
quietly weeping	barking and growling	through all our time together
long ago and far away	taking his good old time	strict but fair
sweeping across the sky	a tough nut to crack	bright green berries
to give thanks	a man ahead of his time	soft and fluffy
knowing the right people	warm and cozy	of all the people I know

Putting It All Together

A sentence must contain at least **one independent clause** in order to be complete. Most sentences also have one or more of the other building blocks: *dependent clauses* and *phrases*.

See how all the parts work together in the following sentences:

- *As the clerk rang up my purchase,* **I noticed** *that she worked* <u>quickly and</u> <u>efficiently</u>.
- *When the alarm sounded,* **the firefighters gathered their gear and jumped** <u>into the waiting fire truck</u>.
- *Lumbering across the road,* **the buffalos** of <u>Yellowstone Park</u> **stopped traffic** *while tourists snapped pictures.*

EXERCISE 14.7 Identify Independent Clauses, Dependent Clauses, and Phrases

Directions: Identify each of the following groups of words as an independent clause (**IC**), a dependent clause (**DC**), or a phrase (**P**).

1. ____ caring for the environment

2. ____ when Samuel returned from vacation

3. ____ which will enable me to find a job

4. ____ sometimes TV commercials seem to go on forever

5. ____ my new interests in genealogy and archeology

6. ____ Esteban visits a chiropractor for relief from back pain

7. ____ to pick the best candidate for the job

8. ____ although the algebra class was challenging

9. ____ if you take the time to review your notes each evening

10. ____ writing is a skill requiring a lot of practice

❷ Understand and create simple sentences.

The Simple Sentence

While a very basic construction, the simple sentence can vary in length and in the number of subjects and verbs it contains. Experienced writers use simple sentences to present key ideas they want to emphasize to their readers.

The Simple Sentence = 1 Independent Clause

For any statement to be able to stand alone as a sentence, it must contain one independent clause.

Three ingredients make up an independent clause:

- **subject**.
- verb.
- complete thought.

These three components must be present for a sentence to be complete. The following are examples of independent clauses:

An **essay** must have a central point.

Strong **writers** practice writing as a process.

Terrain determines tactics.

In each of these examples there is only one independent clause. We call this kind of construction a **simple sentence**.

The Simple Sentence—Not So "Simple"

You might think that something *simple* is not very complicated or not very elaborate, but that is not how to think of a simple sentence.

Simple refers to a basic type of construction. As you learned about in the previous section, a simple sentence has only one clause—an independent clause. However, that clause may be embellished with additional words and phrases, and it may express a significant idea, as the following simple sentences illustrate:

- Even now after years of writing, *I can still be terrified* when faced with a blank page.
- *I can conquer that fear* by writing what comes to mind and not worrying about correcting sentence errors, being organized, or even making sense to anyone but myself.
- Through revision, *my paper becomes a polished work*, engaging and informing readers.

EXERCISE 14.8 Write Descriptive Simple Sentences

Directions: Add descriptive words and phrases to the following simple sentences. The questions after the sentences will help you determine the kinds of details to add. Be careful not to add additional clauses to the constructions. Keep them simple!

EXAMPLES: My **report** <u>was</u> well received. (Which one? On what subject? By whom?)

My *final* **report** *on plant safety* <u>was</u> well received *by my supervisor*.

The **dog** <u>barked</u>. (What kind? How did it bark? At what? Where?)

The *black* **Lab** <u>barked</u> *loudly and incessantly at the chunky squirrel atop the swing set in my neighbor's backyard.*

1. The **commercial** <u>caught</u> my attention. (Which one? By doing what?)

2. The **accident** <u>shut</u> down the highway. (Involving what? Which highway? For how long, causing what to occur?)

3. The **child** <u>felt</u> sick. (Which child? After doing what?)

4. The **band** <u>played</u>. (Which band? From where? What kind of music?)

5. The **mechanic** <u>checked</u> the noise. (What kind? Coming from where?)

The Simple Sentence: Compound Subjects and Verbs

A common type of simple sentence is one that has multiple subjects and/or verbs. Being able to write simple sentences with multiple, or compound, subjects and verbs will help to solidify your understanding of subjects and verbs as well as improve your overall writing style.

Simple Sentences with Two Subjects

Each of the following simple sentences has two subjects performing one action:

- **Freewriting** *and* **brainstorming** <u>help</u> writers generate ideas.
- **Spellcheck** *and* **Grammar check** <u>will</u> not <u>catch</u> all the sentence errors in a paper.
- **Transitions** *and* **repetition** of key words <u>help</u> to connect ideas in writing.

EXERCISE 14.9 Write Simple Sentences with Two Subjects

Directions: Write simple sentences that have two subjects performing a single action. Connect the two subjects with *and*. Also, try to use a strong action verb in each sentence.

EXAMPLE: Write a simple sentence that describes an activity you and a friend do together.

Carlos *and* **I** <u>design</u> web pages for small businesses.

1. Write a simple sentence that describes two students engaged in a single classroom activity.

2. Write a simple sentence that tells the kind of work two of your courses require.

3. Write a simple sentence that tells the kind of meal you and a date would enjoy.

4. Write a simple sentence that explains why two athletes are successful.

5. Write a simple sentence that describes a hobby you share with a friend or family member.

PUNCTUATION TIP

Notice that there is no comma in front of the coordinating conjunction *and* when it joins a compound subject or verb.

Simple Sentences with Two Verbs

Each of the following simple sentences has a single subject performing two actions:

- **Thesis statements** go beyond general statements and provide direction for what's to come in the paper.
- **Writers** must grab the readers' attention and keep it.
- Careless **proofreading** can annoy readers and raise questions about the writer's competence.

EXERCISE 14.10 Write Simple Sentences with Two Verbs

Directions: Write simple sentences that have one subject performing two actions. Also, try to use strong action verbs in each sentence.

EXAMPLE: Write a simple sentence that describes two activities your mechanic performs when he works on your car.

The **mechanic** changes the oil *and* rotates the tires.

1. Write a simple sentence that names two benefits of regular exercise.

2. Write a simple sentence that describes two activities students should do to improve their grades.

3. Write a simple sentence that describes two typical behaviors of fans at a football game.

4. Write a simple sentence that describes two behaviors parents can expect from their newborn.

5. Write a simple sentence that describes two annoying habits of neighbors.

Simple Sentences with Multiple Subjects and Multiple Verbs

If you need further evidence to see that simple sentences are not so simple, try writing a couple of simple sentences that have multiple subjects performing multiple actions such as the following:

- My **aunts** and **uncles** went to the same high school and still live in the same neighborhood.
- **Students**, **parents**, and **teachers** should determine a policy on bullying, make the policy known to everyone, and strictly enforce it.
- **Mike** and **Stuart** go to school during the day, work at night, and party on weekends.

EXERCISE 14.11   **Write Simple Sentences with Two or More Subjects and Verbs**

Directions: Write two simple sentences that have two or more subjects performing two or more actions. Use strong action verbs in each sentence.

❸ Understand and write compound sentences.

Compound Sentences

The compound sentence is one of the most frequently used types of sentences in the English language. An effective **compound sentence** *connects two separate independent clauses or complete sentences that contain ideas of equal importance.*

There are *three* ways you can correctly join two independent clauses, which is how you create a compound sentence. Here is the basic formula: independent clause + independent clause = compound sentence.

Three Ways to Connect Two Independent Clauses

1. Independent Clause, [coordinating conjunction] Independent Clause   The most common way to connect two independent clauses is by using one of the coordinating conjunctions, sometimes remembered by using the acronym **fanboys** (*for, and, nor, but, or, yet, so*), **and a comma**. Here are a couple of sets of sentences that could easily be combined by using one of the "fanboys" with a comma between the complete sentences.

- Descriptive writing often relies on visual images.
- Good writers evoke the other four senses as well.

  Descriptive writing often relies on visual images**, *but*** good writers evoke the other four senses as well.

- Strong action verbs make descriptive writing more vivid.
- Writers should avoid overusing weak "to be" verbs like *is* and *was*.

  Strong action verbs make descriptive writing more vivid**, *so*** writers should avoid overusing weak "to be" verbs like *is* and *was*.

PUNCTUATION TIP

Avoid Misusing Commas with Coordinating Conjunctions

Think of how often you use coordinating conjunctions when you write. If you put a comma before every one of them, you will have a lot of unnecessary commas. Before putting a comma in front of one of the "fanboys," be sure the coordinating conjunction connects two independent clauses (remember—subject, verb, complete thought).

Notice how the following sentences contain coordinating conjunctions, but since they do not link independent clauses, there are no commas.

Strong descriptive **and** observational writing uses the senses.

Active learners keep track of their grades **and** think of ways to improve.

---

2. Independent Clause; [adverbial conjunction], Independent Clause Another way to join two sentences in a compound construction is to use another type of connecting word: an **adverbial conjunction**. These special conjunctions used to connect equally important ideas are usually more formal sounding than the "fanboys," and there are more of them. Adverbial conjunctions also require more complex punctuation. As you can see in the following examples, when an adverbial conjunction connects two sentences, you must put a semicolon before the conjunction and a comma after it.

- The yellow ribbons of the dandelion look like petals.
- Each is actually an individual flower.

  The yellow ribbons of the dandelion look like petals*; **however***, each is actually an individual flower.

- "Phib freaks" follow winding trails into deep forests.
- They search for streams and logs inhabited by frogs and amphibians.

  "Phib freaks" follow winding trails into deep forests*; **then***, they search for streams and logs inhabited by frogs and amphibians.

PUNCTUATION TIP   Avoid Comma Splices and Run-ons

If you use an adverbial conjunction to connect independent clauses and you put only a comma before it or you put no punctuation at all, you have a serious mistake: a comma splice or a run-on. The following sentences illustrate these errors:

CS	**Mark Twain** <u>gained</u> knowledge of the river, however, **he** <u>lost</u> his appreciation of its beauty.
CORRECT	**Mark Twain** <u>gained</u> knowledge of the river**; however, he** <u>lost</u> his appreciation of its beauty.
RO	Descriptive **writing** <u>needs</u> to make the subject "real" for the readers **therefore** a **writer** *should use* concrete details.
CORRECT	Descriptive **writing** <u>needs</u> to make the subject "real" for the readers**; therefore,** a **writer** <u>should use</u> concrete details.

---

3. Independent Clause; Independent Clause If you want to stress a particularly close connection between the ideas in two sentences, you may connect them with only a semicolon. Since this construction is used for emphasis, you should use it very sparingly in your writing. The following examples illustrate this method.

- The dancing men smile constantly.
- The women are serious.

  The dancing men smile constantly; the women are serious.

- Mark Twain gained knowledge of the river's intricacies.
- He lost a full appreciation of its beauty.

  Mark Twain gained knowledge of the river's intricacies; he lost a full appreciation of its beauty.

*Note: You do not capitalize the word after the semicolon unless it is a word that is always capitalized like a name or the pronoun *I*.

EXERCISE 14.12   Combine Sentences to Create a Compound Sentence

Directions: Combine each of the following sets of sentences to create a single compound sentence. You may reverse the order of the independent clauses, but you should use the type of connector indicated along with the proper punctuation. Be sure the connector you choose indicates a clear relationship between the ideas in the two clauses.

1. Writers should use concrete details in descriptive writing.

   Concrete details can make the subject "real" for readers. (semicolon)

2. "Grammar freaks" seem obsessed with correcting every sentence error.

   They need to remember the importance of a paper's content as well. (adverbial conjunction)

3. The gazebo in my backyard provides a quiet sanctuary.

   I retreat there to gather my thoughts after a long day. (adverbial conjunction)

4. Bats may have a bad reputation thanks to rabies scares and horror movies.

   Without its bat population, Austin, Texas would be overrun with mosquitoes. (coordinating conjunction)

5. I used to pull all the dandelions out of my yard.

   After reading "Dandelion: A Virtuous Weed," I have a new respect for this plant. (coordinating conjunction)

6. For the whirling dervishes, dancing becomes a kind of prayer.

   It sends them into a trancelike state. (semicolon)

Complex Sentences

Sometimes writers will try to emphasize ideas by bolding text, using all capital letters, or adding lots of exclamation points. The complex sentence is a particularly important construction because it allows writers to emphasize and de-emphasize ideas without resorting to such distracting tactics.

Subordination

When you use a highlighter to remind yourself of key points in a page of text, do you mark every single word on the page? Does a speaker who wants to emphasize a key point raise his voice throughout the entire speech? Using all simple and compound sentences is the written equivalent of highlighting the whole page, or shouting at readers.

Look at the following sentence that emphasizes both points as being equally important:

I walked into my kitchen, and I saw Bigfoot raiding my refrigerator.

Is walking into the kitchen—something everyone does all the time—as significant as seeing Bigfoot raiding the refrigerator? Of course not!

Since every detail in a piece of writing is not equally important, effective writers place relevant but less important ideas in phrases and dependent clauses. A sentence that contains an independent clause and one or more dependent clauses is called a **complex sentence**. A complex sentence shows that a writer has prioritized ideas. For example, here is a revision of the Bigfoot sentence:

┌────── Dependent Clause──────┐ ┌────── Independent Clause──────┐
When I walked into my kitchen, I saw Bigfoot raiding my refrigerator.

The less significant point about walking into the kitchen is de-emphasized as a dependent clause, and the more important point of seeing Bigfoot is emphasized as an independent clause.

Notice that both dependent and independent clauses have subjects and verbs. The dependent clause cannot stand alone as a sentence because it lacks a complete thought. When a **subordinating conjunction**—like *when*—is placed in front of an independent clause, it *subordinates* or makes the clause dependent.

Following are some of the words and phrases that can create dependent clauses in complex sentences. They are arranged by purpose:

Subordinating Conjunctions	
Comparison	as, as if, just as
Condition	as long as, if, in case, provided that, unless
Concession	although, even though, if, though, while
Contingency	if, once
Contrast	whereas, while
Reason	as long as, because, since
Result	so, so that
Time	after, as, as long as, as soon as, before, now that, till, until, when, whenever

Dependent Clauses

While they may not contain the *most* important information in a sentence, dependent clauses allow the writer to include relevant details and examples that add clarity and interest to the ideas expressed in the independent clause. Writers can include dependent clauses in a variety of ways.

1. **Dependent clauses can begin sentences.**

   Although information may appear in a book, there is no guarantee it will be accurate.

2. **Dependent clauses can also come at the end of sentences.**

   We could tear down a very nice wall *if all we see are the two bad bricks.*

3. **Dependent clauses can also come in the middle of independent clauses**. Often these are a particular type of dependent clause called a relative clause. **Relative clauses**—which begin with a relative pronoun like *who, whom, which,* or *that*—typically add information to a noun in a sentence. Like all dependent clauses, relative clauses cannot stand alone as a complete sentence.

   • Wright Thompson, *who loves the southern traditions of Oxford,* gets fired up for football season.

   • Oxford, Mississippi, *which is the home of the University of Mississippi,* gets fired up for football every fall.

> **PUNCTUATION TIP**   **Use Commas Correctly with Dependent Clauses**
>
> 1. If a dependent clause begins a sentence, you need to use a comma to set it off from the independent clause unless the initial clause is very short (say four words or less).
>
>   **EXAMPLE**   Because I usually do not catch mistakes just by reading through the paper silently, I make sure to read my papers out loud to catch grammatical mistakes and misspellings.
>
> 2. In contrast, if a dependent clause ends a sentence, you usually do not have to use a comma.
>
>   **EXAMPLE**   I make sure to read my papers out loud to catch grammatical mistakes and misspellings because I usually do not catch mistakes just by reading through the paper silently.
>
> 3. Dependent clauses that interrupt the independent clause are typically set off with commas.
>
>   **EXAMPLE**   Reflective **writing, which** is useful in both academic and workplace settings, helps writers discover their own ideas.

EXERCISE 14.13 Combine Dependent and Independent Clauses to Create Complex Sentences

Directions: Combine each of the following sets of sentences into one sentence. Put the less important information in a dependent clause and the key information in an independent clause. Vary your constructions by putting the dependent clause at the beginning, in the middle, and at the end of the sentences you create.

In the following examples, the independent clause is highlighted in tan. Notice the word used to subordinate the clause.

EXAMPLE   Sherman Alexie felt a critic was wrong about the influence of young adult literature.

Sherman Alexie wrote an article that drew from his personal experience to show how these books are important to young people.

COMPLEX SENTENCES   • **Sherman Alexie** wrote an article that drew from his personal experience to show how books are important to young people **because** he felt a critic was wrong about the influence of young adult literature.

- *Because* **Sherman Alexie** felt a critic was wrong about the influence of young adult literature, **he** wrote an article that drew from his personal experience to show how these books are important to young people.
- **Sherman Alexie**, **who** felt a critic was wrong about the influence of young adult literature, wrote an article that drew from personal experience to show how these books are important to young people.

1. You write for readers.

    You must capture and hold their attention.

2. No one has ever died from eating traditionally cured hams.

    The USDA considers traditionally cured hams dangerous.

3. The monk built a nearly perfect wall.

    The monk noticed only two bricks.

    The two bricks were not aligned.

4. Malcolm X was in prison.

    He expanded his vocabulary and reading comprehension.

    The ability to read made him feel free.

5. I am now thinking about the books I read when I was younger.

    I read "Why the Best Kids Books Are Written in Blood."

Compound-Complex Sentences

❺ Understand and write compound-complex sentences.

Compound sentences contain two or more independent clauses, and complex sentences contain at least one dependent and one independent clause. As its name indicates, the compound-complex sentence combines both sentence structures.

Combining Clauses

A **compound-complex sentence** has at least two key ideas that are in at least two independent clauses and then at least one less important idea that is in a dependent clause. The sentences may contain additional phrases and descriptive words as well.

EXAMPLE
┌──────────────── Dependent clause ────────────────┐ ┌Independent clause
If **you** relate inaccurate information in your paper, your **readers** will
┌──────────────────────┐ ┌── Independent clause ──┐
become skeptical, and **they** will not trust you.

EXAMPLE
┌──────────── Independent clause ────────────┐ ┌──── Dependent clause ────
A **writer** must be willing to revise a paper when **it** does not connect
┌──────────────┐ ┌──────────── Independent clause ────────────┐
to the readers, for the best **writing** keeps readers interested.

EXAMPLE
┌──────────── Independent clause ────────────
Writers need to think about what information readers might
┌── Independent clause ──┐┌─ Dependent clause ──
already know, and **they** must consider what will be new and sur-

prising information to the audience because strong informative

writing sparks interest in readers.

Remember, all clauses have subjects and verbs. However, when a clause begins with a subordinating word, it no longer expresses a complete thought. The following words make clauses dependent:

Subordinating Words

after	although	as, as if	as long as	as though	because
before	even though	if, even if	in order that	rather than	since
so that	that	though	unless	until	when
whenever	where	wherever	whether	which	while
who					

EXERCISE 14.14   Combine Sentences into a Compound-Complex Sentence

Directions: Combine each of the following sets of sentences into one compound-complex sentence. Put the less important information in a dependent clause and the key information in at least two independent clauses. Underline the dependent clause once and place a bracket over the independent clauses.

EXAMPLE
An informative paper often begins with familiar information.

The writer moves on to new information.

The new information may surprise or engage the readers.

COMPOUND-
COMPLEX
SENTENCE
┌──────────────── Independent clause ────────────────
An informative **paper** often begins with familiar information, and then the
┌──── Independent clause ────┐ ┌──── Dependent clause ────┐
writer moves on to new information **that** may surprise or engage the readers.

EXAMPLE   Organization is crucial in all writing.

Writers must consider what examples and details are the most important ones.

They have to play with the organization of the paragraphs as they revise.

COMPOUND-
COMPLEX
SENTENCE

        — Dependent clause ——————— ┌Independent clause ——
Because **organization** is crucial in all writing, **writers** must consider
       — Independent clause ———————— ┌—Independent clause ——
the most important examples and details, and **they** have to play with
       ————————— ┌—Dependent clause ┐
organization as **they** revise.

1. Young birds remain in a nest.

   Young nursing bats cling to their mother.

   The mother is in flight.

2. There is romance in Indian movies.

   The lovers will not kiss.

   Such an act would offend Indian audiences.

3. Colonial Americans used apples for cider.

   Even children drank this alcoholic beverage.

   At the time it was more sanitary than water.

4. Customers stand patiently in long lines.

   Customers tolerate Yeganeh's strict policies.

   Yeganeh's soup is the best.

5. Libraries are democratic.

   Libraries provide all citizens equal access to information.

   Libraries bring diverse groups of people together in a noncommercial public space.

❻ Write sentences that contain well-placed modifiers.

Using Effective Modifiers

To modify something means to change, revise, or transform it. A builder, for example, may modify the plans for a home—perhaps adding another bath or enlarging the garage—to suit the needs of the buyer. Writers use modifiers to transform basic sentence structures.

Modifiers are words, phrases, and clauses that add details to other words in a sentence. Modifiers may also qualify or limit the meaning of other words. Well-chosen and well-placed modifiers lend interest and variety to basic sentences.

Beginning Modifiers

Varying the ways you begin sentences can make your sentences flow and sound smoother. The following examples illustrate some ways you can use modifiers to begin sentences:

DEPENDENT CLAUSE	*As they learn to joke*, women are often taken more seriously by men.
PREPOSITIONAL PHRASE	*To establish rapport with colleagues*, women will initiate "troubles talk."
	By understanding conversation rituals, men and women may begin to share a common language in the workplace.
-ed WORD	*Frustrated by Lester's lack of praise*, two women were ready to quit the company.
-ing WORD	*Assuming her apology is the first step in a two-part ritual*, a woman may find herself instead taking the entire blame for a situation.
-ly WORD	*Reluctantly*, the female doctor attacked her colleague's position.

PUNCTUATION TIP   Use Commas to Set Off Introductory Elements

Remember to use a comma to set off a dependent clause, a long phrase, introductory words or transitions when they begin a sentence.

Notice the comma comes before the subject of the independent clause in each of the above sample sentences.

EXERCISE 14.15   Combine Sentences Using Beginning Modifiers

Directions: Combine each of the following sets of sentences into one sentence by using the suggested opener. Be sure to use a comma to set off the opener from the rest of the sentence.

1. People can be very self-absorbed. They can be so self-absorbed they don't notice the needs of people around them. They are rude. (dependent clause)

2. The female engineer wanted to be accepted and taken seriously by the men in her company. She learned to argue effectively. (prepositional phrase)

3. The mother felt ashamed. She felt humiliated. She went to the government agency to get help for her children. (*-ed* word)

4. The principal laughed out loud at the teacher's joke. He found her playful insult funny. (*-ing* word)

5. Physical activity can improve physical health. I was surprised to learn physical activity can also help kids do well in school. (*-ly* word)

GRAMMAR TIP   Avoid Dangling Modifiers

When you begin a sentence with a modifier, make sure the word it modifies immediately follows. When the word following the modifier is missing or is not a word logically described, the modifier is said to be "dangling."

DANGLING	After waiting for two months, **the tennis shoes went on sale, and Andy could afford to buy them.**
CORRECT	After Andy waited for two months, the tennis shoes went on sale, and he could afford to **buy them.**
	Shoes do not wait; Andy did.
DANGLING	Believing they are the center of the universe, **rude behavior** is all around us.
CORRECT	Believing they are the center of the universe, **rude people** are all around us.
	"Behavior" doesn't believe it is the center of the universe; "rude people" do.

Middle Modifiers

Modifying phrases and clauses can also come in the middle of a sentence.

People **who have strong analytical skills** will use those skills in all areas of their lives.

Exercise, **which has well-known physical benefits**, may have mental benefits as well.

The mother, **thinking of her children**, seeks financial help.

The baby, **hungry and missing her mother**, cried in the corner.

An essay **that has a variety of sentence structures** will appeal to readers.

PUNCTUATION TIP

Do Not Put Commas Around "Restrictive" Modifiers that Present Essential Information about the Word They Modify

In the following sentence the modifier presents optional or nonrestrictive information about author Deborah Tannen, so it is properly set off with commas.

> Deborah Tannen, *who has studied the rituals of conversation*, believes women are at a disadvantage in the workplace.

In the following sentence the modifier restricts the subject to a particular kind of people, so it is not set off with commas.

> People *who simply stop walking in a crowded airport terminal* frustrate hurried travelers.

EXERCISE 14.16   Combine Sentences with a Middle Modifier

Directions: Eliminate unnecessary wordiness by combining each of the following sets of sentences into one sentence. Your final sentence should contain at least one modifier in the middle. Remember to use commas correctly.

1. Physical fitness programs benefit children physically.

   Physical fitness programs benefit children mentally.

   Physical fitness programs should be a priority in schools.

2. Children living in extreme poverty have no school supplies.

   Children living in extreme poverty are often sick.

   Children living in extreme poverty do not do well in school.

3. Some people believe America is like ancient Rome.

   Some people believe America has reached its peak and is now going downhill.

4. Lester thought he showed women confidence by leaving them alone.

   Lester was surprised the women were unhappy.

   These were the women who reported to him.

5. Some writers are reader focused.

   These writers connect with their readers.

   These writers are successful critical thinkers.

Ending Modifiers

Modifiers may also conclude a sentence.

- Reducing environmental stress creates a more pleasant work environment, which can improve employees' performance.
- Caryn was unable to concentrate on her work, distracted by all the background noise around her.
- Caryn spoke about her discomfort to her manager, who arranged for her to move to a quieter workspace.
- Poor air quality is also an environmental stressor, triggering headaches and an inability to concentrate.
- Employees can become fatigued if they work in lighting that is insufficient or too bright.

EXERCISE 14.17   Combine Sentences with an Ending Modifier

Directions: Eliminate unnecessary wordiness by combining each of the following sets of sentences into one sentence. Your final sentence should contain a modifier at the end. Remember, do not put a comma before a restrictive modifier.

1. Nora always arrives to work fifteen minutes early.

   She avoids the stress of rushing to work.

2. Blake had surgery on his wrist.

   Blake's wrist was injured by the repetitious motion of his job.

3. Audrey is a successful manager.

   Audrey delegates responsibility.

   Audrey is willing to compromise.

4. Adric works in a factory.

   The factory is clean.

   The factory is well-ventilated.

5. Ian tries to prevent spreading germs in the workplace.

   Ian washes his hands regularly.

   Ian keeps hand sanitizer on his desk.

❼ Write sentences containing appropriate appositives and parallel constructions.

Appositives and Parallel Constructions

By using a variety of sentence constructions, you can keep your reader more interested and engaged as you convey your ideas more clearly and concisely. Appositives, for example, can reduce unnecessary words while parallel constructions can add memorable rhythm to related points.

Appositives

Each of the following sentences contains an example of what it defines: an **appositive**.

- *Usually a phrase that modifies or clarifies something else,* an **appositive** can make your writing more concise and stylistic.
- An **appositive,** *a phrase that modifies or clarifies something else,* can make your writing more concise and stylistic.
- To make your writing more concise and stylistic, use **appositives,** *phrases that modify or clarify something else.*

Writers often use appositives so they can present information in a concise way without having to write two sentences. For example, read the following sets of sentences:

- Mary is a firefighter from Ladder 12. Mary has two days off.
- The Delta Blues is listened to around the world. That music was born in Mississippi.

You might notice that the sentences are a little wordy, but a bigger concern has to do with emphasis.

Remember, writers use sentence construction to emphasize key ideas. The information that appears in independent clauses is usually the information writers want to emphasize the most. In these sets of sentences, all of the information is given equal emphasis because it is all presented in independent clauses—in separate complete sentences.

The Middle Appositive

Now look at how a writer can use middle appositives to make material more concise and to give more emphasis to key ideas. The **independent clause** contains the most important information. The information in the *appositive* is helpful and descriptive but not as crucial as the other information in the sentence:

- **Mary,** *the firefighter from Ladder 12,* **has two days off**.
- **The Delta Blues,** *music born in Mississippi,* **is listened to around the world**.

The **middle appositive**, a phrase surrounded by commas that modifies or clarifies something, is the most common one in the English language. However, appositives may also begin or end sentences.

The End Appositive

Like its name indicates, the *end appositive* is at the end of the sentence, such as in these examples:

- For our anniversary we went to **Edisto Island,** *a beautiful coastal area in South Carolina.*
- The best sandwich on the menu is the **Meat Monster,** *a mile-high stack of ham, turkey, and roast beef.*

As you can see, the end appositives are set off with a single comma. End appositives modify—or give additional information about the nouns they follow: **Edisto Island** and **Meat Monster.**

The Beginning Appositive

The most advanced appositive is the *beginning appositive,* and writers should use it sparingly even though it can be stylistically sophisticated. This sentence construction is also called a periodic sentence. Here are two examples:

- *A stern man with no tolerance for incompetence,* **my boss** makes the workplace very uncomfortable.
- *Trust, deep communication, good listening skills, mutual attraction,* **these** are all what we want in our partners.

Beginning appositives are also set off with commas and modify the noun or pronoun directly after them: **my boss** and **these.**

EXERCISE 14.18   Combining Sentences Using Appositives

Directions: Combine each of the following pairs of sentences into one sentence containing an appositive in the indicated position.

USE A MIDDLE APPOSITIVE

1. The pot roast tasted as bad as it looked. It was a fatty sludge with overcooked potatoes and carrots.

2. Lee Zimmerman wrote a very favorable review of Amanda Shires's album. He is a critic for *Blurt Online*.

3. Jake broke up with Megyn because he was frustrated. Megyn cheated on him.

USE AN END APPOSITIVE

4. People use technology to keep each other at a controllable distance. Sherry Turkle calls this a "Goldilocks effect."

5. Amanda Shires is a singer and a well-known fiddle player. The critic from *Blurt Online* describes the highlights and strengths of *Carrying Lightning* by Amanda Shires.

6. The play produced by the theatre department received a favorable review from Kwon Hutchins. He is a film critic for the campus newspaper.

USE A BEGINNING APPOSITIVE

7. Social networking should be a limited part of college students' lives. It can be a time-consuming, addicting, and potentially destructive pastime.

8. Poultry byproducts are chicken heads, feet, and intestines. Poultry byproducts are a key ingredient in some dog foods.

9. Criteria are the standards by which something is judged. Criteria should be determined before you begin to write an evaluation essay.

Parallel Constructions

If you think back to math class, you probably learned that parallel lines "never meet" and that they are lined up perfectly with each other. **Parallel constructions** are also important to writing. In writing, having a parallel construction means you have lined up the items in a pair or in a series. When your prose aligns, you avoid creating confusion or awkwardness for your reader.

For example, take a look at the basic sentences below and notice how all parts of a pair or a series line up using the same grammatical forms:

A PARALLEL SERIES OF VERBS

- When I go on vacation, I **relax, sightsee,** and **eat** good food. (Present Tense)
- When I went on vacation, I **relaxed, saw** the sights, and **ate** good food. (Past Tense)

A PARALLEL SERIES OF INFINITIVE PHRASES
When I go on vacation, I like **to relax, to sightsee,** and **to eat** good food.

A PARALLEL SERIES OF PARTICIPLES
When I go on vacation, I like **relaxing, sightseeing,** and **eating** good food.

A PARALLEL SERIES OF INDEPENDENT CLAUSES
The critic disliked the movie because **the plot moved too slowly, the characters lacked charisma,** and **the ending was predictable.**

A PARALLEL SERIES OF NOUN PHRASES
The website has **credible sources, accurate information,** and **easy navigation.**

A PARALLEL SERIES OF ADJECTIVES
The dog food was **cheese-colored, fat-drenched,** and **stinky.**

A PARALLEL PAIR OF DEPENDENT CLAUSES
I enjoy browsing social networking sites **after I have finished schoolwork** and **when I have extra free time.**

A PARALLEL PAIR OF INDEPENDENT CLAUSES
I prefer Facebook, and **my sister prefers Twitter.**

All of these sentences work effectively because the items in the series are parallel—they are all the same form. However, when a writer mixes up the forms, awkward sentences result. Read these examples out loud and notice how they do not sound as smooth as the previous ones:

- When I go on vacation, I like **to relax, sightseeing,** and **ate good food.**
- The critic disliked the movie because **the plot moved too slowly, had a predictable ending,** and **characters were lacking in charisma.**
- The website has **credible sources, accurate information,** and **I could navigate it easily.**
- The dog food was **cheese-colored, fat-drenched,** and **smelled stinky.**
- I enjoy browsing social networking sites **after I have finished schoolwork, and I use it during extra free time.**
- **I prefer Facebook,** and **Twitter is my sister's preference.**

All pairs and series in writing should be balanced and aligned—that is, they should have the same grammatical construction.

EXERCISE 14.19   Write Parallel Sentences

Directions: Use parallel constructions to write a sentence for each of the following prompts.

EXAMPLE: Write a sentence that names three preparations you make before sitting down to do homework.

Before beginning my homework, I **remove myself from distractions, gather all my materials,** and **find a comfortable place to work.**

1. Write a sentence that names three qualities you admire about a person.

2. Write a sentence that names three criteria a computer must have before you will consider purchasing it.

3. Write a sentence that describes three features of a place where you would like to go on vacation.

4. Write a bulleted list that uses sentences to describe ideal co-workers.

5. Write a bulleted list that uses phrases to describe ideal co-workers.

❽ Eliminate wordy constructions to make sentences concise.

Concision—Eliminating Wordiness

Writing cluttered with more words than necessary can confuse and frustrate readers. You can make your writing concise by cutting the "clutter"—words that take up space without contributing to the message in your writing.

For some examples of clutter, here are some wordy sentences with the number of words indicated after each sentence followed by examples showing them after being cut for fluff and repetition.

Wordy Constructions	Revisions	Words Cut
In today's society, people tend to multitask all the time at work and at home. (**15 words**)	Today people multitask at work and home. (**7 words**)	-8 words
The students were greeted by the teacher who had a smile on her face. (**13 words**)	The smiling teacher greeted the students. (**6 words**)	-7 words
This research article includes a discussion of how bottled water is not cleaner and is damaging to the environment and nature. (**21 words**)	This research article discusses how bottled water is not cleaner and damages the environment. (**14 words**)	-7 words

As you can see, all of the sentences had fewer words while presenting the same information more clearly.

Strategies for Concision

The following methods provide some easy tactics to make your writing healthier by eliminating clutter.

1. Eliminate Redundant Words

Some commonly paired words suggest each other, so one of the words can be eliminated without changing meaning. Think, for example, of "free gift." A gift is not something you would pay for, so, of course, it has to be free.

EXAMPLES: The student wrote a ~~brief~~ summary of the article.

We made ~~advance~~ reservations at our favorite restaurant.

I want to ~~entirely~~ eliminate redundancy in my writing.

EXERCISE 14.20   Eliminate Redundant Words

Directions: Revise each of the following sentences by eliminating any redundant paired constructions.

1. After he completely finished his writing assignment, Travon made future plans to see a movie with his friends.

2. Finding five dollars in my coat pocket was an unexpected surprise.

3. The Glee Club members were totally unanimous in their decision to cooperate together with the Business Club to gather donations for the local food pantry.

4. Luis made an inadvertent error on his past history test when he could not recall the true fact that Abraham Lincoln was shot in Ford's Theatre on April 14, 1865.

5. You must understand the basic fundamentals of technology if you hope to grasp the concepts behind recent new innovations.

2. Eliminate Filler Phrases

Writers often include filler phrases that can easily be expressed with one word, thinking they make their writing sound more sophisticated, but most readers recognize them as merely clutter.

Notice how the following statements can be made more concise by replacing filler phrases with a single word.

EXAMPLE	A large proportion of students wait until the night before an exam to begin studying.
REVISION	Many students wait until the night before an exam to begin studying.
EXAMPLE	The campus Academic Center would like to extend an invitation to students for the purpose of attending a study skills workshop.
REVISION	The campus Academic Center invites students to attend a study skills workshop.
EXAMPLE	There is a high probability that the professor will include that question on the midterm exam.
REVISION	The professor will probably include that question on the midterm exam.

Other filler phrases can be eliminated without any other changes to a sentence, as you can see in the following sentences:

EXAMPLE	The point I am trying to make is that being a good multi-tasker has made me more successful at my job.
REVISION	Being a good multi-tasker has made me more successful at my job.
EXAMPLE	As anyone can plainly see, I am actually doing quite well in my classes.
REVISION	I am doing quite well in my classes.
EXAMPLE	I think that you should really make an effort to eliminate filler words.
REVISION	You should make an effort to eliminate filler words.

EXERCISE 14.21   Eliminate Filler Phrases

Directions: Find a single word that can replace each of the following phrases.

EXAMPLE	for the purpose of	<u>so</u>

wordy phrase	one-word replacement
at this point in time	_____
due to the fact that	_____
in the vicinity of	_____
in the near future	_____
in a situation in which	_____
have a tendency to	_____

EXERCISE 14.22   Eliminate Filler Phrases

Directions: Revise each of the following sentences by eliminating filler phrases.

1. In my opinion, some gun laws overlook the rights of hunters.

2. Relying on stereotypes, as a matter of fact, can diminish our ability to think independently.

3. I think, for the most part, that readers often respond more to appeals to their emotions than appeals to their logic.

4. I feel my parents, for the most part, have provided some good reasons why texting and driving is a bad idea.

5. It seems to me that for all intents and purposes, political advertisements rely on emotional appeals to make their points.

3. Avoid Expletive Constructions

Expletive constructions are sentences that begin with *There is, There are,* and *It is.* Besides being unnecessarily wordy, these constructions use weak linking verbs (see page 417 for more on linking verbs). Eliminating expletives during the revision stage of writing will strengthen your style.

EXAMPLE	There are several ways you can eliminate wordiness in your writing.
REVISION	You can eliminate wordiness in your writing in several ways.
EXAMPLE	It is the policy of this course that students attend class regularly.
REVISION	Course policy requires that students attend class regularly.

EXERCISE 14.23   Avoid Expletive Constructions

Directions: Revise each of the following sentences to eliminate the expletive.

1. It is apparent that my state representative supports restrictions on gun ownership.

2. There are several steps you can take to avoid stereotypical thinking.

3. There is evidence that suggests we experience true pleasure when focused on one thing.

4. There are steps society must take to prevent criminal acts.

5. It is education that will keep young people from turning to lives of crime.

4. Avoid Passive Constructions

In **passive sentence constructions**, the subject of the sentence does not perform the action but instead is acted upon. In less wordy active constructions, the subject performs the action. Notice, too, the following revisions eliminate unnecessary linking verbs.

EXAMPLE	The car's **battery** was replaced by the mechanic.
REVISION	The **mechanic** replaced the car's battery.
EXAMPLE	The winning **essay** was written by a first-year composition student.
REVISION	A first-year composition **student** wrote the winning essay.
EXAMPLE	Canned **goods** were collected by the students for the campus food drive.
REVISION	The **students** collected canned goods for the campus food drive.

EXERCISE 14.24   Avoid Passive Constructions

Directions: Revise each of the following sentences to make the passive construction active.

1. The house's roof was lifted off by the high winds.

2. The best papers are written by students willing to revise their work.

3. The accident victim was taken by ambulance to the hospital.

4. The scandal was covered by every tabloid in the country.

5. The race was won by the horse considered a long-shot by most gamblers.

5. Replace *is, are, was, were,* + an *-ing* Word with a Simple Present or Past Tense Verb

Strong and clear verbs will make your prose sound more polished and confident. You do not want to use wordy verb constructions. See how the revisions in the following examples strengthen the sentences.

EXAMPLE	**Deven** is hoping to do better on his next test.
REVISION	**Deven** hopes to do better on his next test.
EXAMPLE	Students **who** were missing too many classes had lower grades than those **who** were attending classes regularly.
REVISION	Students **who** missed too many classes had lower grades than those **who** attended class regularly.

EXAMPLE   **We** are hoping to spend spring break somewhere warm and relaxing.

REVISION   **We** hope to spend spring break somewhere warm and relaxing.

EXERCISE 14.25   Use the Simple Present or Past Tense

Directions: Replace *is, are, was, were,* + an *-ing* word with a simple present or past tense verb. Revise each of the following sentences to avoid wordy verb constructions.

1. Young urban terrorists are committing most of the nation's random crimes.

2. Ben was scanning his email while he was talking on the phone.

3. Reading Is Fundamental (RIF) is depending upon volunteers to distribute books throughout the community.

4. TV commercials are screaming for our attention.

5. Over spring break, the students were volunteering to build houses with Habitat for Humanity.

6. Combine Closely Related Short Sentences

Another way to make your writing more concise is to combine the key ideas of two sentences into one sentence that eliminates repeated words as the following example illustrates.

EXAMPLE   We can speed up the process of avoiding stereotypes. One way we can speed up the process of avoiding stereotypes is by questioning generalizations about people.

REVISION   We can speed up the process of avoiding stereotypes by questioning generalizations about people.

You can also use colon constructions to avoid wordy combinations of sentences.

EXAMPLE   I look for several features in a car. I consider its economy, its comfort, and its safety.

REVISION   I look for several features in a car: economy, comfort, and safety.

EXERCISE 14.26   Combine Closely Related Short Sentences

Directions: Combine the following pairs of short sentences to make them less wordy.

1. Our attention is valuable. The proof is all the money spent on advertising.

2. We can avoid stereotyping. We can avoid stereotyping by questioning generalizations about people.

3. Former inmate Wilbert Rideau concedes that there are some people who belong in prison for life. These people who belong in prison for life include serial killers, serial rapists, and professional hit men.

4. Writers can use several appeals in a persuasive essay. One appeal is *ethos*. Another is *logos*. The last is *pathos*.

5. Using personal experience as support in a persuasive essay may not be a good idea. It may not be a good idea if the instructor wants evidence from articles in the field, research studies, and statistical analysis.

EXERCISE 14.27   Revise Wordiness in Your Own Writing.

Directions: Find examples of wordy sentences from some of your early writing. Revise each sentence using some of the techniques you have practiced in this section.

15

Handbook for Correcting Sentence Errors

Learning Objectives

In this chapter, you will learn how to . . .

1. Identify and correct fragments, run-ons, and comma splices.

2. Identify and correct shifts in person and in verbs.

3. Identify and correct pronoun case, pronoun reference, and agreement errors.

4. Identify and correct apostrophe, comma, quotation marks, semicolon, and colon errors.

5. Identify and correct misplaced and dangling modifiers and non-parallel constructions.

6. Identify and correct abbreviation, capitalization, number, and title errors.

7. Understand usage and avoid the spell check trap.

MyWritingLab All of the exercises and activities in this chapter can be completed in MyWritingLab.

Introduction

This handbook offers illustrations of and corrections for some of the most common kinds of sentence errors in writing. Often, seeing what the error is will be enough to help you find and fix the mistake in your own writing.

If you find that you need additional explanation and practice, you can go to MyWritingLab. There you will find short video explanations and a variety of practice exercises to help you understand how to find and fix the errors in your writing.

Keep in mind, though, that the best way to improve your sentence skills is to find and fix *your* own errors in *your* writing. You may find the editing strategies suggested in Chapter 3 helpful during those final stages of the writing process when you focus on correcting errors. You may also want to use the correction symbols in the Quick Reference Editing Guide as you edit and proofread your writing.

Quick Reference Editing Guide

Correction Symbol	Error	Page	Correction Symbol	Error	Page
Abbrev	abbreviation error	499	Number	number	503
Apos	apostrophe	483	//	parallelism	497
Cap	capitalization	500	PA Agr	pronoun/antecedent agreement	477
Case	pronoun case	471			
:	colon	494	Quote	quotation marks/ dialogue	490
C1	main clause comma	487			
C2	introductory comma	487	Ref	pronoun reference	474
C3	interrupter comma	488	RO	run-on	457
C4	series comma	488	;	semicolon	493
C5	other commas	488	Shift	shift in point of view	462
CS	comma splice	457	SV Agr	subject-verb agreement	479
Frag	fragment	454	Tense	verb tense	464
M	modifier misplaced/ dangling	496	Title	title error ("" or ___)	506
			Usage	usage	508

❶ Identify and correct fragments, run-ons, and comma splices.

A. Catch the Big Three: Fragments, Run-Ons, and Comma Splices

Many writing teachers consider fragments, run-ons, and comma splices to be among the most serious sentence errors. These errors often indicate that a writer does not fully understand sentence boundaries. Generally, you should make finding and fixing these mistakes your first priority during editing.

A.1 Fragment (Frag)

In order to be a complete sentence—an **independent clause**—a group of words must have a subject and a verb and must express a complete thought. A "sentence" that is missing any of these parts is not really a sentence but instead is a **fragment**—only part of a sentence. The following examples illustrate how to correct some typical kinds of fragments.

Dependent Clause Fragment

Because dependent clauses have subjects and verbs, you may mistake them for complete sentences. However, a **dependent clause** does not express a complete thought, so it cannot stand alone as a sentence. You can correct a dependent clause fragment by adding an independent clause to it.

Incorrect	Correct
When I am driving and my cell phone rings.	When I am driving and my cell phone rings, *I will not take the call.*
Until I can safely stop the car.	*When driving, I will not accept a call on my cell phone* until I can safely stop the car.

Relative Clause Fragment

A relative clause is another type of dependent clause. **Relative clauses** begin with words like *who, whom, whose, that, which, when,* and *where.* Since a relative clause typically *modifies* or describes another word or group of words, you can usually correct this kind of fragment by adding the clause to the sentence containing the word or words the relative clause modifies.

Incorrect	Correct
My mom works out at the gym and attends yoga classes. **Which is why she is still so spry at seventy-five years of age.**	My mom works out at the gym and attends yoga classes, which is why she is still so spry at seventy-five years of age.
I read an article about Zisha Breitbart. **Who may have inspired the comic book hero Superman.**	I read an article about Zisha Breitbart, who may have inspired the comic book hero Superman.

-ing Fragment

An *-ing* verb without a helper verb—like *is, has been, was, had been*—functions as a participle, not as a verb. A participle introduces a phrase that describes a word or group of words. One way to correct an *-ing* fragment is by adding a helping verb to the participle, or, when appropriate, by making the participle a past tense verb. (See page 417 for a list of helping verbs.) You can also leave the participle in the sentence and add a new verb and complete the thought.

Incorrect	Correct
Fatima singing to herself as she worked in the garden.	Fatima **was singing** to herself as she worked in the garden.
	Fatima **sang** to herself as she worked in the garden.
	Fatima, singing to herself as she worked in the garden, **put the cares of the past week behind her.**
The squirrel scurrying across the baseball field.	The squirrel **is scurrying** across the baseball field.
	The squirrel **scurried** across the baseball field.
	The squirrel, scurrying across the baseball field, **distracted the pitcher but amused the fans.**

To Fragment

A verb with the preposition *to* in front of it is called an **infinitive**. An infinitive may not function as a verb in a sentence, nor may it stand alone as a sentence. You can correct this kind of fragment by removing the *to* and adding a helping verb. You can also add the infinitive phrase to a complete sentence.

Incorrect	Correct
A tax incentive to help small businesses.	A tax incentive **may help** small businesses.
	A tax incentive to help small businesses **was passed by Congress.**
To feel more confident when taking an exam.	A student **can feel** more confident when taking an exam by thoroughly preparing for it.
	To feel more confident when taking an exam, **a student should study material thoroughly over several days and get plenty of rest the night before.**

Afterthought or Added Detail Fragment

Sometimes fragments happen when a phrase—a group of words that adds detail—somehow gets separated as its own sentence. This kind of fragment can often be corrected by adding it to the complete sentence that precedes it.

Incorrect	Correct
Job applicants can jeopardize their chances of getting hired by making foolish mistakes. **Such as not showing up on time for their interviews.**	Job applicants can jeopardize their chances of getting hired by making foolish mistakes, such as not showing up on time for their interviews.
Students can avoid cramming the night before an exam. **For example, by reviewing their notes on a daily basis.**	Students can avoid cramming the night before an exam, for example, by reviewing their notes on a daily basis.

EXERCISE 15.1   Find and Correct Fragments

Directions: The following paragraph contains ten fragments. Find, underline, and correct them.

I have three obstacles that will cause me a lot of frustration as I attend college. These obstacles being my job, my friends, and my learning disability. First of all, my job at a landscaping company takes up a lot of my time and energy. I work four hours after my classes Monday through Friday. Then another eight hours on Saturday. The work is hard, dirty, and exhausting. Sometimes I'm so tired I can't pay attention in class. Or stay awake to do my homework at night. Another obstacle is my friends. When I have a lot of homework and they call me up and want to go partying. I have a hard time turning them down. If I am suffering from a hangover the next day. I once again can't pay attention in class. Or do my homework that evening. My biggest obstacle is my learning disability. I have dyslexia. This learning disability causes me difficulty with reading and comprehension. Which then makes me frustrated when I try to do my homework. If I get too frustrated, I just give up. And just don't do it. It's not easy. Having these obstacles and trying to go to school. But I have a goal. To succeed in college and have a successful career. I will work hard to overcome these obstacles.

A.2 Run-On (RO) and Comma Splice (CS)

A **run-on** occurs when two independent clauses (complete sentences) run together with no punctuation or connecting words.

Punctuation is confusing at first **it** becomes simple with practice. (IC IC)

A **comma splice** occurs when a writer connects two independent clauses with only a comma.

Punctuation is confusing at first, **it** becomes simple with practice. (IC; IC)

You cannot fix a run-on by adding a comma because that only creates a comma splice. Nor can you fix a comma splice by crossing out the comma because that only creates a run-on. There are five possible ways to fix run-ons and comma splices.

1. **Make two separate sentences.**

Punctuation is confusing at first. It becomes simple with practice.

Avoid overusing this method as it may lead to your having too many short, choppy sentences in your writing.

2. **Connect the two independent clauses with a semicolon.**

   Punctuation is confusing at first; it becomes simple with practice.

   Use the semicolon *only* when you want to emphasize a close relationship between the ideas in the two independent clauses. Like any emphasis device, this one fails when it is overused.

3. **Connect the independent clauses with a comma and a *coordinating conjunction*.**

   Punctuation is confusing at first, **but** it becomes simple with practice.

   Again, this method works best if the ideas in the two independent clauses are equally important. Do not overuse coordination and string too many unequal ideas together.

Coordinating Conjunctions
(fanboys)
for, and, nor, but, or, yet, so

4. **Connect the independent clauses with a semicolon and an *adverbial conjunction* followed by a comma.**

   Punctuation is confusing at first; **however,** it becomes simple with practice.

   This creates a compound sentence just like joining two independent clauses with a coordinating conjunction, so the same considerations apply.

Adverbial Conjunctions				
accordingly	furthermore	likewise	nonetheless	therefore
also	however	meanwhile	otherwise	
besides	indeed	moreover	then	
consequently	instead	nevertheless	thus	

5. **Make one of the two independent clauses dependent (subordinate) by placing a *subordinating conjunction* in front of it.**

Even though punctuation is confusing at first, it becomes simple with practice.

Punctuation is confusing at first **although** it becomes simple with practice.

This is often a preferred method of correcting a run-on because it demonstrates not only an awareness of sentence boundaries, but shows you have prioritized ideas.

Subordinating Conjunction (Dependent Words)				
after	because	rather than	unless	wherever
although	before	since	until	whether
as, as if	even though	so that	when	which
as long as	if, even if	that	whenever	while
as though	in order that	though	where	who

EXERCISE 15.2 Correct Run-Ons and Comma Splices

Directions: Practice using the five methods of correcting run-ons and comma splices in the following exercise. Be sure to use correct punctuation for each method. Refer to the preceding lists for the conjunctions you will need for each method.

RUN-ON: The goal of first drafting is to get ideas organized on paper the writer should not worry about proofreading and editing at this stage.

1. Write the two independent clauses as two separate sentences.

2. Connect the independent clauses with a comma and coordinating conjunction.

3. Connect the independent clauses with a semicolon and adverbial conjunction followed by a comma.

4. Make one of the two independent clauses dependent (subordinate) by placing a subordinating conjunction in front of it. (DC, IC or IC DC)

5. Connect the independent clauses with only a semicolon.

COMMA SPLICE: Students can be outstanding writers, poor time management skills can limit their success.

1. Connect the two independent clauses with a semicolon.

2. Connect the independent clauses with a comma and coordinating conjunction.

3. Connect the independent clauses with a semicolon and adverbial conjunction followed by a comma.

4. Make one of the two independent clauses dependent (subordinate) by placing a subordinating conjunction in front of it. (DC, IC or IC DC)

5. Connect the independent clauses with only a semicolon.

EXERCISE 15.3   Find and Correct Fragments, Run-Ons, and Comma Splices

Directions: The following short essay contains fifteen fragments, run-ons, and comma splices. Find, underline, and fix the errors using a variety of corrections methods.

You have had a long, busy day and now want only to get home and relax. First, though, you have to run to the grocery store to pick up "just a few" items. Maybe a carton of milk and some bread. Thirty minutes later you leave the store with a full cart; then, you stare at the foot-long receipt in your hand and wonder, "How did this happen?" Most likely you have fallen for the tactics your friendly neighborhood supermarket employs to encourage consumer spending. By making a few adjustments in your shopping habits and being more aware of grocery store tactics to encourage spending. You can be a smart shopper with more money in your pocket.

With a busy lifestyle that combines work, school and family, you may have to shop on the run between obligations. Which means you often go into the store hungry and without a shopping list. As you walk into the store, the smell of freshly baked bread hits your nose. You are further bombarded by the tangy scent of chicken wings kept warm at the hot food bar next to them kettles of simmering vegetable soup and lobster bisque make your mouth water. As your eyes take in the colorful fruits, vegetables and mounds of salad embellishments. You're hooked. You cannot resist a stop by the hot food and salad bars now that your brain is screaming, "Feed me!" Supermarket retailers know consumers often come into the stores hungry, they take advantage of this by using the layout of the store to steer shoppers by attractive food bars. Now considering you have also gone to the store without a shopping list. It should be no surprise that you're on your way to overbuying and overspending. When you can plan your trip to the supermarket. You should avoid going when you are hungry. You might consider keeping a box of energy bars handy and eat one before you go into the store. When you must make a quick unplanned stop, you should always take a list. Even a short one you jot down before leaving your car. Your list can be the map that takes you directly to the items you need and away from tempting distractions.

Although you go to the grocery store having a list and a full stomach. You can still be lured into spending more than you should. One tactic retailers use is product placement. They place the higher priced brand name products at eye level toward the right, because you read from left to right, your eyes will tend to settle on the higher priced items. If you look above and below the eye-level shelves, you will find the less expensive brands. Another trick is to link two or more products, usually on displays at the end of shopping aisles, retailers know consumers are drawn to these displays and often expect to find bargains there. For example, you will often find an eye-catching display of chips and salsa at the end of an aisle. Or perhaps tea and coffee with cookies. You will find yourself purchasing these "pairs" of items, not even realizing they are not on sale. The trickery continues even at the checkout. Have you ever started to read a magazine while waiting to check out then find you need to buy it in order to finish reading? Many parents find themselves buying gum or a candy bar those products line the shelves of checkout lanes right at the eye level of impatient children.

You will probably fall victim to at least some grocery store ploys, however, a little planning and awareness of retail strategies may make you a savvier shopper.

❷ Identify and correct shifts in person and in verbs.

B. Avoid Shifts

Shifts in point of view and shifts in verb tense often occur in writing because many of us are careless with these matters in our speech. We can read right over these errors during editing because they "sound" all right to us. As you train your eyes to catch and correct these errors in your writing, you will start to notice you are more careful in your speech as well.

B.1 Shifts in Point of View (Shift)

Depending upon a writer's topic and purpose, three different "persons" can be used.

1. **First person:** *I, we*

   Use first person when writing about yourself as an individual (*I*) or as part of a group (*we*). You may have already encountered a "First-Person Narrative" assignment in which a teacher has asked you to write about an event in your life. Sometimes you may even use first person in more formal assignments if you include examples of your own experience with an issue or a problem.

2. **Second Person:** *you*

   Use second person when you directly address your reader or readers. Most frequently you will find writers use second person when giving directions or explanations. (Notice, for example, how frequently second person is used in this textbook.) Writers sometimes use second person when they engage in direct appeals to their readers as part of a persuasive piece of writing. An editorial in a local paper might urge voters to get out and vote on an election day in such a direct manner: "Voting is **your** right and **your** duty as a citizen. **You** must let your voice be heard."

      A common mistake writers make is using *you* to refer to people in general. You have probably heard or made statements like "It's frustrating when you have a long commute," or "Before the invention of antibiotics, you could die from a simple infection," or "When you work and take classes, life gets hectic." In all these cases, the word *you* is used in a very general way. Be specific in writing. Use *you* only to refer directly to your specific readers when it is appropriate to do so.

3. **Third Person:** anyone who is not the writer or the reader—Bob, people, students, politicians, and so on.

   When you are not writing about yourself or directly addressing your readers, you use third person. Because it is more objective, third person is preferred in most academic and professional writing.

      While it is all right to use more than one person in a paper, the shifts should be logical. The following examples illustrate some logical shifts in person:

   I have exercised my right to vote, and **you** should as well.

   You should be cautious when opening your door to strangers. **People** are not always what they seem. **I** have a neighbor who was robbed by someone she thought was a utility inspector.

These next examples, however, show illogical shifts in person and the misuse of *you*.

Incorrect	Correct
When I went into the auditorium, **you** could hear a pin drop.	When I went into the auditorium, **I** could hear a pin drop.
At my high school, **you** had to follow a strict dress code.	At my high school, **students** had to follow a strict dress code.
During the Civil War, **you** could encounter your own family members on the side of the enemy.	During the Civil War, **soldiers** could encounter **their** own family members on the side of the enemy.

EXERCISE 15.4   Change a Paragraph's Point of View

Directions: Imagine that you work at a customer service desk for Big Box Store. Your supervisor has been so impressed with how well you handle customers that she asks you to describe the process you use to calm customers down. You write the following paragraph:

How I Resolve Problems at the Customer Service Desk

Working at a customer service desk is not always easy, especially when I have to deal with an angry, rude customer. I have learned some strategies for dealing with these unruly customers. First, I try to stay calm even if the customer yells at me. Usually, if I remain calm and keep my voice at a quiet, even tone, a customer will settle down. Once the customer is calm, I try to understand what the problem is by listening carefully. To reassure the customer that I am truly listening, I maintain eye contact, nod my head and say, "I understand" or "I see what you mean." Once the customer has explained the problem, I ask, "What can I do to help?" If I can resolve the problem to the customer's satisfaction without violating store policy, that's what I will do. This process works nearly every time I deal with unhappy customers. On those occasions when a customer does not settle down and becomes increasingly abusive, I maintain my composure and direct the customer to my manager. Although my day at the customer service desk can have some rough moments, I remind myself that most customers are polite, and I begin each encounter with a smile.

Directions: Your supervisor is so impressed with your process that she asks you to rewrite this paragraph as a set of instructions for other customer service representatives. Rewrite the paragraph in **second person**. The beginning has been started for you.

How You Can Resolve Problems at the Customer Service Desk
Working at a customer service desk is not always easy, especially when you have to deal with an angry, rude customer. Fortunately, you can deal with most unruly customers by using the following techniques.

Directions: Your supervisor then asks you to revise the paragraph yet again, so it can be published in a trade journal. She wants you to rewrite the paragraph in **third person** so it refers to all the customer service representatives—men and women—at your store. The beginning has been started for you. (You can avoid pronoun agreement errors and wordy constructions if you use plurals when possible.)

Resolving Problems at the Customer Service Desk
Working at a customer service desk is not always easy, especially when representatives have to deal with an angry, rude customer. Fortunately, customer service representatives at Big Box Store have strategies they use to effectively handle such a customer.

B.2 Shifts in Verb Tense (Tense)

Another faulty shift occurs when a writer does not use a consistent verb tense. For example, when writing about the past, a writer may use a present tense verb. Sometimes these errors occur because the writer does not know the proper verb forms.

Verbs have four principal parts or tenses: *present, present participle, past,* and *past participle*. Here are examples of those tenses, using the regular verb *talk*:

PRESENT	Today I *talk.*
PRESENT PARTICIPLE	Right now, I *am talking.*
PAST	Yesterday, I *talked.*
PAST PARTICIPLE	In the past, I *have talked.*

When you write, you must be sure any shifts between past and present tense verbs are logical and intentional as in the following example:

┌── past tense verbs ──┐   present tense verb
Last year my dad ate junk food and was out of shape, but now he eats right and
present tense verb
exercises daily.

Avoid illogical and unnecessary shifts between present and past tense verbs as the following examples illustrate.

Incorrect	Correct
Preparing for a marathon **demands** energy and **required** commitment.	Preparing for a marathon **demands** energy and **requires** commitment.
In 490 B.C.E. Pheidippides **ran** from the battlefield at Marathon, Greece to Athens, **delivered** the message "Victory!" **collapses** and **dies**.	In 490 B.C. Pheidippides **ran** from the battlefield at Marathon, Greece to Athens, **delivered** the message "Victory!" **collapsed** and **died**.
Abebe Bikila **became** the first person representing a country from Africa to win an Olympic gold medal in the marathon, and he **does** it barefoot and **sets** a world record.	Abebe Bikila **became** the first person representing a country from Africa to win an Olympic gold medal in the marathon, and he **did** it barefoot and **set** a world record.

EXERCISE 15.5 Identify the Correct Verb Tense

Directions: Underline the appropriate verb in each of the following sentences.

1. Perhaps the most disastrous Olympic marathon (is, was) held during the 1904 St. Louis World's Fair.

2. The modern Olympic marathon (is, was) a long distance run of just over 26 miles. An extra distance of 385 yards (is, was) added during the 1908 Olympics in London so runners (finish, finished) in front of the royal family's viewing box.

3. The temperature on that August afternoon in 1904 (reached, reaches) the mid nineties with high humidity.

4. The athletes (run, ran) over hilly, unpaved roads up seven steep hills as they (choked, choke) on dust kicked up by a team of horses that (go, went) ahead to clear the course.

5. Officials, handlers and reporters (rode, ride) in automobiles behind the runners.

6. In 1904 the newly invented automobiles (emitted, emits) exhaust fumes and (kicks, kicked) up more dust, which (adds, added) to the runners' misery.

7. One runner (is, was) hospitalized after inhaling dust that nearly (destroyed, destroys) his stomach lining, and two officials (are, were) seriously hurt when their car (rolls, rolled) over in a ditch when they (swerve, swerved) to avoid hitting a runner.

8. Endurance (was, is) the key to success in running any marathon.

9. Three hours and fifteen minutes after the start of the race, Fred Lorz (runs, ran) into the stadium and (crossed, crosses) the finish line.

10. Just as the President's daughter Alice Roosevelt (is, was) about to place a laurel wreath on his head, Lorz (confessed, confesses) that he (hitches, hitched) a ride in an automobile for eleven miles of the race.

11. Almost fifteen minutes later, the actual winner of the race, Thomas Hicks, (arrives, arrived) at the stadium and (passed, passes) out because his trainers (gave, give, had given) him several does of strychnine sulfate mixed with egg whites and brandy to keep him on his feet during the race.

12. Modern Olympic marathon runners (pace, paced) themselves and (drank, drink) plenty of water during the run, but runners (were, are) allowed to take refreshments only at authorized stations along the route.

EXERCISE 15.6   Edit for Correct Verb Tense

Directions: The following paragraph describes the experiences of Felix Carvajal, a young Cuban who ran in the 1904 Olympic Marathon in St. Louis. The paragraph describes Carvajal's experience using present tense verbs as though it were happening right now. Cross out and replace the present tense verbs with appropriate past tense verbs.

A five-foot-tall mailman in Havana Cuba, Felix Carvajal, hears about the 1904 Olympic marathon in St. Louis, Missouri and decides to enter the race. He has no money but finds a way to raise funds in the central square in Havana. For several days, he runs in circles around the square until a crowd gathers. He then announces his plan to travel to St. Louis and win the marathon for the glory of Cuba. Eventually, Carvajal manages to secure enough donations to make the journey. He boards a steamer to New Orleans and begins his journey to Olympic glory. Unfortunately, once Carvajal reaches New Orleans, he loses his remaining money and his equipment in a dice game. Not discouraged, he walks and hitchhikes the rest of the way to St. Louis. Carvajal reaches the race but has no running gear. In the ninety-degree weather, he arrives wearing wool trousers, a long sleeve shirt, a felt beret, and street shoes. Officials postpone the race while Carvajal cuts off his shirt sleeves and pants legs. Without equipment, training or strategy, Caravajal runs leisurely along, sometimes backwards while he speaks to the crowd, practicing his English. He detours at one point into an apple orchard, where he snatches and eats some green apples. The green apples give him excruciating stomach cramps, so he lies down for awhile by the roadside until he feels better. When he recovers, he continues the race and actually finishes fourth in the marathon. The international press praises the friendly and determined Carvajal. He returns to Cuba and his mail route and enters no more international competitions.

B.3 Shifts in Irregular Verb Tense

Another problem with verbs arises when writers do not recognize the proper tense for irregular verbs.

For most verbs, the past and past participle are formed by adding -ed to the verb. But there are some verbs that are **irregular**. They change form with each tense. Here is an example of an irregular verb:

PRESENT	Today I *see*.
PRESENT PARTICIPLE	Right now, I am *seeing*.
PAST	Yesterday, I *saw*.
PAST PARTICIPLE	In the past I have *seen*.

This chart contains some of the most common irregular verbs.

Present Tense	Past Tense	Past Participle
be	was, were	(have) been
beat	beat	(have) beaten
became	become	(have) become
begin	began	(have) begun
bite	bit	(have) bitten
blow	blew	(have) blown
break	broke	(have) broken
bring	brought	(have) brought
buy	bought	(have) bought
catch	caught	(have) caught
choose	chose	(have) chosen
come	came	(have) come
dig	dug	(have) dug
dive	dived, dove	(have) dived
do	did	(have) done
draw	drew	(have) drawn
dream	dreamed, dreamt	(have) dreamed, dreamt
drink	drank	(have) drunk
drive	drove	(have) driven
eat	ate	(have) eaten
fall	fell	(have) fallen
fly	flew	(have) flown
forget	forgot	(have) forgotten
freeze	froze	(have) frozen
get	got	(have) gotten
go	went	(have) gone
grow	grew	(have) grown
hang (an object)	hung	(have) hung
hang (a person)	hanged	(have) hanged

continued

Continued

Present Tense	Past Tense	Past Participle
lay	laid	(have) laid
lead	led	(have) led
lend	lent	(have) lent
lie (recline)	lay	(have) lain
light	lighted, lit	(have) lighted, lit
ride	rode	(have) ridden
ring	rang	(have) rung
rise	rose	(have) risen
run	ran	(have) run
see	saw	(have) seen
set	set	(have) set
shake	shook	(have) shaken
shine	shone	(have) shone
sing	sang	(have) sung
sink	sank, sunk	(have) sunk
sit	sat	(have) sat
speed	sped	(have) sped
speak	spoke	(have) spoken
spring	sprang, sprung	(have) sprung
steal	stole	(have) stolen
swear	swore	(have) sworn
swim	swam	(have) swum
take	took	(have) taken
teach	taught	(have) taught
tear	tore	(have) torn
think	thought	(have) thought
wake	waked, woke	(have) waked, woke, woken
wear	wore	(have) worn
write	wrote	(have) written

Be particularly careful with the following irregular verbs, which are often confused.

These verbs describe actions you can perform by yourself.	These verbs describe actions that require an object. You do these acts *to something*.
sit (to rest the body on the buttocks)	**set** (to put something down)
Today, I *sit* down.	Today I *set* down the pen.
Yesterday, I *sat* down.	Yesterday, I *set* down the pen.
In the past I **have *sat*** down.	In the past, I **have *set*** down the pen.
lie (to recline)	**lay** (to put something down)
Today, I *lie* down.	Today, I *lay* the book down.
Yesterday, I *lay* down.	Yesterday, I *laid* the book down.
In the past, I **have *lain*** down.	In the past, I **have *laid*** the book down.
rise (to get up)	**raise** (to lift something up)
Today, I *rise* from bed.	Today, I *raise* the window.
Yesterday I *rose* from bed.	Yesterday, I *raised* the window
In the past I **have *risen*** from bed.	In the past, I **have *raised*** the window.

EXERCISE 15.7   Identify Correct Forms of Irregular Verbs

Directions: In each of the following sentences, fill in the blanks with the correct form of the irregular verb.

1. Fred Lorz claimed he was joking when he **run** (_____) into the stadium and **break** (_____) the tape across the finish line at the 1904 Olympic Marathon.

2. Several marathon competitors had **see** (_____) Lorz waving from a car as he passed them on the route.

3. Because the crowd had already **rise** (_____) and cheered when Lorz entered the stadium, few people **rise** (_____) when the real winner, Thomas Hicks, dragged himself across the finish line.

4. Hicks was sick because he had **drink** (_____) strychnine sulfate with raw eggs and a brandy chaser which his trainer **think** (_____) would improve Hicks's stamina.

5. One runner **fall** (_____) by the roadside when fumes from automobiles overcame him.

6. One exhausted runner had to be **drive** (_____) back to the stadium at the end of the race.

7. Felix Cavajal **lie** (_____) by the side of the road to settle his stomach cramps.

8. If Felix Cavajal had not **eat** (_____) green apples, he might have won the marathon.

9. Jan Mashiani, one of the first black Africans to participate in an Olympics, might have **do** (_____) better than ninth place if he had not been chased a mile off course by a dog.

10. In his book *The Olympic Games 1904*, Charles J. P. Lucas **write** (_____), "At no time during the race was the Greek record for the distance in danger."

❸ Identify and correct pronoun case, pronoun reference, and agreement errors.

C. Master Grammar: Pronoun Case, Pronoun Reference, and Agreement

Once again, you will be working with errors that often occur in spoken English without causing too many problems. Few people are going to correct you for saying, "Someone left their book in the classroom." If your friends do not understand to whom you are referring when you say, "In that town they make you feel welcome," they will simply ask you who "they" are, and the conversation will move on. However, the rules of written English are not so forgiving. You must be precise, accurate, and consistent. Mastering these rules is a step in that direction.

C.1 Pronoun Case (Case)

Pronouns are words that can take the place of nouns or other pronouns in a sentence. **Case** refers to the form a pronoun takes depending on its relationship to the other words in a sentence. Here are three common forms of pronouns.

1. **Possessive Pronouns** show ownership or possession.

my	mine	That is **my** book.
your	yours	Is that **your** car?
his	her	**His** dog bit **her** cat.
our	ours	**Our** picnic was canceled.
its	whose	**Whose** book lost **its** cover?
their	theirs	The students voiced **their** concerns.

2. **Subjective pronouns** can function as subjects of verbs. These pronouns can perform actions:

I	**I** ran to the store for milk.
you	**You** took the last box of paper clips.
he / she	**He** does not run as fast as **she** does.
they	**They** took the puppy to the veterinarian.
it	**It** is time to show what you know.
who	**Who** turned off the lights?
we	**We** want to win this game.

3. **Objective pronouns** cannot be subjects; instead, they are receivers of action or objects of prepositions:

me	Xavier gave **me** directions.
you	I told **you** to let out the cat.
him / her	When Jack called, Rudy told **him** about the accident.
them	Calling my neighbors, I told **them** about their barking dog.
it	My car broke down; you have an hour to fix **it**.
whom	You are addressing that letter to **whom**?
us	Sung took **us** to the zoo on Saturday.

How Can You Avoid Errors?

A pronoun case error occurs when a writer uses the wrong form of a pronoun. The following examples show some of the most common kinds of pronoun case errors and how to avoid them in your writing.

1. **Don't confuse a contraction with a possessive pronoun.** Look back at the list of possessive pronouns. You should notice that none of them have apostrophes. So remember, for example, when you write *it's*, you have written a contraction for *it is*, not the possessive pronoun *its* as in *The dog buried its bone*.

2. **Don't be confused by compound constructions.** If you break the sentence down and look at each subject individually, you may find it easier to see that you need a subjective case pronoun, as shown in the following example.

Tomas and (I, me) are going to the ballgame.

> Tomas is going to the ballgame.

> **I** am going to the ballgame.

Tomas and **I** are going to the ballgame.

Similarly, if you break the following sentence down, you can more easily see that each person is receiving rather than performing an action, so you need the objective case.

Give Maria and (I, me) directions to the park.

> Give Maria directions.

> Give **me** directions.

Give Maria and **me** directions to the park.

3. **Don't be confused by words after *we* and *us*.** Most writers know *we* functions as a subject. So don't be confused when a noun follows *we* or *us*. The pronoun's case does not change because it precedes a noun.

(Us, We) students are going on spring break.

> **We** are going on spring break.

> **We** students are going on spring break.

> Be sure to tell (us, we) parents when you'll be back.

> Be sure to tell **us** when you'll be back.

> Be sure to tell **us** parents when you'll be back.

4. **Always use objective case pronouns after prepositions.**

The instructor spoke *with* **him** and **me**.

Just *between* **you** and **me**, I think the election was fixed.

5. **Always use subjective case pronouns after linking verbs.**

The person who let the air out of your tires was **I**.

The winners of the school spirit contest were **we** sophomores.

6. **Avoid using *that* or *which* to refer to people.** Use *who* or *whom* to refer to human beings and *that* and *which* to refer to non-humans and non-living things.

| INCORRECT | Rosa is the only friend **that** helped me move to a new apartment. |
| CORRECT | Rosa is the only friend **who** helped me move to a new apartment. |

7. **Avoid these "pronouns" that do not exist:**

theirselves   hisself   theirself   themself   thereselves   herselves   thereself

EXERCISE 15.8   Correct Pronouns

Directions: Check the underlined pronoun in each of the following sentences. If it is incorrect, cross it out and write the correct pronoun above it.

1. It will be up to <u>us</u> community members to form a neighborhood watch association.

2. My dog growled when I took away <u>it's</u> bone.

3. The manager asked Sophie and <u>I</u> to work overtime.

4. Who is the doctor <u>that</u> performed open heart surgery on <u>you're</u> uncle?

5. <u>We</u> employees are most concerned about job safety.

6. The librarian showed Inés and <u>I</u> how to use the various databases.

7. The person <u>who</u> tried to call you after ten o'clock last night was <u>me</u>.

8. The kindergartener insisted upon tying his shoes <u>hisself</u>.

9. Just between you and <u>I</u>, this season's new fashions for women are too matronly.

10. Damian and <u>him</u> will umpire next week's baseball tournament.

C.2 Pronoun Reference (Ref)

A **pronoun** is a word that takes the place of a noun or another pronoun. The word the pronoun replaces is called its **antecedent**. In the following sentence the pronoun clearly refers to its antecedent:

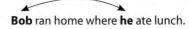

Bob ran home where **he** ate lunch.   (He clearly refers to Bob.)

EXERCISE 15.9   Identify Pronouns and Their Antecedents

Directions: In each of the following sentences, circle the pronoun and draw a line to its antecedent.

1. The tiny, almost transparent Alabama Cave shrimp is found in just two Alabama cave systems. It is an endangered species.

2. Infants can be taught American Sign Language when they are as young as six months.

3. Tupac Shakur wrote the song "Dear Mama" for his own mother.

4. In 1940, Batman's sidekick Robin became the first major child character in comics. He was so popular that soon other superheroes were given young partners.

5. Frida Kahlo began painting in 1925 as she recovered from a streetcar accident. The paintings from this time reflect her intense physical pain.

What Causes Pronoun Reference Errors?

A sentence may be confusing and unclear if a pronoun could refer to more than one antecedent or if the pronoun does not refer to any specific antecedent at all.

Incorrect	Problem	Correct
Angel and **Alejandro** ran home where **he** ate lunch.	Who ate lunch, Angel or Alejandro?	Angel and Alejandro ran home where **Angel** ate lunch.
Bridget told **Mary she** could no longer babysit **her** children.	Who can no longer babysit whose children?	"I can no longer babysit your children," Bridget told Mary.

continued

Continued

Incorrect	Problem	Correct
When **Taj** registered for classes, **they** told **him** that **he** needed to take a placement test.	*He* and *him* refer to Taj, but who are *they*?	When Taj registered for classes, **advisors** told him that he needed to take a placement test.
Carol had excellent references and strong interview skills, **which** got her hired by a major corporation.	What got Carol the job— the references, the skills, or both?	Because of her excellent references and strong interview skills, Carol was hired by a major corporation.
Drew takes occupational therapy classes because he plans to be **one** when he graduates.	What does Drew plan to be? The pronoun *one* cannot be replaced by *occupational therapy*.	Drew takes occupational therapy classes because he plans to be an **occupational therapist** when he graduates.

EXERCISE 15.10   Identify and Correct Pronoun Reference Errors

Directions: Rewrite the following sentences to correct any pronoun reference errors.

1. Andre is taking courses in public speaking and business management because he believes it will help him get a job.

2. Some parents may not help their children pay off credit card debts because they want to teach them a lesson in fiscal responsibility.

3. Because coal mining is such a dangerous occupation, my brother decided not to be one.

4. We called the fire department, and they arrived five minutes later to put out the fire.

5. When the honey badger fought the deadly cobra, it was quickly killed.

6. Pet breeders in Florida have released Burmese pythons into the wild, and now they are threatening native species.

7. After Allen Pinkerton broke up a plot to assassinate President Abraham Lincoln, he was put in charge of forming the Secret Service.

8. Ajani always wears a suit and a tie to work because he thinks it makes him look more professional.

9. Madeline taught her eight-month-old daughter sign language, and now she is not so frustrated and seldom cries.

10. When the hometown player hit a grand slam, the stadium was rocked by their cheers.

C.3 Pronoun Antecedent Agreement (PA Agr)

The word a pronoun takes the place of is called its **antecedent.** A pronoun must *agree* in number with its antecedent. A singular antecedent requires a singular pronoun. A plural antecedent requires a plural pronoun.

Deshi took **his** dog to the vet. (The pronoun **his** refers to the single male Deshi.)

Deshi and Hayden turned in **their** papers early. (The pronoun **their** refers to the plural Deshi and Hayden.)

How Can You Avoid Errors?

Most pronoun/antecedent agreement errors occur because the writer does not realize a subject is singular. The following examples show how to avoid this confusion.

1. **Do not be confused by subjects joined with <u>or</u>.**

   Al or **Jack** will let us borrow **his** truck to pick up the furniture. (Only one man lends a truck.)

   Al and **Jack** are bringing **their** trucks to help us move. (Both men are bringing trucks.)

2. **Remember that indefinite pronouns are always singular.**

   Perhaps the most common pronoun-antecedent agreement errors involve trying to replace a singular indefinite pronoun with the plural pronoun *their*. You cannot replace a singular with a plural.

Indefinite Pronouns			
(-*one* words)	(-*body* words)	(-*thing* words)	
one	nobody	anything	each
anyone	anybody	everything	every
everyone	everybody	nothing	either
someone	somebody	something	neither

Notice how most indefinite pronouns contain "clues" indicating they are singular. *One* is most clearly singular. *Body* and *thing* are also singular with *bodies* and *things* being plural. So when you see a pronoun ending in *one, body,* or *thing*—remember, it is singular. Also, notice that when you put *each, every, either,* or *neither* in front of a word, the word keeps its singular form.

When each **dog** (not *dogs*) arrives at the shelter, **it** (not *they*) is given a check-up.

Every **tomato** (not *tomatoes*) is hand picked to be sure **it** (not *they*) is not bruised.

Either **Donna** or **Judy** (not both) will bring **her** (not *their*) class to the library.

Neither **man** (not *men*) was willing to give up **his** (not *their*) place in line.

Since agreeing in number with indefinite pronouns often leads to wordy constructions, as you will see in the following chart, it is better to avoid using them when possible.

Incorrect	Correct	Better
Every student is responsible for doing **their** work.	**Every student** is responsible for doing **his or her** own work.	**Students** are responsible for doing **their** own work.
Each of the Boy Scouts received a special badge for their community work.	**Each** of the Boy Scouts received a special badge for **his** community work.	
Everybody at this company participates in training to improve **their** skills.	**Everybody** at this company participates in training to improve **his or her** skills.	The **employees** at this company participate in training to improve **their** skills.
Anyone can take **their** papers to the College Writing Center for help.	**Anyone** can take **his or her** papers to the College Writing Center for help.	**Students** can take **their** papers to the College Writing Center for help.
Either of the cell phone plans has **their** drawbacks.	**Either** of the cell phone plans has **its** drawbacks.	

EXERCISE 15.11   Identify Pronouns that Agree with Their Antecedents

Directions: Circle the correct pronouns in the following sentences.

1. Since neither of my cars passed (its, their) safety inspection, I will be riding my bike to work.

2. Everyone who texts and drives should have (his or her, their) driver's license revoked.

3. Each of the nominated actresses held (her, their) breath while the winner was announced.

4. Everybody is expected to do (his or her, their) share in keeping the town streets free of litter.

5. One of the members of the men's figure skating team broke (his, their) ankle in a fall on the ice.

C.4 Subject Verb Agreement (SV Agr)

Verbs must agree in number with their subjects. Singular subjects require singular verbs and plural subjects require plural verbs, as you can see in the following examples:

> **Chen** is coming to the party.
> **Chen** and **Andy** are coming to the party.

This rule seems simple enough, yet subject verb agreement errors are not uncommon. You can avoid most of them by understanding some of the sentence basics covered at the beginning of Chapter 14.

1. **First, identify the verb in a sentence and know the difference between the singular and plural forms of a verb.**

   Notice that most singular verbs end in the letter *s*. Remember the word *singular* starts with *s*, and singular verbs end in *s*.

He (singular)	We (plural)
runs	run
is	are
was	were
has	have
laughs	laugh

EXERCISE 15.12   Choosing Verbs to Agree with Subjects

Directions: Circle the subject of each sentence and underline the verb that agrees in number with it.

1. Celebrities often (endorses, endorse) commercial products.

2. The library (provides, provide) quiet study spaces for students.

3. Anti-virus software products (protects, protect) computers from viruses, worms, and trojans.

4. Employers (hires, hire) the candidates who will best meet the organizations' needs.

5. Common sense (is, are) the best guide for deciding what to wear to an interview.

2. **Be sure you have correctly identified the subject. Do not be confused by prepositional phrases that come between the subject and verb.** (See pages 418–419 in this handbook to review subjects and prepositional phrases.)

A **basket** of peaches was delivered to my house.

The rock **star** along with his entourage of stylists, body guards, and roadies is traveling around the country in a bus.

The sweet **sound** of young children's voices fills the church every Sunday morning.

EXERCISE 15.13   Choosing Verbs to Agree with Subjects

Directions: Cross out the prepositional phrases, circle the subject of each sentence, and underline the verb that agrees in number with it.

1. A stack of overdue library books (sits, sit) on my desk.

2. The success of Superman and Batman movies (has, have) led to many more superheroes appearing on the big screen.

3. Buckets of water (was, were) poured over the beached whale.

4. A system of canyons on Mars (is, are) so large, it could stretch across the continental United States.

5. The President along with his advisors (decides, decide) when to tap our oil reserves to lower prices.

---

3. **Don't be confused by subjects joined with *or*.**

PLURAL SUBJECT	Sarah *and* Josh take out the trash. (Two people take out the trash.)
SINGULAR SUBJECT	Sarah *or* Josh takes out the trash. (Only one person takes out the trash.)

When *or* connects a singular and a plural, the subject closest to the verb determines its number.

Either the **coach or his assistants** are holding practice in the gym.
Either the **assistants or the coach** is holding practice in the gym.

EXERCISE 15.14   Choosing Verbs to Agree with Subjects

Directions: Underline the verb that agrees in number with its subject.

1. Either a parent or a teacher (supervises, supervise) the playground each afternoon.

2. Kamran and Amber (disagrees, disagree) on how to best organize the inventory.

3. Eating spicy food or dealing with stress (has, have) upset my stomach.

4. The ambulance and the fire truck (responds, respond) to all emergency calls.

5. The students or the teacher (takes, take) care of the class hamster on weekends.

4. **Remember, the subject can come after the verb.**

There <u>are</u> two **ways** to solve this problem.

From off in the distance <u>comes</u> the **howl** of a lone coyote.

Under my sofa cushions <u>were</u> two **nickels**, a **penny**, a **button**, and some **kernels** of popcorn.

EXERCISE 15.15   Choosing Verbs to Agree with Subjects

Directions: Circle the subject of each sentence and underline the verb that agrees in number with it. (Don't be fooled by prepositional phrases!)

1. Where (is, are) all the students this morning?

2. Backed up for miles (was, were) cars full of frustrated commuters.

3. Running down the street (comes, come) the mail carrier with my dog snapping at his heels.

4. In the center of the town square (stands, stand) a statue of the town's founder.

5. There (is, are) plenty of job opportunities for those in the medical professions.

❹ Identify and correct apostrophe, comma, quotation mark, semicolon, and colon errors.

D. Pay Attention to Punctuation: Apostrophes, Commas, Quotation Marks, Semicolons, and Colons

Punctuation errors are among the most common kinds of errors in most people's writing. Although a comma error, for instance, may not be as serious as a sentence fragment, an abundance of comma errors can distract a reader.

D.1 Apostrophes (Apos)

Apostrophes are used to indicate omitted letters in contractions and to indicate ownership or possession.

1. **Use apostrophes to show that one or more letters have been left out in a contraction.**

	Incorrect	Correct
are not	There **arent** penguins at the North Pole.	There **aren't** penguins at the North Pole.
can not	Most domestic turkeys **cant** fly	Most domestic turkeys **can't** fly.
do not	Honey bees **dont** sleep.	Honey bees **don't** sleep.
does not	A duck's quack **doesnt** echo.	A duck's quack **doesn't** echo.
I have	**Ive** read several books on animal behavior.	**I've** read several books on animal behavior.
it is	**Its** a fascinating subject.	**It's** a fascinating subject.
of the clock	**Jon** goes bird-watching at six **oclock**.	Jon goes bird-watching at six **o'clock**.
you are	**Youre** welcome to join our nature club.	**You're** welcome to join our nature club.

EXERCISE 15.16 **Use Apostrophes in Contractions**

Directions: Compose your own sentences using the contraction form of the following word groups. Be sure to place the apostrophe where the letter or letters have been left out.

EXAMPLE   he is
                   He's the one who won the writing contest.

1. has not _____

2. I am _____

3. is not _____

4. let us _____

5. who is _____

2. **Use an apostrophe and an *s* to indicate ownership by a *single* object or being.**

Ownership Situation	Possessive with Apostrophe
The rays belong to the **sun**.	The **sun's** bright rays woke me up.
The car belongs to **Mike**.	**Mike's** car broke down on the highway.
The ball belongs to the **dog**.	The **dog's** ball rolled under the couch.
It is the notice of a **moment**.	We were ready to leave in a **moment's** notice.

EXERCISE 15.17   Use Apostrophes to Indicate Singular Possessive Constructions

Directions: Compose your own sentences that use possessive constructions from the following ownership situations.

EXAMPLE   It is being ready in the notice of a minute.
             The firefighters could be ready in a **minute's** notice.

1. It is the vacation of a week.

2. The victory belongs to the team.

3. The report belongs to a manager.

4. The tire belongs to your car.

5. It is the sale of a store.

3. **Use an apostrophe and an *s* to indicate ownership by objects or beings (plural) if the plural word does not already end in *s*.**

Ownership Situation	Possessive with Apostrophe
The books belong to the **children**.	The **children's** books lined the shelves.
The department belongs to the **men**.	I looked for a tie in the **men's** department.
The nests belong to the **geese**.	The **geese's** nests lined the lakeshore.

EXERCISE 15.18   Use Apostrophes to Indicate Plural Possessive Constructions

Directions: Compose your own sentences that use plural possessive constructions from the following ownership situations.

EXAMPLE   The clothing store belongs to men.
The **men's** clothing store is having a sale on business suits.

1. The soccer team belongs to women.

2. The wool belongs to sheep.

3. The cages belong to the mice.

4. The coverage belongs to the media.

5. The cars belong to the people.

4. **Use only an apostrophe to indicate ownership by objects or beings (plural) if the plural word already ends in s.**

Ownership Situation	Possessive with Apostrophe
It is the supper club of the **ladies.**	The **ladies'** supper club meets monthly.
The papers belong to the **students.**	The teacher returned the **students'** papers.
It is the vacation of two **weeks.**	Jamal took two **weeks'** vacation.
It is the home of the **Adamskis.**	The **Adamskis'** home is on this street.

EXERCISE 15.19   Use Apostrophes to Indicate Plural Possessive Constructions

Directions: Compose your own sentences that use plural possessive constructions from the following ownership situations.

EXAMPLE   They are the leaves of trees.
The **trees'** leaves are exceptionally colorful this fall.

1. They are the diplomats of **countries.**

2. It is the family car of the **Smiths.**

3. They are the cheers of the **fans.**

4. It is the screeching of the **monkeys.**

5. They are the benefits of **employees.**

Avoid these two common misuses of the apostrophe.

5. **Do not use apostrophes in possessive pronouns.**

Incorrect	Correct
The car hit a pothole and lost **it's** muffler.	The car hit a pothole and lost **its** muffler.
Turn off **you're** cell phone in the theater.	Turn off **your** cell phone in the theater.
Who's turn is it to change the baby's diaper?	**Whose** turn is it to change the baby's diaper?
Those who take **they're** time make fewer mistakes.	Those who take **their** time make fewer mistakes.
Helen said the scarf found in the class-room is **her's**.	Helen said the scarf found in the class-room is **hers**.

6. **Do not use apostrophes to indicate plurals. (*Plural* means more than one.)**

Incorrect	Correct
The **boy's** and **girl's** drove their **bike's** to the **store's**.	The **boys** and **girls** drove their **bikes** to the **stores**.
The old woman put out **dish's** of food for the stray **cat's** and **dog's**.	The old woman put out **dishes** of food for the stray **cats** and **dogs**.
Family's flock to the **park's** on sunny **day's**.	**Families** flock to the **parks** on sunny **days**.
Many commuter's cut travel **expense's** by joining **carpool's**.	Many **commuters** cut travel **expenses** by joining **carpools**.

EXERCISE 15.20   Correct Apostrophe Errors

Directions: Correct any apostrophe errors in the following sentences.

1. His lawyer's continuous objections' did not help Bart's case in the jury's eye's.

2. If you're credit cards' have reached they're maximum limit's, it's time to look for way's to reduce you're spending.

3. Growing flower's and vegetable's in one's own garden can be rewarding in many ways'.

4. Who's paper's were left on the teacher's desk?

5. It's time for supervisors' to turn in they're yearly report's on each employee's performance in meeting the company's goal's.

D.2 Commas (C)

Writers sometimes claim to be confused by *all* the comma rules, but as you will see, there are about five rules that cover most uses of the comma. Understanding clauses and phrases will help you a great deal as you learn to use the comma correctly.

1. **Comma Rule 1 (C1):** When two independent clauses are separated by a coordinating conjunction (see page 427), a comma goes **before** the conjunction.

> Kayla works a full-time job, **and** she takes night classes.
>
> Coming up with a topic is hard, **but** writing the paper is easy.
>
> No one fishes at that lake, **for** pollution has made the fish toxic.

2. **Comma Rule 2 (C2):** Use a comma to set off transitional or introductory words, dependent clauses, and long phrases that come at the beginning of sentences.

TRANSITIONAL AND INTRODUCTORY WORDS	**In conclusion,** I think we should all recycle whenever possible.
	Supposedly, we will be compensated for working overtime.
	First, you should set some realistic goals.
	Also, I learned that it's not a good idea to miss class.
DEPENDENT CLAUSES	**Although Sam practices daily,** his golf swing is still terrible.
	Because it was so hot, we decided to go to the pool.
	If Forrest Gump is right, life is like a box of chocolates.
	After she paid her tuition, Kim went to the bookstore.

LONG PHRASES   **After taking a long nap,** Alex felt ready to face the world.

Wiping the sweat from her brow, Toni weeded the garden.

Quickly and effortlessly, Khalid did one hundred push-ups.

3. **Comma Rule 3 (C3):** Use commas to set off **nonrestrictive** words and phrases. Nonrestrictive means you could leave out the word or phrase and not change the meaning of the sentence.

My dog, **a purebred poodle,** gets along well with my three cats.

Amela has the flu, **which is why she missed class.**

Do we want Todd, **who is always late,** to go with us?

Do not put commas around **restrictive** words and phrases. These are words and phrases that present essential information about the subject.

Students **who register early** will have the best choice of classes.

The bookstore has sold out of the text **that I need for class.**

The girl **sitting to the right of the speaker** is our class president.

4. **Comma Rule 4 (C4):** Use commas to separate the parts of a series.

Turn in prewriting, outlines, drafts, and revisions.

I signed up for algebra, chemistry, and English classes.

The farmer proudly drove his brand-new, cherry-red tractor.

5. **Comma Rule 5 (C5):** Other common comma uses include the following:

- Always put a comma between a city and state.

My family went on vacation to **Orlando, Florida.**

- Use a comma to set off the tag in a dialogue sentence.

Connor asked, "Do you want to carpool to work?"

"I hope the traffic is not too bad," said Jim.

EXERCISE 15.21   Find and Correct Comma Errors

Directions: Correct the comma errors in the following sentences. In the space before each sentence, put the number of the comma rule you followed in correcting the error.

_____ 1. Hetty Green known as the "Witch of Wall Street was worth more than $100 million when she died in 1916.

_____ 2. Hetty Howland Robinson was born in New Bedford Massachusetts to a ruthless businessman and his invalid wife.

_____ 3. When she was only eight years old Hetty opened her first bank account.

_____ 4. She learned about finance by reading the financial pages to her elderly grandfather and she learned about ruthless business deals from her father.

_____ 5. When Hetty celebrated her twenty-first birthday she did not light the candles but wiped off the cake and returned the candles to the store for a refund.

_____ 6. Hetty's dying father said "I have been poisoned. You will be next."

_____ 7. For years Hetty ate only hard-boiled eggs which she believed could not be poisoned.

_____ 8. At a time when most families lived on $500 per year Hetty inherited $7.5 million.

_____ 9. Hetty hated to spend her money so she lived in small rented rooms for as little as $5 per week.

_____10. She further kept her expenses down by wearing the same clothes for days eating oatmeal cooked on office radiators for lunch and disputing every bill she received.

_____11. Thinking suitors were only after her money Hetty did not marry until age thirty-three.

_____12. After Edward Henry Green ran up debts several times Hetty divorced him.

_____13. Because Hetty had her husband sign a prenuptial agreement her money was safe.

_____14. Hetty was a shrewd investor and once said "I never buy anything just to hold it. There is a price on everything I have."

____15. Hetty's fourteen-year-old son injured his leg in a sledding accident and Hetty tried to treat it herself before taking him to a free clinic.

____16. Gangrene set it so Ned's leg had to be amputated.

____17. Ned who got around by using a cork leg worked as an unpaid clerk for his mother.

____18. Hetty lived for a time with only her dog in a cold-water flat in Hoboken New Jersey.

____19. Ned received all of his mother's money upon her death and spent as much as he could on yachts mansions female companions and other luxuries.

____ 20. After Ned's death the estate's remaining $125 million went to his sister.

D.3 Quotation Marks/Dialogue (Quote)

When you use the exact words of another writer or speaker in your writing, you must use **quotation marks** to set those words off from your own.

Direct and Indirect Quotations

You can tell your reader what someone else has said by presenting the information as a direct or an indirect quotation. A **direct quotation** tells exactly what someone said or wrote, using the original words. An **indirect quotation** tells what was said, but not in the speaker's or writer's exact words. Only direct quotations are in quotation marks. Here are examples of direct and indirect quotations:

INDIRECT	Maddy said her company is hiring.
DIRECT	Maddy said, "My company is hiring."
	"I will begin interviewing candidates next week," she added.
INDIRECT	In *Life on the Mississippi*, Mark Twain wrote that he did not see the river in the same way once he became a riverboat pilot.
DIRECT	Once he became a riverboat pilot, Mark Twain said, "All the grace, the beauty, the poetry had gone out of the majestic river."

EXERCISE 15.22   Use Quotation Marks to Indicate Direct Quotations

Directions: Add quotation marks to the following sentences that contain direct quotes. Not all of the sentences contain direct quotes.

1. Cora said that job candidates who consider themselves shoo-ins for a job can be very annoying.

2. One candidate asked me what his salary and benefits would be before I asked my first question, Cora complained.

3. I was inspired by Richard N. Bolles's book *What Color Is Your Parachute?* when I read the words, Hope can give you wings, persistence, and energy.

4. Human resource directors like Margery say they want job candidates to be completely honest.

5. In their book *Guerilla Marketing for Job Hunters 3.0*, authors Levinson and Perry claim that it's not always the most qualified candidate who gets the job. They write, The positions invariably go to the person who does the best job at positioning himself or herself as the solution to an employer's problem.

6. Cora shook her head and chuckled, Sometimes it is the candidates who are my biggest problem.

Punctuation in Dialogue Sentences

Often you will want to write sentences that contain direct dialogue—the exact spoken words of a person. In order to write these sentences correctly, you will need to familiarize yourself with the following rules for capitalizing and punctuating dialogue sentences.

1. **Be sure to capitalize the first word of spoken dialogue.**

   Tonya asked, "**D**o you think it's all right to wear flip flops to a job interview?"

   Shaking his head, Mark asked, "**A**re you going to a job interview at the beach?"

   "**N**ext you will be telling me to take out my nose ring," Tonya muttered.

2. **Use punctuation to set off the tag from the spoken words of a dialogue sentence.**

- The **tag** is the part of a dialogue sentence that tells who is speaking and how the words are being said.

"This movie is boring," **whispered Monica.**

"You never let me go anywhere," **whined Angie to her parents.**

The crowd cheered, "Go Cardinals!"

The child asked, "Do I have to go to bed?"

- **Set off tags with commas, question marks, or exclamation points.**

EXAMPLES OF STATEMENTS	"Let's move the sofa," said Mary.
	Mary said, "Let's move the sofa."
EXAMPLES OF QUESTIONS	"Where do you want it?" asked Jack.
	Jack asked, "Where do you want it?"
EXAMPLES OF EXCLAMATIONS	"Oh, no! I sprained my back!" cried Jack.
	Jack cried, "Oh, no! I sprained my back!"

3. **Follow the guidelines for using punctuation with quotation marks.**
   - Periods and commas always go inside quotation marks.
   - Question marks and exclamation points may go inside or outside.

Have you read the article "In a Tough Job Market, Teens Are Suffering Most"?

Tom asked, "Is that article in *Time*?"

EXERCISE 15.23   Write Direct Quotations

Directions: Change the following indirect quotations into direct quotations. Be sure to use correct punctuation and capitalization.

EXAMPLE   Sakina said that she is looking for a new job.
            "I am looking for a new job," said Sakina.

1. Ann said that she is often surprised when candidates show up late for a job interview.

2. Harry quietly asked if someone could proofread his resume.

3. Brianna yelled across the room that she could look over Harry's resume.

4. Ms. Whitney asked if Harry is looking for a new job.

5. Harry assured his boss, Ms. Whitney, that he is happy working for her.

EXERCISE 15.24 Correcting Errors in Dialogue Sentences

Directions: Correct any errors in the following dialogue sentences.

1. Why are you looking for a new job the recruiter asked.

2. Rolling his eyes, Harry replied my boss, Ms. Whitney, does not understand me.

3. She complains when I need extra time to finish lunch and never lets me leave work early   Harry explained.

4. I cannot believe you would criticize your boss like this during an interview the recruiter exclaimed.

5. Rising from her chair, the recruiter told Harry this interview is over.

D.4 Semicolon (;)

If you want to emphasize a close connection between the ideas in two independent clauses, you may join the two clauses with a semicolon. Because this is an emphasis device, it should be used very sparingly in your writing.

> Punctuation may seem confusing at first; it becomes simple with practice.
>
> Mia hoped to make the dean's list; Kara hoped only to pass her courses.

The semicolon is also used along with an **adverbial conjunction** to link two independent clauses. Adverbial conjunctions are special kinds of connectors that are stronger and more emphatic than coordinating conjunctions. See a list of adverbial conjunctions on page 458.

> Tim thought he could afford a new car; **however,** he forgot to consider the high cost of insurance.
>
> Fatima highlighted key passages as she read her text; **then,** she copied the most important material into her notebook.

A less common use of the semicolon is to indicate breaks between parts of a series when the parts themselves contain commas. The semicolon makes the parts of the series clearer for the reader.

> As I cleaned out my closet, I found a ring, which had been my grandmother's; a box of ribbons, medals, and trophies from my days with the bowling league; a formal gown, which I had worn to my senior prom; and an old photo album.

EXERCISE 15.25   Practice Using Semicolons

Directions: Add any necessary semicolons to the following sentences.

1. Believing readers open themselves up to listen and to understand an author's perspective doubting readers question and judge an author's perspective.

2. A good thesis may excite readers however, a thesis without adequate support will only disappoint readers.

3. Good writers use examples, which make writing real for readers concrete details, which create drama for the readers and facts, which make writing more credible for readers.

4. All readers have beliefs that are important to them writers tap into these beliefs as a way to connect with readers.

5. We dress differently for different occasions similarly, we adjust our style of writing for different situations.

D.5 Colon (:)

A **colon** is used at the end of a complete statement to introduce a word, a list, a phrase, a long quote, or an explanation.

> Rudy has one great fear when he writes a paper: commas.
>
> The following students have received <u>A</u>'s in the class: Uma, Asher, Brittany, and Mike.
>
> My English teacher has two pet peeves: sloppy work and incomplete work.

Notice that before the colon there is a complete thought—a complete sentence. What comes after the colon explains or illustrates something in that sentence.

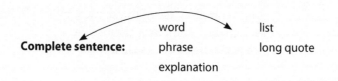

	word	list
Complete sentence:	phrase	long quote
	explanation	

Do not use a colon to interrupt a flow of thought. Make sure that what comes before the colon is a complete thought.

Incorrect	Correct
The mechanic told me that my car needed: a tune-up new tires and an oil change.	The mechanic told me that my car needed a tune-up, new tires, and an oil change.
	or
	The mechanic told me my car needed the following work: a tune-up, new tires, and an oil change.
Before I could leave town, I had to: have my mail held, take my dog to the kennel, and arrange for a ride to the airport.	Before I could leave town, I had to have my mail held, take my dog to the kennel, and arrange for a ride to the airport.

EXERCISE 15.26   Practice Using Colons

Directions: Add colons to the following sentences.

1. There is only one way to stop compulsive shopping self-control.

2. Several signs can indicate you might be living beyond your means a low credit score, no savings, and rising credit card debt.

3. Every community has a resource for low-cost entertainment the library.

4. Benjamin Franklin had good advice for all of us during these hard economic times "Be studious in your profession, and you will be learned. Be industrious and frugal, and you will be rich."

5. I found a way to stop spending so much money at restaurants I learned to cook.

❺ Identify and correct misplaced and dangling modifiers and non-parallel constructions.

E. Avoid Bungled Sentences: Modifiers and Parallelism

Sometimes writers create "bungled" or awkward sentence constructions that can be easily overlooked if proofreading is too hurried. Your goal is to be aware of these kinds of mistakes and catch them with careful proofreading.

E.1 Modifier Errors—Misplaced and Dangling (M)

A **modifier** is a word or group of words in a sentence that describes another word. A modifier is **misplaced** when it does not describe the word the writer intended. A writer can correct a misplaced modifier by moving it next to the word or words it describes.

Incorrect	Problem	Correct
We bought a cake from the *bakery* **that was rich chocolate.**	In this sentence the modifier describes "the bakery" when the writer no doubt intended it to describe the cake. To fix a misplaced modifier, the writer should place the modifier by the word it describes.	We bought a *cake* **that was rich chocolate** from the bakery.
"As a menace to society, *we* must lock up this repeat offender," said the lawyer.	This lawyer is calling himself and perhaps the judge and jury "a menace."	"We must lock up this repeat *offender*, **who is a menace to society**," said the lawyer.
Flying across the green and landing in a sand trap, *the golfer* watched his ball.	Is this a flying golfer?	The golfer watched his *ball* flying across the green and landing in a sand trap.
I read about recent *bear attacks* **in the library.**	Is this a safe place to study?	In the library, *I* read about recent bear attacks.

EXERCISE 15.27   Find and Correct Misplaced Modifiers

Directions: Rewrite the following sentences to correct the misplaced modifier errors.

1. Tumbling down the mountain, the climbers avoided the rocks.

2. The cat belongs to my neighbor that answers to "Kitty, Kitty."

3. The waiter served sandwiches to customers on cracked plates.

4. The motorist was stopped by the policeman who was speeding.

5. I felt relieved when my teacher returned my quiz with a smile.

A **dangling modifier** occurs when the word a modifier is describing is missing. It's nowhere to be found in the sentence. Dangling modifiers usually occur at the beginning of sentences. A writer can correct a dangling modifier by adding to the sentence the word that the modifier describes.

Incorrect	Problem	Correct
After walking the streets and calling his name, *our dog* could not be found.	This sentence says the dog was walking the streets and calling its own name—probably not what the writer intended to say. But notice that the ones doing the walking and calling are not in the sentence, so there is no place to move the modifier in order to fix the error. Instead the sentence has to be rewritten and the word that is being modified must be added.	**After walking the streets and calling his name,** *we* could not find our dog. After *we* walked the streets and called its name, our dog could not be found.
Having not studied the night before, *the test* was a disaster.	The test did not study for itself?	**Since *I* had not studied the night before,** the test was a disaster.

EXERCISE 15.28   Find and Correct Dangling Modifiers

Directions: Rewrite the following sentences to correct the dangling modifier errors.

1. When purchasing a new car, a variety of financing options must be considered.

2. After brushing its coat and trimming its nails, my cat was ready for the big show.

3. Only six years old, my father showed me how to shoot a gun.

4. Jogging down the trail, a growling Rottweiler startled me.

5. Drinking my morning coffee, my cat purred contentedly on my lap.

E.2 Parallelism (//)

Parts of a sentence that are written in pairs or in a series must follow the same grammatical pattern in order to be **parallel** with each other. Parallel sentences have a rhythm—a flow. When a pair or a series lacks this balanced construction, the sentence can sound stilted or awkward.

Not Parallel	Parallel
So far today, my little brother *stuck* a jelly bean in his nose, *is putting tape on the dog*, and *flushed* an action figure down the toilet.	So far today, my little brother *stuck* a jelly bean in his nose, **put** *tape on the dog*, and *flushed* an action figure down the toilet.
After completing his first full day at his factory job, Drew felt *dirty, hungry,* and *wanted to sleep*.	After completing his first full day at his factory job, Drew felt **dirty, hungry,** and **sleepy**.
I enjoy classic novels, but *nonfiction is preferred* by my husband.	*I enjoy* classic novels, but **my husband prefers nonfiction.**
For Valentine's Day, Rosa's boyfriend gave her *red roses, a ring with a diamond,* and *chocolate candy*.	For Valentine's Day, Rosa's boyfriend gave her *red roses,* **a diamond ring**, and *chocolate candy.*

EXERCISE 15.29   Correct Non-Parallel Sentence Constructions

Directions: Rewrite the following sentences so that each has a parallel structure.

1. You can incorporate outside material into your papers by summarizing, to paraphrase, and quoting.

2. Some of the aims described in this textbook include description, reflecting, analyzing, evaluation, and persuading.

3. Well-written paragraphs must have unity, support, and be coherent.

4. My paper had specific details, its ideas were clearly connected, and relevant examples.

5. I used freewriting to generate ideas for my description paper, but brainstorming is what I used to generate ideas for my reflective paper.

❻ Identify and correct abbreviation, capitalization, number, and title errors.

F. Mind Your Mechanics: Abbreviations, Capitals, Numbers, and Titles

Unlike some of the more difficult grammar and punctuation errors, these errors in the *mechanics* of writing do not require a strong understanding of sentence structure to correct. Most of them involve remembering and following a few straightforward rules. When a paper has excessive mechanical errors, the problem is often careless proofreading. Review these rules for *abbreviations, capitals, numbers*, and *titles*. Then you should make a point of carefully proofreading for them during the editing stage of writing.

F.1 Abbreviations (Abbrev)

Avoid most abbreviations in formal writing. This includes the abbreviations commonly used in text messaging, such as *u* for *you* and *b/c* for *because*. However, some abbreviations are acceptable.

1. You may use titles like Mr., Mrs., Ms., and Dr. as long as the titles come before the person's name.

2. You may use the abbreviation U.S. as an adjective only. "United States" should be used as a noun.

   - I am a U.S. citizen.
   - I live in the United States.

3. Some words are known more commonly by their abbreviations. For example, you may use abbreviations such as FBI, CD, NATO, NBC, and DVD.

Incorrect	Correct
Next **Sat.** I am going shopping.	Next **Saturday** I am going shopping.
I am starting college in **Sept.**	I am starting college in **September**.
We moved from **TX** to **MO** last year.	We moved from **Texas** to **Missouri** last year.
This semester I am taking **econ. &** biology.	This semester I am taking **economics and** biology.
Joe is taking off work **b/c** today is his **b-day**.	Joe took off work **because** today is his **birthday**.

EXERCISE 15.30   **Correct Abbreviation Errors**

Directions: Correct the abbreviation errors in the following sentences.

1. Last Tues. I bought paper, folders, pens, etc. at a back-to-school sale.

2. Weighing 1,840 lbs., the world's largest silver nugget was found near Aspen, CO.

3. I plan to visit my dr. B4 this sore throat gets much worse.

4. Flying back to the U.S. & going through security at the airport was easier than I expected.

5. Many consider Dec. 28 the unluckiest day of the yr. b/c it is the anniversary of the massacre of the innocents by King Herod.

6. To celebrate my sister's h.s. grad, we bought three ft. long sandwiches.

7. R u planning to go to FL during Jan. & Feb?

8. On Mon. Nov. 28, my uncle will be sworn in as a United States citizen.

9. I plan 2 write 2 my state gov. & U.S. sen. about the proposed health care plan.

10. I LOL when I read your txt. BTW were u serious?

F.2 Capitalization (Cap)

Due, in part, to the influence of text messaging, some writers are being careless in their use of capitals. You should proofread carefully to catch these errors. Readers, especially professors and employers, will notice if you do not capitalize proper nouns or the pronoun *I*, for example. Such carelessness will hurt your credibility.

The following chart shows how to correct some of the more common errors in capitalization.

Rule	Incorrect	Correct
1. Capitalize the first word in a sentence or direct quotation.	the panhandler asked, "do you have any change?"	The panhandler asked, "Do you have any change?"
2. Capitalize names of persons and the pronoun *I*.	Last night i ran into tony and carol.	Last night I ran into Tony and Carol.
3. Capitalize names of specific places and geographical regions.	After I visit new york city, I plan to fly across the atlantic to europe where I will visit spain and france.	After I visit New York City, I plan to fly across the Atlantic to Europe where I will visit Spain and France.

continued

Continued

Rule	Incorrect	Correct
4. Capitalize names of days of the week, months, and holidays.	We celebrate **thanksgiving** on the fourth **thursday** in **november**.	We celebrate **Thanksgiving** on the fourth **Thursday** in **November**.
5. Capitalize names of commercial products.	My brother drove his **harley davidson** to the store to buy **crest toothpaste**.	My brother drove his **Harley Davidson** to the store to buy **Crest Toothpaste**.
6. Capitalize names of political, social, athletic and other organizations.	My father belongs to the **republican party**, my mother is a member of the **sierra club**, my brother is a **boy scout**, and I am a **yankees** fan.	My father belongs to the **Republican Party**, my mother is a member of the **Sierra Club**, my brother is a **Boy Scout**, and I am a **Yankees** fan.
7. Capitalize races, nationalities and languages.	I earned a higher grade in my **german** conversation class than I did in my **english** class.	I earned a higher grade in my **German** conversation class than I did in my **English** class.
8. Capitalize names of religions, their followers, sacred books, deities.	At the conference to promote religious tolerance, **christians**, **muslims**, and **jews** discussed the sacred teachings of the **bible**, the **Koran**, and the **torah**.	At the conference to promote religious tolerance, **Christians**, **Muslims**, and **Jews** discussed the sacred teachings of the **Bible**, the **Koran**, and the **Torah**.
9. Capitalize historical events, documents, periods.	As part of my American history exam, I had to explain the significance of the **emancipation proclamation**, the **civil war**, and the **gettysburg address** to the presidency of Abraham Lincoln.	As part of my American history exam, I had to explain the significance of the **Emancipation Proclamation**, the **Civil War**, and the **Gettysburg Address** to the presidency of Abraham Lincoln.
10. Capitalize common nouns when used as essential parts of proper nouns.	Sumner **high school** is the oldest high school for African Americans west of the Mississippi **river**.	Sumner **High School** is the oldest high school for African Americans west of the Mississippi **River**.

Capitalizing Titles

Since you frequently must put titles on papers you write for your college classes, pay particular attention to the rules for capitalizing titles.

1. Capitalize the principal words of a title of books, magazines, newspapers, articles, stories, poems, films, television shows, songs, and papers that you write.

2. Do not capitalize the following kinds of words in a title *unless* they are the first or last word of the title:

- articles: *a, an, the*
- coordinating conjunctions: *for, and, nor, but, or, yet, so*
- prepositions: *of, by, at, for, to, etc.* (See the list of prepositions on page 419.)

  - *I Know Why the Caged Bird Sings* (a novel)
  - *New York Times* (a newspaper)
  - "When Lilacs Last in the Dooryard Bloom'd" (a poem)
  - *Modern Family* (a TV show)
  - *Vanity Fair* (a magazine)
  - "How I Connect to Cronon" (an essay)

3. Capitalize the titles of specific school courses.

| CAPITALIZE | This semester I'm taking **Criminal Psychology** 101. |
| DON'T CAPITALIZE | This semester I'm taking a **psychology** course. |

The names of languages and countries are always capitalized in course titles.

I'm taking an **English** class.
British history covers more material than **American** history.

Capitalizing Family Names

Finally, if you are writing about family members, capitalize the words that indicate the relationship of the person to you only if the relationship is used as part of the name or the name itself.

CAPITALIZE	Hand **Grandpa** his walking stick. (Grandpa is used as a name.)
DON'T CAPITALIZE	Hand your **grandpa** his walking stick.
CAPITALIZE	I'm going to the symphony with **Aunt** Betty.
DON'T CAPITALIZE	I'm going to the symphony with my **aunt**.

EXERCISE 15.31   Identify and Correct Capitalization Errors

Directions: Correct the capitalization errors in the following sentences.

1. Last semester in introduction to the short story 201, we read *the curious incident of the dog in the night-time*.

2. I plan to spend the fourth of july holiday with my uncle henry in appleton, wisconsin.

3. Professor Gupta, who teaches asian philosophy, required his students to read the upanishads and the *bhagavadgītā*, both holy texts of the hindu religion.

4. The art class visited florence, italy to see michelangelo's *david*, a masterpiece from the renaissance.

5. I wanted a new mustang for my birthday; instead, i got a ten-year-old volvo.

6. Each student at truman elementary school must bring a box of kleenex tissues and a roll of bounty paper towels on the first day of school.

7. During world war II, asian americans were rounded up and sent to prison camps.

8. My grandpa went to mercy hospital when he had an allergic reaction to tylenol.

9. The st. louis cardinals and the chicago cubs have a long-standing rivalry.

10. Halfway through the movie, Maggie leaned over and whispered, "let's leave this boring movie."

F.3 Numbers (Number)

In your English classes, you will most often be required to follow the Modern Language Association (MLA) guidelines for using numbers. Other disciplines, such as business and journalism, will have different rules regarding numbers. Always learn the expectations of your discourse community before writing a paper.

The following chart illustrates how to correct number errors using MLA guidelines.

Rule	Incorrect	Correct
1. Spell out numbers that can be expressed in one or two words.	During the past two years, my brother has gotten **25** speeding tickets.	During the past two years, my brother has gotten **twenty-five** speeding tickets.
	There is no admission fee for the zoo, but parking costs **$10**.	There is no admission fee for the zoo, but parking costs **ten dollars**.
	My senior class had about **400** students.	My senior class had about **four hundred** students.
2. Numbers that would require three or more words to express should be written as numerals.	Last semester, Goren spent over **three hundred and fifty dollars** on textbooks.	Last semester, Goren spent over **$350** on textbooks.
	The contestants on *The Biggest Loser* lost a combined total of **five hundred and ninety-eight** pounds.	The contestants on *The Biggest Loser* lost a combined total of **598** pounds.
	Last year my daughter's Girl Scout troop sold **one thousand two hundred and fifty-eight** boxes of cookies.	Last year my daughter's Girl Scout troop sold **1,258** boxes of cookies.
3. Use numerals for dates, times, addresses, percentages, scores and statistics, and parts of a book.	At precisely **three forty-five** p.m. the bell rang.	At precisely **3:45 p.m.** the bell rang.
	Mark Twain was born on November **thirtieth eighteen thirty-five**.	Mark Twain was born on November **30, 1835**.
	The President lives at **sixteen hundred** Pennsylvania Avenue.	The President lives at **1600** Pennsylvania Avenue.
	I scored an **eighty-seven percent** on my history test.	I scored an **87%** on my history test.
	Our team won the game with a score of **twenty-one** to **seven**.	Our team won the game with a score of **21** to **7**.
	Turn to page **sixty-eight** in Chapter **Twelve** and complete exercises **one to ten**.	Turn to page **68** in Chapter **12** and complete exercises **1 to 10**.
4. Do not begin a sentence with a numeral.	**80%** of Americans will be crime victims at some point during their lifetimes.	During their lifetimes, **80%** of Americans will be victims of crime.

If you are writing a paragraph in which you use a series of numbers, some of which would be written as words and others as numerals, write them all as numerals. In other words, be consistent.

Incorrect	Correct
During the winter clothing drive at my school, students collected over 250 coats, **fifty** jackets, **twenty-five** pairs of boots, 126 sweaters, and **one** earmuff.	During the winter clothing drive at my school, students collected over 250 coats, **50** jackets, **25** pairs of boots, 126 sweaters, and **1** earmuff.

EXERCISE 15.32   Identify and Correct Number Errors

Directions: Correct the number errors in the following sentences.

1. The Munsters, a creepy family featured in a nineteen sixties television comedy show, lived at thirteen thirteen Mockingbird Lane.

2. A single oak tree can produce two thousand and two hundred acorns in a single season.

3. 3 consecutive strikes in bowling are called a "turkey."

4. Complete the writing exercise on page fifty-eight in Chapter Two of your text.

5. The Egyptian pharaoh Ramses II fathered more than one hundred and sixty children.

6. Lightning strike victims survive 9 out of 10 times.

7. More than twenty percent of the world's oxygen is produced by the Amazon rain forest.

8. Every year the North Atlantic Ocean gets two and a half centimeters wider.

9. The *Titanic* struck the iceberg just thirty seconds after it was first sighted. Among the survivors of the *Titanic* were 2 dogs.

10. Ernest Vincent Wright's novel *Gadsby* contains over 50,000 words, and not one word contains the letter E.

F.4 Titles (Title)

For those occasions when you must cite or mention a title of an artistic work—written, audio, painting, or sculpture—in your writing, use the following rules:

1. **Titles must be properly capitalized.** Review the rules on page 502 of this chapter.

2. **Titles of long works are italicized in electronic documents** or underlined if you are writing by hand.

• books	*Of Mice and Men*	<u>Of Mice and Men</u>
• magazines	*Sports Illustrated*	
• newspapers	*St. Louis Post-Dispatch*	
• epic poems	*Beowulf* (Epics are extremely long, book-length poems.)	
• movies	*Gone with the Wind*	
• TV series	*Star Trek*	
• plays	*Annie Get Your Gun*	
• albums	*Thriller*	

3. **Titles of short works are set off in quotation marks.**

• short story	"The Tell-Tale Heart"
• article	"Are the Chicago Cubs Really Cursed?"
• chapter	"Paragraph Unity"
• poem	"Tiger"
• TV series episode	"Spock's Brain"
• song	"Beat It"

4. **Italics have other uses that may be required in your writing.**

• names of ships	*Caribbean Princess* (ocean vessel)
	U.S.S. Enterprise (space craft)
• names of trains	*Orient Express*
• sculptures	*Little Dancer of Fourteen Years*
• paintings	*Mona Lisa*
• foreign words	*c'est la vie*
• words used as words	You overuse *and* in your writing.

EXERCISE 15.33   Correcting Titles

Directions: Correctly capitalize each title and then decide if it should be in quotation marks or italicized (underlined).

1. new muppet highlights hunger   (magazine article)   _____

2. to build a fire   (short story)   _____

3. epic of gilgamesh   (epic poem)   _____

4. entertainment weekly   (magazine)   _____

5. let america be america again   (poem)   _____

6. the simpsons   (TV series)   _____

7. o brother, where bart thou?   (episode of a TV series)   _____

8. the sound and the fury   (novel)   _____

9. fan throws hot dog at woods   (newspaper article)   _____

10. miami herald   (newspaper)   _____

11. money honey   (song)   _____

12. the discus thrower   (sculpture)   _____

13. the fame monster   (album)   _____

14. phantom of the opera   (musical)   _____

15. writing and the process of writing   (textbook chapter)   _____

16. death of a salesman   (play)   _____

17. the scream   (painting)   _____

18. caribbean princess   (cruise ship)   _____

19. très bien   (French phrase)   _____

20. bayeux tapestry   (famous tapestry)   _____

❼ Understand usage and avoid the spellcheck trap.

G. Understand Usage and Avoid the Spellcheck Trap

Here are some typical words that writers often confuse. Usage errors disrupt the meaning of sentences and can hurt your credibility as a writer.

Usage (Usage)

a and *an*

Both **a** and **an** are used before other words to mean, approximately, "one."

a book	**an** opinion
a whale	an eagle
a city	an ice cube

Generally, you should use **an** before words starting with a vowel (*a, e, i, o, u*) or a vowel sound:

an ache	**an** experiment	**an** elephant	**an** ox
an honor	**an** heir	**an** honest mistake	

Generally, you should use **a** before words starting with consonants (all other letters):

a Coke	**a** brain	**a** television	**a** gambler

affect and *effect*

Affect is usually an action verb meaning "to influence." (*Affect* and *action* both start with *a*.)

The weather **affects** my mood.

The strong storm **affected** my TV reception.

Too many absences will **affect** my grade.

Effect is usually used as a noun and means "a result."

The drug had no **effect** on his medical condition.

The moon has a strange **effect** on werewolves.

High gas prices affect all of us; one **effect** is higher prices for shipped products.

its and *it's*

Its is a possessive pronoun.

The dog wagged **its** tail when I gave it a treat.

My old comb has lost some of **its** teeth.

I saw the house after **its** roof blew off in the storm.

It's is a contraction standing for the words *it is*.

> **It's** never too late to expand your knowledge.

> I hope **it's** all right for me to park here.

> **It's** time to take my cat in for its shots.

principal and *principle*

Principal is an adjective meaning "major." It also is a noun that refers to the head of a school.

> The **principal** reason for my doing well at my job is I'm a fast learner.

> The **principal** at my school was a strict disciplinarian.

Principle is a noun only, meaning a "rule." Ru**le** and princip**le** both end in **le**.

> I follow my **principles** of right and wrong when making a decision.

> We learned the basic **principles** of economics in my finance class.

than and *then*

Than is a conjunction used in comparisons.

> April is taller **than** Deanna.

> I would rather take a walk in the park **than** rake leaves in my yard.

> The karate instructor was stronger **than** she looked.

Then can indicate a point in time or it can mean "in addition."

> I will complete my general education requirements and **then** transfer to a university.

> Dan works eight hours every day, **then** takes evening classes four nights a week.

> College tuition is expensive; **then**, there is the cost of textbooks.

> Brenda put the turkey in the oven, **then** began peeling potatoes.

there, their and *they're*

There indicates "in that place" or functions as an expletive.

> The ball rolled over **there**.

> I hope **there** are still classes open.

> **There** is little hope that I will be a millionaire.

Their is a plural possessive pronoun.

The students packed up **their** books.

The patients' hopes rested with **their** doctor.

Over there is where my parents will build **their** dream house.

They're is a contraction for the words *they are.*

If students think college is easy, **they're** in for a surprise.

They're more likely to be successful if they learn to use the library.

Their chances for success fade if **they're** too intimidated to go there for help.

to, too, and two

To is a preposition or part of an infinitive verb.

I have **to** go to work.

Mark tried **to** think of a good excuse for being late.

To get **to** the bank, drive **to** the corner and turn left.

Too is an adverb meaning "also" or "excessively."

It's **too** cold to work outside.

Your brother wants to go to the store, **too**.

I, **too**, have had to work my way through school.

Sometimes it's just **too** hard to combine work and school.

Two refers to the number 2.

It will take **two** people to haul that couch; it's too heavy for one.

I too have to leave for a meeting at **two** o'clock.

I have to write **two** papers for my history class.

weather and whether

Weather has to do with such atmospheric concerns as temperature, moisture, wind velocity, and barometric pressure. It can also be used as a verb, meaning to "hold up" or "withstand."

The **weather** can be extreme at the Earth's two polar regions.

Check the **weather** before planning your picnic.

The old house **weathered** the storm with little damage.

Whether is usually used to refer to one of two choices.

> **Whether** I attend college or go straight to work after high school depends upon my getting a scholarship.
>
> I don't know **whether** I should buy a new car or a pre-owned car.

who's and whose

Who's is a contraction for the words *who is* or *who has.*

> **Who's** calling me at this late hour?
>
> Is Al the mechanic **who's** fixing your car?
>
> Carrie, **who's** visiting her grandma, asked me to water her plants.

Whose is a possessive pronoun.

> **Whose** turn is it to work overtime?
>
> That's the neighbor **whose** dog keeps barking all night.
>
> I tried to find out **whose** book was left in the classroom.

your and you're

Your is a possessive pronoun.

> **Your** schedule is posted in the break room.
>
> Take **your** time while writing a paper.
>
> It's **your** choice whether to stay or leave.

You're is the contraction for the words *you are.*

> **You're** too late for the tryouts.
>
> If **you're** tired, take a nap.
>
> **You're** responsible for taking the classes required for your degree.

EXERCISE 15.34   Identify and Correct Usage Errors

Directions: Correct the twelve usage errors in the following passage.

Food can effect you're mood because of it's ability to altar neurotransmitters in the brain. Neurotransmitters carry the brain's chemical messages. If they're insufficient levels of certain nutrients in your diet, the brain cannot manufacture proper levels of neurotransmitters, and you may feel more stress and anxiety. For example, people who lack sufficient selenium in there diets may be more irritable and depressed then those who's diets are not deficient. Its easy to get selenium, to. Weather you eat a hole grain cereal for breakfast or eat a tuna sandwich for lunch or even snack on Brazil nuts, you can get enough selenium.

Credits

Text

Abinader, Elmaz. "Just Off Main Street." U.S. Department of State's Bureau of International Information Programs: Writers on America.

Adams, Glade Byron. "It is of course possible to dance a prayer."

Alexie, Sherman. "Why the Best Kid Books are Written in Blood." *Wall Street Journal*, April 9, 2011.

Barry, Dave. "Nobody cares if you can't dance well. Just get up and dance."

Brahm, Ajahn. "Two Bad Bricks" from *Who Ordered This Truckload of Dung?: Inspiring Stories for Welcoming Life's Difficulties*. Copyright © 2005 by Ajahn Brahm. Reprinted with the permission of The Permissions Company, Inc., on behalf of Wisdom Publications, www.wisdompubs.org.

Brooks, David. "Marshmallows and Public Policy." *The New York Times*, 5/7/2006.

Cohen, Sarah. "A Night of Lynching, a Life of Remembering" Associated Press, February 23, 2003.

Coniff, Richard. From "The Cave of Bats" in *Every Creeping Thing*, by Richard Conniff. ©1998 by Richard Conniff. First published by Henry Holt and Companies, Inc. in 1998. Reprinted by permission of the author.

Constanze. "Dancing is like dreaming with your feet!"

Cronon, William. "The Goals of a Liberal Education" *The American Scholar*, Volume 67, No. 4, Autumn 1998.

De Mille, Agnes. "The truest expression of a people is in its dance and in its music. Bodies never lie."

De Mille, Agnes. "To dance is to be out of yourself. Larger, more beautiful, more powerful."

Denby, Edwin. "There is a bit of insanity in dancing that does everybody a great deal of good."

Devet, Bonnie. "The Day I Met Bruce Lee". Copyright 2007.

Durning, Alan Thein. "Seven Sustainable Wonders of the World." *Society for the Advancement of Education/USA Today Magazine*, Vol. 124, No. 2602, July 1995.

Dryden, John. "Dancing is the poetry of the foot."

Eastern Illinois University. Search page and search results from Eastern Illinois University online catalog.

EBSCO. Screenshot showing EBSCO logo icon.

Egerton, John. "Country Ham." Excerpt from *Pleasures of the Smokehouse*.

Erin, Adrienne. "Reality Check: Your Social Media May Be Putting You in Danger." Reprinted by permission from AL. com.

Glater, Jonathan D. "To: Professor@University.edu Subject:Why It's All About Me." *The New York Times*, 2/21/2006.

Greer, Jeff. "4 Reasons Why The Library Should Affect Your College Choice" *U.S. News,* July 17, 2010.

Heilbroner, Robert L. "Don't Let Stereotypes Warp Your Judgment." *Think Magazine*, 1962.

Holdrege, Craig. "Dandelion: A Virtuous Weed" in *Cosmos Doogood's Urban Almanac*. Eric Utne (Publisher), 2006. p. 143.

Little, Jane Braxton. Excerpt from "The Trail Winds."

Mrs. Chili. "The Attendance Policy." *A Teacher's Education*. December 7, 2008.

Nietzsche, Friedrich. "And those who were seen dancing were thought to be insane by those who could not hear the music."

Pitts, Leonard. "Put the Brakes on Driving While Texting." Miami Herald, 8/9/2009.

Pollan, Michael, "The Botany of Desire: A Plant's-Eye View of the World", Random House.

Prud'Homme, Alex. "Slave." *The New Yorker*, January 23, 1989, p. 24.

Roosevelt, Max. "Student Expectations Seen as Causing Grade Disputes." *The New York Times*, 2/18/2009.

Selzer, Richard. *Mortal Lessons: Notes on the Art of Surgery* by Richard Selzer. Copyright © 1974, 1975, 1976, 1987 by Richard Selzer. Reprinted by permission of Georges Borchardt, Inc., on behalf of the author.

Simon, Robin W. "Bundle of Trouble: Kids are Supposed to Bring Joy. So Why are Parents So Unhappy." Excerpted from Simon, R. "The Joys of Parenthood, Reconsidered" *Contexts*, May 2008, Vol. 7, Number 2, p. 40–45. Copyright 2008 by American Sociological Association. Reprinted by permission of SAGE Publications, Inc.

Stafford, William. "Kids: they dance before they learn there is anything that isn't music."

Staples, Brent. "Black Men and Public Space." *Harper's Magazine*, December 1986.

Stengel, Richard. "Space Invaders." *The New Yorker Magazine/ Conde Nast*, 71, 1995 2-3.

Deborah Tannen. "But What Do You mean?" *Redbook*, vol. 183, October 1, 1994. Copyright Deborah Tannen. Adapted from Talking from 9 to 5: Women and Men at Work, HarperCollins. Reprinted with Permission.

Taylor, Tim and Linda Copeland. "A Close Look at 'Why Prisons Don't Work.'"

Taylor, Tim and Linda Copeland. "Coach Pick."

Taylor, Tim and Linda Copeland. " Curling."

Taylor, Tim and Linda Copeland. "I-Search Abstract.

Taylor, Tim and Linda Copeland. "A Kennel for Bud."

Taylor, Tim and Linda Copeland. "Letter."

Taylor, Tim and Linda Copeland. "No %#@$&*: Profanity on Campus Should Be Banned."

Taylor, Tim and Linda Copeland. "The Real Marlboro Man."

Taylor, Tim and Linda Copeland. "'Sorry It's Late'"—Seeing Both Sides of an Age-old Homework Dilemma."

Taylor, Tim and Linda Copeland. "Stop the Cyberbully."

"The School Smarts Effect." Excerpt from "Fit Body, Fit Brain." From *Current Health*, January 2008. Copyright 2008 by The Weekly Reader Corporation. Reprinted by permission of Scholastic Inc.

Turkle, Sherry, "The Flight from Conversation" from *The New York Times*, 4/22/2012.

Twain, Mark. Excerpt from "Life on the Mississippi."

Vonnegut, Kurt. "Dance, even if you have nowhere to do it but your living room."

Wallace, David Foster. "Clog Dancing at the Illinois State Fair." Copyright 1994, David Foster Wallace. Originally published in *Harper's*. Used by permission of the David Foster Wallace Literary Trust.

Youssef, Soha. "I Dream of Egypt Even When I Dream in English." 2014.

Zimmerman, Lee. "Amanda Shires—*Carrying Lightning*." *Blurt Online*, May 3, 2011.

Photos and Illustrations

1: Monkey Business/Fotolia. 2: Diego Cervo/Fotolia. 3: doble.d/Getty. 7: United Feature Syndicate. 8: ktsdesign/Fotolia. 9: Lgor Mojzes/Fotolia. 14: oneblink1/Fotolia. 18: Black Currant/Fotolia. 23: mediaphotos/Getty Images. 24: Photographee/Fotolia. 32 top: WavebreakMediaMicro/Fotolia. 32 bottom: Singkham/Fotolia. 34: Bonniemarie/Fotolia. 46: gwimages/Fotolia. 55: Ammentorp/Fotolia. 59 top: Charles taylor/Fotolia. 59 bottom: Monkey Business/Shutterstock. 64: iQoncept/Fotolia. 68: Anna Gorin/Getty Images. 93: Leekris/Fotolia. 99: Jaimie Duplass/Fotolia. 101: Tim Taylor/Linda Copeland. 105: Rabbit75/Fotolia. 106: Lebrecht Authors/Lebrecht Music & Arts/Lebrecht Music & Arts/Corbis. 107: Pefkos/Fotolia. 127: Paul Fleet/Fotolia. 128: Hurst/Shutterstock. 130: Kena Betancur/Getty. 136: Freshidea/Fotolia. 138: Bobby Bank/Getty Images. 141: Plusone/Shutterstock. 146: kreizihorse/Fotolia. 153: Ferrerilavarialiotti/Fotolia. 155 left: Lgor Mojzes/Fotolia. 155 middle: Steven Greaves/Dorling Kindersley Limited. 155 right: Steven Greaves/Dorling Kindersley Limited. 156: Aleksandar Mijatovic/Fotolia. 157: krsmanovic/Fotolia. 158: Linda Copeland/Pearson Education. 165: cosma/Fotolia. 167: Photobyjimshane/Fotolia. 168: Owen Franken/Corbis. 184 left and right: House Plan Gallery, Inc. 187: JupiterImages/Getty Images. 188: Georgios Kollidas/Shutterstock. 189: Krasimira Nevenova/Fotolia. 191: Nomad_Soul/Fotolia. 192: Peshkov/Fotolia. 194: effe45/Fotolia. 199: Andrei/Fotolia. 221: Alexey Stiop/Fotolia. 222: Rawpixel/Fotolia. 224: nickolae/Fotolia. 226: Marcin Sadlowski/Fotolia. 227: ddgrigg/Fotolia. 231: volff/Fotolia. 234: Andrea lzzotti/Fotolia. 240: Doble.D/Fotolia. 245: Marco Mayer/Fotolia. 248: Tim Taylor/Linda Copeland/Pearson Education. 253: Pressmaster/Fotolia. 254: Andrewgenn/Fotolia. 260: California Tobacco Control Program. 268: Mat Hayward/Fotolia. 269: Thepoeticimage/Fotolia. 285: IQoncept/Fotolia. 286: Trekandphoto/Fotolia. 288: andrewgenn/Fotolia. 292: PackShot/Fotolia. 296: Silver Knife Records. 303: Fmarsicano/Fotolia. 313: Innovated Captures/Fotolia. 314: Intheskies/Fotolia. 317: Stockyimages/Fotolia. 319: Ninared/Fotolia. 322: Fotolia. 325 top: Anuchai Secharunputong/Thai Health Promotion Foundation. 325 middle: James Pozarik/The LIFE Images Collection/Getty Images. 325 bottom: TobaccoFreeCA/Calfiornia Department of Health. 340: IQoncept/Fotolia. 350: Minerva Studio/Fotolia. 351: Login/Fotolia. 356: Thinglass/Fotolia. 358: Chris McDermott/Fotolia. 377: Focus Pocus LTD/Fotolia. 386: Pearson Education. 398: Pearson Education. 413 top and 414: Aihumnoi/Fotolia. 413 bottom and 452: chris2766/Fotolia.

Works Cited

Adelstein, Michael E. "The Writing Process." *Strategies for Business and Technical Writing,* edited by Kevin J. Harty, Pearson, 2005, pp. 15-20.

Bean, John C. *Engaging Ideas: The Professor's Guide to Integrating Writing, Critical Thinking, and Active Learning in the Classroom,* Jossey-Bass, 2001.

Elbow, Peter. *Writing without Teachers.* Oxford UP, 1973.

Fulkerson, Richard. *Teaching the Argument in Writing.* NCTE, 1996.

Raymond, James C. *Moves Writers Make.* Prentice-Hall, 1999.

Stolley, Karl, et al. "Is It Plagiarism Yet?" *Purdue Online Writing Lab.* Purdue University. 13 Feb. 2013, owl.english.purdue.edu/owl/resource/589/2/.

Thais, Chris and Terry Myers Zawacki. *Engaged Writers, Dynamic Disciplines: Research on the Academic Writing Life.* Heinemann, 2006.

Index